China's Emerging Cities

Urbanism has become a key driver of socioeconomic change in China, with rapid housing privatization, commodification, and urban redevelopment transforming the face of Chinese cities. The Chinese experience challenges the received wisdom of Chinese "gradualism" in economic reform, and goes beyond classical Western notions of "new urbanism" as gentrification, diversity, and higher-density living. This book investigates China's urban reform, demonstrating how it transcends the centrally planned model of economic growth, and assessing the extent to which it has gone beyond the common wisdom of Chinese "gradualism." It covers a wide range of important topics, including local land development, the local state, private-public partnership, foreign investment, urbanization, ageing and home ownership. This book provides a clear appraisal of recent trends in Chinese urbanism, putting forward important new conceptual resources to fill the gap between the outdated model of the "Third World" city and the globalizing cities of the West.

Fulong Wu is Professor of East Asian Planning and Development and the Director of the Urban China Research Centre at the School of City and Regional Planning of Cardiff University. He is co-editor (with Laurence Ma) of *Restructuring the Chinese City* (Routledge, 2005), editor of *Globalization and the Chinese City* (Routledge, 2006), and co-author (with Jiang Xu and Anthony Gar-On Yeh) of *Urban Development in Post-Reform China: State, Market, and Space* (Routledge, 2007).

Routledge Contemporary China Series

China's Emerging Cities

The making of new urbanism

Edited by
Fulong Wu

Routledge
Taylor & Francis Group

LONDON AND NEW YORK

First published 2007
by Routledge
2 Park Square, Milton Park, Abingdon, Oxon OX14 4RN

Simultaneously published in the USA and Canada
by Routledge
605 Third Avenue, New York, NY 10017

*Routledge is an imprint of the Taylor & Francis Group,
an informa business*

Typeset in Times New Roman by
Newgen Imaging Systems (P) Ltd, Chennai, India

British Library Cataloguing in Publication Data
A catalogue record for this book is available from the British Library

Library of Congress Cataloging in Publication Data
A catalog record for this book has been requested

ISBN13: 978–0–415–41617–7 (hbk)
ISBN13: 978–0–203–93780–8 (ebk)

Contents

Figures

Tables

Contributors

Daniel Benjamin Abramson is Assistant Professor of Urban Design and Planning and is also on the China Studies Faculty of the University of Washington, Seattle, USA. He received a doctorate in urban planning from Tsinghua University, Beijing, in 1998, and has combined research, teaching and consulting work in China primarily in Beijing and Quanzhou, Fujian Province, with partners at the Chinese Academy of Urban Planning and Design and numerous universities in the PRC and Taiwan, Canada, and the USA. His papers on this work have appeared in *Planning Perspectives Journal of the American Planning Association* and *Journal of Planning Education and Research*.

Xiangming Chen is Dean and Director of the Center for Urban and Global Studies and the Paul E. Raether distinguished Professor of Sociology and International Studies at Trinity College in Connecticut. His research focuses on the multiple facets of global–local relations in the urban and regional contexts of China and Asia. He co-authored *The World of Cities: Places in Comparative and Historical Perspective* (Blackwell, 2003) and published *As Borders Bend: Transnational Spaces on the Pacific Rim* (Rowman & Littlefield, 2005). His articles have appeared in a variety of international social sciences and urban studies journals.

Ian G. Cook is Professor of Human Geography, program leader in Geography and head of the Centre for Pacific Rim Studies at Liverpool John Moores University. His main research interests are aspects of spatial transformation in China. His books include the co-edited volumes on *Fragmented Asia* (Avebury 1996) and *Dynamic Asia* (Ashgate 1998), and he co-authored *China's Third Revolution: Tensions in the Transition to Post-communism* (Curzon 2001) and *Green China: Seeking Ecological Alternatives* (RoutledgeCurzon 2002). He has also contributed to a number of recent and forthcoming edited volumes and journals on such topics as the active elderly in China, Chinese TVEs, and urban and regional pressures of development.

Guillaume Giroir is Professor in the Department of Geography at University of Orléans (France). He has published many works – both theoretical and empirical – relating to a geographical approach of transition and globalization process in China. His main areas of interest include Chinese megacities (especially Beijing and Shanghai), satellite towns, state farms, high tech parks, theme parks, and especially gated communities (*bieshu qu*). More recently he has also studied the environment, particularly natural reserves and biodiversity.

Chongyi Guo received his PhD from the Department of Geography at Peking University, China. After two years of working as a retail consultant, he was appointed Lecturer of Marketing and Distribution Science at Beijing Technology and Business University. His teaching and research interests include retail chain management, location analysis, and strategic planning. He has written and published widely in China, and is a regular contributor to *China Chain Store Almanac*.

Shenjing He is a Research Fellow at the School of City and Regional Planning at Cardiff University. She has published articles on *TEGS*, *Journal of Urban Affairs, China Information and Cities*, and book reviews on *China's Urban Transition* and *Emerging Land and Housing Markets in China*. Her major research interests focus on the political economy of urban redevelopment, spaces of neoliberalism, neighborhood change and new urban poverty.

Sunil Kumar lectures on the MSc in Social Policy and Development at the Department of Social Policy, London School of Economics and Political Science. He is an urban social planner with interests in housing, poverty, livelihoods, and informal institutions. He has undertaken work for the United Nations Centre for Human Settlements (UNCHS Habitat) and the UK Department for International Development (DFID). He has written widely on housing and housing tenure and his most recent research publication is entitled 'Social Relations, Rental Housing Markets and the Poor in Urban India, 2001'. He is currently working on issues regarding social security and social protection in relation to those working in the informal economy in India.

Seungho Lee is Lecturer at the School of Contemporary Chinese Studies, University of Nottingham. His research interests are water industry, water policy, environmental NGOs, environmental politics, and water conflicts in China. His recent publications include *Water and Development in China – Political Economy of Shanghai Water Policy* (*World Scientific*, 2006), "Private Sector Participation in the Shanghai Water Sector" and "Environmental Movements of Social Organizations in Shanghai." He also works as consultant in water policy, particularly for the South Korean government, and often advises NGOs, the media and governmental organizations in the UK on China's water issues.

Bingqin Li is Lecturer on Social Policy at the Department of Social Policy, London School of Economics. She lectures on social economics and policy and international housing courses. Her research interests include urban poverty and social exclusion, and rural urban linkage in China. Her latest publication is on social protection of rural construction workers in Chinese cities (2006).

Si-ming Li is Chair Professor of Geography and Director of the Centre for China Urban and Regional Studies, Hong Kong Baptist University. His current research focuses on housing and residential change in China. He recently co-edited a special theme issue in *Housing Studies* (2006, with Youqin Huang) and another one in *Environment and Planning A* (2004, with Fulong Wu) on urban housing in China. He is a board member of the Urban China Research Network based in the University at Albany.

Jason L. Powell is Lecturer in Sociology and Social Policy at the University of Liverpool. He has 75 published papers on social gerontology and the recent book *Social Theory and Aging* (Rowman & Littlefield).

Hyun Bang Shin received his doctorate from the London School of Economics and Political Science (LSE). He is a postdoctoral research fellow at the White Rose East Asia Centre, University of Leeds, and is also associated with the ESRC Centre for Analysis of Social Exclusion at the LSE. His research interests include urban planning and regeneration, neighborhood renewal and social impacts, urban housing and homeownership, and comparative social policy in developing countries.

Jiaming Sun is Assistant Professor in the Department of Sociology and Criminal Justice at Texas A&M University-Commerce. He had been a faculty member of Sociology Department, International Politics Department in Fudan University for 11 years before coming to the United States. He is author of *Generation Gaps: The Background of Transition Period 1991–1994*. He has also published a number of book chapters and papers on globalization, urban residential life, cultural study, and youth problems in the last twenty years. His recent publications include *Global Sociology: Analysis of Transnational Phenomena* (Tsinghua University Press, 2005); "Personal Global Connections and a New Residential Differentiation in Shanghai, China" (*China: an International Journal*, 2005); "Sociological Perspectives on Urban China: From Familiar Territories to Complex Terrains" (*Contemporary China Studies*, 2006); and "Personal Global Connectivity and Consumer Behavior: A Study in Shanghai" (*Journal of International Consumer Marketing*, 2006).

Ying Ying Tian received her PhD from the Department of Civic Design, University of Liverpool. Her thesis is on institutionalist approach to the analysis of built environment change in housing regeneration in central Shanghai. She was a qualified architect and experienced masterplanner working for Tongji University. Currently she is working for one of the UK's leading community planning and urban design practices, John Thompson and Partners, committing herself to the creation of sustainable communities.

Hung-Kai Wang is a Professor at the Graduate Institute of Building and Planning at the National Taiwan University. His research interests include urban planning in developing countries, local development in postreform China, and sustainable cities. He has published numerous papers on subjects such as urban land use patterns in Taipei and Shanghai, local land property rights in China, and sustainable tourism in Taiwan.

Shuguang Wang is Professor and Chair of the Department of Geography at Ryerson University, Canada. His research interests include the changing retail structure in Chinese cities and the impacts of foreign retailers on China's retail sector. His recent publications include "The New Retail Economy of Shanghai," "Penetrating the Great Wall and Conquering the Middle Kingdom: Wal-Mart in China," and "Opportunities and Challenges of Shopping Centre Development in China: A Case Study of Shanghai." He is currently conducting policy research to examine how China has responded to the new challenges brought about by the foreign retailers after its admission to the WTO.

Cecilia Wong is Professor of Spatial Planning and Director of the Centre for Urban Policy Studies at the University of Manchester. Her research interests include quantitative measures, socioeconomic analysis, strategic and spatial planning, national spatial planning frameworks, and policy monitoring and evaluation.

Fulong Wu is Professor of East Asian Planning and Development and the Director of the Urban China Research Centre at the School of City and Regional Planning of Cardiff University. His recent research is urban poverty and transition. He is co-editor (with Laurence Ma) of *Restructuring the Chinese City* (Routledge, 2005), editor of *Globalization and the Chinese City* (Routledge, 2006), and co-author (with Jiang Xu and Anthony Gar-On Yeh) of *Urban Development in Post-Reform China: State, Market, and Space* (Routledge, 2007).

Chun Yang is Research Assistant Professor in the Department of Geography at the University of Hong Kong. Her research interests include cross-border interaction and governance between Hong Kong and China (especially the Pearl River Delta), industrial clustering of Hong Kong and Taiwan investment in the Pearl River Delta and the Yangtze River Delta. She has recently published papers on cross-border integration and governance of the Greater Pearl River Delta and transition of overseas Chinese investment in China, in *Political Geography*, *Environment and Planning A*, *Eurasian Geography and Economics*, *Habitat International* and *International Development Planning Review*.

You-Ren Yang is a post-doctoral researcher in the Department of Geography at National Taiwan University. His research interests include geography of production, land use regulation in postreform China and geography of innovation. He has published papers on Taiwanese IT companies' trans-border investment in China in *Environment and Planning A*.

Preface

More than 25 years have passed since China's embarking on economic reform. China seemingly adopted a different trajectory of market transition – in contrast to the shock therapy in Central and Eastern Europe, a gradualism approach allows political and social stability while the economy is experiencing rapid growth. But market reform has dramatically transformed urban landscapes. It is now the time to assess whether the idea of gradualism still fits to the reality of Chinese cities. Within China, the thought of the so-called New Left claims the radical nature of marketization. It is therefore important to explore whether the Chinese city is becoming an emerging space of new institutions, new working and living practices.

With the development of several networks of urban China scholars, the chance is ripe for this endeavor. Among these networks, I would like to particularly mention the Urban China Research Network based in Albany, of which I am a member of the steering committee, a British Higher Education Link project with China on urban poverty, of which I am the coordinator, and more recently the Urban China Research International Network (UCRIN) under the Leverhulme Trust, of which I am the project director. The financial support from the Leverhulme Trust (F/00 407/AM) is acknowledged.

The majority of chapters in this volume are revised versions initially presented at the RGS/IBG 2005 Annual Conference. I would like to thank Dr Shenjing He for helping organize China sessions in the conference. I also want to thank many people for helping the development of this edited volume, in particular John Logan, Laurence Ma, Anthony Gar-On Yeh, George Lin, Weiping Wu, Jiang Xu, Binqin Li, You-Ren Yang, Chun Yang, Eric Heikkila, Christian Kesteloot, Alana Boland, Canfei He, Shuguang Wang, and Hyun Bang Shin. The support from Peter Sowden, editor at Routledge, is critical to the completion of this publishing journey. I appreciate his long-term collegial trust.

Part I

Cities as emerging institution

1 Beyond gradualism

China's urban revolution and emerging cities

Fulong Wu

Urban revolution

Chinese cities are the country's engine of economic growth. The level of urbanization increased from 18 percent in 1978 to over 43 percent in 2005 (State Statistical Bureau 2006). Driving rapid urban growth is the inflow of foreign capital into coastal China. Since gaining World Trade Organization (WTO) membership in 2001, China has been speeding up its pace of becoming a world factory. But where is the world factory physically located? Many factories for global commodity production in China are located in the cities, or more precisely within the metropolitan region. Global economic production is becoming part of urban economies, concentrated in the cities of the Pearl River Delta and the Yangtze River Delta but also widespread all over the country. Accompanying economic growth is the emergence of cities on the world stage of super-affairs or mega-events: Beijing will be hosting the Olympic Games in 2008; Shanghai the World Expo 2010; Guangzhou the Asian Games in 2010; and Shenzhen the 2011 Summer World University Games. With the development of international airports, deep-water ports and information port and logistics centers, Chinese cities are rebuilding themselves towards becoming "global cities" (Wu 2006).

China's urban landscapes are being forcefully transformed: in first-tier cities such as Beijing, Shanghai and Guangzhou but also in many other large cities such as Chongqing, Dalian, Shenzhen, Suzhou, Nanjing and Xi'an, skyscrapers mushroom in central areas; fast elevated multilane roads extend to suburbs where gated communities, development zones, and high-tech parks are scattered. Infrastructure is being built at an unbelievable pace.

Large-scale urban redevelopment schemes have converted old neighborhoods into modern office blocks. For example, in Shanghai, the government initiated a redevelopment program to demolish and rebuild 3.65 million square meters of old lane housing, which was achieved in 2000 (see He and Wu, Chapter 10 of this book; Tian and Wong, Chapter 11 of this book). The government then swiftly launched the second phase of the redevelopment program, involving the redevelopment of 20 million square meters of old housing. With the boom in real estate development, suddenly Chinese cities began to see the formation of a multilayer structure: old prerevolutionary lane housing remains in residual poverty neighborhoods; workers' welfare housing, built in the prereform or early reform era, is deteriorating into low-quality residential areas; and new luxury condominiums have upgraded some parts of the city into gentrified residences. In the suburbs, gated high-standard commodity housing estates sometimes even flaunt ostentatious and magnificent gates, demarcating emerging "consumer clubs" in response to the retreat of the state from the provision of public goods (Wu 2005).

Chinese cities are now perhaps seeing the "newest" form of urban development reported in advanced Western market economies: sports-led property redevelopment near Nanjing Olympic Sport Center, leisure-led redevelopment to pursue the nostalgia for colonial or prerevolutionary republic era in Shanghai's Xintiandi and Nanjing's 1912, arts-led regeneration near the Great Tang Dynasty Garden in Xi'an, and artists' enclaves in Beijing's Factory 798. These landscapes can take a variety of forms: some transplant classical Western styles that are alien to China; some repackage Chinese architectural motifs of imperial palaces into playful fun parks, while others like Beijing's Factory 798 reuse derelict industrial buildings and adapt them to postmodern cultural production and consumption. Chinese cities are also becoming experimental sites for global signature architects and their firms, ranging from Paul Andreu to Rem Koolhaas.

While Chinese cities are modernizing, or even postmodernizing themselves, classical components of the Third World City have reemerged. Some quasi-slum areas or deteriorated neighborhoods accommodate millions of "floating population" or migrant workers. Former rural villages encroached on by urban expansion are becoming "villages in the city" (*chengzhongcun*), spontaneously built by farmers into very high density areas. Farmers rent out their houses, often now with multiple floors, to migrants from other places. But these buildings are so close to each other, because each owner of a land plot wants to maximize the use of the land, that the streets between them barely allow fire engines and ambulances to enter. The infrastructure and public facilities of these neighborhoods are completely missing. However, these villages provide cheap housing for migrants, and are becoming virtually migrant enclaves.

It is now even possible to depict a general model of the new Chinese city. While Chinese cities vary greatly according to their geographical locations and histories of development, some generic elements are present almost everywhere, including

- Central Business Districts (CBDs) or financial streets such as Shanghai's Bund and Lujiazui Financial and Trade Zone, or Beijing's CBD in Chaoyang district and Xidan financial street;
- Bar street and night-time entertainment places such as Shishahai and Sanlitun in Beijing, Hengshan road and Xintiandi in Shanghai, Hunan road and 1912 in Nanjing, Kundu in Kunming, and the Great Tang Dynasty Garden in Xi'an;
- Boulevards, pedestrian streets, and magnificent city squares such as the Century Avenue in Shanghai and Jiefangbei in Chongqing;
- High-tech parks and economic development zones such as Beijing's Haidian university and science park and Shanghai's Zhangjiang high-tech park;

- Gated communities in Western styles such as the Orange County, Yosemite, and McAllen in Beijing, Fontainebleau in Shanghai, and Creative Britain in Kunming;
- "Villages in the city," widely seen in almost every Chinese city, with varying qualities of built environment.

What are the factors that contribute to China's urban revolution? The remainder of this chapter will look into this radical nature of postreform urban development, in contrast to the common wisdom of Chinese gradualism.

The catalyst factor of globalization

Since the adoption of an open-door policy, China has seen phenomenal growth in foreign direct investment (FDI). China is the second largest country in terms of absorbed FDI (Nolan 2004), and in 2005 FDI amounted to 60.33 billion US dollars, growing from 3.39 billion US dollars in 1989 (State Statistical Bureau 2006). Since China joined the WTO in 2001, the pace of integration into the global economy has quickened. Globalization is becoming a major driving force for China's economic growth (see Yang, Chapter 5 of this book).

However, China's growth is not totally determined by the agenda of globalization. The influence of globalization on the locality is mediated by the state at various levels. In contrast to India, where the demographic political setup allows more bottom-up development, China's urban development is still very top-down, in the sense that the state plays a much more important role. Many ambitious development projects, including the building of global cities, are initiated out of the strategic considerations of the national state. For example, the development of Shanghai as a global city is part of an overall strategy to revitalize the Yangtze River region (Wu 2000). Thus, the central government has provided much support, both institutionally and financially (in terms of changing the tax regime), to the city. While the development of Shanghai reveals the role of the central state, the development of China-Singapore Suzhou Industrial Park (Pereira 2003) shows another example of the importance of the local state. Reading China as an authoritarian state, the Singapore government negotiated the project mainly with the central government in Beijing. Because the Suzhou municipality was placed in a peripheral position in the Park development, it decided to set up its own development zone – the Suzhou New District, an industrial zone controlled by the local government. The two parks are in competition, with the latter having the advantages of low-cost land development. The example shows that foreign investment cannot act on its own without the support of the local state, even with nominal approval from the central state. Foreign capital has to be embedded into local politics. This global–local nexus means that globalization is not simply a "homogenization" process through which the global overcomes the local.

This perspective of locally initiated globalization is particularly important to the understanding of the spread of Western architectural styles in China. Drawing from the examples in *Globalization and the Chinese City* (Wu 2006), this section will decode the factor of globalization. Western building styles are often selectively adopted and mixed (e.g. "continental European style"), and are becoming very popular in China. Gated residential enclaves, built in the style of American "gated communities," are spreading out in the suburbs of Chinese cities. Some are so "exotic" that they do not really belong to any single American, French or Dutch style, but rather display a mélange of Western architectural motifs. They bear fantasy Western place names such as Orange County and Venice Garden, but in fact they are imagined forms of the West.

In the design of landmark buildings, Western architects and their firms are invited to apply various sorts of new concepts. The Western style also deeply penetrates "ordinary" residential landscapes. The Orange County (Beijing) is such an example. Located 16 kilometers into the northern suburbs of Beijing, the Orange County is one of Beijing's luxury gated communities along the belt of villa compounds near the Wenyu River. What is unusual is that the project boasts that it adopts "100 percent authentic North American design" (Wu 2004). According to the promotional materials, the design uses a new visionary concept that helps to maintain an atmosphere of "community." This sense of community is also, it is claimed, derived from "mimicking a French town on the River Seine," and therefore it fully "presents exotic characteristics of the foreign country" (from promotional web page). The construction materials, including doors, windows and ventilation systems, are in fact imported from overseas. Some houses in the Orange County are built in a townhouse style, which is a kind of product innovation. In the prereform period the dominant form of housing was multistorey matchbox-style walk-ups. In the 1980s (the early stage of reform), high-rise and high-density commodity housing estates began to emerge. They are built in the form of residential districts (micro-regions), a concept originating from the Soviet residential plan (French and Hamilton 1979). While the large modern housing estates developed in the 1980s are better than the workers' villages built in the 1950s, market reform has raised the aspirations of the middle class that has benefited from marketization.

Driven by the desire for lower density, more green space and private car travel, those "who want to own a plot of land under the feet and a piece of sky overhead" began to seek the villa type of living, which would bring them "land, sky, garden, and garage," a lifestyle which has not previously been seen in China. But the form of the villa demands more land, which is scarce in densely populated Chinese cities. The government in Beijing also tightened control over villa projects after the villa market collapsed in the Asian Financial Crisis. The townhouse, as an "economic villa," fills the gap between luxury villas and ordinary high-rise commodity housing, and is becoming popular with the upwardly mobile middle class. These townhouses mostly follow Western styles, as do the luxury villas.

In addition to the clustering of luxury villas, the villa compounds that are targeted at foreign tenants (mostly expatriates) are built close to each other, forming "foreign gated communities." This spatial concentration, it appears, reflects the rising demand for high-quality expatriate housing due to globalization. However, looking into the formation of concentrated foreigners' villa areas, it is revealed that such a separation of foreign and local housing is due to the historical requirement for the special approval of "foreign housing" or "housing for foreign sales." Domestic and foreign properties are separate submarkets. The latter is a kind of market that is unsubsidized. But the customers of foreign gated communities are not limited to expatriates. Now, since the category of foreign housing sales was abolished and merged into local sales (i.e. there is no difference between foreign and domestic sales), the gated form is becoming popular, promoted by the developer as well as the government to meet the increasing demand for better and safer residential space. In fact, while the gate has existed in China for many dynasties, it has now been rediscovered as an instrument for the partitioning of derelict socialist landscapes produced by "economizing the cost of urban development" and a postsocialist imagined good life (Wu 2005).

More recently, under the notion of "new urbanism" and "transit-oriented development" (TOD), developers emphasize the small-town atmosphere and the value of "community" to boast their product innovation. Again, they selectively package the elements of neo-traditionalist design, originally advocated by Duany and Plater-Zyberk (1993), such as a walkable community, compact urban form, neighborhood, or small town social relations, into a theme-park-like residence. For example, the McAllen Courtyard Villa claims that the project was named by Elizabeth Plater-Zyberk. These kinds of Chinese versions of "new urbanism" designs, however, intentionally forget about the advocacy of their originals for a "compact" urban form and higher reliance on public transit. The American version of new urbanism, as a kind of "smart growth," at least has an environmental agenda in the context of American suburban sprawl. But the Chinese traditional city form is more compact. The adoption of American new urbanism in the Chinese context is leading to urban expansion and the loss of more agricultural land (see Giroir, Chapter 12 of this book, for golf communities, which occupy excessive land).

How to explain this spread of Western residential forms? Do they reflect the hegemony of "globalization" or the imperialism of Western culture along with economic globalization? Did Chinese cities jump over the linear stages of modernization into "postmodern urbanism" (Dear and Flusty 1998), given that the basic elements of the latter (e.g. de-contextualized building styles, gated communities, thematically preserved heritages, and playful nightscapes) are all present in Chinese cities? These questions will lead to a more fundamental question, that is, what is the role of globalization in China's urban development?

Does this reflect globalization? Not really. This is at least different from so-called McDonaldization, as it is not Western styles that overwhelm and diminish Chinese styles. This is more a sort of "imagined globalization," using global motifs to sell off "local" products. Some tenants in Western-style communities might be translocal migrants, but the landlords are almost all the Chinese new rich. Globalization provides the possibility (such as the transplanting of different building styles), but how to turn this possibility into reality (e.g. the construction of the Orange County, Beijing) depends greatly on local conditions and politics. The local conditions for the development of exotic Western-style gated communities are, first, from the supply side, the development of a real estate market in China, and second, from the demand side, the preference for new projects and the requirement for product differentiation from mass-produced walk-ups to enclosed villas.

Rather than examining the impact of globalization on the city, as if globalization were independent of and superimposed on the latter, we need to address how globalization can be imagined, pursued and exploited in the process of local development of real estate. Through examining the emergence of Western architectural motifs and gated residential forms, we can understand the motivation underlying transplanted cityscapes. The developers of these Western-style buildings are in fact mostly locally based rather than global firms. They use transplanted Western forms to sell their products. This helps them to overcome the constraint of local property markets: that is, the lack of demand for "ordinary" properties. These new building forms are innovated products. By associating themselves with globalization, the development elite hope to give themselves the credibility that they are the builders of a vision of the good life (here it becomes similar to the notion of "urbanism"). Thus the globalization of Western forms is achieved through the conscious action of local players.

The factor of globalization therefore acts as a catalyst or enabling factor, triggering two major aspects of change. The first is that under globalization, space itself is being transformed; or, in a way, space is becoming transformative, in a very similar sense to Lefebvre's (1991) "révolution urbaine." Instead of treating space as a container of economic and social change, space itself becomes a critical element of/media for capital production and circulation. This is more fundamentally related to how the city is "reconceptualized" in a global context. This reconceptualization is embodied in recent notions about the basic nature of the city, that is, "urbanism" as a diverse, tolerant and hence innovative way of life – a new kind of "urbanism" that brings creativity and innovation (Florida 2002). The following section will further elaborate how Chinese urban space is used as a "fix" and how this has led to the emergence of cities.

The second is the change in politics, or "neoliberalization with Chinese characteristics" (Harvey 2005). But in China this neoliberal ethos is more than financial deregulation. In China, the coalition between the capital and the (local) state is more "strategic," rather than capital-driven civic boosterism. For multinationals and FDI, the low cost of the labor force and land resources as well as the potentially huge market are major reasons for relocating into mainland China. For the state, foreign capital provides additional resources to expand investment. The alliance between the state and capital, therefore, is more based on complementary need (and is hence fragile). This complementary relation can change from place to place and from time to time. For example, when the state needs capital to renovate dilapidated neighborhoods, the former can provide various institutional supports such as assisting with the relocation of households. But when housing demotion causes social tension, which is deemed potentially threatening to social stability and political legitimacy, the state can turn the other way and restrain the inflow of capital. Sometimes this restraint can be applied to a particular sector, such as real estate, if house price inflation becomes politicized. This complementary relation has led to a very strange dynamic between the two: they are closely intertwined, while not necessarily compatible with each other. This coalition is different from American civic boosterism. In the United States, capital exerts greater influence over the state, in the sense that the state itself is more or less the machine of capital, while capital is the "community builder" involved in the shaping of places. The alliance is also different from quango-based entrepreneurialism in the United Kingdom, in which the central state still exerts influence over local issues (Jessop *et al.* 1999).

Space as "fix": from state-led industrialization to urban-based accumulation

To understand China's urban revolution, we need to examine the role of space. Space, or more concretely, the built environment upon which urbanism is physically sustained, is critical to this movement. This importance has been acknowledged in the literature of "urbanization of neoliberalism" in the West (Brenner and Theodore 2002: 28). But this has not been fully explored in other contexts. As an emerging and transitional market, China sees urbanization as the important pathway to its economic rise.

China has been witnessing a tendency to over-accumulation. This is measured in terms of suppressed labor costs, which have been pushed to the minimum, while the redistributive function of the state has been significantly scaled down (e.g. the state has totally retreated from public housing provision, and about 80 percent of housing stock is privately owned, though a significant proportion is ex-public housing; see Li, Chapter 8 of this book). As a result, the pressure for capital to find an outlet is very high in China. The combination of suppressed labor cost and the lack of a redistributive state not only creates social inequality but also challenges economic growth: because of the repressed rewards at the bottom social stratum, before China can further develop the Fordist type of mass consumption to sustain its mass production, it has to shift to particular niches, or fragment in order to advance demand. The continuing expansion of the overseas market has already triggered trade conflicts with trade partners in the West. On the other hand, in order to sustain growth, a very high rate of capital investment has to be maintained. Now investment must be absorbed in the built environment so as to avoid an over-accumulation crisis. That the built environment (now including the rural environment under the so-called new countryside movement, which advocates the construction of roads and houses in rural areas) is increasingly used as the medium to absorb capital is the central thread throughout postreform urban development in China.

Along the way, the function of the city has been transformed in the postreform era. Looking retrospectively, the city as the physical/built environment is increasingly used as a means to overcome the constraint of accumulation in state-led industrialization (Wu and Ma 2005). This transformation is a change corresponding to the overall change in the regime of accumulation. The city is used as a fix to absorb capital. The commodification of urban assets exerts a powerful effect on economic growth. The opening up of the real estate sector as an investment venue has injected a strong impetus into almost saturated industrial development. The windfall profits generated by land development are in sharp contrast to declining profitability in state-owned enterprises (SOEs). Factories have begun to sell their sites to develop real estate business. Along with the "consumer revolution" (Davis 2000), niche markets have been expanded, of which the housing market is a major new area for consumption. Housing consumption has boosted urban-based accumulation by absorbing capital into the production of the built environment.

Economic restructuring, starting in the late 1970s, accelerated in the late 1990s. The state enterprise system established under the planned regime was scaled down; SOEs that produced nonconsumer products have been replaced by hybrid economic entities that produce "commodities." The rationale of production organization under marketization is based on the demand for "commodities." In order to achieve this aim, property rights are rebundled, for example, separating land ownership from land use rights. The latter can be transacted as commodities. Shareholding companies are established. Quasi-privatization separates the state as the ultimate owner from the leaseholder or shareholder who can draw legitimate benefits (see Lee, Chapter 3 of this book). This often leads to a transfer of state assets to private hands. Disguised by state ownership in name and strong political control, China has entered a process of radical privatization (see Yang and Huang, Chapter 2 of this book, also Abramson, Chapter 4 of this book).

This urban-based accumulation regime relies more and more on developing and exploiting niche markets. Targeting those who can afford the commodity is becoming a tactic of producers. Therefore, commodities require their unique selling points. Products need to be branded, and so does the city. Because the demand comes from the marketized segments, the more closely production is associated with commodification, the more profitable it becomes. While developers claim to be producing housing for "ordinary people," it is the upper end of luxury housing that actually generates a profit (see Shin, Chapter 9 of this book; Tian and Wong, Chapter 11 of this book). This is why in the building boom, while the state attempts to control the construction of "luxury properties," they are still produced in horrendously massive quantities. Similarly, new cultural industries are pursued by cities, just as the individual developer pursues a product's identity. Conspicuous consumption has driven the production of more and more spectacular urban spaces (Giroir, Chapter 12 of this book, for leisure space; Wang and Guo, Chapter 13 of this book, for retail space). Recently, China has put forward a slogan to suggest that economic development should be based on "human needs"; politically this is a very elegant proposal. But there are different readings of this rationale by local government officials and developers: because the city, as a space of new urbanism, agglomerates "need" (read consumer/purchasing power), the best way of satisfying human needs is to promote urban growth.

The shift in accumulation methods requires institutional twists to sustain its structural coherence. For example, the central city is strengthened by enlarging its jurisdiction over nearby counties (Ma 2005). At a more macro level, the state plays an active role in facilitating the development of the market. This capacity is due to several factors: (1) the historical legacy that provides some means of maneuver (e.g. in the land leasing market); (2) the influence of the "developmental state" (see the discussion on this perspective later); (3) the essential requirement for market order. The last point is often neglected. In fact, in this urban-based accumulation regime, social conflict and potential contentions are so strong that the state has to play a visible role so as to develop the basic conditions for the market to operate. The state also plays an indispensable role in maintaining social stability, which is not unique to China. For example, Smith (2002) reveals that neoliberal discourse in the US contradicts the reality of heavy-handed intervention through policies such as zero-tolerance policing and maintaining social reproduction (e.g. importing Spanish teachers from Spain to New York, where there are more than two million native Spanish speakers).

My argument is that, regardless of whether Shanghai or Beijing is a truly global city using the narrow definition of "global command center," Chinese cities have been integrated into global commodity production. It is this tight association with global production circuits that has laid down political economic conditions similar to those of the core Western economies. As a result, globalization in the Chinese city should be seen as being as much an indigenously generated process (the changing regime of accumulation) as an externally imposed one (influx of FDI). The production of urban space is part of this function of using space as a new medium to expand accumulation. The mode of regulation is consequently changed in order to meet such a requirement.

Besides the change in the fiscal regime, which has given greater autonomy to the locality, urban land and housing are "commodified," allowing rent/profit to be legitimately drawn. The components of productive infrastructure – airport, deep-water port, metro system, elevated roads and highways, fast rail, info-ports – are becoming the indispensable elements for building the entrepreneurial city. As the city is staged at the center of accumulation, the outcome is severe economic competition between cities and within the city. The local "entrepreneurial agent" leads this process to facilitate the realization of the shift in accumulation strategy.

The result of this shifting accumulation strategy is intensified competition for space. In particular, China is seeing the "replication" of land enclosure (*quan di*) in history: local government attempts to acquire rural land under the collective owner- ship of farmers to, for example, set up a development zone or a "university town"; developers requisition land to increase their land bank, causing a property boom; rural collectives transfer land, formally or informally, to various businesses so as to get land rents; farmers rebuild their houses into private rentals for migrants. Some of these large-scale redevelopments are truly on a grand scale. According to the *People's Daily* (August 22, 2004), up to July 2004 a total of 6,866 development zones had been identified, amounting to 38,600 square kilometers. Guangzhou University Town is one of the largest university towns in China. A so-called uni- versity town is not just a town of universities – it accommodates a whole range of commercial development. In the case of the widely criticized "Oriental Uni- versity" in Langfang Economic and Technological Development Zone, a 108-hole golf course was even built.

Land enclosure has led to millions of "landless farmers." Relentless and illegal land-grabs cause displacement and discontent. Land-related corruption is also a major abuse, involving large sums of money. The well-publicized case of Zhou Zhengyi involves forced house demolition in Shanghai. More recently, in 2006, Mr Cheng Liangyu, the Party Secretary of Shanghai, was sacked and arrested for land-related corruption. The amount involved is claimed to be as high as 300 million Yuan. What is more appalling is that the corruption included the misuse of the recently established social security fund.

Such space competition has profound social implications. In the beginning of 2006, Mr Ren Zhiqiang, the CEO of Huayuan Corporation, also China's most outspoken developer, openly claimed, "I only build for the rich," and asserted that "the poor should be segregated from the rich," triggering a widespread debate in the media and Internet-based discussion forums. Within a couple of weeks, his vision of rich/poor separation led to over 3,000 replies on one of China's largest news web sites (sina.com). Mr Ren's argument however reflects a reality in China: building for the poor cannot make money. As a developer, he cannot reasonably be expected to act as a charity – pursuing profit is the goal of his company. Housing provision for the poor should be the responsibility of the government. However, the question is why, as a developer, he feels that development, to make money, has to disperse the poor – that is the money can only be made through demolition of the housing of the poor. Because the space is used as a fix to solve the problem of capital accumulation, the exchange of value of land is regarded as more important than the use value. As a consequence, the poor have to be dispensed in order to redevelop the old areas.

Theoretical relevance

Possible theoretical explanations

How to explain China's urban transition? To put urban China in a comparative perspective, Logan and Fainstein (2007) propose four theoretical perspectives that might be relevant: modernization, dependency theory, the developmental state, and postsocialist transition. The theory of modernization (Rostow 1960), starting from neoclassical development studies, views Third World urbanization as a process mimicking that in advanced Western economies. It focuses on the change in economic structure (i.e. industrialization) and its consequent change (urbanization). But the theory of modernization fails to explain the phenomenon of "over-urbanization" in Third World countries, and the fact that cities are not becoming engines of economic growth but rather sources of social conflict and retarded infrastructure and rural development.

The world system and dependency theory looks at problems such as squatter settlements, informal economies, high rate unemployment, and under-serviced population and over-urbanization in Third World cities beyond these countries themselves. The developed Western economies subject the under-developed Third World to a state of dependency: the latter becomes an exporter of raw materials; the modern export sector is juxtaposed with the retarded traditional sector, continuing to siphon out resources and impoverish weak countries into a peripheral position (Wallerstein 1976).

The developmental state theory explains why the newly industrializing economies (NIEs) of East Asia have been able to catch up with developed economies, through highlighting the role of the state (Wade 1990). The state promotes export-oriented growth through strong intervention measures and a close link between domestic capital and the state bureaucratic system. Modeled after the successful catching-up experience of the Japanese economy, the developmental state turns the modern urban sector into the growth engine of the national economy.

The theory of (post)socialist transition, mostly derived from the experience of former socialist countries in Eastern and Central Europe, points to the factor of "marketization," in particular the emergence of the private sector, and the history of state socialism in determining current social and political characteristics, as "path-dependency" (Harloe 1996; Stark and Bruszt 1998).

The four "paradigms" that start from very different theoretical stances are as follows:

1 Modernization theory views the social structure as essentially being determined by economic structure (including the level of urbanization), which assumes that the change in the former corresponds to the stage of the latter; for example, Kuznets' (1955) inverted U-shaped curve argues that inequality initially rises with economic growth and later declines.
2 Dependency theory views the social structure as conditioned by relationships between nation states – that is a world system – and regards the economic structure of the nation as serving as a functional part of that world system.
3 The development state theory emphasizes the role of the nation state, and argues that economic structure can be boosted by the interventionist state, thus running against the "determinist" view of dependency theory – that is emphasizing national sovereignty in the system of inter-nation relations.
4 The postsocialist transition theory emphasizes the root of socialism and argues that social structure is determined and continues to be determined by internal political structure.

These paradigms are theorized out of particular contexts and do not necessarily fit into a different context of development. They have strengths and weaknesses in explaining different contexts.

Modernization theory's strength lies in its view of temporal change in a national economy (especially its economic structure and urbanization); while it is oriented towards neoclassical economic explanation, its stance seems to be closer to the "structuralist" view and has that view's merit – that is, how the production force creates corresponding social relations. Its problem is, in contrast to the structuralist view, the direct connection between economic stages and social structure, leaving out the essential mode of production, and thus a whole range of national and international politics.

To explain China's increasing regional and rural/urban inequalities, modernization theory duly invokes changing economic structure. The Kuznets-inspired paradigm can be viewed as a model using modernity or economic restructuring to explain spatial inequalities. However, the theory of modernization is problematic in the sense that it "naturalizes" economic structure change, whereas reindustrialization and consequent urbanization are closely related to state policies. The underdevelopment of inner regions and rural areas is related to deliberate state policy, starting in the socialist period, to catch up with the modern industrial powers in the West. Recently the Chinese government initiated the "going-west" strategy to develop China's western regions, and the "new countryside movement" to revitalize rural infrastructure and reduce rural and urban differences. Thus regional and urban–rural inequalities are not only determined by the economic stage but are also influenced by state strategies and policies.

Dependency theory goes beyond local/national politics and views the nation in the world context. The theory was invented ahead of its time – globalization and the global economy are only becoming more substantial in the twenty-first century; but its view of the capitalist world system neglects the fact that the globalization of production forces is a process rather than an end product, and there is no such thing as a "united" class of capitalists in the world; rather they are embedded into local and national politics.

To explain regional inequality, dependency theory finds the historical root of regional imbalance in China's being a peripheral developing country; and indeed the reorientation of China's economy towards an export-oriented one in the reform period led to the booming of coastal regions. To explain urban inequality, dependency theory reminds us of rural migrants as the labor force in the process of global commodity production, going beyond "local" inequalities between rural and urban households. Despite foreign investment flowing into the coastal region, bringing economic prosperity to the coastal cities, much profit is controlled by multinationals and their agents and does not spread out to the "direct producers" – those who actually provide the labor for the production of global commodities. Migrants are engaged in market-based production but receive economic rewards below a livable wage in the market (see Kumar and Li, Chapter 6 of this book, for the social protection problem). Their own labor force thus cannot be reproduced in a market way. For example, they cannot afford so-called commodity housing and tend to live in private rentals in urban villages – a contributing factor to increasing intra-urban differentiation.

The developmental state duly points out the local dimension of growth, but its explanation of this state role suffers from the lack of a detailed anthropological account of the agents behind the developmental state, albeit the original version does implicitly relate the development mentality to elite bureaucrats. That is, the developmental state theory emphasizes the role of the state but from an economic perspective. In this aspect, it is closer to modernization theory.

The developmental state theory would appear to have strong appeal in that the Chinese Communist Party (CCP) and the state maintain rather strong control over society. Indeed, the remaking of large Chinese cities such as Beijing and Shanghai is more like a "state-project" (Wu 2003) than the outcome of global trade flows that is identified in the classical global city thesis (Sassen 1991). But it is not clear why state agents can be described as developmental rather than "predatory," given the recent proliferation of corruption. To understand urban governance and transition, the developmental state theory has difficulty in using the local government as the autonomous agent, because the theory is developed at the national state level – or the city-state in the case of Singapore where the state has autonomy in determining fiscal, financial, industrial, and import/export policies. Not only do the rules of the WTO reduce such autonomy, but local governments do not have it. In addition, they are becoming more "entrepreneurial" (read "neo-liberal") than "developmental," because they tend to make coalitions with capital rather than using industrial and banking policies to restrain it.

Postsocialist transition theory probes deeply into the power structure of the socialist and postsocialist state. But the key problem is that it examines the socialist state narrowly without situating it in, first, the particular stage of economic development of the nation (late development) and, second, its position in the world system (semi-periphery).

The transition from socialism perhaps not only offers an explanation for the postsocialist urban pattern but also links current urban forms to their origins in historical state socialism. Many present divisions – urban versus rural inequalities for instance – are often the legacies of socialism. The movement of rural laborers into the city brings this urban/rural division to the intra-urban level. This legacy is evident in the creation of new urban poverty neighborhoods, either as deteriorating workers' districts or vibrant but chaotic migrant enclaves (Liu and Wu 2006). China has not officially ended its socialism, hence the term is not denominated "post"; state power persists (Bian and Logan 1996), and the mentality will continue to influence urban development for many years to come. The problem of transition theory is that it recognizes the feature of "path-dependency" without understanding its path-breaking tendency.

Although the differences in theoretical stances mean these theories are not compatible, the elements upon which they build can be recombined to form a new explanation. We disagree with the modernization theory in its determinism of economic stages; we disagree with the world system in its determinism of world politics; we disagree with the developmental state in its rosy picture of the state capacity; and we disagree with postsocialist transition in its notion of "socialist legacies."

Reading this picture of urban emergence, we believe that China's transition is moving towards a very "advanced" stage of capitalist development – which is why Chinese cities can provide a laboratory for observing some recent trends in contemporary urban restructuring. The "newness" has so far not been fully recognized in the literature, a point highlighted in our previous work.

> [Pulling all these threads together], we see a picture of "advanced" market-oriented urban growth in transitional China. Such a mode of regulation is a profound shift from the "developmental" state, which emphasizes the use of

industrial policies to guide national economic growth in late industrializing countries, to the "entrepreneurial" city, which commodifies "place" as a space commodity. Along with such a shift is the changing role of the state itself, from resource manager to market actor. The "legacies" of state socialism define many of the parameters of market engineering, and the development of a fully-fledged *market* society is facilitated by the high capacity of "political mobilization." It is the distinctive combination of "path-dependent" politics and a vibrant market economy that demands future scholarship.

(emphasis in original, Wu *et al.* 2007: 309)

Related to China's urban revolution, we attempt to formulate a new hybrid theory as follows. In this particular historical stage of economic development (under-urbanization) and the world system (globalization extending from the new international division of labor to socialist countries), the socialist state, for its own considerations of legitimacy, uses governance instruments to boost economic growth, acts like a developmental state but without the coherence of the latter, and subsequently turns the particular forms of social structure (rural/urban division) existing in history into the conditions for the capitalist mode of production for the global economy (e.g. the pool of rural migrants as pure and abstracted cheap labor without regarding them as social subjects), and brings both the inequalities within the world system and the inequalities within the nation (rural/urban division) into the urban realm, further shaping inter- and intra-urban inequalities as new forms of "uneven spatial development."

The test ground for urbanism

Smith (2002: 427) argues that "the true global cities may be the rapidly growing metropolitan economies of Asia, Latin America, and (to a lesser extent) Africa, as much as the command centers of Europe, North America and Japan." He bases his argument on the *scale* of change – the extent to which neoliberal urbanism is adopted during globalization rather than the existing function nodes. In a sense, his view of global cities is more process oriented – perhaps they are more appropriate as globalizing cities.

I want to argue that in the context of a refashioned globalism, widely (if partially) expressed via the ideological discourses of "globalization," we are also seeing a broad redefinition of the urban scale – in effect, a new urbanism – that refocuses the criteria of scale construction, in this case toward processes of production and toward the extraordinary urban growth in Asia, Latin America, and Africa.

(p. 430)

As argued in an earlier section, China is at the forefront of making this global "new urbanism" through radical space commodification and strong if not "revanchist" state participation in market development. Chinese cities are now the test ground for this new urbanism, as whatever can be found in the world, you can find it there – in a similar fashion to "it all comes to LA" (Soja 1989). Such a sense of ever-present newness is vividly illustrated by a senior planner in Shenzhen, talking about his attitude towards "foreign expertise" in urban design.

> If foreigners want to come here to exchange their view, that's fine. If they want to teach us how to do urban design, I don't buy it. Here [in Shenzhen] we have done all the fanciest stuffs that are just being talked of in the West.
>
> (Personal communication)

Chinese cities are now becoming experimental sites for various sorts of avant-garde as well as prestigious architectural styles. On the one hand, China is still a pre-modern developing country that is experiencing modernity and urbanization; on the other, the most ostentatious self-expression of postmodern architecture, which is not even possible in Western economies, is solicited for place-making. In the common wisdom of the West, China is still an authoritarian country with strong state control. But place entrepreneurs have more "freedom" to test and advance their urbanism than they would have in a "free-market" economy elsewhere in the world.

New concepts such as the eco-city and the creative city are popular with Chinese city officials and planners. In Shanghai's Chongming Island, the world's first eco-city is being built by Arup, a multinational engineering consulting firm based in London. Shanghai, Beijing and Shenzhen are testing the idea of "creative industries," along with their experiments in the commodification of culture and in using culture as a means of consumption (see Sun and Chen, Chapter 14 of this book, for globally oriented consumption behavior). These experiments are now becoming possible, because Chinese cities are "too rich" – not measured by per capita income or household consumption, but in terms of surplus capital that is leading to capital "hyper-liquidity," both domestically and internationally.

Practical implications

China's urban revolution has a series of practical implications for the world. These implications range from political and environmental to social challenges.

First, there is a political implication for governance at the city level – that is, reshaping the regulatory regime. The injection of China's vast human resources into global production imposes a new condition for urban governance at the global scale. The condition of neoliberal governance has been laid down by the new international division of labor starting in the 1970s. Under economic globalization, it has given capital greater mobility across the boundaries of the nation state. But China's scale of human resources brings this division to a new stage. The impact of China's labor costs can be felt in many places in the world, including Western Europe today. Competitive-minded local states, commodified land, under-mobilized labor rights protection, together with various institutional legacies (such as *hukou*) that restrain the rights of the migrant population, are making Chinese cities very "competitive" production sites, in terms of economic costs, for global commodity production. Neoliberalism with Chinese characteristics, at least at the city level, is making the continuing adoption of the welfare state in the world more difficult. China's "strange" combination of strong state "intervention" and radical market orientation (in particular in terms of the labor regime) reflects the stage of "rolling out" neoliberalism (Peck and Tickell 2002) in which state intervention moves away from redistribution to supporting the market by putting in place relevant conditions for it (see also Smith 2002).

Second, there is a huge environmental challenge. This urban-based development strategy is energy-intensive. On the one hand, the motorization of transport (i.e. the wide use of the car), large-scale construction of highways and roads, encroachment on rural land for industries and urban leisure (e.g. golf courses), wide adoption of refrigerators and air-conditioning all enhance the quality of life in the cities; on the other hand they create environmental problems. China has a very low per capita resource endowment, especially in terms of nonrenewable resources. Its energy endowment is unlikely to be self-sustaining. This urban-centered growth model will inevitably force China to go down the path of global energy search. But this revolution is unfolding under the name of development, and what complicates the environmental issue is the right to development: why should more developed market economies enjoy a high quality of life while the under-developed nations have to put their urban development on hold?

Third, there is an implication for global or transnational immigration. China has a potential pool of labor. Its outflow is only a matter of time, when the huddle for international migration is reduced. Developed economies are experiencing an ageing problem (as does China: see Cook and Powell, Chapter 7 of this book). Along with the ageing population, there is a need for a younger labor force. While the current phase of globalization is biased towards capital mobility and a limited number of upper-end professionals and global elite transnationals, the advent of the mobility of people seems inevitable. More fundamentally this is related to labor mobility, the constraining of which is a worldwide practice. Transnational migration may begin with undocumented immigrants, but increasingly the border cannot be sustained. There are officially about 10,000 workers in the sweatshops in Italy (personal communication). Transnationalism will not only occur among highly skilled professionals (such as nurses and engineers) but also at the bottom of the labor market.

Fourth, there is an implication for the global market in higher value-added goods such as high-tech products. The WTO opened the gate for Chinese goods to flow into the world; Europe has now seen competition from labor-intensive products such as shoes and textiles. But China has been strategically investing in R&D and technological innovation. The cost of high-end and skilled labor is also competitive in China. The development of scientific and research bases can be dated back to the centrally planned era, when the state strategically invested in nuclear technology and defense-related industries. While it still remains to be seen how effective this state-led research and innovation will be, the upgrading of the export structure from labor-intensive goods to higher value-added items such as electronics products has already begun. There is a possibility that in the next two decades Europe as well as the world will see the coming of competitive high-tech goods from China.

Fifth, there is an implication for emerging consumer markets. China's urban revolution is driven by its consumer revolution. China opened its vast domestic market to the world under WTO, especially in the services sector when the last restriction expired in December 2006. Chinese consumers are becoming a new driving force for the development of global consumer markets, in particular specific markets such as overseas tourism, overseas education, and niche luxury consumer goods. Universities in Britain have already seen the potential of postgraduate education for Chinese students; the trend will continue, to include undergraduate education, enhanced by the increasing domestic costs of education in China and a rising income for the middle class.

In sum, these implications are presented as speculative thoughts; nevertheless, they are practical for the world. China's emerging cities will become an important subject of study not just because of the interest in these cities themselves, but also because they have profound theoretical relevance and practical implications for the rest of the world.

Organization of this volume

This volume is divided into four parts, reflecting the contributors' efforts to grapple with institutional emergence accompanied by phenomenal urban growth, transition in economic and social spheres, rebuilding residential space, and emerging leisure, retailing and consumption practices.

The first part identifies the city as an emerging institution through which land property rights are delineated and distributed, public-private partnerships are built to provide new infrastructure (in this case the water sector), and property rights lead to the construction of place-based interests, or so-called community building, which transforms the premises of how the city is managed and planned. You-Ren Yang and Hung-Kai Huang (Chapter 2 of this book) discuss the regime of land property rights in Suzhou and Dongguan. They compare detailed practices of land rights management in these two cities and highlight the dynamics of the institutional arrangement that leads to different outcomes in land development. Beyond the known effect of using the city as a growth machine (Logan and Molotch 1987) built by city development officials to generate land revenue, they reveal that the promotion of cadres is heavily based on achievement in GDP growth, and thus various ways of allocating growth quotas affect development behaviors. They seem to suggest that Suzhou is more aggressive in land development than Dongguan because of these local differences.

Seungho Lee (Chapter 3) explores the emerging institutions in the water sector, namely public and private partnership (PPP). The chapter is revealing in the sense that it suggests the level of privatization in infrastructure development – an aspect previously overlooked. On the other hand, such a mode of privatization is subject to intense negotiation and intervention from various tiers of government. The government of Shanghai strives to privatize the water sector and use PPP to strengthen its financial capacity in water provision. As a result, the partnership is highly volatile. But with WTO membership and the opening of the service sector to the world market, Chinese cities are being invested in by transitional corporations and becoming the assets of multiple ownerships.

Property-based interests and communities were overlooked in the prereform era. Daniel Abramson (Chapter 4) highlights some dramatic challenges facing the Chinese city planning profession. The traditional premises of city planning in China – that planning was used to legitimize government commands, that planning was advocated for stimulating growth or with a "developmentalist" justification – are becoming recognized as defective. The awareness of "community" is not just fostered by the state in order to continue and supplement its traditional work-unit based governance, but also emerges from "commodity housing" development, which has created millions of homeowners (see also Si-ming Li, Chapter 8 of this book). This "dialectics" of urban planning surprisingly realigns the regulatory aspect of the Chinese city according to the logic of market capitalism. Even though his example of the city of Quanzhou in Fujian province is a unique case, having historically strong private property awareness due to the fact that Quanzhou historically was the origin of many overseas Chinese, it well illustrates the difficulty in initiating and regulating urban development.

The city as institutional emergence is accompanied by a series of transitions in economic and social spheres. Part II begins to explore how the inflow of foreign or overseas investment transforms the city; how the urban labor market is transformed by the arrival of increasing numbers of migrant workers; how demographically Chinese cities are becoming ageing communities; and how housing provision is dramatically reshaped by the transition to homeownership. Chun Yang (Chapter 5), for example, illustrates how Taiwanese investment is different from that of Hong Kong, in that the coming of Taiwanese investment in the later development stages of Dongguan, a city in the core of the Pearl River Delta, has driven the city onto a different trajectory. While Hong Kong investment focuses on small- and medium-scale labor-intensive and export-oriented manufacturing, Taiwanese investment has helped the city link with global brand-name producers and thus become the "supply- chain city." This transformation again shows the profound nature of change – from initially an "export-enclave" to a globally integrated production complex.

Sunil Kumar and Bingqin Li (Chapter 6) reveal significant change in the urban labor market, comparable with that in urban India, both of which have experienced increases in the sector outside the salaried state sector. The growth in China is not so much in the form of the "self-employed" as in India, but the challenge is similar – how to protect vast numbers of informal urban workers. This requires not only a paternalist state but also a mobilized civil society to fill the gap in the state's institutionalized protection. But the obstacle to increasing self-provision by informal/migrant workers lies in not only the state's reluctance but also the imperative to constrain labor costs, deeply associated with the changing role of the city as the production site for global commodities (see earlier discussion on accumulation strategy).

Ian Cook and Jason Powell (Chapter 7) identify an important trend in China's emerging cities becoming an ageing urban society. The unique feature of China's urbanization is that before China even enters a medium level of urbanization the process of ageing has started. However, they argue that we should not see the issue of "ageing" as a problem through the bio-medical gaze – that is, the elderly being disabled, "vulnerable" and a burden on society. Instead, the issue of ageing is intermingled with changing lifestyles and social marginalization. It is the poorest elderly in the poorest parts of the city who become potentially vulnerable. Cook and Powell thus argue that, rather than a broad-brush approach to social policy, support should be ensured for the most vulnerable of the elderly.

Perhaps the most dramatic change is in housing provision. China is now a nation of "homeowners." Si-ming Li (Chapter 8) studies the transition to homeownership and assesses the implications for wealth redistribution. Using longitudinal data gathered from Beijing and Guangzhou, he identifies the fact that the structure of inequalities in a socialist redistributive system is further strengthened under market transition, because the beneficiaries of housing reform, through the conferment of full ownership on buyers of reform housing, are managerial and professional staff and the cadres of Party and government organizations. What is the most striking is that while the private rental sector remains undeveloped, the public rental sector is dwindling.

The making of China's new urbanism proceeds through rebuilding residential space. Part III includes three closely related chapters focusing on residential rede-velopment, neighborhood changes, and sociospatial stratification. These chapters extend the understanding of social and housing tenure inequalities revealed in the earlier chapters into that of spatial segregation. Hyun Bang Shin (Chapter 9) examines Beijing's "Old and Dilapidated Housing Redevelopment Program" and the change of practice from in-kind to monetary compensation. He identifies that the poor have been squeezed both financially and spatially: reduced cash compen-sation, increased housing costs, the unaffordable price of "affordable housing," limited housing finance, and displacement to the suburbs. He argues that for ex-public-housing tenants in the new emerging city, residential redevelopment is no longer the pathway to homeownership but "simply becomes an exit to the much constrained private rental sector," while the sector is marginal in Beijing's housing tenure.

Similarly, Shenjing He and Fulong Wu (Chapter 10) have studied urban rede-velopment programs in Shanghai and population redistribution through population census and a tailored questionnaire survey. They gathered detailed neighborhood-level statistics in three neighborhoods and assessed the impact of redevelopment on these neighborhoods. They argue that residential redevelopment is a direct cause of intensification of residential differentiation. There are significant differences in neighborhood profiles pre- and post-development. Residents of redeveloped neighborhoods are sorted through different routes into different residential spaces.

Further, Ying Ying Tian and Cecilia Wong (Chapter 11) investigate two adjacent redevelopment projects. They find that not only the low-income group but also the medium-income group are both displaced by super-wealthy elites in Shanghai's premium locations such as International Ladoll. In purely profit-making large urban redevelopment projects, market forces continue to dominate the urban landscape. The state has to make concessions to lure in private capital. They make comparisons with Smith's (1996) thesis of gentrification as the "return of capital" to the inner city in the Western economies. All these chapters reveal a very "novel" aspect of Chinese cities: they are emerging not through the natural course of residential invasion and succession, but as a result of capital's engineering over space.

Part IV begins to examine emerging practices in China's new urbanism: leisure, shopping and consumption. These practices might not be brand new to Western cities as they have existed for some time now (e.g. gated communities and shopping malls). However, in the context of urban China, they show the extension of urban functionality as a (new) way of life: golf associated with gated villa compounds, shopping at the shopping center, living in luxury flats, and enjoying a "globally oriented lifestyle" with brand clothing and Western-style entertainment. Indeed, even in the Western context, they continue to trigger debates; for example, for gated communities, the concern over fear (Low 2003) and social segregation; for shopping malls, privatization and the end of public space (Zukin 2004).

Guillaume Giroir (Chapter 12 of this book) explores "gated golf communities" as new leisure spaces. These communities, such as Tomson Golf Villas in Shanghai and Mission Hills in Shenzhen, are not stealth spaces. They are publicized in the media, most vividly revealing the "new" urbanism to the emerging middle class. Themed by large-scale green space together with clubhouses, five-star hotels and luxury villas, these gated golf communities present not only income inequalities but also the divide of lifestyles. Ironically, the spread of golf courses, often associated with the struggle to expand green space in eco-friendly cities, in the context of Chinese cities, which are more compact than their American counterparts, causes problems of overconsumption of land, water and chemical products. Greening the emerging city contradicts the basic principle of sustainable development.

The production of new retail spaces is examined in detail by Shuguang Wang and Chongyi Guo (Chapter 13 of this book). They demonstrate that behind this are retail deregulation and restructuring of retail capital. They depict the waves of "department store boom," "hypermarket boom," and "shopping center boom" sweeping over Beijing and Shanghai. Their tale of two cities shows the reorientation of emerging Chinese cities to a consumer society. They predict the cannibalization of retail space, which has already begun in some areas of these two cities, through which competition weeds out the weak players, leading to the consolidation of retail capital in the hands of a smaller number of players.

This reorientation towards a consumer society is further explored through the changing behavior of consumers by Jiaming Sun and Xiangming Chen (Chapter 14). They establish the link between residential categories, connection to the global economy, and consumption behavior. They find that the different patterns of behavior are attributable not only to socioeconomic or demographic variables but also to "personal global connections" (e.g. having worked for a foreign company, having been abroad, or having relatives or friends overseas). Their study highlights how global influences act locally and transform emerging Chinese cities through a global/local nexus (see the earlier discussion on the catalyst factor of globalization).

Conclusion: beyond gradualism

China is moving towards an urban society. Chinese cities are emerging social, political and economic entities. The meaning of "emergence" is twofold. First, it is an urban scene that is emerging outside mature Western economies. In this sense, the term is used interchangeably with "emerging markets." Second, China is experiencing "urban revolution": the emergence of Chinese cities is breaking the gradualist trajectory of market-oriented reform. This is not to deny the path-dependent features that are readily identifiable in Chinese cities (e.g. prereform housing inequalities manifested in new sociospatial divides). But Chinese cities are facing many problems that at the same time confront the developed Western economies. In fact, many "novel" aspects of the emergence can be seen to reflect the most recent trends witnessed in developed market economies. The city is becoming the driver for socioeconomic transformation. This book strives to demonstrate this "radical" side of transformation – institutional changes behind urban emergence, and the spaces and practices that make the new urbanism. This "new urbanism" in the title of the book refers to something much broader than walkable and compact communities in American suburbs, promoted by neo-traditionalist design – indeed, it refers back to Louis Wirth's classic study of the nature of the city: "urbanism as a way of life," to see how a new way of life is under formation in China.

Acknowledgments

This chapter has a long intellectual journey. Some initial ideas originated from my co-editing the book *Restructuring the Chinese City* (Routledge) with Laurence Ma. Subsequently, the theme has been developed in various workshops and conferences, including The New Chinese Urbanism (2005, organized by Neil Smith), China's Urban Transition (2005, organized by John Logan), and Workshop for Chinese Urbanization: Theories and Approaches (2005, organized by Chaolin Gu). More recently the paper has been presented as the ninth Annual Lecture of Globalization and World Cities (GaWC) Network (2007). I would like to thank, in particular, Laurence Ma, George Lin, Neil Smith, John Logan, Chaolin Gu, Anthony Yeh, and Peter Taylor.

References

Bian, Y. and Logan, J. R. (1996) "Market transition and the persistence of power: the changing stratification system in urban China," *American Sociological Review*, 61: 739–758.

Brenner, N. and Theodore, N. (2002) *Spaces of Neoliberalism: Urban Restructuring in North America and West Europe*, Oxford: Blackwell.

Davis, D. (ed.) (2000) *The Consumer Revolution in Urban China*, Berkeley, CA: University of California Press.

Dear, M. and Flusty, S. (1998) "Postmodern urbanism," *Annals of the Association of American Geographers*, 88(1): 50–72.

Duany, A. and Plater-Zyberk, E. (1993) "The neighbourhood, the district, and the corridor," in P. Katz and J. V. Scully (eds) *The New Urbanism: Toward an Architecture of Community*, New York: McGraw-Hill, xvii–xxi.

Florida, R. (2002) *The Rise of the Creative Class*, New York: Basic Books.

French, R. A. and Hamilton, F. E. I. (eds) (1979) *The Socialist City*, Chichester: John Wiley and Sons.

Harloe, M. (1996) "Cities in transition," in G. M. Andrusz, M. Harloe and I. Szelenyi (eds) *Cities after Socialism: Urban and Regional Change and Conflict in Post-Socialist Societies*, Oxford: Blackwell, 1–29.

Harvey, D. (2005) *A Brief History of Neoliberalism*, Oxford: Oxford University Press.

Jessop, B., Peck, J. and Tickell, A. (1999) "Retooling the machine: economic crisis, state restructuring, and urban politics," in A. Jonas and D. Wilson (eds) *The Urban Growth Machine: Critical Perspectives Two Decades Later*, Albany, NY: SUNY Press, 141–159.

Kuznets, S. (1955) "Economic growth and income inequality," *American Economic Review*, 65: 1–28.

Lefebvre, H. (1991) *The Production of Space*, London: Blackwell.

Liu, Y. and Wu, F. (2006) "Urban poverty neighbourhoods: typology and spatial concentration under China's market transition, a case study of Nanjing," *Geoforum*, 37: 610–626.

Logan, J. and Fainstein, S. (forthcoming) "Urban China in comparative perspective," in J. Logan (ed.) *Urban China in Transition*, Oxford: Blackwell.

Logan, J. R. and Molotch, H. L. (1987) *Urban Fortunes: The Political Economy of Place*, Berkeley, CA: University of California Press.

Low, S. (2003) *Behind the Gates: Life, Security, and the Pursuit of Happiness in Fortress America*, London: Routledge.

Ma, L. J. C. (2005) "Urban administrative restructuring, changing scale relations and local economic development in China," *Political Geography*, 24(4): 477–497.

Nolan, P. (2004) *Transforming China: Globalization, Transition and Development*, London: Anthem Press.

Peck, J. and Tickell, A. (2002) "Neoliberalizing space," *Antipode*, 34(3): 380–404.

Pereira, A. (2003) *State Collaboration and Development Strategies in China: The Case of China-Singapore Suzhou Industrial Park (1992–2002)*, London: RoutledgeCurzon.

Rostow, W. (1960) *The Stages of Economic Growth*, Cambridge: Cambridge University Press.

Sassen, S. (1991) *The Global City*, Princeton, NJ: Princeton University Press.

Smith, N. (1996) *The New Urban Frontier: Gentrification and the Revanchist City*, London: Routledge.

Smith, N. (2002) "New globalism, new urbanism: gentrification as global urban strategy," *Antipode*, 34(3): 427–450.

Soja, E. (1989) *Postmodern Geography: The Reassertion of Space in Critical Social Theory*, New York: Verso.

State Statistical Bureau (2006) *China statistic yearbook*, 2005, Beijing: China Statistic Press.

Wade, R. (1990) *Governing the Market: Economic Theory and the Role of Government in East Asian Industrialization*, Princeton, NJ: Princeton University Press.

Wallerstein, I. (1976) *The Modern World-System: Capitalist Agriculture and the Origins of the European World-Economy in the Sixteenth Century*, New York: Academic Press.

Wu, F. (2000) "The global and local dimensions of place-making: remaking Shanghai as a world city," *Urban Studies*, 37(8): 1359–1377.

Wu, F. (2003) "The (post-) socialist entrepreneurial city as a state project: Shanghai's reglobalisation in question," *Urban Studies*, 40(9): 1673–1698.

Wu, F. (2004) "Transplanting cityscapes: the use of imagined globalization in housing commodification in Beijing," *Area*, 36(3): 227–234.

Wu, F. (2005) "Rediscovering the 'gate' under market transition: from work-unit compounds to commodity housing enclaves," *Housing Studies*, 20(2): 235–254.

Wu, F. (ed.) (2006) *Globalization and the Chinese City*, London: Routledge.

Wu, F. and Ma, L. J. C. (2005) "The Chinese city in transition: towards theorizing China's urban restructuring," in L. J. C. Ma and F. Wu (eds) *Restructuring the Chinese City: Changing Society, Economy and Space*, London: Routledge, 260–286.

Wu, F., Xu, J. and Yeh, A. G. O. (2007) *Urban Development in Post-Reform China: State, Market, and Space*, London: Routledge.

Zukin, S. (2004) *Point of Purchase: How Shopping Changed American Culture*, London: Routledge.

2 Land property rights regimes in China

A comparative study of Suzhou and Dongguan

You-Ren Yang and Hung-Kai Wang

Introduction

Since the beginning of economic reform in 1979, China has set up many economic development zones and opened up numerous cities for foreign investment. At the same time, trying to provide incentives to promote regional economic development, local governments in coastal areas have been granted certain administrative powers in land-use conversion. With regard to industrial land use and development mechanisms in these fast industrializing regions of China, we observe that there are different institutional arrangement of land-use system in Dongguan and Suzhou. Such variations between different areas serve as the point of departure for this research undertaking.[1]

This chapter intends to explore the divergent pattern of the transformation of land property rights (from farmland to industrial land) in Suzhou and Dongguan, China, and investigates the factors of such divergence from the perspective of the interaction between institutional arrangements and "tiao (central/local sectoral command)–kuai (territorial jurisdictions)" agents. We will analyze the evolution of the land property system in Suzhou and Dongguan as well as the concrete modes of governing practices within the local governments. Through the comparative study of the formation of divergent local land property regimes in China, this article hopes to understand the political process concerning land development, and proposes an institutional-political perspective which should be helpful in the study of local economic evolution in post-reform China.

Analytical framework

The issue of agricultural land loss in China has attracted attention in academia (Brown 1995; Cartier 2001; Skinner *et al.* 2001; Tan *et al.* 2005; Xu 2004; Yang and Li 2000; Yeh and Li 1999). Some scholars have pointed out that institutional factors as well as local governments are important forces behind this phenomenon (Cartier 2001; Xu 2004; Wu 2002; Yeh and Li 1999). However, few of these studies have taken the dimension of "spatial differentiation" into account. On the other hand, the "institutional turn" in geography postulates a methodology based on studying institutions to comprehend divergent economic activities in different areas. It proposes that institutions are the intermediaries in shaping trajectories of economic development in different localities, thereby becoming important elements of further institutional variances (Jessop 2001; Martin 2000). This perspective is quite appropriate for our purpose in investigating the institutional factors that influence local land property rights regimes.

Martin (2000) further categorizes the conception of the institution into institutional environments and institutional arrangements. The former include systems of informal conventions, customs, norms and socialized routines, as well as formal rules and regulations, and act as frameworks for reconciliation among socio-economic behaviors. The latter encompasses specific organizational formations, such as markets, firms, unions and the state. Therefore, the institutional approach in geography focuses on the "institutional regime" constituted by institutional environments and arrangements in particular localities and the interactions between them. It heeds the evolution of different local institutional regimes and how they interact with local economic activities.

Based on such a perspective, we thus try to provide a preliminary conceptualization of the "local land property rights regime." Our primary concern is both the transfer of land-use rights (such as converting collectively owned land into state-owned lands by compulsory purchase, leasing state-owned land to private enterprises, transferring collectively owned land to private enterprises, etc.) and the conversion of land uses (such as turning farmland into construction land) in China. Thus we define a "local land property rights regime" as a set of dynamic systems that comprises varied formal institutional environments as well as arrangements, and informal rules concerning land property rights transfer and land-use conversion in a particular geographic region.

Furthermore, from the perspective of "path dependence," special attention should be paid to the structural influences of post-socialist reform on institutional transformation, especially with regard to the fiscal system, decentralization and the "quota system" between different levels of government. For example, Montinola *et al.* (1995) emphasize that the reform and devolution of the fiscal system have had great consequences for China's economic development. They propose the concept of "market-preserving federalism" as an important political foundation in China's economic reform, and assert that devolution and competition among localities ensured the success of economic reform in China. Oi (1992, 1995) also recognizes that reforms in China's fiscal system have established strong advantageous factors to entice local government officials to strive for local economic development. She introduces the notion of "local state corporatism," and argues that the governments at higher levels assign economic "quotas" to be accomplished by lower-level governments, and establish connections between local officials' personal rewards and the economic development they help to achieve. However, Whiting (2001) maintains that the motivation/supervision system of the local governments is very complicated in practice, including performance evaluation, a promotion system and an objective responsibility system. Thus, in addition to the economic incentives induced by the new fiscal system, the political factors of party organizations' promotion mechanisms should also be taken into account.

This kind of socialist heritage results in variables that we have to explore while investigating local land property rights regimes, especially regarding the role of local governments.

In the following sections, we try to elaborate on this framework while systematically analyzing the formation and transformation of the land property rights regimes in Suzhou and Dongguan. Our analysis will focus on five more inclusive dimensions of the local land property regime. First, we analyze the formal regulations of China's land-use management system and their interactions with the Ministry of Construction, as well as related local regulatory mechanisms. Second, we scrutinize the allocation arrangements of land-related incomes between different levels of governments and analyze some specific modes of land development derived from such arrangements. Third, we examine the distribution problems of farmland acquisition, and some local institutions derived from unique contexts in Suzhou and Dongguan that are relevant for local farmers. Fourth, we try to compare the local financial structures in Suzhou and Dongguan that might influence their different practices in the transformation of farmland property rights. Finally, we try to understand the divergent assignment and examination system of related quota systems between different levels of government and its influences on local land property rights regimes.

The empirical data for this research was gathered by face-to-face interviews with local authorities in Suzhou, Kunshan, Wujiang and Dongguan (Figure 2.1; Figure 2.2), as well as participatory observation of some land development projects, accompanied by secondary data from related regulations and reports in China. Fieldwork began in May 2003 and ended in April 2004. The interviews were carried out with people from different agencies of local government (including planning, land management, finance, taxation, foreign trade and customs affairs departments), as well as village committees, leaders of villagers' groups and land developers, in a total of 92 meetings.[2]

Institutional environment of land property rights transformation in China

After the economic reform in 1979, local governments in China were granted certain administrative powers in land-use conversion in order to attract foreign investment. However, the vast majority of local governments levied great amounts of farmland, and this caused a wide variety of problems, including the omnipresent "development zone fever" and a severe waste of prime agricultural land. Thus, the central government made a decision to establish, in 1986, a unified land management system in urban areas, and passed the 1986 Land Management Act. Furthermore, the state created a new central-level Land Management Bureau to be charged with national land-related affairs, and established its local branches at each level of local government. However, the problem of the loss of cultivated land remained severe after 1986 (Cartier 2001).

The attention of China's central government to land resource management was expressed in the issuance and implementation of a new Land Management Act

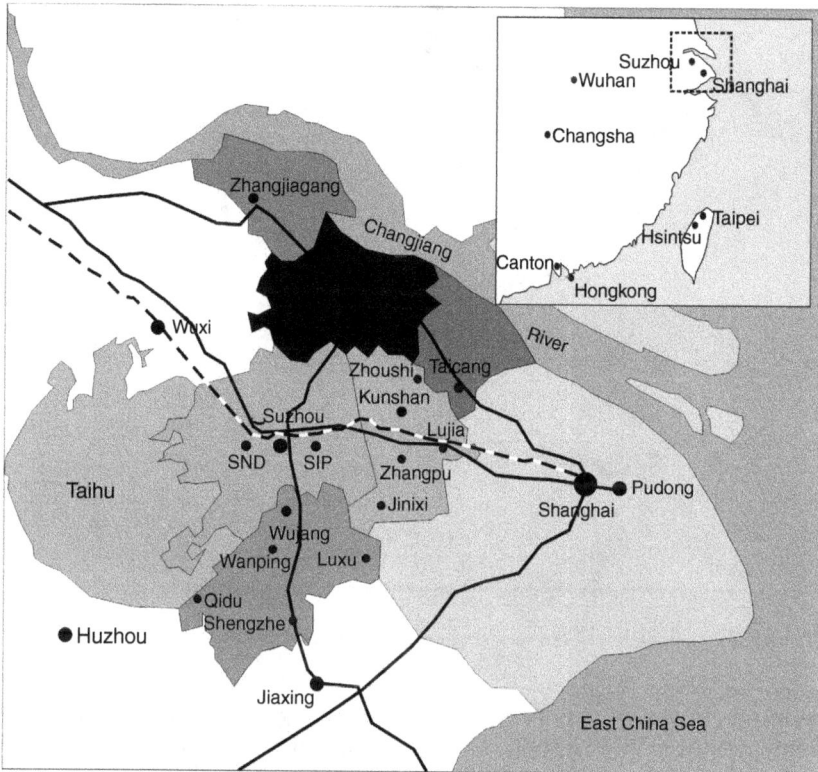

Figure 2.1 The location of the case studies in Suzhou.

in 1998. The 1998 Act requires governments at each level to adopt a Land Use Master Plan, prepared according to the all-important National Economic and Social Development Plan, as well as geological features, environmental resources, conservation considerations, land provision ability and land requirements of construction projects. The land-use schemes of lower-level governments should be established according to the schemes of higher-level governments.[3] The total amount of construction land in the land-use scheme compiled by any local government should not exceed the control indicator defined in the scheme compiled by the higher-level government above it, and the amount of agricultural land must not be less than the control indicator defined by the same higher-level government.[4] The central government also implemented a policy of compensation for farmland displacement (named "agriculture land-use balance, *zhan bu ping heng*") to keep stable the total amount of agricultural land (especially that of high quality) by controlling the hitherto unruly process of land-use conversion.[5]

The transformation of the regulations related to land-use approval shows that China's central government is tending to re-centralize land management

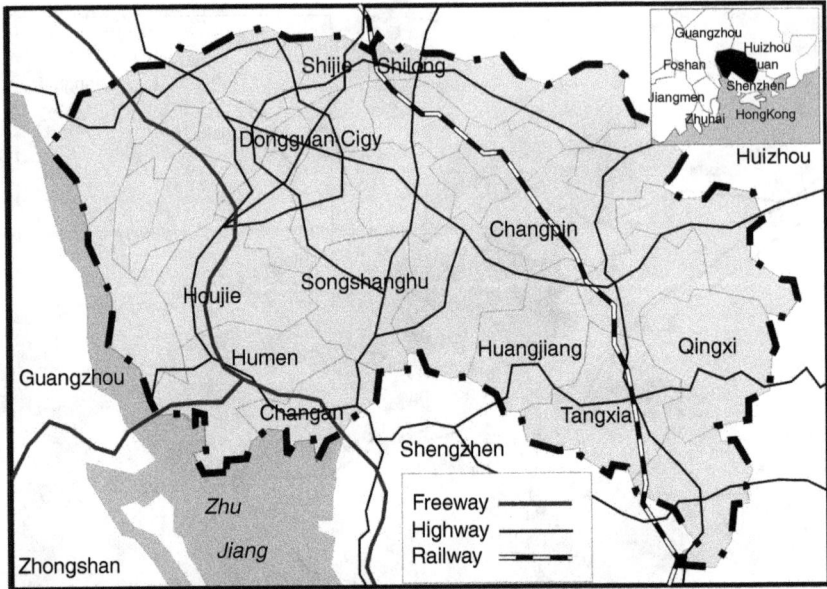

Figure 2.2 The location of the case studies in Dongguan.

powers from their previously decentralized pattern. However, such attempts face restrictions from other institutions at different scales. This is our next focus of concern. Under the dual system of land ownership in China, there are two ways of changing the agricultural use of farmland in the countryside. The first is through acquisition by compulsory purchase on the part of the government, thus trans-ferring the land ownership to the state, and then transfer to the final land user; and the second way is to transfer the land-use rights from the collective owner-ship body, which is usually the village, to the final land user, such as investors in the manufacturing sector. In the Suzhou area, the first way is most commonly employed. In terms of local government, such transformation of land property rights involves several regulatory mechanisms, including the "agriculture land use balance" policy and the "construction land index (*jian she yong di zhi biao*)" system.

When levying collectively owned farmland (say, for the purpose of estab-lishing an economic development zone) local governments must follow a specified approval process, and must satisfy the principle of the compensation-for-displacement balance, which is mainly to be achieved at the provincial level. Local governments below the provincial level should also keep the balance them-selves. The way it works is that when a piece of prime farmland is taken, a piece of nonagricultural land of equal productivity must be converted into the farm-land category. However, such an institution results in the "trans-jurisdiction index exchange" phenomenon. That is, some fast-developing areas would have to "buy" index quotas from areas that are developing more slowly. For example, when there is a shortage of 10,000 acres of farmland in Suzhou, the city government may pay the Jiangsu provincial government to convert or reclaim an amount of land that is equivalent in agricultural productivity somewhere in, say, northern Jiangsu, where development is going at a much slower pace. According to our interviews, the index fee for farmland compensation is about 6,000 Yuan per hectare.

As for the control of construction land supply, the high-level governments would allocate quotas to lower-level governments each year. For example, Jiangsu Province establishes annually a total amount of construction land allowance, and distributes quotas to each city, county and township. The actual land use must correspond with the relevant "urban planning" and "land use master plan." Such planning and control systems are basically the heritage of the bygone age of the planned economy. However, in the case of rapid development, planning can seldom keep up with the mounting requirements of economic development. This is especially true in areas such as Suzhou, where the policy emphasis is on attracting foreign investment. We notice that agencies related to economic development at all levels of local government often break the restrictions stipulated by their land management counterparts, expecting to obtain as large a construction land quota as possible. Many industrial parks in townships in the Suzhou region do not exactly follow urban planning and the land-use master plan as required. What is obvious is that local government at all levels (but especially in the townships) considers the quota allocations from upper-level governments as restrictions instead of instructions to be followed. Their emphasis on attracting foreign investors is so great that many of the local officials interviewed by us indicated that all the investment projects could certainly get the land they need, even when the present quota was already used up.

Furthermore, the historical formation of the land property rights regime in Dongguan reveals the process of institutionalization of the conversion of farmland into construction land use. The new Land Management Act adopted in 1998 can be seen as an institutional watershed. In respect of formal institutions at the national scale, there have been two ways of transforming the use of farmland. One is to add "new construction land" by allowing farmland to be converted into construction use with allocated "construction quotas." The other is using "inventory land," which means clearing and managing old construction land, since a lot of land was assigned for construction use before the implementation of the 1998 Land Management Act. According to the 1998 Land Management Act, collective construction land includes land occupied by "township and village enterprises (TVEs)" and public facilities at the village level, as well as villagers' housing land. The stipulations in the Land Management Law before 1998 (enacted in 1986) were loose regarding the conversion of collectively owned land from agricultural to construction use. Collective organizations can ask for a change of land use in the name of establishing TVEs. Many such TVEs are so-called *san lai yi bu* (processing supplied materials) enterprises. As many "*san lai yi bu*" enterprises with capital from Hong Kong, Macau or Taiwan come to the Pearl River Delta, many collective organizations seek this type of land-use change.

Before 1998, the approval process for farmland transformation was indeed flexible. Moreover, there was no limitation on the size of the land involved. Our surveys also indicate that "construction land quotas" did not exist before 1998. At the level of Dongguan city, construction land obtained by collective organizations before 1998 was still entitled to be used for development. This would not be allowed under the new 1998 Land Management Act. But approval can be granted with some remedial measures, such as paying certain local fees. Much collective construction land maintains its current status with these measures. Much is still waiting to be developed, while some already has factories built upon it to attract foreign investors.

The 1998 version of the Land Management Act also has some implications especially for the so-called agriculture land-use balance policy and the construction land quotas system. Until 2010, Dongguan city has to keep 600,000 mu (1 mu = 666.7 square meters) of farmland, among which 520,000 mu must be of the more critical "essential farmland" category. When an imbalance arises, additional farmland has to be supplemented somewhere in a certain jurisdiction (usually in areas where nonconstruction land supplies are ample). The "balance fee" – that is, the cost involved in providing new agricultural land – for 1 mu is about 5,000 Yuan. The local governments that receive the balance fees are those in Guangdong Province where urbanization and industrialization are not progressing so fast. The amounts of essential farmland cannot be changed without permission from the national State Council. Thus the regulations of the new law tend to increase the costs and limit the locations of developments.

Since the declaration of the new law, new construction land cannot be obtained without the assignment of quotas from the land management bureaus. In fast-developing areas such as Dongguan, there is a certain degree of "imbalance" in the demand and supply of construction land. For example, in 2002 the statistics for construction land in Dongguan started to show signs of shortage. After some negotiation, the Guangdong provincial government allowed its quotas for 2010 to be used up in 2005. Dongguan city government then allocated the quotas among townships within its jurisdiction according to their demands and speed of development. However, there are no specific rules concerning the allocation, and the city government does not reserve any quota allowance for possible unforeseen additional demands from the townships. As a result, there are under-the-table deals on quotas among the townships.

The development mechanisms of industrial land

Furthermore, county and township governments in the Suzhou region tend to discourage the villages' long-established practice of promoting investment by transferring collective construction land. What really happens is that these local governments usually establish large development zones by converting farmland into state-owned land by compulsory acquisition, and this is what distinguishes the mode of development in the Suzhou region from that in the Dongguan region. We also found cases where villages tried to attract investment with collectively owned construction land, but the upper-level governments discouraged such undertakings by eliminating these villages' construction land quotas.

For local governments in the Suzhou region, investment in industrial land construction was not great, nor were the extra-budgetary funds involved large. For example, in Kunshan city the total extra-budgetary funds excluding land transfer fee were 0.4 billion Yuan in 2002, and this was distributed among a large number of agencies. With such a financial structure, income from land transfer fees and bank loans become important funding means for construction and development for local governments.

The land transfer fee is not enough to cover the costs of infrastructure and relocation of farmers in the developing zone. The income from land transfer fees (including industrial, commercial, and residential categories) of Kunshan in 2002 was about 2 billion Yuan, more than the 1.6 billion Yuan of budgetary revenues kept by Kunshan city. Though this seems to be a large amount of income, it has to be shared with the Suzhou city and township governments. According to our investigation, the fees paid to the upper-level government exceeded $700 \sim 800$ million Yuan in 2002, with more than 80 percent of the rest being returned to the townships. Therefore, the funds available for the city of Kunshan from land transfer fees of 2 billion Yuan amounted to only about 100–200 million Yuan.

Furthermore, town governments often lower the actual land transfer cost to attract investment. Although Jiangsu Province established the lowest allowable land price and stipulated that the lowest land transfer price must exceed 200 Yuan per square meter (or about 133,000 Yuan per mu), the lowest land prices tend to occur at lower levels of government. For example, Kunshan city adopted the lowest land price of 105,000 Yuan per mu (including the related charge to each of the upper-level governments) in 2002. After the basic price was established, Kunshan city required the town governments to pay 105,000 Yuan per mu to the land management bureau when transferring land. This would be returned to the townships that actually transferred land, according to a specified proportion after payments to the upper-level governments. However, the strategy of low price transfer was commonly adopted in the drastic competition for investment.

According to the regulations of the fiscal agency in the central government, the income from land transfer fees can only be used for two purposes. The first is for land compensation and relocation expenses, and the second is for the development of the land involved. Basically, according to our investigation, land transfer fees could not pay for the expenses of infrastructure provision, for which, therefore, some local governments need to arrange budgetary financing or loans from financial institutions. Therefore, land-secured bank loans have become an essential means of funding local development. As for the banks, before lending to a development zone, they need to consider the development prospects of the area, and it is basically a business undertaking. Therefore, the land-use type designated by the planning system is a crucial factor. Utilizing the usually high-priced transfer fees of commercial and residential districts to compensate for the generally reduced industrial land transfer fees has gradually become a new common practice in land development in many townships. For example, we observe that

Huguan township in Suzhou New District adopted this development model. It started a development zone of 10 square kilometers, and invested 2 billion Yuan in two years (2003–2004). The funding is kept in balance in three ways. The first is through the sale of commercial and residential properties, the second is from the rental of standard plants, and the third is by collection of revenues from local joint enterprises. This mode of development could be described as borrowing on the one hand, and selling property on the other. The 10 square kilometers of land "enclosed" by the government could be said to be the key to the future success of the development zone.

In Dongguan, collective ownership is one of the distinctive features. The entities of collective ownership can be the village committee or the villagers' group, which is a sub-unit under a village. The distinction between the two used to be vague and was not clarified until the start of the development process of converting farmland to construction land. The method of clarification is the application and issuance of land permits, also known as "collectively owned land permits." Both the village committee and the group can apply for the permit rights, but whichever gets the permit should sign a contract to be responsible for the welfare of the villagers involved.

Village committees have two ways of handling their collectively owned land. They can directly lease it out to manufacturers or developers (including private companies) and let the lessee develop the land, or they can build factory spaces (standard factory buildings) and then lease them to manufacturers. Either way, the committee needs to apply for the permit before carrying out the development. Once the necessary lands have been amassed, the committee can start the development process. In earlier days, when village committees did not have much financial means, they usually directly leased the land to the final land user. The land user was liable for the permit fee and the "land payment" made to the committee. In addition, the land user had to pay a monthly land rent to the committee. Such schemes still exist in some underdeveloped areas in Dongguan. The income from land payment and rent thus becomes the village's financial means of undertaking future land developments.

Once village committees had accumulated sufficient capital, direct investment in building factories for lease became a more common method of land development. Some of the capital would come from a "Stock-sharing Cooperative" (SSC) of the committee, some from bank loans. For example, the committee in Shigu village invested 50 million Yuan in building 100,000 square meters of standard factory plants. The cost is 500 Yuan per square meter, and the monthly rent is 9 Yuan. With the influx of foreign investment (especially from Hong Kong and Taiwan) since the 1980s, huge demand for plants has created considerable profit margins for these village committees, some of which even exceed the returns on direct leases of lands. Such economic incentives lure the committees to invest directly in the development and leasing of factory spaces. Villagers' groups with resources also participate actively in the process of land development by adopting similar strategies, with the precondition that they maintain a good relationship with the village committee.

Village committees have to obtain agreements from villagers' groups before carrying out collectivized land development schemes. However, unlike government land expropriations often seen in the Suzhou region, the methods of obtaining land in Dongguan are through negotiation, or more directly, through concrete land/welfare interest exchange agreements. All villagers' groups have their representatives on the committee to reflect and express the group's opinion about the handling of their land. Apart from negotiations, villagers' groups have to obtain permission from the committee before leasing out the group's land for development. However, if villagers' groups have sufficient capital and decide to build factories on their own and lease them out for developments, the committee would not oppose it. This enables groups with resources to use self-controlled collectively owned land in ways they see fit.

The distribution of land rent

Although central government established the compensation standards for farmland nationalization, according to our fieldwork there are varied local institutions emerging in different areas in this regard. For example, the compensation standard of Kunshan city does not make full payment at once, but adopts a so-called three-six-nine system to issue the payment annually of 300, 600, and 900 Yuan per acre/year to the affected peasants according to the land category: responsibility field (*ze-ren-tian*), family land (*zi-liu-di*), and staple field (*kou-liang-tian*), respectively. This significantly reduces the financial burdens on the local government.

How would the "three-six-nine" system affect farmers in a village where the upper-level government took all the land away? The illustrative village is located in Huaqiao township in Kunshan, with a total area of 2,800 mu, and a population of about 1,800. Our calculations show that if the government obtained all the agricultural land of the village, each farmer would only receive a compensation payment of 817 Yuan per year, an amount lower than the average income from cultivation. In other words, this "three-six-nine" mechanism is to a certain degree disadvantageous to the village and the farmers.

How to cover such benefit differences has become an important issue in the Suzhou region. Kunshan city has proposed an experimental system which promotes the so-called Enrich-the-People Cooperative (EPC) (*fu min he zuo she*) at the village level, makes the villagers shareholders in the cooperative, and reserves 3–5 percent of the expropriated land for the EPC to build rental standard factory plants or workers' dormitories. For example, the development zone of Changpu township in Kunshan set aside 2,000 mu for EPCs to build standard factory plants. They also assembled the collectively owned constructive lands in nearby villages and transferred their development rights to the development zones. The rent payments of standard factory plants on those 2,000 mu were made to the EPCs. So we can see that, for the development of the village economy, the local governments are trying to make good use of the opportunities provided by upper-level governments' investment-luring policies.

The EPCs tested in Kunshan are very different from the village-level SSCs in the past. The SSCs managed the public assets accumulated in the village, villagers obtained stock shares automatically due to their household registration in the village, and the share rights could not be sold or reassigned. Now, the villagers can join or withdraw from the EPC freely, and the shares are transferable; in other words, it operates in a free cooperative spirit. Basically, the system of EPCs can be regarded as a remedy for large-scale farmland acquisition by compulsory purchase in Suzhou. The local governments hope the farmers who have lost their land will join the EPCs with compensation payments and obtain a certain ratio of return through the business of standard factory buildings and dormitory rentals to secure their future livelihood. However, according to our investigation, successful cases of EPCs are few, and the villages that set up EPCs are economically better off. For example, although Changpu township had put aside land for an EPC on which to build standard factory plants, there was no EPC start-up in any of the villages in the township. The key to the success of such strategies lies in the villagers' trust in the collective organizations that would manage the collective properties. Villagers in some areas had no confidence in propositions put forward by collective leaderships, owing to past experiences of failure in TVEs.

In Dongguan, compared to Suzhou, local farmers' welfare under collectively owned land property rights is much better. For example, it is a common practice for villagers' groups to accumulate sufficient capital to build standard factory plants for lease. Apart from SSCs, wherein shares cannot be traded, some villagers' groups can run "Share-holding Cooperatives" for specific development projects, with free exchange and trade in shares being allowed. Whenever there is a new investment project, and the need for more factory space is anticipated, the villagers' group will set up a new share-holding cooperative to raise the required funds. Take a villagers' group in Humen township, for example. The population of the villagers' group was about 2,000 people, collectively holding about 40,000 square meters of construction land. The land-use quotas were carryovers from past applications. As the villagers estimated that they would need nearly 20 million Yuan to fully develop the land, the villagers' group established a share-holding cooperative. Since the expected return of investment would be over 10 percent, villagers were willing to buy the shares.

In Dongguan, the user of the collectively owned land has to pay the "land fee," which is mainly used to pay for the welfare of the villagers and the basic infrastructure involved. Dongguan City and township governments do not get any part of the payment, nor do they regulate its magnitude and use, which is entirely up to the land user and the "landlord" (e.g. the village committee or villagers' group). The "land fee" is one of the important sources of revenues for the village. In addition to paying the permit fee to the land management bureau and the "land fee," the land user also has to pay land rent to the "landlord" if the former builds facilities on its own. Our surveys show that wealthy village committees in Dongguan could receive nearly 10 million Yuan every year from the above-mentioned sources of revenues. Some villagers' groups could even receive up to 30 million Yuan.

How are these rents allocated within the collective organizations? The collective bodies pay a certain amount of their income to all the people whose households are officially registered as residing in the village. The reason for this is that every collective body has its own "Share-holding Cooperative." These cooperatives are charged with the management and allocation of all collectively owned assets. The per capita amount paid by the cooperative varies according to the financial capability of each organization. Some wealthier villages pay people up to 600 or 700 Yuan per person per month, but immigrant workers who are not considered official residents of the village cannot enjoy the benefits.

In the above discussions, we illustrate how the welfare distributed to local farmers in Dongguan is far better than in Suzhou. In other words, we argue that the collectively owned land property rights regime protects local farmers' interests to a significantly higher degree.

A comparison of local financial structures in Suzhou and Dongguan

In this section, we try to investigate, from a financial perspective, the mechanisms that influence the different practices of local governments in Suzhou and Dongguan with regard to the transformation of farmland property rights. Although Suzhou and Dongguan are both locations that attract a great deal of foreign investment, the property rights arrangements for investing companies are very different. In the Suzhou region, most of the foreign companies are sole owners, and the tax these companies pay is mainly value added tax (VAT), a means of governmental income to be shared between central and local governments. Our interviews with staff in fiscal agencies in the city of Kunshan reveal that the tax revenues contributed by foreign investors amount to 60 percent of total tax income. The total tax revenue in 2002 was about 4.1 billion Yuan, but the share kept in Kunshan was only 1.6 billion Yuan, of which the contribution of foreign companies was less than 40 percent. In other words, the fruit of attracting foreign investment to Kunshan made a great contribution to the national tax revenue, but less so to the financial status of Kunshan. The reason for such results is closely related to the local revenue-sharing system in China.

According to the tax revenue-sharing system as defined by the central government, in the period from 1993 to 2001 75 percent of VAT income was allocated to the central government, 12.5 percent to the province, 4 percent to Suzhou city, and 8.5 percent to Kunshan city (including the townships). After 2001 the proportion shared by Kunshan city (including the townships) increased to 12.5 percent, while leaving the central and provincial shares intact and squeezing the city of Suzhou totally out of the picture. Suzhou city had to share 0.6 percent of the total tax revenues of the county-level cities under its jurisdiction, with a reduced total amount of intake. As for the tax-sharing situation of Kunshan city and its townships, we find that the basic principle is a 40/60 split, that is, 40 percent of the tax revenue is for the city of Kunshan, and the townships receive 60 percent.

At the township level, the current revenue-sharing system often results in financial deficits and lack of construction funds for townships that depend on land development to draw in investment. For example, the total financial revenue of Luchia township is 0.38 billion Yuan, but the amount kept in the township is only 74 million Yuan. We find that the budgets in the investigated areas only cover so-called meals finance or basic personnel expenses.

The property rights composition of foreign investment in Dongguan is very different from that in the Suzhou area. A great number of manufacturers in Dongguan operate as "contracted materials processors." "Contracted materials processing" factories do not have to pay the VAT imposed by the central government. They only pay the so-called processing fees. The most common formula is to levy a fixed percentage from the processing budget stipulated in the contract. The current "rate" is about "100/80" – that is, the local contracted processor gets 80 Yuan for every 100 Hong Kong dollars that the foreign company transmits to him/her. If calculated at an exchange rate of 1 Hong Kong dollar to 1.06 Yuan, the processing cost would be 26 Yuan, which is treated as "off-budget revenue" and does not have to be shared with the central and provincial governments. It is allocated among the relevant municipal-level and township-level governments (each getting roughly 4 Yuan), minus the handling charges levied by some banks. The remaining 17 Yuan are paid to units under the village committee. If the village committee is the "landlord," it gets all of the remaining 17 Yuan. If the villagers' group or a private company is the landlord, the committee and the landlord share the 17 Yuan. Basically, only sole-owner companies pay VAT. As there is no county-level authority between Dongguan City and the townships, revenues from VAT are shared by these two levels of governments, and each gets half (12.5 percent) of the total amount of the revenues, which is about twice the 5–6 percent levied by townships in Suzhou. This is of course financially more beneficial to the townships.

After comparing the financial structures in Suzhou and Dongguan, we observe that under different patterns of foreign investment and institutional arrangements for revenue-sharing, the financial conditions in the townships of Suzhou are much worse than in Dongguan. Furthermore, the local governments in Suzhou have to invest considerably in the construction of infrastructure in industrial zones. However, the strategy of low-priced land-use rights is commonly adopted in the drastic competition for investment in the county and township governments in Suzhou. Under the current tax-sharing system, land transfer operations do not contribute to the financial capabilities of local governments in Suzhou. Furthermore, the economic-development-related agencies in Suzhou, due to the pressure from the quota of registered capital, usually try to attract investors by lowering the land price, but without understanding the fact that the land transfer fees are not enough to pay for the land acquisition and supply the funds needed for the provision of infrastructure. Thus we find that it is a convention in Suzhou's local government to achieve the goal of economic development through large-scale farmland acquisition accompanied by loans from banks to build the infrastructure. From an economic perspective, this seems to be a contradictory phenomenon. Therefore, we would like to explore further some of the factors that induce "development zone fever" in Suzhou.

A comparison of economic indicator and Chinese Communist Party (CCP) cadres' promotion/evaluation systems in Suzhou and Dongguan

China's economic indicator system is a legacy from the era of the planned economy. At that time, there were very definite quotas for almost every governmental function at each administrative echelon, and such a governing mechanism has been retained up to the present. Differently from supervision through the ballot in Western democratic societies, the efficiency of local governments in China is managed with "*zh-biao*" (indicator or quota) systems, which cover various administrative functions. Though some areas pay special attention to development-related indices, such as the growth of GDP and quantities of incoming foreign capital, the indices differ in different regions, and the central government does not have a definite, overarching index control system. Totals may not be thoroughly distributed among lower-level governments by the upper levels. The lower-echelon governments still have a certain leeway, and define their annual objectives after answering to the demands from the upper level.

The responsibility for quota assignment belongs to the planning commission, which in the planned-economy era would define a five-year economic and social development plan, carry out certain annual reviews and adjustments, and assign "solid" economic quotas. However, the indices defined by planning commission in recent years have tended to become "estimates." Generally, they are only predictions, and not the single reference for a party member's promotion/evaluation.

According to our investigation, Jiangsu Province has stopped assigning quotas to lower-level governments; therefore the highest level of government that assigns quotas is cities such as Suzhou. Although the pressure from the indices given by the city government seems much less, the pressure from the lower-level governments has increased. We observe a contradictory phenomenon, which city-level governments have noticed: "solid" indices are in disaccord with the market economy, and investment growth that depends on international capital movements is much too hard to predict. But it is possible for areas below the city level to define targets higher than the predictions by the upper level, and some even relate the promotion/evaluation of lower-level government leadership to the rate of quota completion.

Is there any connection between the completion rate of assigned indices and the promotion/evaluation of local leadership? The personnel and organization department primarily manages the party cadres' promotion/evaluation. The quota completion rate is just one of the references. In theory, the accomplishment of indices is not connected to the party cadres' evaluation, but it seems otherwise in practice. We further notice the practice of so-called pressing the quotas most noticeable below the county level. The indices become very "solid" after being distributed through the echelons, especially to the townships, and are more commonly combined with party members' evaluation. In Suzhou, we observed that township officials seldom have a chance to be promoted to the county level, and their county-level counterparts were usually dispatched from the relevant department in the Suzhou city government. Their term of office is usually not very long. Therefore, when they serve as county officials their achievements (especially in economic development) usually become the major reference for future promotion. Thus, these county officials are the driving forces behind the practice of "pressing the quotas."

The mechanism of "pressing the quotas" at the county level provides an important motive for attracting investment through large-scale farmland conversion in the Suzhou region. In other words, even though the land administration department establishes land use regulations, the party cadres' evaluation system below the county level drives the local government leadership to breach the index regulations. Thus we argue that the economic index system, combined with the party cadres' promotion/evaluation system, has become the predominant driving factor in Suzhou's land property rights transformation.

The main reason why Suzhou's intra-governmental quota systems result in local areas quickly renting out land to attract foreign investors is that economic and financial achievements are linked to officials' promotion assessment. We still need to examine two issues: (1) Do higher-level governments in Dongguan issue quotas to lower-level governments? Are they "hard" quotas? (2) Is the accomplishment of these quotas linked to officials' promotion assessment? Dongguan had at one time assigned economy-related quotas to township governments, but "softened" them (i.e. made them toothless) after the 1990s. Recently, Dongguan scrapped economic and financial quotas for township governments and replaced them with predictive quotas, which are only for reference purposes, allowing township governments to set their own annual development goals. At the scale of Dongguan city, such a trend of "softening the quotas" is similar to the trend in Suzhou, but, as discussed above, Suzhou's quotas "harden" as we descend the administrative hierarchy. However, we find these phenomena absent in Dongguan, probably for three reasons. One is that Dongguan's upper-level government, Guangdong provincial government, no longer issues economy-related quotas to Dongguan, and all numbers are now set by Dongguan itself based on its own conditions. In addition, beneath Dongguan city there are no county-level cities; therefore, unlike the case of Suzhou, there would not be any prefecture-level department heads "going rural" to work as heads of county-level cities. These "going rural" leaders are some of the most important drivers of "pressing the quotas" (manipulating or skillfully bypassing the restrictive numbers). Such differences in administrative structure make the phenomenon of "pressing the quotas" not as frequent as in Dongguan. Third, our field research shows that township governments in Dongguan did not allocate economy-related quotas to village committees, as the latter are fundamentally not government organizations. Thus, village committee leaders' economic motivations were less driven by "pressing the quotas."

If "pressing the quotas" is not a frequent phenomenon in Dongguan, the question becomes whether Dongguan officials' promotions are linked to economy-related quota performance. We discover that there were some assessments that were related to the economic performance of lower-level governments, but these assessments were not combined with the promotions of lower-level leaders. In other words, economic and finance-related quotas are not linked to officials' promotion assessment in Dongguan, and these quotas are themselves being downplayed. Thus, comparing Suzhou with Dongguan, we believe that the latter's tax-sharing system and the land-use fee appropriation arrangement are already enough for encouraging local leaders to attract business through land development, and the distribution of local revenues facilitates the reproduction of local social-political relations.

Conclusion

Spatial variation is always an interesting topic for geographers. From an institutional geographic perspective, we try to clarify the institutional arrangements that sustain the divergent local land property rights regimes in Suzhou and Dongguan. Although these two industrializing regions are under the regulation of the same nationwide Land Management Law, the pattern of land property rights transformation (from farmland to industrial land) is quite different.

Two factors can be seen as exogenous explanations. The first is administrative hierarchy. Dongguan has an administrative setting of prefecture – townships (two levels), while another is prefecture – counties (county-level cities) – townships (three levels). This factor influences the local financial structure and the incentive structure of the leaders of counties (county-level cities) that were embedded in CCP cadres' promotion/evaluation systems. The second explanation is the pattern of foreign investment. A great number of manufacturers in Dongguan operate as "contracted materials processors," while in Suzhou more are sole-owners. This factor also influences local financial structure and the incentive structure of village committees.

More interestingly, emergent local institutions – such as the practices of "pressing the quotas," "Share-holding Cooperatives," "three-six-nine" and others – could be regarded as endogenous causes of the variation in the transformation of farmland property rights in these two regions. As this study shows, these local institutions played an important role in shaping the local land property rights regime. Under the transition of China's political-economic systems as well as in their interplay, we believe that such local institutions are relevant factors that influence the divergent patterns of China's local development.

Which model is more successful? The answer requires much more investigation with different insights. However, it is quite obvious that in the process of industrialization, the collectively owned land property system in Dongguan is much more desirable than nationalization (levying collectively owned land into state-ownership) in terms of farmers' welfare. Furthermore, we argue that there exists a "dilemma of governance" that reinforces the "development zone fever" in Suzhou, especially the interplay among economic quota assignment, the party cadres' promotion/evaluation system, and the revenue-sharing system. We suggest that such land property regimes, which rely on attracting foreign investment through low

42 *You-Ren Yang and Hung-Kai Wang*

land prices made possible by land-ownership conversion, is not really beneficial to short-term (and even midterm) local fiscal operations, and there are consequential "governance deficits," such as the resettlement of landless peasants, abuse/waste of land resources, and so on.

Finally, on the theoretical level, we try to draw a "political turn" in the studies of China's local development. Apart from the "economic paradigm" that focuses on fiscal reforms and decentralization, scholars might pay more attention to political-institutional factors, such as intra-party promotion systems, tensions between the two evaluative indicator systems maintained by the "tiao (central/local sec-toral command)" and "kuai (territorial jurisdictions)," and the regulation as well as the political governance of "government–village" relations. The perspectives mentioned above might be helpful to further understanding of the dynamics and contradictions in China's local development.

Notes

1 Some exceptions exist, as one reviewer has reminded us. For example, Dongguan city government recently converted rural land into state land by expropriation to build the Song Shan Lake Science Park. But such cases are few. Furthermore, although cases of converting rural land into construction land exist in Suzhou, according to our fieldwork, such cases are usually because of the reuse of former TVE sites, not a transformation from farmland to construction land in terms of land use nor a main source of industrial land supply. Thus, regarding industrial land supply, we believe that it is appropriate to recognize Dongguan and Suzhou as two different models.
2 These samples were carefully and systematically selected, since the first author of this article, who is a planning consultant to local government as well as a consultant to Tai-wanese trade unions, conducted the interviews through planning and policy consultation intended to build a sense of partnership with the interviewees.
3 Article 17, Land Management Act.
4 Article 18, Land Management Act.
5 Article 31, Land Management Act.

References

Brown, L. (1995) *Who Will Feed China: Wake Up Call for a Small Planet*, New York: W. W. Norton and Company.
Cartier, C. (2001) " 'Zone Fever,' the arable land debate, and real estate speculation: China's evolving land use regime and its geographical contradictions," *Journal of Contemporary China*, 10(28): 445–469.
Cox, K. (1998) "Spaces of dependence, spaces of engagement and the politics of scale, or: Looking for local politics," *Political Geography,* 17(1): 1–23.
Jessop, B. (2001) "Institutional re(turns) and the strategic-relational approach," *Environment and Planning A*, 33: 1213–1235.
Martin, R. (2000) "Institutional approaches in economic geography," in Sheppard, E. and T. J. Barnes (eds) *A Companion to Economic Geography*, Oxford: Blackwell, 77–94.
Montinola, G., Qian, Y. and Weingast, B. (1995) "Federalism, Chinese style – The political basis for economic success in China," *World Politics*, 48: 61–81.

Oi, J. C. (1992) "Fiscal reform and the economic foundations of local state corporatism in China," *World Politics*, 45: 99–126.

Oi, J. C. (1995) "The Role of the local state in China's transitional economy," *The China Quarterly*, 145: 1132–1149.

Putterman, L. (1995) "The role of ownership and property rights in China's economic transition," *The China Quarterly*, 144: 1047–1059.

Skinner, M. W., Kuhn, R. G. and Joseph, A. E. (2001) "Agricultural land protection in China: A case study of local governance in Zhejiang Province," *Land Use Policy*, 18: 329–340.

Tan, M., Li, X., Xie, H. and Lu, C. (2005) "Urban land expansion and arable land loss in China – a case study of Beijing-Tianjin-Hebei region," *Land Use Policy*, 22: 187–196.

Whiting, S. H. (2001) *Power and Wealth in Rural China: The Political Economy of Institutional Change*, New York: Cambridge University Press.

Wu, F. L. (2002) "China's changing urban governance in the transition towards a more market-oriented economy," *Urban Studies,* 39(7): 1071–1093.

Xu, W. (2004) "The changing dynamics of land-use change in rural China: A case study of Yuhang, Zhejiang Province," *Environment and Planning A*, 36(9): 1595–1615.

Yang, H. and Li, X. (2000) "Cultivated land and food supply in China," *Land Use Policy*, 17: 73–88.

Yeh, A. G. O. and Li, X. (1999) "Economic development and land loss in the Pearl River Delta, China," *Habitat International*, 23(3): 373–390.

3 Public–private partnership in the urban water sector in Shanghai

Seungho Lee

Introduction

The chapter analyzes the extent to which commercialization of urban infrastructure in China has brought about a new way to formulate cities, with a particular focus on the water sector in Shanghai since the late 1990s. The study focuses on the evolution and progress of Shanghai's initiative to bring the private sector into urban infrastructure development through Public–Private Partnership (PPP). This initiative has resulted from new political and economic circumstances and has had significant impacts on the improvement of urban infrastructure. In the 1990s a number of industrial cities in China started looking at options they could adopt to renovate dilapidated urban infrastructure, including water service facilities. Shanghai became one of the pioneering cities to introduce the PPP option to improve water facilities on the basis of its economic strength as well as political willingness to rectify problems remaining in the water sector. International and local water companies quickly marched into Shanghai with a strategy to take some share of the largest water markets in China in the late 1990s (Industrial Map of China 2004–2005).

It was imperative for the Shanghai government to enhance urban infrastructure including water services in the reform era, because good urban infrastructure could influence household welfare, public health and sanitation, foreign direct investment and overall socioeconomic development in the city (Wu 1999). Recent observation, and findings based on fieldwork and data from 2000 to 2004, disclose that the Shanghai government had been committed to implementing reforms to improve urban infrastructure, particularly in the water sector, including the introduction of private investment. Such governmental policy was due to major challenges in urban infrastructure provision in China: "unmet demand; deficiencies in cost recovery; and inadequate maintenance" (Wu 1999). In response, private companies have taken an active part in the process of urban infrastructure development.

Transnational Corporations (TNCs) have been spearheading PPP, although some Chinese companies have won a few water contracts. Such transformation of ownership structure in urban infrastructure provision is unlikely to continue on a smooth path unless the Shanghai government establishes adequate institutional frameworks for private sector involvement. It is concluded in the study that a new way of urban infrastructure development in the Shanghai water sector has been possible through the introduction of PPP. Such new development will be an unavoidable process for the rationalization of water services stimulated by the program of economic reforms initiated in the late 1970s. However, this process has been, and will continue to be, balanced and bolstered first by the government's role in regulating privatized water services, secondly by the contribution of private companies to service provision, and thirdly by the continuous interaction between the government and private companies to achieve provision of high quality water.

Institutional reform

The public utility sector in Chinese cities, including Shanghai, had remained "a sacred cow" even under the rapid and wide range of economic reforms since the late 1970s (*Business China-EIU* November 10, 1997). The monopoly of the Shanghai government in the provision of water services continued until the late 1990s. Such monopoly brought about inefficient management of facilities, out-of-date management skills and technologies, and no incentive to conduct institutional reform for cost-recovery water pricing. These problems also caused losses of more than 800 million yuan (97 million US dollars) in 1999 and caused the municipal government to run out of its public fund to keep the water service system going (*China Daily* May 23, 2002).

Confronted with such challenges, from the mid-1990s, the Shanghai government began to consider the option of bringing in investment from the private sector. The introduction of private investment in urban infrastructure, particularly the water sector, stemmed from not only the internal factor but also an external factor. There has been a global trend in water service privatization, advocated by international development agencies such as the World Bank and the Asian Development Bank. For instance, the World Bank has pushed forward two main policies in the global water sector, particularly to developing countries: first, reforms in infrastructure in relation to the process of deregulation and privatization; and second, environmental concerns related to water stress (Fingers and Allouche 2002). In response to such trends, in the late 1990s a radical reform of the Shanghai water supply sector was introduced. This resulted in integrating ten waterworks companies into four limited ones, covering Minhang area, Pudong area, southern city, and northern city, respectively (see Table 3.1). The Shanghai Water Authority (SWA) was also established to operate water and sewage services in an integrated way after the conversion of various water related bureaus into one in May 2000 after following the step of Shenzhen in 1993 (*China Environment News* December 10, 2001; Nickum and Lee 2006). In terms of legal instruments, there are national laws related to water services, such as the PRC Water Law (1988, revised 2002) and the PRC Water Pollution Prevention Law (1984, revised 1996), which indirectly encourage PPP by promoting the protection of water resources. In Articles 6, 7, and 8, the PRC Water Law encourages entities and individuals to develop water resources and promotes the development of a water conservation industry. Article 22 in the

Table 3.1 Four waterworks companies in Shanghai in 2003

	Shanghai Northern Water Supply Co. Ltd.	Shanghai Southern Water Supply Co. Ltd.	Shanghai Minhang Water Supply Co. Ltd.	Shanghai Pudong Veolia Water Supply Co. Ltd.
Population served	4 million	3 million	0.6 million	1.7 million
Area served	North-western suburbs (industrial center – Baoshan Steel)	South-western city center (old commercial and residential areas)	Southern suburbs (small-scale farms and new industrial areas)	Eastern city center and suburbs (Financial, commercial and industrial district)
Capacity (m³/day)	3 million	2.5 million	0.7 million	1.3 million
Capital (yuan)	1.8 billion	1.1 billion	1.1 billion	1.4 billion

Source: Lee (2003).

Table 3.2 Laws and regulations related to public–private partnership in the Chinese Water Sector

Year	Name
1995	The Certain Matters Relating to Project Financing by Domestic Institutions Notice
1995	The Several Issues Concerning the Examination, Approval & Administration of Experimental Foreign Invested Concession Projects Circular (the BOT Circular)
1995	The PRC Security Law
1997	The Catalogue for Guiding Foreign Investment in Industry
1997	The Administration of Project Financing Conducted Outside China's Tentative Procedures (The Interim Procedures)
1998	The Administration of Borrowing International Commercial Loans by Domestic Organisations Procedures
1999	The PRC Contract Law

Source: Rozner (1998) and Sorab and Rogers (1999).

PRC Water Pollution Prevention Law requires enterprises to use clean production techniques for reduction of pollutants, which indirectly attracts more TNCs to enter the water market, equipped with cutting-edge sewage treatment technologies. The Build–Operate–Transfer (BOT) Circular in 1995 and the Catalogue for Guiding Foreign Investment in Industry in 1997 are regarded as the regulation and guideline to be applicable to PPP projects in the water sector (see Table 3.2).

Even though it was reported that the Shanghai water industry began to make profits in 2001, the Shanghai authorities came to realize the need to enhance operational and management efficiency concerning the accumulated deficit of

Table 3.3 Options for public–private partnership and responsibility

Option	Asset ownership	Operations and Maintenance	Capital investment	Commercial risk	Usual duration
Service contract	Public	Public and private	Public	Public	1–2 years
Management contract	Public	Private	Public	Public	3–5 years
Lease	Public	Private	Public	Shared	8–15 years
BOT	Private	Private	Private	Private	20–30 years
Concession	Public	Private	Private	Private	25–30 years
Joint venture	Joint corporate	Joint corporate	Joint corporate	Joint corporate	Indefinite
Divestiture	Private	Private	Private	Private	Indefinite

Source: Modified from Johnstone *et al.* (2001).

water sector services over the previous two decades. Chi Jianguo of the Shanghai Water Assets Operation and Development Corporation commented, "To break the monopoly is the first step in reform. We have to import foreign technology and management to create more value to increase our competitiveness in the local market" (*China Daily* May 23, 2002). It is argued that these problems have generated favorable conditions for the launch of partnership between the public and private sector. This development illustrates the beginning of municipal governmental recognition of the need to bring in new elements (private companies with investment and technology) that can rejuvenate the existent urban infrastructure system.

Increasing loans from international development agencies such as the World Bank and private banking consortiums have continued to pressure the Shanghai government to repay its debts. The loans channeled from the World Bank, the Asian Development Bank and other commercial banking consortiums coupled with tight public financing became a budgetary problem for the Shanghai government (*China Daily* July 23, 2002). Therefore financing through other channels, such as the BOT scheme and joint ventures in Shanghai, was considered (see Table 3.3). This phenomenon is also linked to the view of the World Bank in favor of water TNCs' involvement in developing countries. The World Bank maintains that water TNCs' abundant experience in different countries, advanced know-how and technical innovations have led to the nurturing of economic and political capacity that can play a part in policy making and implement the development strategies of the World Bank (Fingers and Allouche 2002).

Overview of water PPP in the Chinese water sector

Chinese water market

The urgent need to bring private investment into urban infrastructure development in China, particularly in the water sector, has been discussed in numerous news articles and research reports. The Chinese Academy of Sciences predicted that freshwater consumption for domestic and industrial uses in China would be expected to rise by 60 percent for 50 years, up to 800 billion cubic meter per year; and the current water supply capacity should be increased by 25 percent by 2010 (*Business China – EIU* February 18, 2002). In addition to such huge potential for investment in the water supply sector, the sewage treatment sector has been recognized as a high potential business field by companies. The Chinese government's investment in sewage treatment has been substantial, culminating in the investment of approximately 25 billion US dollars in the sewage treatment sector during the Ninth Five Year Plan (1996–2000) (Horton 2000). China's winning of the competition to host the 2008 Olympic Games had also driven the central government to push forward its sewage treatment schemes. The Ministry of Construction drew up a blueprint that all cities in China should establish sewage treatment facilities that can deal with 60 percent by 2010 (*Xinhua Net* June 19, 2002).

Major water transnational corporations

Aware of these business opportunities and calls from the Chinese government, water TNCs, such as Suez, Veolia, Thames Water, and Bouygues (SAUR), have scrambled to enter the Chinese water market since the 1980s. However, their active participation began to take place in the 1990s. Equipped with international experience, management expertise and technologies, these water TNCs surpassed their Chinese counterparts that did not have competitive cutting-edge technologies and advanced management expertise (*China Water Conservancy News* May 24, 2002).

Among these water TNCs in China, the Suez Group is one of the leaders in terms of the number of water contracts won and the scale of accumulated investment. In China, Ondeo Degremont, an engineering subsidiary of the Suez Group, began to enter the market in 1975 and has so far commissioned more than 100 water and sewage treatment construction contracts. Such a business record implies that the Suez Group is responsible for about 10 percent of China's water and sewage treatment facilities. The unique stance of the Suez Group in China can be found in its cautious strategy of doing business in China in collaboration with the New World Development Co. Ltd, based in Hong Kong, under the name of Sino-French Water Development (Owen 2002, 2003; *Water Market China* 2004). Employing this strategy of entering the Chinese market with a guide (New World Development), Suez, by 2004, had set up 19 joint ventures in many parts of China and had a total investment of 522 million US dollars (*Water Market China* 2004). In the joint ventures, the partners of Suez have always been local municipal water authorities. This strategy has been regarded as "the best insurance to avoid legal, regulatory, and political risks" (*Business China-EIU* November 10, 1997). The Suez Group's territorial influence now reaches Shanghai, and the company built two joint ventures in the Pudong New Development Zone in the years 2001 and 2002 (*China Daily* March 27, 2002).

The other most influential water TNC in China is the Veolia Group. Veolia entered the Chinese water market in the late 1990s and began to establish its strong position through its China office in Beijing (*Beijing Review* February 2, 1998). The company won the contract for the Chengdu BOT Water Supply Project in 1998. This drew much attention, because, with the total investment of 106.5 million US dollars, it was the first BOT based water supply project in China (Wei 2001). Considering its late entry to the Chinese water market, the recent record of Veolia has been impressive. As of 2004, Veolia was providing water services through 12 projects in China with a total investment of 450 million US dollars, and implementing water projects in Shanghai, Beijing, Baoji, Zhuhai, Chengdu, and Tianjin (Owen 2002, 2003; *Water Market China* 2004).

In addition to these powerful water TNCs in China, there are a few foreign players from France and the United Kingdom (Owen 2002, 2003), though their influence is not as significant as that of Suez and Veolia. Bouygues (SAUR) is a leading French water TNC active in the Chinese market. The company first entered the market by signing a contract with the Harbin municipality to construct a sewage treatment plant (Owen 2002). Thames Water, which was sold by the German RWE Group to the Macquerie-led consortium in October 2006, penetrated the Chinese water market in 1989 (Boles 2006). One of its greatest successes would have been the 1995 BOT contract with the Shanghai government in Da Chang to provide water treatment services (Owen 2002); but Thames Water withdrew from the market due to the implementation of governmental regulations in relation to the Da Chang Project which ban guaranteed returns for foreign invested projects (Public Citizen 2005).

Chinese companies

Although it is difficult to define Chinese companies as privately owned and free from any relationship with governmental bureaus and agencies, they are gradually becoming major competitors with water TNCs in China. It is observed that in order to meet local water service needs, numerous local municipalities have established their subsidiary water companies, and some of them have begun to be partially privatized. Exemplary companies, to name a few, are the Beijing Sound Environmental Industry Group, Shanghai Liangqiao Tap Water Corporation, Shanghai Municipal Raw Water Corporation, Shenyang Public Utilities, and Wuhan Shanzheng Industry Holding (Owen 2002, 2003).

Among them, the recent performance of Beijing Sound Environmental Industry Group (Sound Group) deserves attention. In 2001, the Sound Group signed agreements in Beijing with 11 local representatives to build sewage treatment plants, including Shanghai, Qinghai Province, and Hubei Province. These large-scale projects require about 240 million US dollars in total, and the company has a responsibility to implement project financing and constructing plants via the form of BOT (*China Daily* June 15, 2002). Another notable achievement by Chinese private companies is the Shanghai Zhuyuan No. 1 Sewage Treatment Project contract undertaken by Youlian Enterprise Development Company with two other Chinese investment companies (*Xinhua Net* June 8, 2002).

The discussion of achievements by TNCs and Chinese companies provides strong evidence of the contribution of the private sector to the Chinese water sector. The reform drive since the late 1970s has started to change the landscape of the political economy of China, and the water sector has needed cutting-edge technology as well as investment from abroad. These factors have spawned the proliferation of water TNCs in many parts of China. The processes of the reforms have also allowed Chinese companies to grow, and their competitiveness has been improved over the past decades. These international and national entrepreneurs have been beneficiaries of a new mode of urban infrastructure development in the reform era. At the same time the companies have influenced national water policies – for instance, by advocating rational water tariffs, providing the opportunity for government bureaus to learn advanced operational and managerial skills and innovating the previous system.

Shanghai water market

The previous section has discussed various water projects performed by water TNCs and Chinese companies at the national level. This section examines water service projects in Shanghai by water TNCs and Chinese companies. The provision of water supply and sewage treatment services in Shanghai was regarded as the responsibility of the government until the late 1990s. The idea that water is an economic good has still not been widely recognized and accepted in Chinese society. In addition, the firm grip of the government over urban infrastructure provision in the communist regime consolidated the state-society duality, whereas the growth and involvement of the private sector was discouraged. In such circumstances, private sector involvement in the water sector had not been noticeable until the early 1990s, although the rapidly changing political economy had strongly influenced many aspects of society and economy in Shanghai since 1978. The slow but gradual shift of the government's policy towards ownership change in urban infrastructure provision, particularly the water sector, developed during the 1990s, mainly because of chronic problems in water supply and sewage treatment services. Management was inefficient, skills and facilities were out-of-date, there was a lack of finance, and raw water sources were polluted.

At the national level, one of the priorities for the reform of water services from the early 1980s was to attract foreign investment. The global trend of water service privatization led by water TNCs and donor agencies paved the way for the central and local governments to consider PPP. The statistics show that the total foreign investment in water resources projects in the period between 1982 and 1997 reached over 4 billion US dollars (Donoghue *et al.* 1999). Foreign investment in the Chinese water sector had increasingly been needed since the mid-1990s. The scale of investment in water services in the Ninth Five Year Plan period (1996–2000) was estimated at 20–25 billion US dollars (Horton 2000). In Shanghai, the total investment plan for water projects in the year 2002 was 7.3 billion yuan (900 million US dollars) (*China Environment News* March 4, 2002). The necessary investment for water services during the 10th Five Year Plan period (2001–2005) was estimated at more than 38 billion yuan (5 billion US dollars) (*China Environment News* June 10, 2002). Furthermore, the Shanghai water industry market expanded on the scale of 500–600 billion US dollars in a few years time from 2002 (*China Water Conservancy News* May 24, 2002).

Public–private partnership water projects in Shanghai began in the late 1990s, the two leading French water TNCs, Veolia and Suez, endeavoring to take advantage of the trend towards the privatization in water supply and sewage treatment services in Shanghai. In spite of its pioneering move, as we have seen, Thames Water disappeared in the game of water PPP because of the Da Chang project failure in 2004. However, some Chinese companies managed to win large-scale sewage treatment plants in Shanghai in 2001 and 2002.

Thames water

The earliest PPP water project in Shanghai was the Da Chang BOT water project begun by the Thames Water and Bovis consortium in 1995. The goal of the project was to build and manage a water treatment plant in Da Chang, Shanghai, with an operation period of 20 years. The capacity of the water treatment plant is 400,000 cubic meters per day (peak at 520,000 cubic meters per day), and the total investment is 78 million US dollars. The water supply service began for two million customers in 1997, and Degrement (the Suez Group) was upgrading a second water treatment plant in 2003 (Wang 2001). The Da Chang water project was regarded as a successful case in terms of limiting financial risks at the municipal level without any of the central government's symbolic support letters or guarantees. This was possible because Thames Water was confident of the political and economic stability and strength of the Shanghai government coupled with the favorable economic conditions for China's infrastructure projects in 1996 (Donoghue *et al.* 1999).

The Da Chang Project, however, illustrates how difficult it is for foreign companies to cope with the uncertain and risky Chinese water market. The Da Chang project was handed over by Thames Water to the Shanghai Shibei (Northern City) Water Treatment Corporation in June 2004. The major reason for this sudden event stemmed from the State Council's decision in 2002 that guaranteed rates of return for infrastructure projects are illegal, and risks and returns in BOT projects should be shared by Chinese as well as foreign partners. The 1996 contract guaranteed a fixed return of 15 percent per annum, but this now became illegal. Although Thames Water tried to negotiate new terms with the Shanghai Waterworks Company (owned by the Shanghai government) the companies could not come to agreement (Public Citizen 2005).

Suez

Compared with their impressive achievements in other cities and provinces in China, the Suez Group's activities in Shanghai had been negligible until 2000. Since 2000, the Suez Group has entered the Shanghai water market more aggressively. In July 2001, Ondeo in the Suez Group won a contract for the management of water services in the Shanghai Pudong Spark Industrial Zone over a 30 year period (*Suez Press Release* March 20, 2002). More extensive activities of Suez in the Shanghai water market were visible in the year 2002. In March, Sino French Water Development, a subsidiary of Ondeo and the Hong Kong based New World Group, set up a joint venture with the Shanghai Chemical Industrial Park on the same site to provide an industrial sewage treatment service. The duration of the contract is 50 years, and the total investment is more than 54 million US dollars for the treatment of sewage at a volume of 50,000 cubic meters per day. Ondeo is in charge of designing, financing, and managing water treatment installations and services (*China Daily* March 27, 2002).

Another successful contribution by Suez was the reconstruction project, signed in 2002, of the Nanshi and Yangshupu drinking water treatment plants. The project cost is estimated at 31.2 million US dollars, and the total capacity of two plants is 860,000 cubic meters per day. On the technical side, the plants will be equipped with more advanced technology in order to provide better drinking water in Shanghai (*Ondeo Press Release* May 22, 2002).

Veolia

Veolia's contract with the Shanghai Pudong Water Supply Corporation was a striking development. Veolia's acquisition of a 50 percent share of the Shanghai Pudong Water Supply Corporation was unprecedented and regarded as a genuine breakthrough for foreign companies to take part in the entire waterworks process, from water processing to water distribution, in Shanghai as well as elsewhere in China. Veolia was selected as the winner of the international bidding for the contract. The contract period is 50 years, and Veolia agreed to invest around 311 million US dollars (*China Environment News* June 24, 2002; *Veolia Water Press Release* May 22, 2002). The Sino-French company is scheduled to make, distribute, and sell running water for domestic use. The service area of the new company covers 319 square kilometers and caters for about 550,000 customers whose average daily drinking water consumption is estimated at 1.2 million cubic meters (*Shanghai Water Authority News* May 26, 2002). The increase in water sales is expected to be up to 3 percent per annum, and Veolia plans to enhance water quality with its advanced technology and know-how.

In addition to its allowing for the first time a foreign company's involvement in the entire water service process and acquisition of state-owned water supply corporations' shares, this project's importance lies in the fact that Veolia will be able to contact Chinese customers directly for the first time as a foreign water company. Direct contact with Chinese water consumers by foreign companies has been banned in the past in accordance with the Catalogue for Guiding Foreign Investment in Industry (1997). The flexibility of the interpretation of laws and regulations by local authorities may allow Veolia to provide customer services through its direct contact with Shanghai customers. To this end, the company will establish customer call centers, as well as making and distributing water customer handbooks (*Shanghai Water Authority News* August 30, 2002).

The company seems to be happy about this new breakthrough, because water prices and distribution systems are more transparent. This may enable Veolia to generate more revenues through price negotiation. However, it is expected that Veolia will be involved in painstaking and long-term negotiations with the Shanghai government about water tariffs. Shanghai authorities have reiterated their policy of maintaining the unitary water price system throughout the Shanghai municipality areas (*Xinwen Evening News* March 11, 2002; *Water Market China* 2004).

Chinese companies

One of the most frequently quoted projects in the media during the summer of 2002 was the Zhuyuan No. 1 Sewage Treatment Project, one of the subprojects in the Shanghai Sewerage Project Phase III which has been underway since 2001 (Lu 2001). The contract winner was the Youlian Consortium, consisting of three Chinese companies, namely Youlian Enterprise Development Company, Huajin Information Industry Investment Company, and the Shanghai Construction and Engineering Group (*Shanghai Water Authority News* June 5, 2002). The Youlian Consortium agreed to invest 870 million yuan (110 million US dollars) for the next 20 years, and the contract was based on the BOT scheme. Sewage treatment capacity is expected to reach 1.7 million cubic meters per day (*Xinhua Net* June 5, 2002). The capacity of the Zhuyuan sewage treatment plant is the biggest of all those in China, except for that of a plant in Hong Kong. It is reported that the Youlian consortium's bidding costs for sewage treatment were much lower than the current market cost, which illustrates the potential of the lucrative sewage treatment market in Shanghai. Jin Zhigang, chief engineer of Youlian Enterprise Development Company, presented his optimistic view that the Youlian Consortium would be able to start payback in the 13th year of the project during the 20 year contract period (*Xinwen Morning News* June 6, 2002).

The Beijing Sound Environment Industry Group (Sound Group), an engineering company specializing in water and sewage treatment facilities, is another Chinese company that is expected to expand its influence in the Shanghai water market. The group's entry to Shanghai was in June 2001 when it agreed to build sewage treatment plants in 11 Chinese cities, including that in the Jinshan District of Shanghai (*China Daily* June 15, 2002). Each of the 11 sewage treatment plants will have a capacity of more than 1.7 million cubic meters per day, which will be equal to that of Zhuyuan No. 1. The contracts were drawn up on the basis of a BOT scheme, and the total investment for all the plants will be around 2 billion yuan (240 million US dollars) during the 25-year concession period (Owen 2002). Considering the financial and engineering capacity confirmed by its simultaneous 11 contracts, it will be interesting to observe if the Sound Group can grow to be one of the major competitors of water TNCs. Table 3.4 summarizes water projects undertaken by water TNCs and Chinese companies in Shanghai since the 1990s, and Figure 3.1 visualizes how water projects in the process of PPP are geographically located in Shanghai.

Table 3.4 Public–private partnership water projects in Shanghai since the 1990s

Name	PJT Name	Contract type	Cost (US$ Mil)	Concession period	Capacity (m³/d)
Thames Water (*Shanghai government**) Suez (*Ondeo*)	Da Chang Water Treatment	BOT	78	20 years from 1996	400,000 (peak 520,000)
	Pudong Spark Industrial Zone Water Supply Services	Joint venture		30 years from 2001	
	Pudong Spark Industrial Zone Industrial Sewage Treatment	Joint venture	54	50 years from 2002	50,000
	Reconstruction of the Nanshi and the Yangshupu Water Treatment Plants	Reconstruct	31	2002–	860,000 (combined capacity)
Veolia	Shanghai Pudong Veolia Water Supply Corporation	Joint venture (Purchase of a 50% share of the Chinese counterpart)	311	50 years from 2002	
Youlian Consortium	Zhuyuan No. 1 Sewage Treatment Plant	BOT	110	20 years from 2002	1.7 million
Beijing Sound Group	Shanghai Jinshan Sewage Treatment Plant	BOT		25 years from 2002	1.7 million

Source: Author's compilation of information from fieldwork.

Note

* Thames Water withdrew the project, which was taken over by the Shanghai government in 2004.

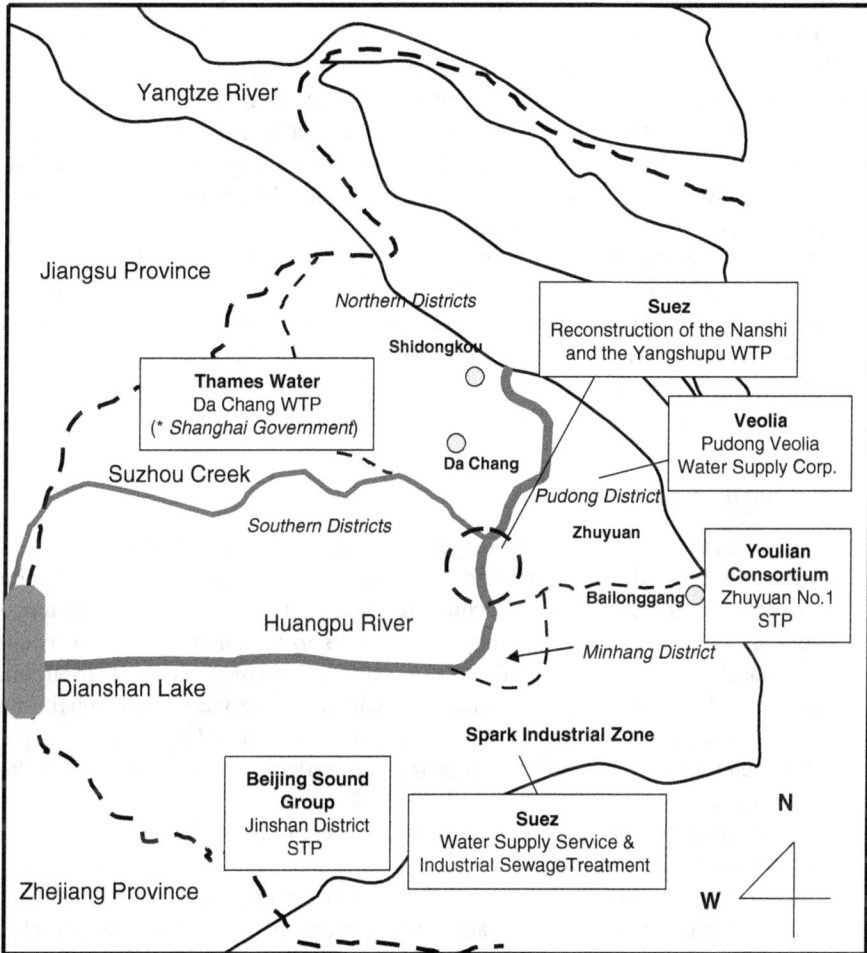

Figure 3.1 Water projects by private companies in Shanghai from the 1990s to 2004.

Source: Author's compilation of information from fieldwork.
Notes
* Thames Water withdrew the project, which was taken over by the Shanghai government in 2004.
WTP: Water Treatment Plant. STP: Sewage Treatment Plant.

Ramifications of PPP in water sector

Challenges

The recent emergence of private companies in urban infrastructure development, particularly in the water sector, indicates that Shanghai is in a new era in which the demarcation between the private and the public sector has become clearer. This process has accelerated since the economic reforms embarked on in the late 1970s. In other words, the willingness to modernize Communist China during the reform era has facilitated the resurgence of the private sector so that private companies have become a constituent of the process in the infrastructure sector since the late 1980s and the early 1990s (Bellier and Zhou 2003). The long disempowered private sector has started to exercise influence on the reformed, but still government-controlled, water sector in Shanghai. However, water TNCs and Chinese companies are not satisfied with the current business environment. Although Shanghai boasts its strategic location, a highly skilled labor force, foreign-investment-favoring policies and institutions, and political stability, private companies perceive a high degree of uncertainty as well as various risks in putting their investment in the Shanghai water sector. Such uncertainty and risks facing PPP in the Shanghai water sector can be analyzed according to three categories: sociopolitical challenges, regulatory uncertainty, and revenue risk.

Sociopolitical challenges

With regard to sociopolitical challenges, attention must first be paid to the issue of challenging the traditional perception of water, which is seen in China as a public and social good, rather than an economic good as it is seen in most developed countries. This situation has caused water prices to be much lower than would be reasonable if they were to reflect the actual costs of construction, distribution, and maintenance of water supply and sewage treatment services in Shanghai. The current water price for domestic use in Shanghai is 1.03 yuan (0.13 US dollars) per cubic meter, and there is no price adjustment to reflect the volume used in 2006, according to the SWA.

Although the water authorities in Shanghai seem to be well aware of inappropriate water prices, it is difficult for them to plan and launch the radical change of water pricing that would recover the costs of water supply and sewage treatment services. Such public sensitivity about water prices has prevented the Shanghai government from allowing private companies to adjust water tariffs in order to achieve commercial gains. Rather, as observed in the negotiations between the Shanghai government and Veolia and Suez, the Shanghai government has shown its explicit will to keep the unitary water tariff system which applies to all areas in the municipality, including the economic development zones in Pudong covered by Veolia and Suez's joint ventures. This implies that the government would not be inclined to provoke public anger or unrest through a sudden increase of water tariffs but keeps the water tariffs low in order to maintain the its legitimacy. Although privatization has been stressed and pursued since the late 1990s in the Shanghai water sector, the political-economic system and state-led society prevent the government from operating private modes of management.

Political uncertainty for private investors in China has continued to make water TNCs seek some form of guarantee from politically influential government bureaus related to water projects, such as the State Development and Reform Commission

(SDRC) and the Ministry of Water Resources. This legally nonbinding guarantee is called a "Government Support Letter/Comfort Letter" (Turner III and Seem 1999). Given political uncertainty and local government's low creditworthiness, water TNCs have no option but to appeal to hierarchically superior central ministries and bureaus for these letters. Since the concept of these guarantees is based on a Chinese tradition of "gentlemen's honor and agreement," it would be difficult for project-concerned local governments, worrying that they would "lose face," to offer unfavorable deals to water TNCs supplied with such documents (Turner III and Seem 1999). The use of these letters has been commonplace in a number of joint venture water projects.

With further decentralization, the central government has become reluctant to provide Government Support Letter/Comfort Letters to local water projects. As for water TNCs involved in water projects in Shanghai, it may not be necessary to gain these letters to avoid political and credit risks, because the relative risks of political unrest and creditworthiness in Shanghai are lower than in other areas in China. However, it can be contended that these letters will remain as important as other essential documents for water projects in Shanghai and China. Previous experience of Chinese politics suggests that nothing can be sure and guaranteed in the future for water TNCs in China, particularly during the water project concession period of about 20–30 years (*Business China-EIU* November 10, 1997). This illustrates the public and private interface in a situation where there is no politically stable environment for private companies. It shows that private companies are adapting to totally different sociopolitical and economic settings. A political guarantee like the Government Support Letters/Comfort Letter has been a device through which private companies try to minimize their risks in complex negotiations and contracts with local and central government agencies, local companies, and other stakeholders.

Legal and regulatory uncertainty

Another challenge in the development of PPP in Shanghai is how to improve the legal and regulatory frameworks. As discussed before, a series of laws and regulations have been enacted regarding water PPP in the China water sector; these include the PRC Water Law and the PRC Water Pollution Prevention Law together with numerous laws and regulations. Although these laws and regulations relate to private sector involvement in Shanghai, none of them specifies any guidelines for foreign investment in the water industry. This legal vacuum is also linked to the lack of "a uniform supervisory legal system" (Blackman 2001) for a coherent legal system in China. Such situation causes water TNCs to feel uncertain and insecure about the Chinese legal system and often discourage them from expanding their activities. Compared with the Chinese market, European markets, in which legal systems are implemented and enforced in a systematic manner, are more predictable . The legal institutions and law enforcement in China have an influence on the organizational behaviors of water TNCs, generating a more prudent market approach and tactics.

As for water projects in Shanghai and China, the process of managing joint
ventures by water TNCs together with Chinese counterparts shows the validity of
the notion "everything is negotiable." Since each joint venture has different administrative and management structures, it is usual for water TNCs to face numerous
negotiations with their Chinese counterparts – as Suez has experienced for more
than two decades. Suez's successful localization through establishment and management of 19 joint ventures over the past decades exemplifies the extent to which
water TNCs can adjust themselves to local customs and norms and at the same time
achieve their primary goal of economic gain. It is noted that such dual successes
have been possible because of a constant adaptive process through protracted
negotiations and compromises between water TNCs and government agencies.

The Shanghai government's private sector administrative structure looks simple but in reality encompasses a complex system dominated by internal politics.
The continuous administrative reforms in the Shanghai government influenced the
water sector and led to the setting-up of the SWA in 2000. With the integration
of different governmental bureaus associated with water services, the SWA oversees the operation of the city's water and sewerage services to which the private
water companies pay special attention. The SWA's efforts to establish PPP, however, are hampered by the fragmented structure of the central administration in
Beijing. Although the SWA's administrative position falls under the Ministry of
Water Resources, the SDRC takes responsibility for assessing projects involving
an investment of over 30 million US dollars as well as setting guidelines for water
prices. The Ministry of Construction deals with water projects in urban areas, and,
in this part of the bureaucratic hierarchy, the Shanghai Bureau of Construction
is responsible for the construction of water projects and water distribution. Furthermore, the State Environmental Protection Administration (SEPA) is involved
in the amelioration of water pollution,. The Shanghai Bureau of Environmental
Protection (SBEP), administered under SEPA, implements various water pollution
control policies together with the SWA. Such complicated mechanisms in water
resource management often discourage private companies from participating more
aggressively in water projects in Shanghai as well as in China at large.

Revenue risk

Whereas the Shanghai government has endeavored to channel foreign investment,
water TNCs do not seem to be fully sure of the creditworthiness of the government regarding various water projects. Because of the 1997 Catalogue for Guiding
Foreign Investment in Industry, any water joint venture has not been allowed to
own and manage the right of water distribution, which makes the project company unable to secure a certain level of profits. The case of Veolia's contract in
Pudong was the unprecedented one. The continued ownership by the government
of the water distribution system prevents the project company from charging users
through proper utilization of metering according to the volume of water they use.

As pointed out before, the public perception of water embedded in Chinese
culture makes it difficult for the government to implement the rationalization of

water prices. As a result, the government has to subsidize water services in order to make up the difference caused by unrealistic water pricing. There is little research on how much the current unitary water price system in Shanghai can cover the cost of water supply and sewage treatment services. The expectation of an increase of water prices in Shanghai is high, and this projected increase is one of the main reasons many water TNCs have been knocking on the door of the Shanghai water market (*China Daily* July 23, 2002). However, it is reasonable to assume that a number of water joint venture projects including the Shanghai Pudong Veolia Water Supply Corporation need long and tough negotiations with the government to make water tariffs realistic.

In spite of the risks and uncertainties discussed above, PPP in the Shanghai water sector has seemed to be going well so far. However, Thames Water's retreat from the Shanghai water market provides a warning signal to foreign water companies. Thames Water's pull-out implies a couple of challenges that foreign companies have to deal with. First, there is still a long way to go to establish transparent policy-making processes in China. It is hard to predict central government political decisions, and, as shown well in the Thames Water's case, foreign companies, including water TNCs, are suspicious of what would have a negative impact on the market. Second, this reflects a prevailing Chinese mode of way of life – based on negotiations. Although Thames Water wished to resort to the previous contract terms and conditions, against the State Council's decision, the Chinese partner did not agree to this, but acquiesced to the new edict from central government. Such behavior appears to be local governments' deference to hierarchy; however, it also implies that the Chinese partner in the project found the edict favorable to itself against Thames Water. These two elements suggest that the Shanghai water market is still risky and uncertain. The Shanghai government faces a big challenge of how to persuade foreign water companies to continue business as usual in spite of constant unpredictable sociopolitical, legal, and economic risks.

Ties between the Shanghai government and companies

Since the 1990s, Shanghai has experienced an influx of TNCs into the water market, and during recent years water TNCs and Chinese companies have rejuvenated the activities and capacity of the private sector in implementing water joint ventures and participating in BOT water projects. Such PPP in the Shanghai water sector seems to develop further and even speed up thanks to China's entry into the World Trade Organization (WTO). This reflects the fast changing picture of the Shanghai water market as well as water policy.

At the national level, the central government has recognized the importance of PPP in the Chinese water sector since the early 1980s. One of the more recent governmental blueprints to attract foreign financing for the improvement of urban water infrastructure was the twenty-first century Urban Water Management Pilot Scheme in 1997. In the scheme, the liberalization of water tariffs on projects funded with foreign capital was scheduled, and foreign financiers were allowed to gain favorable rates of return for water projects in China (Rozner 1998). Following the

Scheme, the Urban Water Price Regulation of 1998 allows foreign investors to gain a net return rate of 12 percent and local governments to decide water prices on the condition that water companies provide detailed information on their costs. These governmental plans and regulations have resulted in an increase in private sector involvement in the water sector since 1998 (Wang and Chen 2001). The central government was willing to reform the water sector in order to remove the irrational management and unrealistic water tariffs that were main causes of the large-scale deficit from the 1980s. Such necessary action induced an influx of foreign investment as well as of water TNCs in the 1980s and 1990s. New demand and requirements in relation to loans from international development agencies, such as the World and Asian Development Banks, have at the same time conditioned institutional rearrangements in favor of privatization. Water TNCs have taken advantage of this trend and influenced Chinese governmental policies in water services with international development agencies.

In response to the central government's new policy, the Shanghai government has also tried to attract many water TNCs, as well as Chinese companies, in water supply and sewage treatment services. The recent governmental report on Shanghai announced various water project schemes during the 10th Five Year Plan (2001–2005) which attracted private water companies' attention. These included: the Shanghai Sewerage Project Phase III, the construction of 10 additional sewage treatment plants in the city center; the construction of a sewage collection network; the renovation of dilapidated sewage treatment plants; and the control of runoff sewage (*Shanghai Water Authority News* June 9, 2002). Most scheduled projects were expected to attract PPP. In addition to many water projects, the Shanghai government had developed a marketing strategy to channel the huge scale of water infrastructure investment required in the future.

These optimistic plans for private investment and project opportunities, however, would not be viable if there had not been much redefinition of governmental roles and responsibilities for the privatization of the water sector in Shanghai. Most importantly, the Shanghai authorities have to be aware that they are no longer the direct providers of water supply and sewage treatment services but only the regulator. The separation of administrative and commercial functions in the government needs to be implemented (Johnstone and Wood 2001; Wang and Chen 2001). The SWA is the likely candidate to become a relatively independent regulatory institution to manage complicated issues related to water services. It is still questionable if the SWA can manage to mediate in conflicts of interest among different bureaus, such as the Bureau of Construction and the Bureau of Environmental Protection, and conduct the regulatory roles effectively. It seems that the Shanghai government still needs more time to redefine its new governmental roles for PPP. The shift to regulator of the governmental role in water services and the establishment of the SWA highlight how the approach of the Shanghai government has changed faced with privatization. Privatization requires that the government should adopt the new role as a regulator in response to PPP and learn technical and managerial expertise from private companies to innovate institutions and facilities. But it is crucial that the government should also take lessons on the customer care service from private companies in water services and consider working together with customers, namely local people, for the achievement of better quality water services.

Conclusion

This chapter explores the dynamics of the commercialization of urban infrastructure in Shanghai in the water sector since the late 1990s. The need for investment, advanced technology, and innovative management pushed the government to adopt PPP in the water sector. The municipal government introduced a series of reforms in favor of private sector involvement in urban water services. Private companies responded by contributing to privatization. These main social actors, however, have faced unprecedented challenges in order to secure their interest, and such conflicts of interest have culminated in a very different political economy landscape. Private companies, mainly water TNCs, have experienced unpredictable and challenging sociopolitical circumstances, uncertainty of laws and regulations, and revenue risk. The case of Thames Water's exit from the Chinese water market is a good example of how risky it is for foreign companies to run their business in China. The continuous demands from the private sector to reform water tariffs and establish sound legal instruments have driven the government to bring about change in its internal organizations.

The analyses of the diverse sociopolitical, legal and regulatory, and revenue risks demonstrate that the Shanghai authorities are required to implement a number of institutional reforms in order to take on their new role as the regulator, not the provider, of water services. The success of privatization in the Shanghai water sector hinges partially on the extent to which the Shanghai government is able to accomplish its work as a regulator based on laws. Otherwise, the early privatization projects become the price the government could pay for such lessons.

The interaction between the public and the private spheres in the Shanghai's water sector reflects the nature of the Chinese mode of privatization. First, the preferred mode of negotiation is an important factor. Negotiation normally slows the process of privatization but, if fully implemented, makes outcomes more secure. Also even though privatization is appropriately "negotiated" at the central government level, it is likely to be different at the lower level of government. Second, the pace of expansion is further affected by the lack of finance available in the course of privatization. The low degree of financial capacity has caused the Shanghai government to invite water TNCs and Chinese private companies to adopt new forms of financing methods such as BOT schemes, joint ventures, and equity sales – as are evident in the deal with Veolia in Pudong. The effort of the Shanghai government to strengthen its financial capacity is an engine to speed up the pace of privatization in the water sector.

Public–private partnership in water services in Shanghai has just begun and seems likely to develop rapidly in the foreseeable future. China's entry to the WTO may become a catalyst to further push the Shanghai government to implement rigorously policies favoring the private sector for water services. Such new environments for the water industry were expected to support the fast growth of the China water market, requiring an investment of around 1,000 billion yuan (120 billion US dollars) until 2005. This investment would include 200–300 billion yuan (24–36 billion US dollars) from central and local governments. The remaining portion, equivalent to more than 70 percent, would be channeled through foreign investment, which would pave the way for water TNCs to extend their market shares (She 2002). Shanghai's blueprint to attract an investment of around 38 billion yuan (5 billion US dollars) for water services before 2005 would be viable only if there were enough foreign investment, particularly through water TNCs, under the WTO system in China (*China Environment News* June 10, 2002). More transparent and internationally standardized laws, regulations, and implementation of policies in Shanghai provide favorable conditions for introduction of private sector involvement in the urban infrastructure sector, including the water sector.

The initiation of PPP in China's cities, shown in the case of the water sector, implies a new path for sustainable urban governance in China. The new mode in urban infrastructure development, PPP, has gradually pushed away the monopoly of government. The private sector has brought in not only expertise, know-how and finance but also the opportunity for the government to learn cutting-edge technology and management skills, renovate its out-of-date facilities, and undertake institutional reform. Private sector involvement has drawn attention to customer satisfaction in service provision. This leads local people to become vocal about municipal services like water supply and sewage treatment services, paving the way for local people in Chinese cities to take an active part in policy making and implementation, thereby having an impact on institutional change in China's urban governance. PPP in the urban water sector has helped form sustainable urban governance in China where the government, private companies and individuals interact and pursue a common goal – the provision of high quality water services, through collaboration.

Acknowledgments

I would like to thank Tony Allan, Richard L. Edmonds, Urooj Amjad and David L. Owen for their invaluable comments and encouragement. This research was not possible without financial support from the School of Oriental and African Studies' Additional Fieldwork Award, the Senate House of the University of London's Central Research Fund, and the Universities China Committee in London.

References

Bellier, M. and Zhou, Y. M. (2003) *Private Participation in Infrastructure in China*, Washington, DC: World Bank.
Blackman, C. (2001) "Local government and foreign business," *China Business Review* 28(7): 26–31.
Boles, T. (October 23, 2006) "RWE's watertight profit on Thames," *The Scotsman*.

China Daily (July 23, 2002) "City waterworks tap foreign pool," *China Daily*.

Donoghue, N., Nelson, S. and Smith, D. (1999) "Water projects: growth for foreign investment, financing problematic," in B. Sorab and R. Benedict (eds) *Project Finance Models for Greater China*, Hong Kong: Asia Law & Practice, pp. 81–87.

Finger, M. and Allouche, J. (2002) *Water Privatisation: Transnational Corporations and the Re-Regulation of the Water Industry*, London: SPON.

"First Private Sector Involvement in the Public Water Service Area," June 5, 2002, *Shuiwu Xinwen (Shanghai Water Authority News)*.

"First Sino-Foreign Running Water Joint Venture Set Up in Shanghai," May 22, 2002, *Xinhua News*.

"First Sino-French Joint Venture Water Supply Corporation – Establishment of the Shanghai Pudong Veolia Water Supply Corporation," May 26, 2002, *Shuiwu Xinwen (Shanghai Water Authority News)*.

"Foreign Investment Entering Shanghai Water Market," June 24, 2002, *Zhongguo Huanjing Bao (China Environment News)*.

"French Group Generale des Eaux adds investment in China," February 2, 1998, *Beijing Review* (5&6): 35–38.

"French Firm Enters Chinese Drinking Water Market," May 23, 2002, *China Daily*.

Horton, P. (2000) "For all the water in China," *Water & Environment International*, 9(66): 14.

Industrial Map of China (2004–2005), Beijing: Social Sciences Academic Press.

Jiang, S. (ed.) (2000) *Directory of Standing Representative Organs of Foreign and Territorial Companies in China*, Beijing: Zhongguo Huaqiao Press.

Johnstone, N. and Wood, L. (eds) (2001) *Private Firms and Public Water: Realising Social and Environmental Objectives in Developing Countries*, Cheltenham: Edward Elgar.

Kohli, H., Mody, A. and Walton, M. (eds) (1997) *Choices for Efficient Private Provision of Infrastructure in East Asia*, Washington, DC: The World Bank.

Lee, S. H. (October 2003) "Shanghai overshadows risks," *Global Water Intelligence* 4(10): 8–10.

Lee, S. H. (2004) "The transformation of Shanghai water sector in the reform era – social actors and institutional change," unpublished Doctor of Philosophy (PhD) Thesis, School of Oriental and African Studies, University of London.

"Love that dirty water – Suez Lyonnaise des Eaux" November 10, 1997, *Business China*, The Economist Intelligence Unit.

Lu, H. (2001) "Retrospect and prediction for the Shanghai Municipality's water environment," *Shanghai Chengshi Fazhan (Shanghai City Development)* (1): 35–37.

"Modernisation of Water Management in the Twenty-first Century in Shanghai," May 24, 2002, *Zhongguo Shuilibao (China Water Conservancy News)*.

Nakagawa, M., Moor, R. and Or, F. (1999) "Financing power in the PRC: whither the 'five China issues?" in B. Sorab and R. Benedict (eds) *Project Finance Models for Greater China*, Hong Kong: Asia Law and Practice, pp. 7–12.

"New Water Joint Venture between Shanghai and Suez Group," November 19, 2001, *Jingji Ribao (Economic Daily)*.

Nickum, J. E. and Lee, Y.-S. F. (2006) "Same longitude, different latitudes: institutional change in urban water in China, North and South," *Environmental Politics*, 15(2): 231–247.

"Official Launch of the Shanghai Pudong Veolia Water Corporation," August 30, 2002, *Shuiwu Xinwen (Shanghai Water Authority News)*.

"Ondeo Strengthens Its Leadership in China with a New Industrial Services Contract Win in Shanghai," March 20, 2002, *Suez Press Release, Year 2002*.

"Ondeo (Suez) Strengthens Its Leading Position in China's Water Market," May 22, 2002, *Ondeo Press Release*.

"Opening of the Shanghai Water Market," June 10, 2002, *Zhongguo Huangjing Bao (China Environment News)*.

Owen, D. L. (2002) *Masons Water Yearbook, 2002–2003*, London: Masons Solicitors.

Owen, D. L. (2003) *Masons Water Yearbook, 2003–2004*, London: Masons Solicitors.

"Public Private Partnerships in Urban Regeneration," *The Royal Institution of Chartered Surveyors website*. Available online at: www.rics.org/AboutRICS/RICSstructureand governance/RICSpolicy/URBACTreport.htm (accessed August 20, 2006).

"Public private partnership will partially be needed for sewage treatment projects in Shanghai," March 4, 2002, *Zhongguo Huanjing Bao (China Environment News)*.

Rozner, S. (ed.) (1998) *Infrastructure Financing Strategies in the PRC, March 1998, A China Law & Practice Guide*. Hong Kong: Asia Law and Practice Publishing Ltd.

"RWE/Thames Water – A Corporate Profile," Public Citizen, October 2005. Available online at: www.citizen.org/documents/RWEProfile.pdf (accessed August 20, 2006).

"Scramble of Foreign Investment for Water Industry in Shanghai," December 10, 2001, *Zhongguo Huanjing Bao (China Environment News)*.

"Sewage Treatment Goes Private," June 15, 2002, *China Daily*.

"Shanghai Gets Its First Joint Waterworks," March 27, 2002, *China Daily*.

"Shanghai's Biggest Sewage Treatment Project Introduced Private Investment," June 6, 2002, *Xinwen Chenbao (Xinwen Morning News)*.

"Shanghai's Full-fledged Sewage Treatment Works – Commencing of Construction of Two 1 million capacity Sewage Treatment Plants," June 9, 2002, *Shuiwu Xinwen (Shanghai Water Authority News)*.

"Shanghai Starts Building New Sewage Treatment Plants," June 8, 2002, *Xinhua Net*.

She, S. (October 14, 2002) "A good time for foreign investment in the Chinese water industry," *Hong Kong Development Trade Council* Website at www.tdctrade.com

Silk, M. A. and Black, S. (2000) "Financing options for PRC water projects," *China Business Review*, 27(4): 28–32.

"Sino-French Joint Venture will Improve Water Quality in Shanghai," March 11, 2002, *Xinwen Wanbao (Xinwen Evening News)*.

Sorab, B. and Benedict, R. (1999) *Project Finance Models for Greater China*, Hong Kong: Asia Law and Practice.

Sun, L. (1999) "The dynamics of the private sector," in L. Sun, E. X. Gu, and R. J. McIntyer (eds) *The Evolutionary Dynamics of China's Small- and Medium-Sized Companies in the 1990s*, Helsinki: The United Nations University, World Institute for Development Economics Research, pp. 75–90.

"Thames Expands Its Chinese Dynasty," June 28, 2002, *Utility Week*, 17(25).

Turner III, E. L. and Seem, A. D. (1999) "The new project finance – legal solutions, legal strategies', in B. Sorab and R. Benedict (eds) *Project Finance Models for Greater China*," Hong Kong: Asia Law and Practice, pp. 13–21.

"Veolia Environment wins the international tender for the 50 year outsourcing contract to operate and manage Pudong water services, Shanghai's leading business district," May 22, 2002, *Veolia Water Press Release*.

Wang, J. and Chen, P. (2001) "China modernises public utilities," *China Business Review*, 28 (4): 44–49.

Wang, X. C. (2001) "Approach on finance raising and performance mechanism of environmental protection fund in Shanghai," *Shanghai Huanjing Kexue* (*Shanghai Environmental Sciences*), 20(6): 297–298.

"Water Guzzlers," February 18, 2002, *Business China*, The Economist Intelligence Unit.

Water Market China (2004), Oxford: Global Water Intelligence Publication.

Wei, H. (2001) "Private sector finance for infrastructure (ADB Report)," July 21, 2001, *The Western Region Development Workshop*, Beijing.

Wu, W. P. (1999) "Reforming China's institutional environment for urban infrastructure provision," *Urban Studies*, 36(13): 2263–2282.

Xinhua Net (2002) "China's largest sewage treatment factory to be run privately," June 5, 2002, *Xinhua Net*.

Xinhua Net (2002) "China seeks foreign investors for sewage treatment," June 19, 2002, *Xinhua Net*.

Zheng, L. (1999) "Making progress – a PRC viewpoint on the opening of project finance to foreign investment," in B. Sorab and R. Benedict (eds) *Project Finance Models for Greater China*, Hong Kong: Asia Law and Practice, pp. 89–95.

4 The dialectics of urban planning in China[1]

Daniel B. Abramson

Introduction – dialecticism versus gradualism

This chapter first focuses on the premises of urban planning in China and the contradictions inherent in planning practice as it has evolved uniquely in the current era of market-oriented reforms. The chapter then examines two concerns that are fundamental considerations for planning in all market-based systems, but of which current Chinese planning practice is not very cognizant: community and property. These concerns nevertheless push planning in China to evolve dialectically. The chapter is organized around the standard dialectical categories of *thesis*, which outlines the chief premises and functions of planning as it is currently practiced in China; *antithesis*, which outlines the problems produced by this practice and the contradictions inherent in it; and *synthesis*, which outlines some of the policy responses to these problems, and speculates on their implications for change in planning practice.

This dialectical view of planning in China also joins the critique of "gradualism" – the notion that market-oriented reform ultimately aims at a stable and unproblematic state of development, even as the way to achieve this state follows an experimental, incremental and pragmatic path that is unpredictable in the short-term. The dialectical view, by contrast, holds that development is inherently incomplete, problematic, and unpredictable in the long-term, and proceeds only according to the resolution of an endless stream of contradictions between sharply conflicting political-economic imperatives.

The discourse of gradualist reform considers local variations in planning and development policy to be temporary in the nation's "transition from plan to market" (Zhu 1999: 535). Similarly temporary are the emergence of "local growth coalitions" that take advantage, for private gain, of the persistence of state ownership of economic assets. Governmental legitimacy is supposed to survive the abuse of authority that emerges in this situation, precisely because such abuse is held to be temporary and even a necessary evil in a government-led development that accords with "the nation's collective aspirations" (Zhu 1999: 537). However, it is possible – some say likely – that the central government will lose control over its decentralized agents, who then become "predatory" instead of developmentalist, creating a crisis of legitimacy for the state (Pei 2006: 44).

According to a dialectical view, governmental legitimacy would depend not only on the pursuit of policies that strive to achieve collective aspirations, but also on the ability of the government to recognize contradictions that arise from these aspirations, and to work to resolve them. The very act of resolving conflict then creates new conflicts, which must themselves be resolved, and so on. Change is still "gradual," but each act of conflict-resolution depends on the immediate application of a set of existing principles – the outcome of which may require a questioning of those principles as well as a redefinition of the developmental goal. In the process, the nature of government itself may be redefined, including, for example, the role of political parties.

Is this happening in China? Certainly it is not according to official rhetoric, which stresses the persistence of Party-led policy for "100 years without change." However, an examination of actual governmental practices may reveal a more nuanced picture, especially at the local level. Urban planning is one such practice the transformation of which during the reform era shows some indication of a dialectical process in action. This process can explain how changes in planning practice relate to changes in urban form itself, for even as plans affect the form of the city, planners eventually respond to the new forms by changing how they plan.

Urban planning in China under reform is the product both of a renewed support of professionalization as well as of the decentralization of development powers. It is both an instrument of developmentalism and also a guarantor of environmental and social imperatives that may conflict with development (e.g. defense of national sovereignty, preservation of cultural heritage, adherence to broad popular notions of fairness as well as Party doctrine, etc.). Planning is a source and expression of governmental legitimacy, as well as a tool for power abuse. In short, urban planning must serve a number of functions, many of which are contradictory. While planning in China still falls short of the self-aware practice of social learning advocated by Friedmann (1993), it nevertheless evolves out of a constant need to resolve these contradictions in individual cases, based on lessons from previous cases. And as a primarily governmental practice in a society that in many aspects is highly "planned," the evolution of urban planning may ultimately indicate broader changes in governance and political culture.

Thesis – the premises of urban planning in China

Governmental legitimization as a function of urban planning

Urban planning serves to legitimize the state by performing both practical (instrumental) and symbolic (expressive) functions. Planning is an instrument of legitimization in the sense that it is necessary to accomplish legitimizing projects. But planning is also an *expression* of legitimization in the sense that the act of planning itself is symbolic of governmental success. Both officials and the general public commonly express approval for environments that are planned and orderly in comparison with those that are organic and chaotic, even when the latter may actually be more economically efficient or even more easily governed.

As a modern profession in China, urban planning has become dominated by its role as an instrument of state-led developmentalist projects. To the extent that these projects justify governmental power, the success of planning in this role is itself a legitimization of the government. However, there were other functions of professional planning which emerged in the 1980s, or which survived from earlier periods, and these cannot be ascribed to developmentalist goals alone. They have remained as elements of practice that serve primarily to legitimize the government and stabilize society; indeed, the maintenance of political legitimacy and social stability – as distinct from support of market activity – may be one of the oldest motives for urban planning in China.

The largest cities in premodern China were typically administrative capitals, not purely commercial centers, and were planned according to principles that legitimized the state through ritual, cosmology, the selective interpretation and application of precedent, and the demonstration of the government's sheer ability to mobilize a large population (Meyer 1991; Rykwert 1976: 184; Steinhardt 1990; Wheatley 1971; Wright 1977; Zhu 2004; Zhu and Kwok 1997). Given that planning conveyed legitimacy, the place of the market in China's traditional planning priorities was often problematic. Uniformity, regularity, hierarchy, cellularity, and the ritual symbolism of urban space have been celebrated as an expression of state power and administrative effectiveness in China since early times, especially at the beginning of new dynasties, and often at the expense of commercial activity (Brook 1985; Hou 1985: 228–230; Knechtges and Xiao 1982: 201–203; Wang 1995; H. Wu 2005: 145; L. Wu 1999: 3–12).

Many of these historic patterns in the spatial administration and design of Chinese cities continue to support governmental control of society. Chinese cities are bound into a regional and national system of governance that extends below the municipal level down to that of the street and household. There are two effects of this hierarchy especially worth noting in this context: first, that *community* is a very spatial concept;[2] second, that *property* (i.e. rights to space) is especially contingent on state power.

China's system of spatial administration is not only hierarchical, but also strikingly cellular (Gaubatz 1995) – that is, there is a tight correspondence between social units and spatial units. Both premodern and modern Chinese cities have been organized to enable the government to monitor and mobilize urban populations, not only by restricting residence (e.g. through *hukou*) but also by compartmentalizing space and making local communities responsible for their own internal law and order (Dray-Novey 1993; Han 1996; Li 1995; Rowe 1989; Wakeman 1993; F.-L. Wang 2004; M. Wang 2004). In modern times, this cellularity reached an extreme expression in the Mao-era work unit (*danwei*) compound, and continues in an eroded form in the Reform-era housing estate (*xiaoqu*) (Bray 2005; Huang 2005).

Premodern Chinese urban structure also persists in the form of complexly layered distinctions between public and private spaces. Private ownership of land existed for centuries in China, but through much of China's history the state was assumed to have "ultimate ownership" or at least control of land

(Clunas 1996: 26–27; Zelin *et al.* 2004). Even under the Communist Party, land was not formally nationalized in the constitution until 1982 (Deng 2003: 230). Private property use and disposition were always subject to broad police powers that continue to the present in the hands of resident committees (Samuels 1986: 61), and tended historically to be subject also to extensive informal and customary rules intended to maintain the integrity of extended families, clans and lineages (Clunas 1996: 200–201; Zelin *et al.* 2004: 26–27).

A corollary of these historic notions of both community and property is the way that public space – that is, space that is accessible to anyone in the society – relates to the spaces of smaller groupings (workplaces, housing estates, or families). Public space historically was not an object of voluntary civic responsibility, except for temples and other formally ritualistic/ideological spaces belonging to specific institutions but used informally for a variety of social activities (Clunas 2004: 159; Y. Xu 2000: 191 ff.). In any case, spaces for informal gathering were not the subject of urban planning as such. The public embellishments of China's cities today do not so much reflect civic pride as symbolize modernist statism as described by Scott (1998). This orientation is reflected today in political showcase projects: the sweeping away of informal markets; the remote, monumental municipal buildings surrounded by vast, empty plazas in nearly every city; the energy- and water-wasting "nightscape" projects and wide expanses of grass; and local governments' efforts to use planning for propaganda (Broudehoux 2004). The modern practice of historic preservation also fulfills many of the legitimizing functions of premodern planning. Much as previous dynasties "invented" the precedents and canons they used to justify the planning of their capitals, urban heritage plans today often aim to restore or copy a simplified premodern ideal rather than preserve the complex historic reality (Abramson 2001; Stille 1998).

Urban planning as a developmentalist profession

Urban planning as a modern profession in China today is inextricably linked to the national goal of market-oriented economic development, based on a Western-inspired definition of "modernization" and decentralized fiscal power. Planning practice in China fundamentally enables growth. It is also part of Deng Xiaoping's reaction against Maoist antiurban and antiprofessional principles of indigenous, self-sufficient, development. The literature on how urban planning in China has served as a tool of local growth coalitions and globally oriented developmentalism since the mid-1990s is well established (Olds 2001; Wu 1997, 2002a, 2003; Zhang 2002; Zhang and Fang 2004; Zhu 1999).

China's planners see their job as one of enabling environmental change. Far from "managing" growth, they very self-consciously serve it. Even historic preservation, which involves more of a regulatory component than other branches of planning, tends to focus more on designing essentially new construction than on restricting development. The dominance of design in planning is reflected in the terms used by the profession. For example, the social and economic five-year plans carried out by the State Planning Commission (renamed the State Development and Reform Commission in 2004) are now called *guihua* (spatial planning, literally "rule and delineate" or "layout") rather than *jihua* (economic programming, literally "calculate and delineate"). Party academics explain this as reflecting a shift away from the discredited, over-prescriptive "planned" economy toward a more flexible, long-range, "strategic" planning suitable for market economies (Baidu 2006). Nevertheless, the term *guihua* continues to present planning as value-neutral, engineering-based, and incapable of addressing the "wicked problems" inherent in market-based development (Abramson *et al.* 2002; Ng and Wu 1997).

Friedmann (1987, 1993) characterizes this view of planning as "orthogonal" or "Euclidean," and particularly unsuited to these "turbulent times, when little can be foreseen"; under such circumstances, planning should be based on social learning and "oriented to values rather than profit" (Friedmann 1987: 21–23, 1993: 484). Yet, it is precisely the design-and-construction orientation of planning in China that best serves the needs of a developmentalist state: by enabling rapid physical change that simultaneously profits and legitimizes the government. Other modes of urban planning that commonly protect public interests in advanced market economies – regulation, incentivization, advocacy, and community enablement – have less obvious applicability in the developmentalist context. As argued below, however, pressures exist in China that tend to favor the emergence of these other planning modes.

Antithesis – contradictions in Chinese urban planning and development

Chinese planning discourse does not present the public good or social justice as normative goals of planning, and distinctions between public and private interests generally are not well articulated (Leaf 1998). Because the Communist Party is defined as the champion of social justice, planning, as an arm of the Party-state, is assumed to advance the public good and follow the principles of social justice. However, as diversity increases among socioeconomic strata and interests in Chinese society, defining and defending the public good becomes a more and more obvious problem. Specifically, a number of contradictions have arisen out of the multiple premises under which urban planning is practiced in China.

First, there is a profound contradiction between the continued hierarchy of spatial administration and the recent fiscal decentralization that has empowered prefecture-level municipalities. The former is manifest in the evolving five-year economic planning system overseen by the Development and Reform Commission and its provincial and municipal branches. The latter is primarily expressed in urban spatial planning overseen by the Ministry of Construction. The social welfare and community governance bureaucracy, the Ministry of Civil Affairs, is responsible for democratic reforms at the village level, for issues of public accountability in government, and for basic services and governance down to the resident committee level. Given the impacts that urban redevelopment and urbanization of rural villages has had on China's local communities, civil affairs has increasing relevance to urban planning, and yet no institutional mechanisms reflect this special relationship.

There is also a tension between the administration of physical planning and that of land management. The latter falls under the Ministry of Land and Resources, which oversees a separate bureaucratic hierarchy from that of the Ministry of Construction, and which is used more to carry out regulatory functions. However, the persistence of a "dual land market" has made land management extremely difficult, and the absence of a straightforward land taxation system has given municipal governments a strong incentive to develop land quickly. Different branches and levels of the approving bureaucracy often have opposing interests in specific projects, the result being inefficiency as well as abuse of the public trust (Hong 2005).

Each of these related but separate vertical hierarchies – Construction (including physical planning), Development and Reform, Civil Affairs, and Land Management – is crosscut by the hierarchy of spatial government. Each level of spatial government – Province, Municipality, County/District – attempts to bend the will of each of these bureaucracies to suit the interests of that level. Although it appears that higher-level/larger-scale plans support policy, and lower-level/smaller-scale plans support regulation, this is deceptive; increased fiscal autonomy on the part of municipalities has taken most of the teeth out of the national five-year plan, and the sheer speed of growth has made long-term policy planning a low priority for most municipal leaders. As a result, much large-scale planning is a *pro forma* exercise. At the smaller scale, truly private development interests have not yet become the norm, and thus there is often no one for the local government to regulate other than companies with some form of government backing. State control of most urban land facilitates land assembly and further exacerbates this close relationship. Therefore local area plans tend either to be subverted by development, or used as blueprints for it. They rarely serve as regulating tools over the long term, and they are compromised from the outset as instruments of the public interest.

These plans set normative goals for physical development but do not account for conflicts of interest among government agencies responsible for their implementation (Deng 2003; Fang and Zhang 2003; Leaf 1998). Both inner-city redevelopment and the development of the urban fringe are extremely controversial because they benefit local government agencies and developers at the expense of residents and villagers who are dislocated. At the least, such dislocation involves disputes over appropriate levels of compensation. At its worst it removes people from their livelihoods and basic services, often concentrating poorer residents at some distance from the newly wealthy, and replacing older, demographically and socially diverse or poorer neighborhoods with more exclusive, uniform, and expensive neighborhoods or commercial projects (Logan 2005; Tan 1997; Wu 2002b, 2004)

China's planning legacy tends to exacerbate these impacts. Designs that rely on traditional axiality, regularity, and monumental scale in the name of celebrating governmental power or just the sheer effectiveness of planning must erase more of the historic human-scaled environment than more flexible designs would, and they tend to make the new public spaces particularly inhospitable to pedestrians.

The lack of a tradition of planning specifically for the public realm and the continued cellular approach to designing and developing new neighborhoods and commercial areas has not only created homogenous gated communities (including those that concentrate lower-income residents together in poorly served parts of the city), but has also inhibited planners from considering the interface of individual projects and the surrounding streets (Marshall 2003; Miao 2003). Such enclaves are usually now off limits to street vendors and others who provide inexpensive services to residents and derive income from them (Zhang 1997).

In broad strokes, since 1949 cellularity can be said to have first served the aims of Maoist state mobilization of the population according to production, in the form of the *danwei* compound, and then also the aims of the Dengist state to mobilize the consumer power of increasingly segmented income groups, in the form of specialized housing estates (*xiaoqu*) and shopping centers. But the design of the housing interacts both with the demographic profile of the residents and the manner of their governance to create different conditions for planning. Even though the *xiaoqu* facilitates the commodification of urban space, planners originally introduced it without anticipating the social stratification and segregation that has also emerged with this form of development. Rather, most Chinese planners in the 1980s and early 1990s viewed the *xiaoqu* simply as an improvement in residential amenity that saved land area and also preserved the cellular organization of communities. The designs of housing redevelopment projects in the early- to mid-1990s, and the reactions to them, demonstrate this: most project designs were ill-prepared for the division of space according to income group or ownership type that quickly emerged (Abramson 1994).

Problems included not only the appropriateness of the design for residents of different habits and means, but also for management in general. In neighborhoods that were redeveloped but which retained original community members – common in early 1990s inner-city redevelopment projects and still common in peri-urban "villages in the city" (*chengzhongcun*) redevelopment – the imposition of a standard *xiaoqu* environment presented many challenges to the neighborhood committee system that other types of design did not. In particular, the multistory walk-up apartment buildings and amorphous open spaces of the *xiaoqu* completely disrupted the delicate balance of household rights to privacy and neighborhood committee rights to intrude that existed in the old one-story environment.

Finally, since urban planning focuses entirely on enabling large-scale redevelopment rather than on regulating small-scale building activity, neighborhoods or villages not officially redeveloped proceed either to accelerated deterioration or to chaotic makeshift improvement and densification. Urban administration and economic policy since the early 1980s have done little to support a community-based, nonprofit, or self-help-enabling sector to "take up the slack" in areas that have been ignored by planned redevelopment (Zhang *et al.* 2003). This situation is especially acute at the urban fringe, to which factories are frequently relocated from the inner city, and where the greatest numbers of provincial migrants tend to concentrate even as the environment is rapidly degraded (Tang and Chung 2002; Zhang 2005). The problem of planning a durable physical environment when individuals are mobile is a new challenge to China's traditional cellular mode of urban social organization and spatial design.

Synthesis – community and property

The contradictions and problems outlined above have already generated policy responses that appear capable of changing planning practice significantly, primarily by creating new potential clients for planners and by requiring new modes of working and defining the practice of planning. Figure 4.1 provides a diagram of the dialectical logic implied by these problems and their responses. In cyclical fashion, a combination of prereform "legacy" functions of planning, and new modes of planning that serve various reform policies, produce both intended and (unintended) problematic sociospatial outcomes; in anticipation of the broader societal reactions to these outcomes (which are mainly just implied in this diagram), the government then responds with a second generation of reforms, which themselves push planning practice toward new modes, and produce new intended and unintended outcomes. Meanwhile, the "legacy" functions of planning continue to influence the way planning-related reforms are carried out.

Two recent government responses to the problematic results of Reform-driven urban development and planning are community-building (*shequ jianshe*) and the legal clarification of property rights – particularly the strengthening of private property rights. Environmental protection has also recently received increased government attention. As a movement in China, environmental protection clearly affects planning practice in the short-term by expanding the scope of its currently dominant engineering mode, and also potentially by enhancing its regulatory mode. In the slightly longer term, as pollution worsens, the cause of environmental protection appears likely to focus popular discontent on the urbanization process itself. Expert groups who advocate on behalf of local communities or the environment itself against rural industrialization and large infrastructure projects are already quite organized.[3] By contrast, the potential impact of community-building and property rights clarification on planning practice is much less clear and much less discussed, despite their relevance to urban development.

Significance of community-building for planning practice

Community-building in China is largely a top-down, policy-driven movement. It may be interpreted as an effort by the state to reduce and concentrate its welfare responsibilities while maintaining its spatially cellular approach to governance (Xu 2005). It is effectively a governmental response to the wholesale removal of old communities, the sudden formation of new ones, the increasing disparities in economic means between them, and indeed the dislocation of communities in the sense that social groupings are increasingly no longer place-based. However, in most cities, the newly constituted "communities" (*shequ*) are little more than a reshuffling of the resident/neighborhood committees (*jumin weiyuanhui*) and street/subdistrict offices (*jiedao banshiqu*) – the lowest levels in the spatial

PERSISTING PRE-REFORM FUNCTIONS OF PLANNING

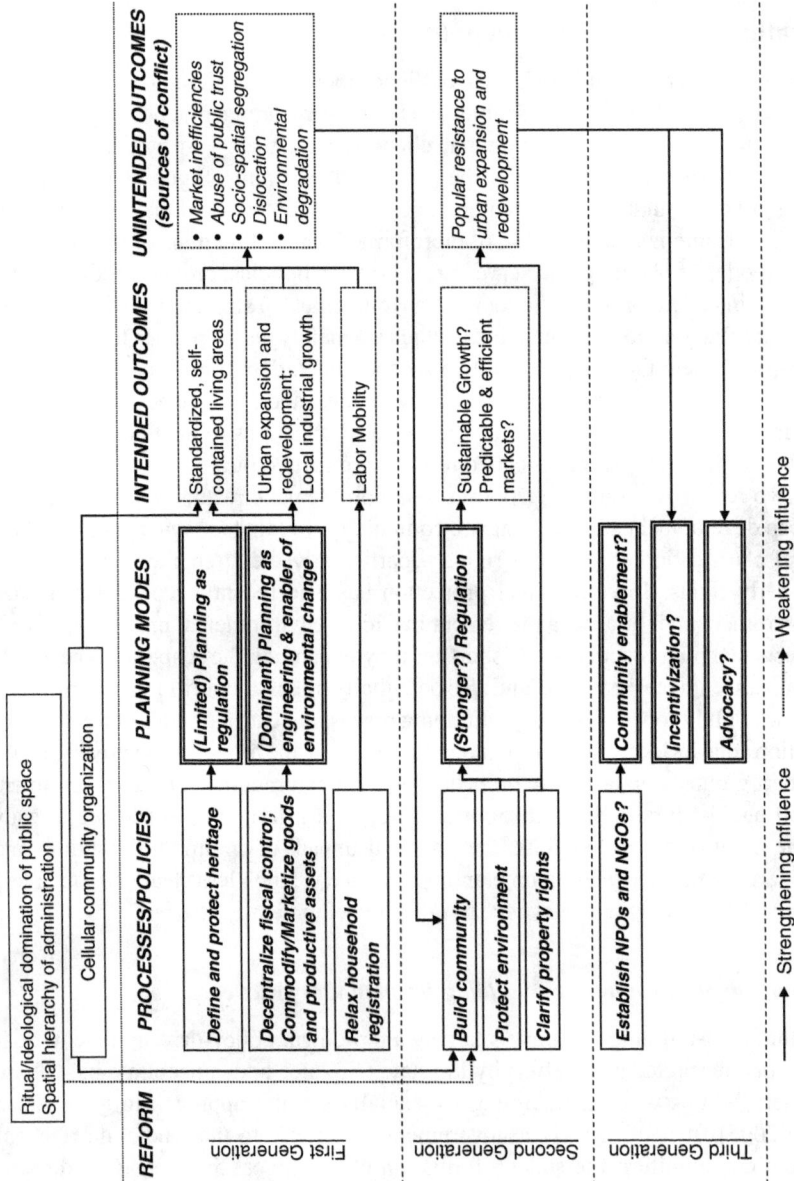

Ritual/ideological domination of public space

Spatial hierarchy of administration

Cellular community organization

REFORM	PROCESSES/POLICIES	PLANNING MODES	INTENDED OUTCOMES	UNINTENDED OUTCOMES (sources of conflict)
First Generation	Define and protect heritage	(Limited) Planning as regulation	Standardized, self-contained living areas	• Market inefficiencies
	Decentralize fiscal control; Commodify/Marketize goods and productive assets	(Dominant) Planning as engineering & enabler of environmental change	Urban expansion and redevelopment; Local industrial growth	• Abuse of public trust
				• Socio-spatial segregation
	Relax household registration		Labor Mobility	• Dislocation
				• Environmental degradation
Second Generation	Build community	(Stronger?) Regulation	Sustainable Growth? Predictable & efficient markets?	Popular resistance to urban expansion and redevelopment
	Protect environment			
	Clarify property rights			
Third Generation	Establish NPOs and NGOs?	Community enablement?		
		Incentivization?		
		Advocacy?		

⟶ Strengthening influence   ┈┈➤ Weakening influence

Figure 4.1 Dialectical logic of changing urban planning practice in China.

administrative hierarchy. The persistence of this hierarchy confounds efforts to make community-building an opportunity for community self-governance, and there is little reason for planners to consider the *shequ* any differently from the previous administrative bodies.

Still, *shequ* can apply for funds to carry out community improvement projects, including facilities for recreation, and activities for adult education, job training, and career placement. Some planners have responded by taking commissions from some of the more established (but not necessarily privileged) communities to develop long-term plans (Zhao 2003). Throughout the entire period of reform, planners have customarily worked only for government agencies above the *jiedao* level, or for work units or developers. Planners now working with this new type of client will need to adopt new skills and redefine their discipline. Such skills would include making planning expertise comprehensible to a broader segment of the public, and reorienting the goals of planning to include community preservation and enablement as well as simple profit-making development or the pursuit of supra-community-level public goods like heritage preservation or infrastructure improvement.

More study is needed to determine which communities are most able to act as direct clients for planning expertise. It seems that even if the hierarchical nature of spatial government tends to disempower communities from engaging planners directly, cellularity – the conflation of spatial and social units – might actually be empowering. Focusing on new, high-density urban estates of commodity apartment-purchasers, Tomba (2005) finds that the sociospatial cellular form of community enhances the perception of autonomy that is necessary to undertake informal socialization and to "mobilize" resources and material interests of the residents themselves. Of course, in communities like that of Tomba's study, the other key determinant of residents' desire and ability to organize is the propertied basis of their interest in their immediate environment.

Significance of property rights for planning practice

A second important arena of recent national policy change is in property law and the rights of citizens to litigate. In China's city centers, housing owned and managed by the local government occupies most land, having been appropriated from private owners during the collectivizing movements of the 1950s and 1960s. This has allowed local governments (sometimes even down to the resident committee level) to mobilize residents easily, relocate them, and profit by redeveloping the centrally located land where they lived. The conversion of agricultural land to urban use is similarly fraught with conflict (Guo 2001). Rural "collective" ownership is vested in agricultural village governments supposedly answerable to all the villagers but often able to act with impunity (Su and Chan 2005). Village governments on the urban fringe may sell land-use rights to adjacent urban governments that then establish development zones on the village land and transfer the rights to developers.

As more newly built housing (especially on redeveloped city-center land) is developed as commodity housing, and as a broader segment of the population invests speculatively in this housing, the government has sought to clarify and protect private property, in order to stabilize the economy, facilitate the operation of the market, and combat corruption. The 2004 revisions to the national constitution may be viewed in this light. While the Chinese constitution is a frequently amended document compared with most Western constitutions (it is considered a programmatic rather than a rights-based constitution), this revision is momentous nevertheless, as it parallels a number of recent court decisions against local government agencies (including the Beijing Planning Bureau) in cases of land-use rights expropriation for urban redevelopment (Phan 2005). The new legal environment has shaken local governments' confidence in their ability to carry out large-scale plans, and has fueled discussions over how to make planning a more transparent, democratic process (Shi 2004).

Enabling resistance to redevelopment through increased litigation may be a means by which the central government is applying brakes on hard-driving local growth coalitions, but it is likely to have some unanticipated effects. Like the professionalization of urban planning itself, new legal formulations were conceived in the 1980s sometimes independently of the larger developmentalist thrust of Dengist Reform (Deng 2003: 231). As such formulations evolve, they will create yet new clients for planners, and new constraints on the conventional mode of engineering- and design-oriented planning. The proliferation and empowerment of property owners strengthens the basis for incentivist as well as regulatory planning, and the concept of rights inherent in property ownership may encourage the development of advocacy planning, even for non-property-owning groups.

As indicated by the diagram in Figure 4.1, these "third generation" reforms are not yet manifest, and so this stage of the dialectical narrative is somewhat abstract. In order to illustrate the narrative more concretely, the following section outlines some key planning experiences in one city, that of Quanzhou, Fujian Province, since the early 1990s. In its own way, planning practice in this city is very clearly a product of the interaction of community and property, and of the balance between historical continuity and the unanticipated consequences of innovation.

An illustrative case: Quanzhou, Fujian

Quanzhou and its prefecture hinterland (including especially Anxi and Jinjiang Counties) has been the subject of historical and contemporary studies of community formation and property rights regimes that mark it as unusual with respect to the broad patterns of urban development alluded to above, while rooting it firmly within broader Minnan (Southern Fujian) regional practices and comparing it with other regions and their own characteristic practices (Abramson *et al*. 2002; Chen 2004; Kuah 2000; Leaf and Abramson 2002; M. Wang 2004; Wang 1995; Zhu 2000, 2002). In other words, Quanzhou is distinct, but probably not more so than any other Chinese city; the very localization of its planning practices is therefore part of a broader pattern, which this chapter argues is dialectical in nature.

Two distinctive features of Quanzhou have special bearing on this argument: first, an historically continuous property structure dominated by private family ownership of most housing and residential land-use rights even in the inner-city of the prefecture seat; and second, a lively practice of traditional neighborhood temple rituals that is almost equally continuous with prerevolutionary practice. Both of these features derive from the cultural, social and economic roles of overseas Chinese (*huaqiao*) who originate from Quanzhou, and who continue to own property, send remittances to family members, invest in local industries and businesses, and donate to temples, schools and hospitals from abroad. In the decades after 1949, the proportion of the local population who had returned from overseas sojourns, or who were dependents of overseas relatives, frequently ranged between 50 and 80 percent (Pan and Chinese Heritage Center 1999: 32).

In order to protect the transnational property interests that were the city's economic and cultural lifeblood, even during the most radical periods of Maoist collectivization, local government avoided expropriation of most small landholdings, and held local private businesses in trust rather than closing them altogether. In the 1980s, local *huaqiao* advocates brokered a series of court cases and negotiations to return many expropriated properties to their original owners or otherwise generously compensate them. Consistent with this position, the government has maintained a generous compensation policy for residents whose neighborhoods are redeveloped, requiring developers to provide owners of demolished housing with new units in their original neighborhood (Lu *et al.* 2004).

These actions by the local state have secured good conditions for attracting a very broad base of investment, but they have also made authoritarian design-oriented planning and urban redevelopment quite difficult. Strong private property rights give residents a rare degree of autonomy at the level of the family. However, "private" should not be taken to mean "individual." Rights to property are a subject of complex negotiation between extended family members, many of whom spend most of their lives abroad and are difficult to reach. Householders themselves, not to mention the government, thus often find it difficult to dispose of property.

It is also difficult for the government to mobilize communities. Communities are organically constituted, with temples serving as focal points for many of the most influential members, and neighborhood committees relatively weak, even in old, longstanding neighborhoods. Many of the temples are in fact territorial, and are relics of an earlier period of cellular spatial organization when, instead of street and neighborhood committees, the city was divided into *pu* and *jing* – jurisdictions that served similar functions of public order, but which had local god cults at their core. These social groupings overlap and sometimes conflict with the contemporary system of spatial administration.

During the 1990s, when the city underwent its first large-scale wave of redevelopment and densification, planners gradually came to incorporate temples into the spatial planning of the new housing areas. Temples were communal property, for which demolition was difficult to compensate except by replacement with a new temple. Even their relocation involved costly and time-consuming rituals. More importantly, it became clear that plans could not be implemented without communicating with residents at all stages of the development. In order to achieve this level of communication, the government would need the cooperation of respected and influential members of the community, many of whom were active in temple committees.

The city's planners did not immediately realize this. Initially, official planners were quite cavalier about residents' concerns and property rights. In 1993, the district government that administered Quanzhou's inner-city core planned to redevelop 65 percent of its land (Tao 1995). By the end of 1999, however, only about 17 percent of the old city had actually been rebuilt. The city's compensation policy for property owners prevented significant displacement, reduced developers' profits, preserved communities, and limited the opportunities to widen streets and create monumental open spaces. Still, enough was destroyed in that 17 percent to cause a policy reaction – an antithesis that created its own new problems which demanded further unanticipated changes in planning attitudes and practice.

Story within a story – the Kaiyuan Temple neighborhood

Perhaps no case so illustrates the evolution of planning attitudes and practices in the city as that of Xijie (West Street), an important but narrow and dilapidated thoroughfare that passed in front of Quanzhou's most important historic landmark and tourist attraction, the Kaiyuan Temple. In the 1980s, planning for the surrounding neighborhood put a priority on preservation, and proposed making Xijie a pedestrian street with its existing width intact. By 1994, the priority was to widen the street to improve traffic flow; to demolish all but a few structures, regardless of their ownership; and to relocate most residents into new large apartment buildings on one side of the neighborhood. The historic quality of the temple would be respected by rebuilding the structures along West Street uniformly in Tang or Song dynasty style. The official planning authorities had no interest in consulting or surveying the residents. After 1998, out of fear that redevelopment and street-widening would destroy the pagodas' sense of historic monumentality and visual prominence, the city adopted a more preservationist policy toward the street, but it also strengthened regulation of private home-building. The current rather draconian ordinance calls for the eventual reduction of all multistory individual houses in the historic core down to two stories, and forbids the enlargement of all existing one-story houses.

By 2004, it was clear that any successful plan would have to take property rights into account, and also clarify them.[4] At this point, the planning bureau proposed two strategies for upgrading and preservation of private properties in Xijie. First, the government could undertake household-by-household negotiations to purchase and resettle the residents or a portion of them (many houses had been subdivided to accommodate separate building activities by relatives of one family); then pay for the upgrading of the housing and sell it back at cost to those residents who remained. However, this approach was deemed too slow and costly. Alternatively, the government could buy up all the properties at once, replat the land and rebuild or upgrade the houses, and either sell back the newly configured properties to their original owners or resettle those owners elsewhere and sell the properties to new buyers, perhaps at a profit. This approach was considered too drastic for the historic character of the street.

In late 2004, the municipal government provisionally decided to revitalize the street under existing ownership, and to explore policies that would encourage residents themselves to upgrade their houses according to the city's regulations for private house building in historic districts. The government paid the municipal planning institute and then a team of outside professionals to produce designs that would both provide improved living conditions and satisfy the regulations, and presented these to each household along the street.

In effect, the local planners of Quanzhou had moved from an approach that mobilized resources for profitable redevelopment (assembly of land and investment of large amounts of capital) to one that regulated and incentivized private initiative in the interest of a public good, with limited potential to generate income.

Residents demurred, however, finding the regulations were unreasonably restrictive (the rules essentially forbade any enlargement of existing building envelopes). Ironically, now the residents themselves need convincing of the new regulatory approach; they actually prefer the favorable compensation that accompanies large-scale redevelopment, and do not share the planning authority's view of the street's historic architectural value. It is thus becoming clear to the planning bureau that planning in this context requires new skills of communication, and attitudes of service, that are normally missing in the planning profession and education.

The logic described in the preceding sections appears to be taking its course in Quanzhou, given the city's own characteristics. A continuity of pre-revolutionary property rights in the hands of householders has produced a stronger regulatory and incentivizing mode of urban development planning and policy than is usual in China. However, these rights are not necessarily clarified in the modern sense: they are still somewhat subject to the complex layering of obligations that accompanies extended family ownership. They therefore do not facilitate development transactions in the way that property rights do in advanced market economies. Rather, they have a kind of frictional effect on development that is forcing planning authorities to adopt new tools of engagement. Also, traditional ritual/ideological domination of public space is expressed in the popular, unofficial sphere by residents' continued observance of the folk-religious meaning of this space, to the exclusion of concern for the quality of urban open space. It is also expressed in the governmental sphere by the focus of political leaders on the monumental, iconic values of historic sites like the Kaiyuan Temple, to the exclusion of other more local and lived values that these public sites may have. As a result, community-building remains a remote concern from the perspective of local planners.

Conclusion

The concepts of community (social and political collectives of various forms and scales) and property (land tenure) present a kind of central opposition for planning in economies that are primarily market-driven. As Roweis (1981) has put it

> The history and development of urban planning under capitalism can thus be seen as the history and development of modes of operation allowing for some measure of collective action (that affects decisions concerning the social utilization of urban land); modes of operation which must be feasible in a society whose basic social and property relations (or institutions) resist such action.
>
> (Roweis 1981: 170–171)

Since the Chinese central government's pursuit of market-driven urbanization is one of the defining premises of urban planning, the roles of property and community in China's urban planning should provide some basis for understanding how China's urbanism compares to that of "advanced" capitalist societies.

In capitalist societies, where planning is defined as the representation of public community interests in determining the form of cities, the disposition of property is its ultimate subject. Planning may take the form of governmental *regulation* of property development or *incentives* for it; governmental or nongovernmental *design* or *advocacy* for it; or, less directly connected to property disposition, the *enablement* of community formation or action. However, the moment a community interest becomes identified with a property through ownership, it essentially becomes "private" with respect to any planning that relates to that property. In capitalist systems, property is the dominant vehicle for the definition and representation of interests; interests that do not operate through the disposition of property are difficult to define and represent. This is especially true in the United States, but it is also essentially the case in capitalist societies everywhere, from Japan to Ireland (see, for example, McGuirk 2000; Yamasaki 2005).

In China, particular forms of diversification and proliferation of planning modes are products both of tensions between central and local government priorities, as well as of the ability and need of local governments increasingly to act according to locally distinct cultural and social constraints and opportunities in order to pursue economic development. Local social and cultural (but not always official) institutions have shaped property rights in dramatically different ways in China (Chen 2004). Not only have these institutional variations produced regional diversity, crucial aspects of them remained continuous with their history, despite the radical nature of Maoist revolution. Yang (1994, 2000) has shown how such continuity can intersect with a booming export-oriented economy to transform (locally) the very meaning of success in the global marketplace, and to challenge both the national developmentalism of the Chinese government as well as theories of global cultural hegemony. Along similar lines, this chapter argues that community and property are emerging as two axial concerns of urban planning in China, for reasons both of participation in the global marketplace and of resurgent local values. These values are as operable as the market in the dialectical process by which urban planning practices change.

Acknowledgments

The author is especially grateful to Michael Leaf and Hao Xin for their help in improving and clarifying the logic illustrated in Figure 4.1. Any remaining faults with this diagram are of course the author's.

Notes

1 Many sections of this chapter were originally published in the article, "Urban Planning in China: Continuity and Change," *Journal of the American Planning Association*, *72*(2): 197–215. The text underwent significant revision for publication in this book.
2 The most commonly used word in modern Chinese for "community," *shequ*, derives from the social-scientific influence of Robert Park and the Chicago School of sociology in the 1920s and 1930s. This influence was distinctly ecological, that is, it conceived of social groupings as environmental phenomena (Xu 2005: 11). Other translations of "community" include the term also used more commonly in Japan than in China, *gong-tongti*, which is also how "gemeinschaft" in Ferdinand Tönnies's *Gemeinschaft und Gesellschaft* is translated (Tönnies 1999). The twentieth-century introduction and translation of modern social science notwithstanding, the practical application of cellular approaches to urban management has centuries of precedent in China.
3 China's first truly grassroots nongovernmental organization (NGO) was the environmentalist Friends of Nature founded by Liang Congjie, who managed to obtain legal registration for the organization by playing one branch of the administration (the Ministry of Culture) against another (the National Environmental Protection Administration), and by appealing to central government concerns that local governments were not obeying the former's directives (United States Embassy in Beijing 2000).
4 In the intervening years, the planning bureau had experimented in other neighborhoods with consultants in participatory community planning and design (Abramson *et al.* 2001). In this work the project team initiated a tentative form of advocacy planning and mediation using design between the bureau, neighborhood committee and property owners (Abramson 2005). Project team members included primarily Tan Ying, Lecturer at Tsinghua University in Beijing; Tao Tao, Senior Planner at the Chinese Academy of Urban Planning and Design; and Professor Michael Leaf and Dan Abramson at the University of British Columbia. The project was independently funded by a grant from the Ford Foundation in Beijing.

References

Abramson, D. (1994) "New housing in old Beijing: a comparative survey of projects completed to date – Beijing's old and dilapidated housing renewal (Part V)," *China City Planning Review*, 10(3): 42–56.
Abramson, D. (2005) "The 'studio abroad' as a mode of trans-cultural engagement in urban planning: a reflection on ten years of Sino-Canadian educational exchange," *Journal of Planning Education and Research*, 25(1): 89–102.
Abramson, D., Leaf, M., Anderson, S. and the students of UBC Plan 545B. (2001) Governance and Design: Participatory Planning, Residential Design Guidelines and Historic

82   *Daniel B. Abramson*

Preservation in Quanzhou, Fujian, China: A Year 2000 Studio Report (No. Asian Urban Research Network Working Paper Series #WP27), Vancouver: UBC Centre for Human Settlements.

Abramson, D., Leaf, M. and Tan, Y. (2002) "Social research and the localization of chinese urban planning practice: some ideas from Quanzhou, Fujian," in J. R. Logan (ed.), *The New Chinese City: Globalization and Market Reform*, Oxford: Blackwell Publishers, 227–245.

Baidu. (2006) "Weishenme shi Shi Yi Wu Guihua, er bu shi Jihua? [Why is it the Eleventh Five (-Year) *Guihua*, and not *Jihua*?]," retrieved November 25, 2006, from http://zhidao.baidu.com/question/15735000.html

Bray, D. (2005) *Social Space and Governance in Urban China: The Danwei System from Origins to Reform*, Stanford, CA: Stanford University Press.

Brook, T. (1985) "The spatial structure of ming local administration," *Late Imperial China*, 6(1): 1–55.

Broudehoux, A.-M. (2004) *The Making and Selling of Post-Mao Beijing*, London; New York: Routledge.

Chen, C.-J. J. (2004) *Transforming Rural China: How Local Institutions Shape Property Rights in Rural China*, New York: Routledge.

Clunas, C. (1996) *Fruitful Sites: Garden Culture in Ming Dynasty China*, Durham: Duke University Press.

Clunas, C. (2004) *Superfluous Things: Material Culture and Social Status in Early Modern China*, Honolulu: University of Hawaii Press.

Deng, F. F. (2003) "Political economy of public land leasing in Beijing, China," in S. C. Bourassa, Y.-H. and Lincoln Institute of Land Policy (eds), *Leasing Public Land: Policy Debates and International Experiences*, Cambridge, MA: Lincoln Institute of Land Policy, 229–250.

Dray-Novey, A. (1993) "Spatial order and police in imperial Beijing," *The Journal of Asian Studies*, 52(4): 885–922.

Fang, K. and Zhang, Y. (2003) "Plan and market mismatch: urban redevelopment in Beijing during a period of transition," *Asia Pacific Viewpoint*, 44(2): 149–162.

Friedmann, J. (1987) *Planning in the Public Domain: From Knowledge to Action*, Princeton, NJ: Princeton University Press.

Friedmann, J. (1993) "Toward a non-Euclidian mode of planning," *Journal of the American Planning Association*, 59(4): 482–485.

Gaubatz, P. R. (1995) "Urban transformation in post-mao China: impacts of the reform era on China's urban form," in D. S. Davis, R. Kraus, B. Naughton and E. J. Perry (eds), *Urban Spaces in Contemporary China: The Potential for Autonomy and Community in Post-Mao China*, New York: Cambridge University Press, 28–60.

Guo, X. (2001) "Land expropriation and rural conflicts in China," *The China Quarterly*, 166, 422–439.

Han, G. (1996) *Beijing Lishi Renkou Dili [Historical Demographic Geography of Beijing]*, Beijing: Beijing Daxue Chubanshe [Beijing University Press].

Hong, Y.-H. (2005) "Taxing publicly owned land in China: a paradox?" *Land Lines: Newsletter of the Lincoln Institute of Land Policy*, 17(1): 9–10.

Hou, R. (1985) "The transformation of the old city of Beijing, China: a concrete manifestation of new china's cultural reconstruction," in C. D. Harris and M. P. Conzen (eds), *World Patterns of Modern Urban Change: Essays in Honor of Chauncy D. Harris*, Chicago: University of Chicago, Dept. of Geography, 217–239.

Huang, Y. (2005) "From work-unit compounds to gated communities: housing inequality and residential segregation in transitional Beijing," in L. J. C. Ma and F. Wu (eds), *Restructuring the Chinese City: Changing Society, Economy and Space*, New York: Routledge, 192–221.

Knechtges, D. R. and Xiao, T. (1982) *Wen Xuan, or, Selections of Refined Literature* (Vol. 1, "Rhapsodies on Metropolises and Capitals"), Princeton, NJ: Princeton University Press.

Kuah, K. E. (2000) *Rebuilding the Ancestral Village: Singaporeans in China*, Aldershot; Brookfield: Ashgate.

Leaf, M. (1998) "Urban planning and urban reality under chinese economic reforms," *Journal of Planning Education and Research*, 18(2): 145–153.

Leaf, M. and Abramson, D. (2002) "Global networks, civil society, and the transformation of the urban core in Quanzhou, China," in E. J. Heikkila and R. Pizarro (eds), *Southern California and the World*, Westport, CT: Praeger, 153–178.

Li, X. and Lamoureux, C. (translator) (1995) "Structure spatiale et identité culturelle des villes chinoises traditionnelles [Spatial Structure and Cultural Identity in Traditional Chinese Cities]," paper presented at *Histoire et identités urbaines: Nouvelles tendences de la recherche urbaine, Table rondée organisée par les revues Dushu et Annales avec le soutien de l'Ambassade de France et de l'École française d'Extrême-Orient* [History and Urban Identities: New Directions in Urban Research, Roundtable organized by the journals *Dushu* and *Annales,* with the support of the Embassy of France and the French School of the Far East], Beijing.

Logan, J. (2005) "Socialism, market reform and neighborhood inequality in urban China," in C. Ding and Y. Song (eds), *Emerging Land and Housing Markets in China*, Cambridge, MA: Lincoln Institute of Land Policy, 233–248.

Lu, S., Chen, Z., Li, Y., Xie, M., Yang, Q. and Zheng, J. (July 22, 2004) "Zhanwang Xi Jie Weilai Muyang: 'Yao Dui Mei Yi Jia Mei Yi Hu Jinxing Sheji' [Looking ahead to the future appearance of Xijie – Carry out design for each family, each household]," *Haixia Dushi Bao (Minnan Ban) [Strait News (Minnan Edition)]*, A6.

Marshall, R. (2003) *Emerging Urbanity: Global Urban Projects in the Asia Pacific Rim*, London; New York: Spon Press.

McGuirk, P. M. (2000) "Power and policy networks in urban governance: local government and property-led regeneration in Dublin," *Urban Studies*, 37(4): 651–672.

Meyer, J. F. (1991) *The Dragons of Tiananmen: Beijing as a Sacred City*, Columbia, SC: University of South Carolina Press.

Miao, P. (2003) "Deserted streets in a Jammed Town: the gated community in Chinese cities and its solution," *Journal of Urban Design*, 8(1): 45–66.

Ng, M.-K. and Wu, F. (1997) "Challenges and opportunities – can Western planning theories inform changing Chinese urban planning practices?," in A. G. O. Yeh, X. Xu and X. Yan (eds), *Urban Planning and Planning Education under Economic Reform in China*, Hong Kong: Centre of Urban Planning and Environmental Management University of Hong Kong, 147–170.

Olds, K. (2001) *Globalization and Urban Change: Capital, Culture, and Pacific Rim Mega-Projects*, Oxford; New York: Oxford University Press.

Pan, L. and Chinese Heritage Center (Singapore) (1999) *The Encyclopedia of the Chinese Overseas*, Cambridge, MA: Harvard University Press.

Pei, M. (2006) *China's Trapped Transition: The Limits of Developmental Autocracy*, Cambridge, MA: Harvard University Press.

Phan, P. N. (2005) "Enriching the Land or the Political Elite? Lessons from China on Democratization of the Urban Renewal Process," *Pacific Rim Law and Policy Journal*, 14(3): 607–657.

Rowe, W. T. (1989) *Hankow: Conflict and Community in a Chinese City, 1796–1895*, Stanford, CA: Stanford University Press.

Roweis, S. T. (1981) "Urban planning in early and late capitalist societies: outline of a theoretical perspective," in M. Dear and A. J. Scott (eds), *Urbanization and Urban Planning in Capitalist Societies*, New York: Methuen, 159–177.

Rykwert, J. (1976) *The Idea of a Town: The Anthropology of Urban Form in Rome, Italy and the Ancient World*, Princeton, NJ: Princeton University Press.

Samuels, C. (1986) *Cultural Ideology and the Landscape of Confucian China: The Traditional Si He Yuan,* Unpublished Master Thesis, University of British Columbia, Vancouver.

Scott, J. C. (1998) *Seeing Like a State: How Certain Schemes to Improve the Human Condition Have Failed*, New Haven: Yale University Press.

Shi, N. (July 16–17, 2004) Opening Address by the Secretary General of the Urban Planning Society of China, paper presented at the *Chengshi Guihua Juece Minzhuhua Yantaohui* [Conference on Democratization of the Urban Planning Decision-making Process], Quanzhou, Fujian.

Steinhardt, N. S. (1990) *Chinese Imperial City Planning*, Honolulu: University of Hawaii Press.

Stille, A. (1998) "Faking it," *The New Yorker*, 74(16): 36–42.

Su, H. and Chan, K. W. (2005) *Tudi Zhengyong yu Difang Zhengfu de Xingwei [Land Expropriation and Local Government Behavior]* (Occasional Paper No. 58), Hong Kong: The Centre for China Urban and Regional Studies, Hong Kong Baptist University.

Tan, Y. (1997) Cong Jumin de Jiaodu Chufa dui Beijing Jiucheng Juzhuqu Gaizao Fangshi de Yanjiu [Redevelopment Practices of Housing Area Renewal in the Old City of Beijing: A Study from the Residents' Perspective], unpublished doctoral dissertation, Tsinghua University, Beijing.

Tang, W.-S. and Chung, H. (2002) "Rural-urban transition in China: illegal land use and construction," *Asia Pacific Viewpoint*, 43(1): 43–62.

Tao, T. (July 6–18, 1995) "Problems in the implementation of Quanzhou's old city redevelopment plan," paper presented at the *International Conference on Renewal and Development in Housing Areas of Traditional Chinese and European Cities [First Year]*, Beijing, Quanzhou and Xi'an.

Tomba, L. (2005) "Residential space and collective interest formation in Beijing's housing disputes," *China Quarterly* (184): 934–951.

Tönnies, F. (1999) Gongtongti yu Shehui: Chuncui Shehuixue de Jiben Gainian [Community and Society: Fundamental Concepts of Pure Sociology (translated from the German, "Gemeinschaft und Gesellschaft: Grundbegriffe der reinen Soziologie")] (R. Lin, trans.), Beijing: Shangwu.

United States Embassy in Beijing (2000) "Chinese Environmentalist Liang Congjie On NGO Life: A February 2000 report from U.S. Embassy Beijing," retrieved November 30, 2006, from http://www.usembassy-china.org.cn/sandt/liangNGO.htm

Wakeman, F., Jr. (1993) "The civil society and public sphere debate: Western reflections on Chinese political culture," *Modern China*, 19(2): 108–138.

Wang, F.-L. (2004) "Reformed migration control and new targeted people: China's *Hukou* System in the 2000s," *The China Quarterly*, 177, 115–132.

Wang, M. (1995) "Place, Administration, and territorial cults in late imperial China: a case study from South Fujian," *Late Imperial China*, 16(1): 33–78.

Wang, M. (2004) "Mapping 'Chaos': the Dong Xi Fo Feuds of Quanzhou, 1644–1839," in S. Feuchtwang (ed.), *Making Place: State Projects, Globalisation and Local Responses in China*, London; Portland, OR: UCL; Cavendish, 33–59.

Wheatley, P. (1971) The pivot of the four quarters: a preliminary enquiry into the origins and character of the ancient Chinese city, Chicago, IL: Aldine.

Wright, A. F. (1977) "The cosmology of the chinese city," in G. W. Skinner (ed.), *The City in Late Imperial China*, Stanford, CA: Stanford University Press, 22–74.

Wu, F. (1997) "Urban restructuring in China's emerging market economy: towards a framework for analysis," *International Journal of Urban and Regional Research*, 21(4): 640.

Wu, F. (2002a) "China's changing urban governance in the transition towards a more market-oriented economy," *Urban Studies*, 39(7): 1071–1093.

Wu, F. (2002b) "Sociospatial differentiation in urban China: evidence from Shanghai's real estate markets," *Environment and Planning A*, 34(9): 1591–1615.

Wu, F. (2003) "The (post-) socialist entrepreneurial city as a state project: Shanghai's reglobalisation in question," *Urban Studies*, 40(9): 1673–1698.

Wu, F. (2004) "Intraurban residential relocation in Shanghai: modes and stratification," *Environment and Planning A*, 36(1): 7–25.

Wu, H. (2005) *Remaking Beijing: Tiananmen Square and the Creation of a Political Space*, Chicago, IL: University of Chicago Press.

Wu, L. (1999) *Rehabilitating the Old City of Beijing: A Project in the Ju'er Hutong Neighbourhood*, Vancouver: UBC Press.

Xu, F. (2005) "Building Community in Post-Socialist China: towards Local Democratic Governance?," *China Colloquium*. University of Washington, Seattle, WA.

Yamasaki, M. (October 17–21, 2005) "Control Tools for Conservation of Historic Townscape with Citizens' Strong Property Right: Experience of Kyoto," paper presented at the *ICOMOS 15th General Assembly and Scientific Symposium: Monuments in their Setting – Conserving Cultural Heritage in Changing Townscapes and Landscapes*, Xi'an, China.

Yang, M. (1994) *Public and Private Realms in Rural Wenzhou, China [Videorecording]: An Ethnographic Video*, Berkeley, CA: University of California Extension Center for Media and Independent Learning.

Yang, M. (2000) "Putting global capitalism in its place – Economic hybridity, bataille, and ritual expenditure," *Current Anthropology*, 41(4): 477–509.

Zelin, M., Ocko, J. K. and Gardella, R. (2004) *Contract and Property in Early Modern China*, Stanford, CA: Stanford University Press.

Zhang, J. (1997) "Informal construction in Beijing's old neighborhoods," *Cities*, 14(2): 85–94.

Zhang, L. (2005) "Migrant enclaves and impacts of redevelopment policy in Chinese cities," in L. J. C. Ma and F. Wu (eds), *Restructuring the Chinese City: Changing Society, Economy and Space*, New York: Routledge, pp. 243–259.

Zhang, L., Zhao, S. X. B. and Tian, J. P. (2003) "Self-help in housing and chengzhongcun in China's urbanization," *International Journal of Urban and Regional Research*, 27(4): 912–937.

Zhang, T. (2002) "Urban development and a socialist pro-growth coalition in Shanghai," *Urban Affairs Review*, 37(4): 475–499.

Zhang, Y. and Fang, K. (2004) "Is history repeating itself ? From urban renewal in the United States to inner-city redevelopment in China," *Journal of Planning Education and Research*, 23(3): 286–298.

Zhao, M. (2003) *Shequ Fazhan Guihua: Lilun yu Shixian [Community Development Planning: Theory and Practice]*, Beijing: Zhongguo Jianzhu Gonghe Chubanshe [China Architecture and Building Press].

Zhongguo Chengshi Guihua Xuehui [Urban Planning Society of China]. (2006) "Guihua Wushi Nian [Fifty Years of Planning]," web site of the *Annual Meeting of the Urban Planning Society of China, Guangzhou, 21–23 September*, retrieved November 25, 2006, from http://www.upsc50.org.cn

Zhu, J. (1999) "Local Growth Coalition: the Context and Implications of China's Gradualist Urban Land Reforms," *International Journal of Urban and Regional Research*, 23(3): 534–548.

Zhu, J. (2004) *Chinese Spatial Strategies: Imperial Beijing, 1420–1911*, London; New York: RoutledgeCurzon.

Zhu, Y. (2000) "In situ urbanization in rural China: case studies from Fujian province," *Development and Change, 31*(2): 413–434.

Zhu, Y. (2002) "Beyond large-city-centred urbanisation: *in situ* transformation of rural areas in Fujian Province," *Asia Pacific Viewpoint*, 43(1): 9–22.

Zhu, Z. and Kwok, R. (1997) "Beijing: the expression of national political ideology," in W. B. Kim, M. Douglass, S.-C. Choe and K. C. Ho (eds), *Culture and the City in East Asia*, Oxford: Oxford University Press, 125–150.

Part II

Transitioning economic and social spheres

5 Hong Kong and Taiwan investment in Dongguan

Divergent trajectories and impacts

Chun Yang

Introduction

Globalization in the twenty-first century is characterized by the increasing integration of a variety of small and medium-sized players in international networks of production, movement of goods, and flows of information and knowledge (Dicken 2000; Mathews 2006). These features of globalization will continue to throw up new opportunities for involvement on the part of innovative small and medium-sized players, who will create constant pressure on incumbents. Industries in the Asian Newly Industrializing Economies (NIEs) have upgraded by building links to international markets and to the necessary sources of technology, expertise, managerial experience, and capital in the advanced countries. Changes emanating from the advanced industrial economies, particularly the United States, have begun to alter substantially the prospects for supplier-oriented industrial development in East Asia (Sturgeon and Lester 2005).The concept of "dragon multinationals" has been advanced to characterize multinational corporations (MNCs) that are relative newcomers on the global economic scene, especially the Asian NIEs with an overseas Chinese connection (Mathews 2002, 2006). Unlike MNCs from advanced industrialized economies, the dragon multinationals from the Asian NIEs are latecomers that internationalize from the periphery rather than from the center, encountering resource shortages and greater distances to consumers and suppliers alike. Recent work has gone beyond just identifying these MNCs: it now concentrates on differentiating between characteristics, strategies, advantages and performance of the groups and their affiliated firms, such as the contrast between Taiwanese and South Korean business groups (Dacin and Delios 2005). Yeung (2006a) argues that the interplay between corporate strategies and home-base advantages within the context of changing global production networks can offer a better explanation for the differentiated competitive transformation of Asian electronics, changing firms from "followers" to "market leaders." Most studies of the distinctive developmental models of the Asian NIEs have been primarily conducted from the perspective of home regions; relatively little has been written on the transformations of cross-border investment from various sources of the Asian NIEs in host countries, such as transitional China.

Recent literature on industrial clusters driven by MNCs in developing countries have attributed to external/transnational linkages the main driving force of local industrialization, either from the perspectives of global value chain (Giuliani *et al.* 2005; Schmitz 2004) or global production networks (Yeung *et al.* 2006). In the context of a changing global economy, it is argued that advantages based on low cost labor and land became less sustainable (Humphrey 1995). The policy emphasis of local development has thus shifted from passive marketization and deregulation in adapting to the requirements of transnational investors or buyers, to actively promoting the construction of localized backward supply chains and promotion of knowledge spillover between foreign agents and local producers (Wang *et al.* 2005). Nevertheless, efforts have seldom been made to separate external linkages into global lead producers/marketers, usually in the advanced economies, and parent firms in the home country/regions of cross-border investment, especially in Asian NIEs. The interaction between the home and host regions and its impact on the local transformation of the host regions lack comprehensive analysis.

Empirical analysis of cross-border production and the impact of foreign investment on economic transformation has primarily concentrated on advanced economies, such as the United States (Florida 1996) and Japan (Florida and Kenny 1991). It is argued that although these MNCs do respond and react to (or anticipate) changing competitive conditions, the path or strategy they choose is most strongly shaped by the national-institutional legacy of their *home* country (Gertler 2001: 14). When a firm "arrives" in a new location inside a new national-institutional space via foreign direct investment (FDI), it is not a blank slate – that is, it continues to bear many strong markings and influences from its origins (Doremus *et al.* 1998). These characteristics interact in dialectical ways to produce a new set of practices which conform to neither "original" model – Abo's (1994 and 2004) "hybrid factory" comes to mind. Since the late 1990s, the concept of "hybridization" has been applied to examine the interaction between the home-host national/regional business systems.[1] Taking overseas Chinese investment in Southeast Asia as a case, Yeung (2004) put forward a pattern of "hybridization" that has emerged in Chinese capitalism, which reflects both the influence of globalization tendencies on nationally or supranationally organized economic systems and the impact of significant participation of key actors from those economic systems in globalization tendencies (Yeung 2004: 43). The growing hybridization is characterized by a transformative process in which traditional and new elements are continuously morphed and recombined into something that resembles neither previous ethnic Chinese capitalism nor global capitalism (Yeung 2006b). The transformation of Taiwanese investment in the Yangtze River Delta (the YRD) during the past two decades provides an example of emerging hybridization in mainland China[2] (Hsu 2005). Taking Dongguan, a municipality in south China, Yang (2006) argues that overseas Chinese investment from different origins – for example, Hong Kong (HK) and Taiwan (TW) – to the same host location exhibit different patterns of change, which may be interpreted as divergent responses to both institutional changes in host regions and the comparative advantages of different home regions, as well as distinctive interactions between home and host regions.

Against the above theoretical and empirical backdrop, this chapter attempts to examine comparatively the evolving patterns of HK and TW investment and their different impacts on the local transformation of Dongguan over the past 25 years. It is argued that the divergent trajectories of evolution result from distinctive home advantages and their interaction with the host regions in the context of the global economy. After this introduction, transformations of overseas Chinese investment in the era of globalization will be overviewed so as to set up a conceptual and empirical background to the study. The paper then examines comparatively the evolution of HK and TW investment in Dongguan, in terms of sectoral composition, entry modes, market orientation, spatial distributions and organization. It further explores the consequent impact on the transformation of Dongguan from an assembly-factory to a supply-chain city. In the concluding section, the paper will discuss some theoretical perspectives and policy implications for the sustainable development of Dongguan in its integration with the global economy.

Overseas Chinese investment in transition: an overview

According to the statistics released by the National Statistical Bureau of China, overseas Chinese[3] investment accounted for 43.3 percent of the total actualized foreign investment in 2004. Nearly 90 percent of such investment came from HK and TW – the first and fourth largest sources of foreign investment in the mainland, accounting for 32.5 and 5.4 percent of the national total (National Statistical Bureau 2005). In general, investments from HK, Macao, TW and ethnic Chinese in Southeast Asia (e.g. Singapore) have been treated as overseas Chinese investment as a whole. In the existing literature on the so-called Greater China economic linkages, Chinese ethnicity and *guanxi* (interpersonal relations) networks have occupied a privileged analytical role in explaining the governance of cross-border economic activities by overseas Chinese entrepreneurs, especially from HK and TW (Yeung 2000, 2004). Recent empirical studies demonstrate the dramatic changes in and transformation of overseas Chinese investment in Southeast Asia (Yeung 2004, 2006b) and mainland China (Hsing 2003; Smart and Hsu 2004). It is argued that the nature of overseas Chinese investment strategies and relationships between home and host countries/regions are becoming quite distinct, although their importance is still maintained (Smart and Hsu 2004).

Owing to the similarity between their cross-border transplantation of labor-intensive, export-oriented manufacturing to the mainland, and particularly to the Pearl River Delta (PRD), HK and TW investments have been generally treated as similar. However, the trajectories of evolution over time are somewhat different. At the national level, the dominant initial HK investments in the PRD were made by labor-intensive manufacturing industries, although after the completion of the transplantation of manufacturing to the PRD, HK investment in the early years of the twenty-first century subsequently turned toward the service sector (Yang 2006). With respect to TW investment, the initial orientation toward investments in labor-intensive manufacturing in PRD appears to have been retained, although their sectoral structure appears to have changed – from the desktop personal computer and peripheral industries in the late 1990s to notebook computers and integrated circuits, in the YRD, since the turn of the century (Wang and Tong 2005; Hsu 2006; Yang and Hsia 2006). Looking particularly at Dongguan, a municipality receiving a major concentration of both HK and TW investment, Yang (2006) argues that industrial development has changed from being predominantly driven by HK investment in the 1980s to being increasingly exposed to TW investment since the 1990s. The latter has contributed significantly to Dongguan's local economic transition from an export orientation, based on cheap labor, in the 1980s, to a domestic market orientation since the late 1990s. HK and TW investors have followed different strategies of adaptation to host-region institutional changes.

Although there is a growing literature on the country/region of origin effects of FDI in China (e.g. He 2003a; Shi *et al.* 2001), comparisons have been primarily made between overseas Chinese investment and Western MNCs (Park and Lee 2003). Rarely have studies been devoted to comparing differences between overseas Chinese investment from different countries/regions. Numerous studies have explored the influx of HK investment into China, especially, during the 1980s and mid-1990s, on its impact on local economic development in the PRD in South China (Leung 1993; Shen *et al.* 2000; Sit and Yang 1997; Smart and Smart 1991, Smart 2000; Yeung 2001); while rather fewer have studied comprehensively TW investment, until recent years (Hsing 1998; Hsu 2005, 2006; Yang and Hsia 2005 and forthcoming). Moreover, previous studies usually treated HK and TW investment equally. As two of the "Four Little Dragons" in East Asia, both HK and TW initiated their cross-border transplantation of small- medium-scale, labor-intensive and export-oriented traditional manufacturing activities to the mainland in the early 1980s and mid-1990s respectively, with major geographical concentration in the PRD at the early stage. Compared to the prevailing locational concentration and main focus on labor-intensive industries of HK investment in the PRD, TW manufacturing investments since the early 2000s have changed focus dramatically, both in industrial structure and spatial concentration. This has been characterized by industrial upgrading to computer-related and integrated circuit-related information technology industries, and investment by large-scale enterprises; and has been associated with geographical relocation from the PRD to the YRD (Hsu 2005, 2006).

Dongguan, located between Guangzhou and Shenzhen on the eastern part of the PRD (Figure 5.1), has witnessed rapid industrialization and urbanization driven by foreign investment, especially from HK and TW. Actualized foreign investment in Dongguan accounted for 4.6 percent and 16.5 percent of the total for China and Guangdong province respectively in 2004. Over the past two decades, HK and TW investment has accounted for over 92 percent of total foreign investment in Dongguan (Figure 5.2). Dongguan has been transformed from a traditional agricultural county to a modern manufacturing city. It has become a world-famous "global factory," not only of labor-intensive manufactures (e.g. textiles and apparel, footwear and toys), but also technology-intensive computer and peripheral products. Dongguan has been widely chosen in previous literature as a useful focus for studying the development of foreign investment and its impact on local economic development

Figure 5.1 Location and administration of Dongguan.

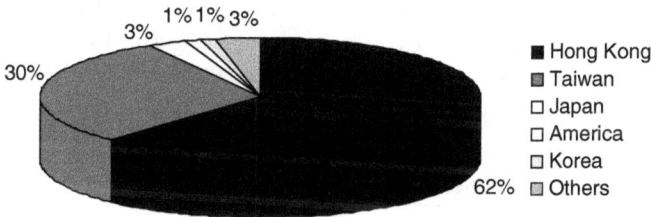

Figure 5.2 Number of foreign-invested firms in Dongguan by sources of origins in 2006.

Source: Dongguan Bureau of Foreign Trade and Economic Cooperation 2006.

(Lin 1997; Sit and Yang 1997; Yeung 2001; Wang and Tong 2005). It provides a typical case of rapid industrialization and urbanization driven by foreign invest-ment, especially from HK and TW. It has been extensively documented that locally specific conditions (e.g. preexisting kinship ties, interpersonal trust and connections) provide shelters within which global capitalism can settle in formerly socialist territory (Hsing 1998; Leung 1993; Lin 1997; Smart and Smart 1991). However, this *guanxi*-based interpretation of HK and TW investment during the 1980s and 1990s has been found insufficient to explain the changes and transforma-tions of HK and TW investment, especially after China's WTO accession (Smart and Hsu 2004). Although following, in the 1980s, the example of HK investment by concentrating most heavily in the PRD, TW investment since the late 1990s has demonstrated salient trajectories of development and transformation which warrant comprehensive examination and careful comparison.

As opposed to the majority of the literature on foreign investment in China, which is based on official statistics (He 2003a,b; Wei *et al.* 1999), throughout this study semistructured interviews and site observations are applied. During the period from April 2005 to August 2006, interviews with local officials involved relevant departments of the Dongguan municipal and Guangdong provincial governments as well as selected official and nongovernmental organizations. All were conducted to obtain information on changes in policies governing HK and TW investment. Firm-level interviews with the CEOs in selected TW- and HK-invested enterprises were conducted to secure information on operations and management. The interviews covered around 30 TW-invested and a similar number of HK-invested firms representing labor- and technology-intensive manufacturing sectors (furniture, footwear, watch making, printing, chemicals, electronic products, and electrical appliances), computer and related peripheral manufacturing sectors, as well as the emerging service sector (restaurants, coffee shops, wedding pictures, travel agencies, etc.) (Table 5.1). All firms were randomly selected from major sectors with HK and TW investments listed in the Directory of Foreign-Invested Enterprises of Dongguan provided by the municipal government. According to the Directory, 67.5 percent of firms with HK investment and 62 percent of TW supported firms are very small, with investments of below 1 million US dollars. In addition to large-scale firms with brand names, a number of small- and medium-scale firms have been selected for interviews in order to increase and diversify the sample. In all instances, we tried to interview the CEOs and managers in Dongguan and at their headquarters in either HK or TW. Each tape-recorded

Table 5.1 A profile of the interviewed HK and TW-invested firms in Dongguan from April 2005 to August 2006

Sector	HK firms	Sector	TW firms
Textile and Apparel	6	Furniture	2
Electronic products	4	Footwear	2
Watches	3	Watch	2
Furniture	3	Textile and apparel	2
Paper products	2	Metals and plastics	5
Bags	2	Communication equipment, computer and other electronic equipment	7
Logistics	3	Electrical machinery and equipment	6
Agent services	3	IC foundry	1
Trading companies	3	Wedding photographing	2
		Coffee shops, restaurants and hotels	2
Total	29	Total	31

Source: Compiled by the author.

interview generally took one to one and half hours. In addition to the interviews, relevant government documents, company directories, and web sites provide valuable information.

Divergent transformation of Hong Kong and Taiwan investment in Dongguan

Similar initiation of investment, but distinction since the 1990s

Both HK and TW initiated their cross-boundary transplantation of small- medium-scale, labor-intensive and export-oriented traditional manufacturing activities to the PRD in the 1980s and 1990s. Cheap and abundant supplies of labor and land were the major attractions for both HK and TW manufacturing industries. Prior to 1990, HK was the only source of foreign investment inflows. TW investment has arrived in Dongguan since the early 1990s and has become the second largest source of foreign investment since 1992. By the end of 2003, although HK's share still covered nearly half (47.8 percent) of the total actualized foreign investment in Dongguan, the contribution of TW investment had risen dramatically from only 2 percent in 1991 to 12 percent in 2003. In some towns (e.g. Qingxi) the amount of TW investment already surpassed HK investment, the share of HK investment being less than 20 percent while that of TW reached over 77 percent of the total actualized foreign investment in 2002 (Figure 5.3). Although in 2004

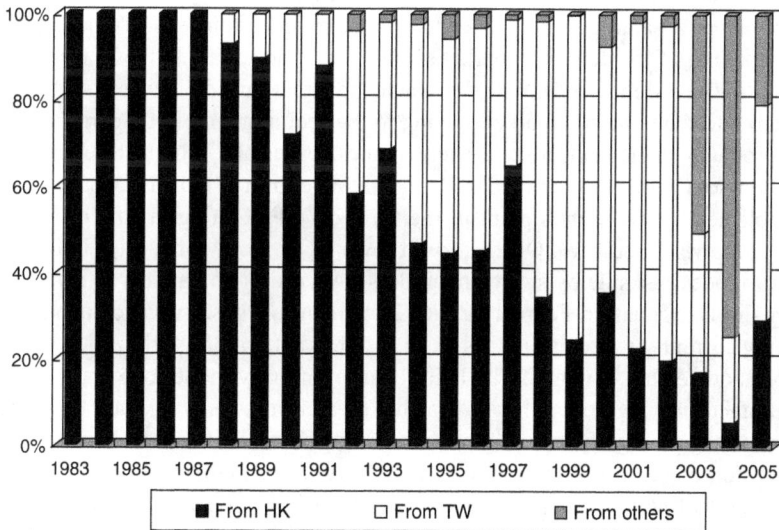

Figure 5.3 Shares of HK and TW investment in Qingxi Town, Dongguan from 1983 to 2005.

Source: Qingxi township government 2006; Dongguan Bureau of Foreign Trade and Economic Cooperation 2006.

70 percent – 9,000 of the total 14,000 – of foreign-invested enterprises in Dongguan were still dominated by the HK-invested firms, 344 (53 percent of the total number of foreign-invested enterprises with investment above 100 million US dollars) were supported by TW investors (Almanac of Dongguan 2005).

Since the late 1990s, the major sources of foreign investment in Dongguan have been under transition. HK investment has lost its predominant position in inflows of foreign investment. As stated by a Hong Kong investor in of Dongguan (Huangjiang town): "We like Dongguan while Dongguan tends to dislike us" (interview in Dongguan in July 2006). Local governments in Dongguan (e.g. Qingxi township government) formulated a FDI policy based on explicit direction of investment from different sources – that is, "setting Taiwan investment; fixing Japanese investment; attracting European and American investment; observing Hong Kong investment (Qingxi township government and Institute of Guangdong Development at Zhongshan University, 2004)."

Different transition of entry modes and market orientations

In the initial stage of cross-border investment from HK and TW, enterprises bene-fiting in the PRD in general and Dongguan in particular were classified as "outward processing and assembly with imported materials and compensation trade" (*sanlai yibu*). The basic requirement is 100 percent import of materials and export of products (so-called *liangtouzaiwai, dajidachu*).[4] In the uncertain regulatory envi-ronment at the initial stage of transplantation, this peculiar form allowed the setting up of enterprises more rapidly, with lower transaction costs.

There is a paradigm shift in China's FDI regime from export-orientation to the opening of the domestic market since China's accession to the WTO in 2001 (Buckley and Meng 2005). With this change, both HK and TW investors attempted to tap into the domestic market. Owing to the requirement of 100 percent export of products, more and more TW companies, especially wholly foreign-owned enterprises (WFOE), attempted to change into the form of FDI. They have usually established a new branch plant in the form of WFOEs (e.g. a *sanlai yibu* fac-tory in town A and a WFOE factory in town B, or the two factories in different entry modes just side by side as neighbors). According to our survey of 150 TW firms in Dongguan in February 2006, 21 percent of those surveyed admitted to taking currently two entry modes. As a result, a pattern of hybridization of entry modes/ownership emerged. The hybridization of entry modes/ownership of TW manufacturing investment has indicated a greater propensity to adapt to environ-ment changes (e.g. the opening of the Chinese domestic market). Moreover, the operation of the TW-invested firms goes beyond the preexisting inter-firm rela-tions prevailing in the early stage of investment in Dongguan. Instead, more and more raw materials and other supplies are procured from local firms. Since the late 1990s, with more Taiwan downstream assemblers moved to China, more materi-als were locally sourced. In consequence, clustering patterns of such industries as furniture, computer and peripherals are emerging in most of the towns in Dong-guan – for example, Shijie, Dalingshan, Qingxi, and Chang'an. The proportion of

TW sourcing has decreased significantly. By the end of 2003, local sourcing from TW firms and from local firms shares similar proportions of procurement orders. Although still 55 percent of the interviewed firms stated that raw materials were coming from Taiwan, 50 percent sourced their imports from other countries, but as high a percentage as 35 percent sourced from the same town and 25 percent from other towns in Dongguan. In terms of inter-firm interaction, most suppliers are TW-invested firms. On the other hand, nearly 45 percent of TW-invested firms in Dongguan perform the functions of marketing/sales and R&D locally, which means that Dongguan is longer only a factory of production.

The transformation is not so obvious for HK firms, since the majority of them are still export orientated. Instead, there emerges a new trend of "localization of HK-firms" – that is, a transition of HK-invested firms from joint ventures to local firms. With the participation of local people, usually the relatives or close friends of the HK investors in Dongguan as partners of the firms, the HK-invested companies thus changed into local businesses. Through this arrangement, the local partners remain largely "silent partners," but may take responsibilities for negotiating with local officials. Through this transition, HK-invested firms escape from the strict customs regulations and tax duties, and tend to access raw materials locally and sell products in domestic markets more easily (Interview in Dongguan, July 2006).

Distinctive trajectories of industrial upgrading

Both HK and TW investment in the 1980s and early 1990s are characterized by export-oriented, labor-intensive traditional manufacturing sectors such as toys, footwear and textiles. A distinction has occurred since the late 1990s. There is an influx of IT investment, particularly personal computer and related peripherals investment from TW. As a result, since the late 1990s, Dongguan has become a "global manufacturing factory" of IT products, especially computer-related products.

The statistical data indicates that TW firms are mainly concentrated in the manufacture of communication and computer-related electronic equipment (17 percent), while HK firms are dominated by plastic (15 percent) and textile and apparel production (14 percent) (Table 5.2). Instead of upgrading in the manufacturing sector, HK investment has turned to the services sectors since the early 2000s. HK services investments benefited from the newly established Closer Economic Partnership Arrangement (CEPA) of 2003 in tapping into the domestic market. The tertiary sector accounted for nearly 5.5 percent of HK investment in Dongguan, but only 2.7 percent of TW investment (Table 5.3).

In terms of industrial upgrading in manufacturing, over the past decade TW firms have been changing proactively from original equipment manufacturing (OEM) to original design manufacturing (ODM) and original brand manufacturing (OBM), while HK-invested firms have stagnated as OEM subcontractors. Thanks to the intensive linkages between parent firms in TW and global brand-name producers, TW electronic firms in Dongguan have become major players in the world market

Table 5.2 Sectoral composition of manufacturing industries by TW and HK investment (top five) in 2005

Sectors	Taiwan		Hong Kong	
	Number	Share (%)	Number	Share (%)
Communication equipment, computer and other electronic equipment	883	17.4	882	8.5
Plastic products	658	12.9	1599	15.4
Textile apparel and footwear	481	9.5	1401	13.5
Metal products	422	8.3	867	8.4
Electrical machinery and equipment	357	7.0	–	–
Toys	–	–	793	7.7

Source: Compiled from firm-level database of foreign enterprises of Dongguan, Dongguan Bureau of Foreign Trade and Economic Cooperation, 2006 (internal document).

Table 5.3 Sectoral composition of HK and TW investment in Dongguan in 2006

Sector	Hong Kong		Taiwan	
	Number of firms	Shares of total investment (%)	Number of firms	Shares of total investment (%)
Primary	31	0.3	15	0.3
Secondary	9755	94.20	4939	97.10
Tertiary	567	**5.5**	136	**2.7**
Total	10353	100.0	5090	100.00

Source: Compiled from firm-level database of foreign enterprises of Dongguan, Dongguan Bureau of Foreign Trade and Economic Cooperation, 2006 (internal document).

and production, while HK firms have remained as followers in low-end production without technological upgrading. The critical differences in industrial upgrading between HK and TW investment in Dongguan could be explained to some extent by the failure of HK manufacturers to upgrade local industrial activities (Davies and Ko 2006). HK's manufacturing sector has remained stuck in low value-added man- ufacturing activities for three decades. The subcontractor model locks HK firms in the OEM role within the buyer-driven global chain. The weakness of the HK elec- tronics industry lies in both brand management and direct distribution to end-users. Most of the interviewed HK firms in Dongguan mentioned that the marketing was mainly handled by their own overseas sales offices/agents. This indicates subcontractors' lack of initiative in going beyond the OEM system. Electronics industries in both HK and Dongguan are thus summarized as "global supplier[s] without a global name" (Lam and Kwok 2004) characterized by "growth with- out catch up" (Chiu and Wong 2004). It is argued that the other three Asian NIEs have experienced industrial upgrading in terms of either product upgrad- ing or process upgrading (or both). By contrast, HK has stagnated in both aspects

(Chiu and Wong, 2004). Taking the electronics industry as an example, the other three NIEs responded to the challenge of global restructuring by a combination of two strategies: first, outward investment and relocation of production processes to other developing countries; second, the upgrading of their domestic industrial structure and increasing the value-added content of the exports. By contrast, HK's electronics industry responded almost exclusively by relying on the relocation strategy and failed to move beyond consumer and low-end electronics.

For survival, HK firms mainly depend on their flexible response and cost advantages to obtain the changing orders of foreign buyers, rather than developing high technology and R&D strategies collectively or fostering close strategic alliance and network resources within the HK firms themselves (Yu 2005). The lack of input in R&D also caused HK manufacturers to be ranked the lowest among the Asian NIEs in the development of technology-intensive and hi-tech products. As a result, HK investment in the PRD and Dongguan in particular is still mainly concentrated on labor-intensive manufacturing, mainly of home electronic appliances such as TV sets and radio receivers, with low entry barriers and fierce competition globally (Table 5.4).

Since the early 1990s, manufacturing industries in TW have tended to become more relatively "high-tech." Taiwan investment in the PRD and Dongguan in particular after the mid-1990s has been transformed to high-value-added industries such as computer-related manufacturing. More importantly, although TW manufacturing firms play the role of OEM manufacturers serving brand-name global buyers, TW and HK firms have adopted different strategies. In addition to fostering the local supply network, TW manufacturers invest in the R&D section to exploit the local labor pool. In addition, the firm network of TW MNCs is more powerful, and is trust or relational based. The networking of TW footwear firms and IT firms is strengthened through both subcontracting networks and so-called cluster-based manufacturing linkages, which are regarded as important strategies for increasing the competitiveness of TW offshore assembly factories. Such networking has been considered one of the important factors in the process of relocation (Yang and Hsia 2005). With the influx of IT investment from TW, Dongguan has become one of the most important manufacturing bases of computer and related products. The major products of TW electronic firms in Dongguan concentrate on computer peripheral equipment and electronics components (see Table 5.4). Nearly one in

Table 5.4 Major products of TW and HK electronics firms in Dongguan in 2006

Rank	Products of TW firms	Products of HK firms
1	Computer peripheral equipment	TV sets and radio receivers
2	Electronic components	Home electrical appliances
3	Other electronic equipment	Electronic components
4	Wires and cables	Wires and cables
5	General electronic appliances (e.g. electronic vacuum appliances)	Other electronic equipment

three disk drives and one in five scanners and mini-power switches are made in Dongguan. Nearly all computer components can be obtained/delivered in this area within an hour and half, and Dongguan is capable of supplying about 95 percent of the parts and components for its computer manufacturing plants. In consequence, Dongguan has become a crucial part of the global IT production network; indeed, local officials claim that "if there is traffic jam between Dongguan and Hong Kong, the supply chain of the computers and global market of computers will paralyze" (interview in Dongguan, May 2005).

Distinctive spatial organizations of HK and TW investment

By mid-2006, there were around 11,380 HK firms and 5,520 TW firms scattered in various towns of Dongguan. HK-invested firms tended to be more dispersed, compared with TW investment (Figure 5.4). The dispersed distribution of HK investment in Donguan is attributed to export-led industrialization which is characterized primarily at the village level (Lin 2006). Industrial development widely scattered among many villages without concentration in urban centers is described by local people as the "spread of numerous stars in the sky without a large shining moon in the center."

The differences may reflect weaker inter-firm linkages between HK firms than between TW firms. Inter-firm linkages among TW investors tend to be more intensive with their preexisting relations established and brought from Taiwan. This observation is supported by our interviews with both HK and TW entrepreneurs: HK entrepreneurs have tended to be more loosely connected with each other, while communications among TW entrepreneurs seem more frequent and intensive. During the fieldwork, TW entrepreneurs tended to be more enthusiastic in introducing other CEOs from TW. Being far away from their shared home territory is one of the reasons for TW firms taking collective action.

HK involvement tends to be largely "going alone investment" by HK investors who are good at networking (interview in Donguan, July 2005) (Chen, 2003). Compared with TW firms in Dongguan, HK entrepreneurs lack long-term development vision. They are more like "traders" who are eager for short-term profits rather than real entrepreneurs. However, since Dongguan is the hometown of most HK-financed entrepreneurs, they establish direct connections with local governments individually more easily than TW investors.

It is noted that the economic interaction between HK and the PRD has changed from being spontaneous and market-driven primarily based on personal relations and cultural affinity in the 1980s, to dependent on inter-governmental communication after 1997, and institution-based since 2003 when CEPA was established (Yang 2004). As opposed to this institutional transition, intensive and direct linkages between host and home governments, as well as between HK entrepreneurs and local officials and residents, may not necessarily lead to organizational and functional incorporation into the local economy. HK firms predominated in *san-lai yibu* formed "export-enclave," although they seem "embedded" in Dongguan

Hong Kong

Taiwan

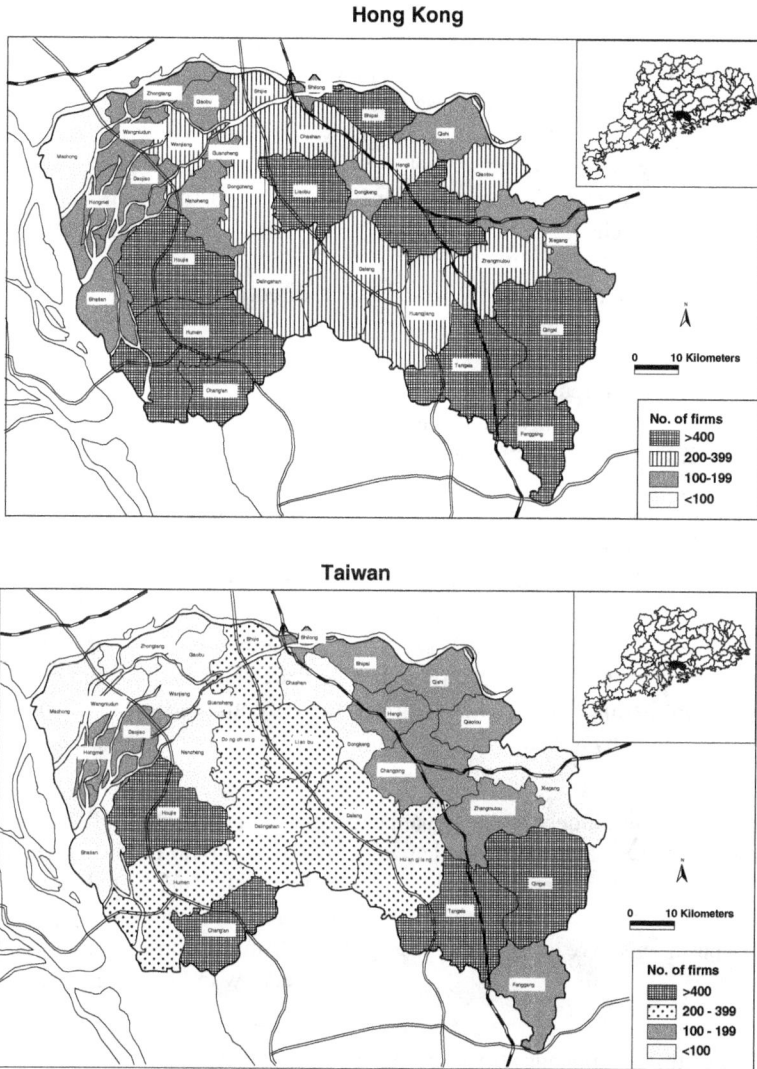

Figure 5.4 Comparison of spatial distributions of HK and TW-invested firms in Dongguan at the town level in 2006.

geographically. A HK entrepreneur suggested:

> The most effective way to resolve disputes is through private channels. Choosing a legal channel is thought to be too naïve, because it will destroy the established personal relations with local government even friends. To some extent, it will bring more trouble for the future development.
>
> (interview in Dongguan, March 2006)

This approach has been shared by the majority of HK investors in Dongguan. The second most effective way is through local government, as indicated by 30 percent of the respondent companies. It is noted that nearly one-third of the companies found no effective way to resolve their disputes (interview in Dongguan, May 2005 and February 2006). Related to these findings, all the problems that HK-invested firms have encountered are connected with government policies. The top three issues listed by the HK investors include: first, customs and import-export regulations; second, customs commodity transfer regulations; and third, collection of various fees and charges by local government agencies (interviews in Dongguan, March 2006).

In comparison with HK which established direct governmental communication with Guangdong provincial government after 1997, there are no direct or official linkages between TW and mainland China across the Straits under the existing political circumstance. As a result, semiofficial organizations, such as the Association of TW-invested Firms, play a significant role in interaction with local government in collective action. The Association of TW-invested Firms of Dongguan, established in 1993, is the first and largest association of TW firms in mainland China. The members increased from only 360 in 1993 to nearly 3,300 in 2005. Moreover, each town of Dongguan has set up its own association of TW firms, while very few towns have an association of HK firms. The major roles of the Associations include three aspects: first, social interaction among TW firms, especially during holidays; second, negotiation with relevant government departments as a group, particularly when there are some new regulations; third, information sharing. They are not platforms for TW entrepreneurs to talk business, as is pointed out by a member of Qingxi town Association of TW firms.

> We really felt lonely in Dongguan, particularly in the early 1990s when there were not so many TW firms here. The Association did provide a venue for us to gather together. In addition, a single firm will usually not be responded to regarding the implementation of new regulations, while the government departments have to reply if we are a group of firms in terms of the Association.
> (interview in Dongguan, May 2005)

Weak institutional linkages between TW firms and Dongguan have led to "institutional dis-embeddedness" (Hsu 2006). Insufficient institutional supports deferred TW firms' proactive adaptability to the changes of the host economic environment (e.g. the opening of the domestic market). TW entrepreneurs in our interviews widely complained about the personal-relation-biased management in some important departments such as customs and taxes. This is listed as one of the major reasons why newly established TW investment in the notebook computer and ITC industries choose to locate in the YRD where the well-regulated government management is widely praised by TW entrepreneurs. Another reason is that there is not an explicit industrial policy in Dongguan to support and stimulate the upgrading and transformation of TW investment.

It is worth noting that the relationship between Taiwan entrepreneurs and local governments is not similar to that of those connected to Hong Kong, which is described as the "coexistence of loving and hating." On the one hand, it is appreciated that Taiwan investment has contributed significantly to employment and export. On the other hand, Taiwan entrepreneurs are quick to appeal to the upper government if their demands cannot be met. Therefore, although belonging to the same ethnic background, these groups show substantial cultural differences owing to the historical barrier of the Straits (interview with local officials in Dongguan, May 2005). More specifically, there are different mechanisms of cross-border communication between HK and Dongguan than between TW and Dongguan.

Dongguan: an emergent supply-chain city

As far as Taiwan investment is concerned, most transborder firms have remained connected with their suppliers and customers in Taiwan, and transferred the whole production networks to the mainland. There is a vertical division of labor across the Taiwan Strait – that is, the technology-intensive sectors, which produce critical components, remain in TW; and the labor-intensive sectors, which process final products, are located on the mainland. With the expansion of TW investment from labor-intensive manufacturing sectors to the computer and peripherals IT industry since the late 1990s Dongguan has been further integrating with global production networks through TW investors.

In order to characterize the consequences of industrial upgrading and insertion into the global production networks, the notion of "supply-chain cities" is suggested (Gereffi 2005). More specifically, the phrase "supply-chain cities" is used in media reports and academic literature to highlight the growth of large-scale production in China and the agglomeration of multiple stages of the value chain in particular locales within China as a key to its upgrading success (Barboza 2004). According to Gereffi (2005), the term encompasses two distinct but related phenomena in China. The first usage refers to giant, vertically integrated factories. These factories are company-specific, and are designed to bring together multiple parts of the firm's supply chain – designers, suppliers, and manufacturers – so as to minimize transaction costs, take advantage of economies of scale, and foster more flexible supply chain management. The second usage of this term is in application to so-called cluster cities, to describe the growing number of single-product industrial clusters that have sprung up in China's coastal regions. These areas dramatically increase production of one specific product, and are churning out massive volume, but are not limited to manufacturing firms. Dongguan, as a global manufacturing factory, has turned from an assembly plant mainly invested in by HK, to an emergent supply-chain city which is dominated by TW-invested manufacturing of computer and related components with intensive linkages to global brand-name producers through the parent firms in TW. TW investment in connection with home advantages and global networks plays a pivotal role in the transformation of Dongguan into a key player in the global economy.

However, the emergent supply-chain city has encountered institutional barriers, especially weak linkages with local institutions and policy supports for sustainable development. In addition, Dongguan, one of the most attractive destinations of migrant labor in the PRD, has been facing serious shortage of workers since the early 2000s (Wang *et al.* 2005). There is a growing tendency for migrant labor to move from Dongguan in the PRD to the YRD, along with the expansion of IT investment from TW. Some interviewed firms have attempted to establish branches in other provinces, such as Anhui, Jiangxi and Sichuan, or other countries, such as Vietnam, where the labor costs are cheaper than in the PRD. In addition, an insufficient supply of electricity becomes another obstacle for the operation and further development of both HK and TW firms. Some of the interviewed firms claimed to operate only four days a week during summer (interview in Dongguan, June 2005 and July 2006). Furthermore, Dongguan is faced with the problem of insufficient land for further industrial development after more than two decades' rapid expansion. It is crucial for the local government to work out solutions in terms of sustainable inflows of foreign investment and the development of the local economy in the long run.

Conclusions

Previous studies on overseas Chinese investment in the mainland generally treated HK and TW investment equally. Taking Dongguan as an example, this study investigated the divergent trajectories of these two major sources of overseas Chinese investment over the past two and half decades in the global economy. Although both HK and TW investment in the mainland started from cross-border transplantation of small and medium-scale labor-intensive and export-oriented manufacturing, they demonstrate different paths of sectoral upgrading, entry mode strategy, and market orientation, as well as organization of cross-border production. While HK investments have turned to services sectors, TW investments tend to IT and related high-tech industries to exploit the mainland domestic market. HK investment, as the largest source of foreign investment in Dongguan for the past 27 consecutive years, played a crucial role in the rapid development of Dongguan during the 1980s and 1990s. However, since the early 2000s, TW investment has replaced that of HK and acted as a major driving force for the economic development of Dongguan. The emergence of a global supply-chain city in Dongguan has resulted from increasing IT investment from TW since the late 1990s and the intensive linkages of parent firms in TW to global brand-name producers. The dynamic of cross-border investment from HK and TW changed from "cheap labor and land" as the first factor in the 1980s to one of "tapping into the domestic market" since the late 1990s. This empirical study of the evolution of HK and TW investment in Dongguan illustrates that a dynamic approach is needed to examine the changes in investment and their impact on local transformation. However, the upgrading and transformation of TW investment does not receive sufficient support from the local institutions in Dongguan. In consequence, while TW investment is identi- fied as an important driving force for local economic development, this source of finance started relocating to the YRD in the early 2000s, raising the concern of local government in Dongguan and Guangdong province.

The interplay between home-base advantages and host-region institutions in the context of a changing global economy and subsidiary firm strategies in Dongguan as a host region provides a better explanation for the divergent trajectories of HK and TW investment in Dongguan. Industrial upgrading of TW investment is driven by efficient firm strategies and proactive industrial policy in the source region as a response to global changes. However, weak linkages with local institutions and insufficient policy supports have failed to keep pace with the upgrading and transformation of TW investment. On the other hand, stagnation of industrial upgrading of HK investment resulted from the lack of explicit industrial policies and insufficient capability, as well as inefficient firm strategies in response to the changing organizational dynamics of global production. It is essential for the local government to recognize the different forms of transformation undergone by HK and TW investment, and the distinctive spatial patterns and interaction between home regions and local institutions. In consequence, policies on FDI and local development should be considered in a holistic manner rather than on a piecemeal basis.

Acknowledgments

This research is sponsored by the Competitive Earmarked Research Grant (HKU7238/04H) from the Research Grant Council of Hong Kong Special Administrative Region, China. Fieldwork is partially supported by the Seed Funding for Basic Research (no. 10206763.20373.04500.302.01) from the University of Hong Kong. I would like to thank the two anonymous reviewers for their helpful comments. My heartfelt thanks go to the senior managers in relevant HK- and TW-invested enterprises for their generous sharing during the firm interviews. The research assistance of Felix Liao is particularly appreciated. The author assumes sole responsibility for any errors or omissions.

Notes

1 The author would like to thank one of the anonymous reviewers for bringing this out.
2 The word "mainland" is used throughout the paper to denote the People's Republic of China (PRC).
3 As discussed by Yeung (2004), the term "overseas Chinese" is usually used to include *huaqiao*, *huaren*, and residents of Taiwan, Hong Kong, and Macau (*tong bao*), who are considered as compatriots residing in parts of the historic territory of China that temporarily fall outside mainland control. *Huaren* (ethnic Chinese) has become the more "politically acceptable" term. No distinction is made in this study between the terms "overseas Chinese" and "ethnic Chinese," although, for the sake of consistency, the term "overseas Chinese" is used throughout.
4 Official statistics of foreign investment in China include three major categories, that is, (1) external loans, which involve loans from foreign governments, international financial institutions and commercial banks, debts and stock issuing, (2) FDI, in the form of equity joint ventures (EJV), cooperate joint ventures (CJV) and WFOEs, and (3) other forms, referring to processing and assembly and compensation trade (PAC) and international leasing (*China Statistical Yearbook*, 2005).

References

Abo, T. (1994) "Application and adaptation of the Japanese production system in Europe," in H. Kumon and T. Abo (eds) *The Hybrid Factory in Europe: The Japanese Management and Production System Transferred*, Basingstoke: Palgrave, 52–72.

Abo, T. (eds) (2004) *Hybrid Factory: The Japanese Production System in the United States*, Oxford: Oxford University Press.

Barboza, D. (December 24, 2004) "In roaring China, sweaters are west of sock city," *New York Times*.

Buckely, P. J. and Meng, C. (2005) "The strategy of foreign-invested manufacturing enterprises in China: export-oriented and market-oriented FDI revisited," *Journal of Chinese Economic and Business Studies*, 3(2): 111–131.

Chen, T. (2003) "Network resources for internationalization: the case of Taiwan's electronics firms," *Journal of Management Studies*, 40(5): 1107–1130.

Chiu, S. W. K. and Wong, K. (2004) "The hollowing-out of Hong Kong electronics: organizational inertia and industrial restructuring in the 1990s," *Comparative Sociology*, 3(2): 199–234.

Dacin, T. and Delios, A. (2005) "Editors' introduction: special issue on networks on Asia pacific business," *Asia Pacific Journal of Management*, 22: 315–320.

Davies, H. and Ko, D. (2006) "Up-grading and performance: the role of design, technology and business strategy in Hong Kong's electronics industry," *Asian Pacific Journal of Manage*, 23: 255–282.

Dicken, P. (2000) "Places and flows: situating international investment," in G. L. Clark, M. P. Feldman and M. S. Gertler (eds) *Oxford Handbook of Economic Geography*, Oxford: Oxford University Press, 275–291.

Dongguan Almanac Editorial Committee (2005) *Almanac of Dongguan 2004*, Beijing: China Book Press.

Dongguan Bureau of Foreign Trade and Economic Cooperation (2006) *Firm-level Database of Foreign-invested Enterprises of Dongguan* (internal document).

Dongguan Statistical Bureau (1991–2005) *Dongguan Statistical Yearbook, 1990–2004*, Beijing: China Statistical Press.

Doremus, P., Keller, W., Paulty, L., and Reich, S. (1998) *The Myth of the Global Corporation*, Princeton, NJ: Princeton University Press.

Florida, R. (1996) "Regional creative destruction: production organization, globalization, and the economic transformation of the Midwest," *Economic Geography*, 72(3): 314–334.

Florida, R. and Kenny, M. (1991) "Transplanted organizations: the transfer of Japanese industrial organization to the U.S.," *American Sociological Review*, 56(3): 381–398.

Gereffi, G. (2005) *The New Offshoring of Jobs and Global Development*, Jamaica: ILO Social Policy Lectures.

Gertler, M. S. (2001) "Best practice? Geography, learning and the institutional limits to strong convergence," *Journal of Economic Geography*, 1(1): 5–26.

Giuliani, E., Rabellotti, R. and Van Dijk, M. P. (eds) (2005) *Clusters Facing Competition: The Importance of External Linkages*, Aldershot: Ashgate.

He, C. (2003a) "Entry mode and location of foreign manufacturing enterprises in China," *Eurasian Geography and Economics*, 44(6): 443–461.

He, C. (2003b) "Location of foreign manufactures in China: agglomeration economies and country of origin effects," *Papers in Regional Science*, 82: 351–372.

Hsing, Y. (1998) *Making Capitalism in China: The Taiwan Connection*, New York: Oxford University Press.

Hsing, Y. (2003) "Ethnic identity and business solidarity: Chinese capitalism revisited," in L. J. C. Ma and C. Cartier (eds) *The Chinese Diaspora: Space, Place, Mobility and Identity*, Lanham, MD: Rowman & Littlefield, 221–236.

Hsu, J. (2005) "From transfer to hybridization: the changing organizations of Taiwanese PC investment in China," in C. G. Alvstam and E. W. Schamp (eds) *Linking Industries Across the World: Processes of Global Networking*, Aldershot: Ashgate, 173–196.

Hsu, J. (2006) "The dynamic firm-territory nexus of Taiwanese informatics industry investments in China," *Growth and Change*, 37(2): 230–254.

Humphrey, J. (1995) "Industrial reorganization in developing countries: from models to trajectories," *World Development*, 23: 149–162.

Lam, H. C. and Kwok, H. (2004) "Global supplier without a global name: a case study of Hong Kong's electronics industry," *Asian Journal of Social Science*, 32(3): 476–500.

Leung, C. K. (1993) "Personal contacts, subcontracting linkages, and development in the Hong Kong Zhujiang Delta region," *Annals of the Association of American Geographers*, 83(2): 272–302.

Lin, G. C. S. (1997) *Red Capitalism in South China: Growth and Development of the Pearl River Delta*, Vancouver: University of British Columbia Press.

Lin, G. C. S. (2006) "Peri-urbanism in globalizing China: a study of new urbanism in Dongguan," *Eurasian Geography and Economics*, 47(1): 28–53.

Mathews, J. (2006) "Dragon multinationals: new players in 21st century globalization," *Asia Pacific Journal of Management*, 23(1): 5–27.

Mathews, J. A. (2002) *Dragon Multinational: A New Model for Global Growth*, New York: Oxford University Press.

National Statistical Bureau (2005) *China Statistical Yearbook 2004*, Beijing: China Statistical Press.

Park, B. and Lee, K. (2003) "Comparative analysis of foreign direct investment in China: firms form South Korea, Hong Kong and the United States in Shandong Province," *Journal of the Asian Pacific Economy*, 8(1): 57–84.

Qingxi Township Government (2006) *The History of Qingxi Town* (Internal document).

Qingxi Township Government and Research Institute of Guangdong Development of Zhongshan University (2004) *Strategic Research on the 'Embeddedness' of Enterprises in Qingxi*.

Schmitz, H. (ed.) (2004) *Local Enterprises in the Global Economy: Issues of Governance and Upgrading*, Cheltenham: Edward Elgar.

Shen, J., Wong, K., Chu, D. and Feng, Z. (2000) "The spatial dynamics of foreign investment in the Pearl River Delta, South China," *The Geographical Journal*, 166(4): 312–322.

Shi, Y., Ho, P., and Siu, W. (2001) "Market entry mode selection: the experience of small Hong Kong firms investing in China," *Asia Pacific Business Review*, 8(1): 19–41.

Sit, V. F. S. and Yang, C. (1997) "Foreign-investment-induced exo-urbanization in the Pearl River Delta, China," *Urban Studies*, 34(4): 647–677.

Smart, A. (2000) "The emergence of local capitalism in China: overseas Chinese investment and patterns of development," in S. M. Li and W. S. Tang (eds) *China's Regions, Polity and Economy: A Study of Spatial Transformation in the Post-Reform Era*, Hong Kong: The Chinese University Press, 65–96.

Smart, A. and Hsu, J. (2004) "The Chinese Diaspora, foreign investment and economic development in China," *The Review of International Affairs*, 3(4): 544–566.

Smart, J. and Smart, A. (1991) "Personal relations and divergent economies: a case study of Hong Kong investment in China," *International Journal of Urban and Regional Research*, 15(2): 216–233.

Strurgeon, T. J. and Lester, R. K. (2005) *The New Global Supply-base: New Challenges for Local Suppliers in East Asia*, Industrial Performance Center, MIT Special Working Paper Series.

Wang, D. W., Cai, F. and Cao, W. S. (2005) *Globalization and Internal Labour Mobility in China: New Trend and Policy Implications*, ABERU Discussion Paper 15: Monash University, Australia.

Wang, J. and Tong, X. (2005) "Industrial clusters in China: embedded or disembedded?" in C. G. Alvstam and E. W. Schamp (eds) *Linking Industries across the World: Processes of Global Networking*, Aldershot: Ashgate, 223–242.

Wang, J., Zhu, H. and Tong, X. (2005) "Industrial districts in a transitional economy: the case of Datang sock and stocking industry in Zhejiang, China," in A. Lagenijk and P. Oinas (eds) *Proximity, Distance and Diversity: Issues on Economic Interaction and Local Development*, Aldershot: Ashgate, 47–69.

Wei, Y., Liu, X., Parker, D. and Vaidya, K. (1999) "The regional distribution of foreign direct investment in China," *Regional Studies*, 33(9): 857–867.

Yang, C. (2004) "From market-led to institution-based economic integration: the case of the Pearl River Delta and Hong Kong, China," *Issues & Studies,* 40(2): 78–119.

Yang, C. (2006) "Overseas Chinese investments in transition: the case of Dongguan," *Eurasian Geography and Economics*, 47(5): 604–621.

Yang, Y. and Hsia, C. (2005) "The local embeddedness of the transborder production networks and the evolution of local institution: a case study of Greater Dongguan Area, China," Paper presented at the 2nd Symposium on Cross-Strait New Economic Geography, June 20–22, 2005, Taipei.

Yang, Y. and Hsia, C. (2007) "Spatial clustering and organizational dynamics of transborder production networks: a case study of Taiwanese IT companies in the Greater Suzhou Area, China," *Environment and Planning A*, 39(6): 1346–1363.

Yeung, G. (2001) *Foreign Investment and Socio-Economic Development in China: The Case of Dongguan*, London: Palgrave.

Yeung, H. W. (2000) "The dynamics of Asian business systems in a globalizing era," *Review of International Political Economy*, 7(3): 399–433.

Yeung, H. W. C. (1997) "Business networks and transnational corporations: a study of Hong Kong Firms in the ASEAN region," *Economic Geography*, 73(1): 1–25.

Yeung, H. W. C. (2004) *Chinese Capitalism in a Global Era: Towards Hybrid Capitalism*, London: Routledge.

Yeung, H. W. C. (2006a) "From followers to market leaders: Asian electronics firms in the global economy," Asian Pacific Viewpoint Lecture, International Geographical Union Regional Congress, Brisbane, Australia, July 3–7, 2006.

Yeung, H. W. C. (2006b) "Change and continuity in southeast Asian ethnic Chinese business," *Asia Pacific Journal of Management*, 23: 229–254.

Yeung, H. W. C., Liu, W. and Dicken, P. (2006) "Transnational corporations and network effects of a local manufacturing cluster in mobile telecommunication equipment in China," *World Development*, 34(3): 520–540.

Yu, F. L. (2005) "Technological strategies and trajectories of Hong Kong's manufacturing firms," *International Journal of Technology Management*, 29(1–2): 21–39.

6 Urban labor market changes and social protection for urban informal workers

Challenges for China and India

Sunil Kumar and Bingqin Li

In the early 1970s, the country missions of the International Labor Organization (ILO) and the ILO World Employment Program's series of city studies sought to move away from a preoccupation with unemployment to a focus on employment (for a review see Moser 1978). Simultaneously, the popularization of the concept of the "informal sector," based on Hart's (1973) research on workers outside the regular waged sector in urban Ghana, produced a vast amount of scholarship on not only how to conceptualize the informal sector but also what policies are needed. This discussion is far from over. Four issues, in particular, are of relevance to contemporary discussions of the informal labor market. First, the evidence points overwhelmingly to the fact that the urban informal economy is not only here to stay but is growing and provides the only livelihood option for a significant proportion of the nonagricultural work force in Asia, Africa and Latin America. Second, concerns relating to the informal economy in the 1970s, such as precarious, low-wage and irregular income, the lack of welfare benefits and poor working environments, remain the same in the twenty-first century. Third, a decline in regular waged work is pushing former salaried employees into the informal economy: in other words, the informal economy is no longer simply a holding ground for those waiting to enter into salaried formal sector jobs. Fourth, changes in employment practices as a result of globalization, especially in new areas of comparative advantage (such as services), are giving rise to contract-based employer–employee relationship with reduced welfare benefits – a process which some have termed "informalization" (Meagher 1995; Sassen 1997; Tabak and Crichlow 2000).

The labor market of China has also experienced informalization. Informal employment increased to more than 50 percent of urban employment by 2004, while the guarantee of welfare benefits has declined. These changes have resulted in less stable and worse paid work as well as poorer labor protection. In order to address these challenges, the state is taking action to address issues of social protection for urban informal workers (see, for instance, Howell 2002). The intention is to gradually integrate informal workers, mainly rural–urban migrants, into a formal social security system (Lu and Yang 2003; Mi 2004). Simultaneously, a number of organizations representing informal sector workers' interests are emerging. The forces against informalization now come from both the state and the nongovernment sector. In the past, the state did not encourage nongovernment organizations

(NGOs). However, the rapid increases in rural–urban migration and other forms of informal employment dwarfed the state's efforts and investment. City governments could hardly cope. Starting from the early 2000s, the state began to acknowledge and work together with NGOs, though not without controls and checks (Zhan and Han 2005). All these changes make the future roles of the state, unions, NGOs, and workers in maintaining "decent" work less clear than when formal work was the single most important source of employment.

India offers a good comparison and reference, not only because of the scale of the labor force and rapid economic growth, but also because of its fairly different employment culture: the dominance of informal employment, less direct intervention from the state, and a tradition of workers' self-organization. Access to work in India's nonagricultural sector has been and continues to be provided by the informal economy (about 83 percent). Following the reports of the Task Force on Employment (Government of India 2001) and the Second National Commission on Labor (Government of India 2002), the government is attempting to bring about legislative reforms aimed at workers in the informal economy. Urban informal workers have had a history of seeking to organize in order to gain a more powerful voice and negotiate a range of benefits from the state and employers with varying degrees of success.

This chapter seeks to explore the challenges that the urban labor market raises for the social welfare of its workers in relation to labor market trends, state intervention, and workers' organizations.

Urban labor market trends

In China, an urban area is defined administratively. A large part of a city's administration area can be periurban and rural. Its population is not officially registered as "urban." A more frequently used measurement of urbanization is based on population registration. The household registration status or the "*hokou*" system has been used to classify who is urban and who is rural. In 1978, China's urban population was 172.5 million (17.9 percent) increasing to 437.5 million (30.4 percent) by 1998. From 1999 the speed of urbanization accelerated and the rural population began to drop for the first time in 20 years. By the end of 2005, the urban population was 562.12 million (43 percent, and more than 2.5 times that of 1980) and it is estimated that it will reach 60 percent by 2020 (Li 2005).

In comparison, in India a geographical area is deemed to be urban only if it meets all of the following three criteria: a population of more than 5,000; a density of more than 400 persons per square kilometer; and having more than 75 percent of its male labor force engaged in nonagricultural activities. Its urban population increased from 62.4 million (17.3 percent) in 1951 to 285.3 million (27.8 percent) in 2001. This slow pace of urbanization is reflected in the decline of average annual urban population growth rates – from 3.79 percent (1971–1981) to 2.71 percent (1991–2001) (Dyson and Visaria 2004: 116). It is predicted that India will be 35.6 percent urban by 2026 and 44.3 percent by 2051 (Dyson and Visaria 2004: 120).

Nonetheless, what is of significance is the size of the urban populations: China with 562.11 million in 2005 and India with 286.12 million in 2001 (Census of

India 2001). This raises the important question of how the poor among these large urban populations seek to establish livelihoods. The pattern of China's urbanization has had profound impacts on its urban employment structure. First, there seems to be an unlimited supply of cheap and unskilled laborers. According to the Rural Household Survey of 2004 (National Bureau of Statistics of China 2005) 102.6 million rural workers migrated to cities. In 2004, 57 percent of those employed in industries were ex-peasants. More specifically, 68 percent of workers in manufacturing, 80 percent in construction, and 52 percent in service industries are rural residents. More than 90 percent of employees in city cleaning, domestic work, and catering services are rural to urban migrants. Second, there has been a dramatic increase in informal employment. For many years, the official *hokou* system discouraged rural labor from seeking employment in urban areas, especially in large cities. However, many urban employers managed to hire rural workers to save on labor costs. They were signed up as "temporary" employees or paid on a piece-rate basis. Third, informal employment has become a practical solution to urban unemployment. People who could not find jobs in the formal sector have taken up self-employment. As a result, more than 70 percent of the urban unemployed are now working under flexible arrangements (Ministry of Labor and Social Security 2002, hereafter MOLSS). In total, urban self-employment accounted for 9.5 percent of total urban employment by the end of 2004 (Li 2006).

The gradual and steady pace of urbanization in India has not created the sudden changes in the urban labor market that China is witnessing. In India as a whole, employment in the formal organized sector has been and continues to be less than 10 percent of the labor force. However, this figure is higher in urban areas, at around 40 percent in 1999–2000, with self-employment accounting for 42 percent and casual employment for 20 percent in the same period (Government of India 2001).

In this broad context of urban labor market changes this chapter considers the ability of informal urban workers to secure welfare benefits – better wages and working conditions as well as social protection – through a range of state and non-state-based mechanisms.

Institutional and legislative arrangements for urban labor and social welfare

This section examines the institutional and legislative arrangements aimed at improving the social welfare of workers in the urban informal sector in urban China and India. The focus is on the levels[1] at which policies are formulated and the challenges to decentralization and adoption. In addition, the extent to which these policies are or are likely to be effective is also explored.

Legislation

For quite a long time since the beginning of economic reform in 1978, the Chinese government did not require new enterprises, especially the privately owned, to offer labor protection. In 1992, the revised Labor Law was published. Later, more than 20 regulations were published to offer implementation and organization details targeting specific social groups. Apart from state regulation, there are also ministerial and local government regulations to give more detailed instructions on enforcement. Over time, China has developed four major elements for the system of labor protection. They are labor relations (labor and collective contracts, and termination of contracts), labor standards (working hours, wages, safety and health, on the job training and protection for women and juvenile workers), social insurance and welfare, and labor law enforcement (Fan 2003).

India has a long history of legislation aimed at protecting the rights of workers. There are about 10 labor laws applicable to workers in the unorganized sector covering wages, contract and migrant workers, child and bonded labor and welfare cases (Ratnam 1999). Some of these, for example, include the Factories Act of 1948 (working conditions, working hours, child labor, health and safety and the working environment, among others); the Employees' State Insurance Act of 1948 (accident compensation and sickness and maternity benefits); the Payment of Bonus Act of 1965; the Employees' Provident Fund and Miscellaneous Provision Act of 1972; and the Payment of Gratuity Act of 1972.

State institutional arrangements

In China, at the central government level, social security is under the control of the MOLSS. In practice, all schemes are managed and administered locally – at or below the provincial level (Saunders and Shang 2001). In the social insurance system, employees contribute jointly with their employers. Each person has an individual account that can be drawn upon for pension or healthcare coverage when certain conditions are met. If a person is unemployed, he or she can receive unemployment benefits for a certain period. For many years, social insurance schemes were only open to urban formal employees. When employees left the formal sector, their membership to the social insurance scheme was terminated (He *et al.* 2003). After 2000, there were various attempts to expand social insurance coverage to urban employees outside full-time formal employment – such as temporary workers, rural–urban migrant workers and foreign workers.

The minimum living standard guarantee is the responsibility of the Ministry of Civil Affairs. It is a noncontributory means-tested social assistance program. Administration of the program is carried out at the provincial level or lower. Funding for the minimum living standard guarantee comes mainly from local budgets. The central government only contributes marginally to support poverty- and unemployment-ridden cities (Cook 2002). So far, only urban citizens are entitled to benefit from the minimum living standard guarantee.

The government of India has initiated about 19 special employment programs since 1970. Only two focused on urban areas. The first of these is the Self-Employment Program for the Urban Poor (SEPUP), 1986–87. The second is the Nehru Rozgar Yojana (NRY), 1989, which has three components: the Scheme for Urban Micro Enterprises (SUME); the Scheme for Urban Wage Employment (SUWE); and the Scheme for Housing and Shelter Upgradation (SHASU) (Agarwala and Khan 2001). A main innovation is the welfare board. The State of Kerala is the most successful in its coverage of unorganized workers (rural and urban). Welfare boards are financed jointly by workers and employers, the state government offering some assistance. The benefits are entitlement based (e.g. retirement, accident, and illness). Some important guarantees (e.g. of either work or unemployment benefits) are not available (see, Nair 2004). A more progressive model of a welfare board has existed in the western State of Maharashtra under the Maharashtra Hamal Mathadi and other unprotected workers (Regulation of Employment and Welfare) Act 1969. The Act requires compulsory registration of employers and workers at the statutory board. Board members include representatives of employers'/traders' associations, trade unions, and the state. Employers pay for the administration costs of the board. The board deals with workers' contribution and pays wages to workers (Chikarmane and Narayan 2000).

Challenges to legislation and institutional arrangements

It is often pointed out that unless legislation can be enforced, the relevance of further legislation is doubtful. As Gosh (2002: 38–39) notes

> it is a common misconception among academics and policy makers, that social realities can be altered by legislative fiat. The relationship between laws and social change ... is always shaped more definitively by political economy and social configurations than by imposition from above, however well intentioned and analytically convincing such imposition may be. . . . Throughout history and across countries, the recognition and granting of workers' rights have not occurred because of the benign intentions of governments, but because workers and other social movements have struggled and fought for such rights. That is also why, even when such rights are "officially" accepted at both national and international levels, they can be systematically denied to large numbers of citizens because of the prevailing political and material realities.

What the Chinese government has been trying to do in relation to informal employment is to remove this informality through the expansion of labor contracts to all employees in the formal sector. Regardless of the terms of contract, any identifiable employment relationship should be recognized and given equal treatment. Theoretically, according to the new Labor Law, all workers are entitled to equal labor rights as long as they can provide evidence of employment. If properly implemented, this may ultimately lead to an integrated social security system for all people working in cities through enforcing employer-based social insurance. In practice, this is far from being achieved.

The Chinese social security system in the past was designed to cater for the needs of urban formal employees. Extending protection to informal employment raises several challenges.

1   The decentralized funding for social security means that local governments do not receive more money for covering more people. Thus, they do not have the incentives to stretch their limited resources to the informal sector and new settlers in the city (Li 2005; Wong 1994).
2   Local governments count on local businesses to boost economic growth. The central government's long lasting strategy of pursuing growth motivates the local government to act in favor of employers rather than employees (Lin and Liu 2000; Zhang and Zou 1998).
3   The Labor Law legislation is not backed up by relevant legislation in other areas. For example, the Labor Law acknowledges protection of workers' rights but other laws continue to facilitate the arbitrary detention and imprisonment of human rights defenders (Amnesty International 2004).
4   It is difficult to tell what is needed for labor protection in the informal employment. The problems can be in the measurement and the special characteristics of informal employment (Li 2006).
5   Some recent research has found that, even if informal employees are allowed to participate in these schemes, it is not always the case that they are willing to join (Zhao and Xu 2002).

The challenges point to the government's limited capacity. However, as workers, especially those from rural areas, are becoming more aware of their rights, if the government continues to fail to fulfill its promises it is constantly inviting dissatisfaction and even resentment.

The problems in India are of a different sort. It is estimated that the Employee Provident Fund, the social protection instrument with the widest coverage, has only reached 10 percent of the workforce (Jain 1997). The government recognized the challenges in policy implementation.

> The laws or welfare systems that we propose for them [unorganized workers – estimated to be 93% of the workforce in India – authors' insertion] cannot be effective unless they themselves are conscious of the laws, and acquire the strength to ensure that laws are brought into force; unless there are effective means to implement, monitor and provide quick redress; unless breaches of the law are punished with deterrent penalties, and unless the organs of public opinion and movements and organizations mount vigil, and intercede to ensure that the provisions of the laws and welfare systems are acted upon.
>
> (Government of India 2002: 594–595)

Clearly, the state on its own does not have the inclination or the ability to ensure access to social protection for informal workers. This raises serious doubts in relation to two proposed pieces of legislation aimed at unorganized workers.

These are the Unorganised Sector Workers' Bill 2004, and the Unorganised Sector Workers' Social Security Bill 2005, modified and presented as the Unorganised Sector Workers' Social Security Bill 2006. The former has mainly a policy and research focus but also calls for the setting up of an Unorganized Sector Workers Welfare Fund. The latter calls for the establishment of a National Social Security Authority (NSSA) for the Unorganized Sector. The act notes that the NSSA shall have the power to allow the Union or State Government to create an appropriate mechanism for collecting contributions from individual employers (or their contractors, wherever applicable), a class of employers, or a whole industry; or to levy a tax on any goods produced or processed or manufactured in order to partly finance the schemes, programs and projects undertaken by NSSA. However, with 93 percent of the work force in the unorganized sector, it is difficult to see how such national- or state-level attempts to provide social security can be successful.

Furthermore, institutional and legislative arrangements in India are subject to a dialectical tension because central and state governments are "partners" in their policy making and financial responsibilities. For example, responsibility for employment is vested in the elected representatives of the state government, who cannot be forced to adopt central government policy. In urban areas, policies and their finance become the responsibility of municipal governments. Thus, although legislation may be passed by the central government, to what extent workers can seek its protection depends upon the state government's willingness to accept and adopt the central government regulations.

In addition, the proposed bill has also received criticism on many fronts: first, for its segmented and narrow focus on social security (Dugal 2006; Jose 2006); second, for recognizing unpaid workers yet proposing to exclude them from social security, with the implications for women that this will have (Neetha 2006); third, for its separation of legislation for conditions of work from social security rather than integration of them (Sankaran 2006); fourth and finally, and in tune with the argument of this chapter, for the failure of the Bill to recognize that the "cart of a social security system needs three galloping horses to take it to the destination of a deprivation free unorganized worker: viable enterprise, successful poverty alleviation progammes and congenial macro policies, none of which is in sight" (Rao *et al.* 2006).

Although both China and India are seeking to legislate for the social protection of their urban informal workers, a key difference is that the Chinese government has taken a more paternalistic approach, with top-down policies, whereas the Indian government rather sees legislation as something that individual workers can seek recourse to. The top-down approach only proves the existence of government failures' while offering individual recourse simply has not worked.

Urban informal workers – organization and representation

State policy and institutional arrangements are necessary; however, they are not sufficient to ensure social protection. The main issue is the extent to which workers are able to successfully contest work-related injustices and have recourse to legislative and other institutional mechanisms.

A brief history of workers' organization

During the central planning era, China's urban workers were organized through state controlled trade unions. The unions represented both the state and organized workers during the prereform era. This made them an important agency for the state to control workers. Since the reforms in the 1970s, the same system has been extended to the nonstate sector. As the state was responsible for the welfare of workers, unions were not active in protecting workers' interests (Chan 1998). However, the role of unions poses challenges in the reform era: first, the fast growing nonstate sector contains a growing proportion of the unorganized urban labor force; second, the inflowing rural–urban migrants, who are largely working as short term informal workers, were not entitled to unionization; third, a shrinking state sector has eroded job security and social protection; and fourth, unlike the state, private employers do not have the incentives to care for workers' interests.

Interwoven with British colonialism, India has had a long history of trade union activity beginning with the Factories Act of 1833 and the Trade Union Act of 1926 (Mathew 2003). The Trade Union Act allows unionization in the formal as well as informal sectors as long as more than seven workers decide collectively to organize (Dasgupta 2002: 2). However, the registration of any union has to be undertaken with each state's Labor Department, which is often reluctant to register unions because of three concerns: the fact that there is no clear employer-employee relationship as is the case in the formal sector, the heterogeneity of the informal sector, and the dispersed work locations of informal workers (Dasgupta 2002). Although the formation of trade unions are recognized under the Trade Union Act of 1926 there is no legal obligation or the part of exployers, ever in the formal sector, to enter into collective bargaining with the unions. It is the strength of some trade unions that brings about widespread collective bargaining, especially in the organized sector (Mathew 2003). As a result, there is limited unionization amongst unorganized workers. Even in the formal sector, the power of trade unions in representing and claiming the work-based rights of their members is being gradually eroded as a result of casualization and a decline in union constituencies (see, for example, Breman 2001; Jhabvala 2005).

Forms and levels of organizing the unorganized

There is general agreement that organization and representation are important in enabling urban informal workers to secure their legally entitled rights and guarantees. One question, however, is – what form the organization should take (Aziz 1997: 49). The simple answer is that there is no one ideal organizational form. The heterogeneity in the forms of work (for instance, own-account, disguised wage, domestic, casual and contract work) gives rise to differing needs and priorities for different groups of workers. A second question relates to local versus national, and formal versus informal forms of organizing.

Unionization

From 2000, the Chinese government began to urge trade unions to offer membership to rural–urban migrants. However, the implementation of the seemingly compassionate regulations is poor. This is largely because of the high costs of enforcing labor law, the inability of the government to monitor policy implementation, the lack of incentives for union leaders to take in rural–urban migrants as members (Howell 2003), and the lack of sufficient protection for people who bargain and fight for workers' rights (Amnesty International 2004). As a result, government-controlled unions often refuse to offer membership to informal employees, mostly rural–urban migrant workers, even if it is against the state regulation.

In India, the unionization of unorganized workers in the informal sector has tended to be trade- or activity-based – such as domestic work, sex work, or street vending. Initiatives to organize unorganized workers in the urban informal economy date back as far as the early 1950s (Sundaram 1997). Of late, there has been an increase in such forms of organizing informal workers, reviving the trade union movement's principles of collective bargaining. For instance, the estimated number of people involved in the collection of recyclable waste in the city of Pune, Maharashtra state, is 7,000, of which 85 percent are waste pickers and the rest itinerant buyers. In 1993, 5,000 of them were organized to form the Kagad Kach Parta Kashtakari Panchayat (Scrap Collectors Association) (Chikarmane and Narayan 2000).

Attempts to organize at the local, regional or national levels with a view to securing the rights of workers is a painfully slow process, due to the laborious processes of negotiation with the state as well as the scattered locations of both workers and employers. This is even worse in the case of domestic workers, with one worker having more than one employer. At the national level, the National Alliance of Street Vendors of India (NASVI) was formed in 1998 with its secretariat in Patna, Bihar. Some highlights of NASVI policy include issues around representation, licensing, spaces for trading, and protection from evictions. The benefit of a national-level federated organization is the strengthening of "voice." NASVI, for example, has been able to bring about litigation for the benefit of street vendors as well as influencing planning decisions (Cohen *et al.* 2000).

Collective self-organizing and provisioning

In China, rural–urban migrant workers are not keen to join the union. They are different from urban workers in many ways. They are often more mobile – they change jobs, move between cities, and travel between cities and their home villages. Thus social protection of rural–urban migrants has different priorities. Organizations set up by rural–urban migrants often have better understanding of their needs and hence tend to be more practical. The state recognized this advantage and began to allow rural–urban migrants to set up separate unions. The first such self-organized union was established in Shenyang in April 2004. By April 2005 it had more than 5,200 members.

Later many unions of this type appeared in other cities. They are now playing an important role in helping migrant workers to protect their rights in cities. Unlike the trade unions for urban workers, unions for migrant workers are not embedded in the workplace. They mainly locate in the local labor market where ex-peasants come to look for jobs. It is easier to organize thus, and ensures independence from employers. This is also convenient for workers who change jobs frequently. Membership is free.

According to the Ministry of Civil Affairs of PRC, by the end of 2004 there were more than 10,736 nonprofit organizations (NPOs) categorized as "labor" related. China's NPOs are in an awkward position. According to current NPO regulations, an NPO should be approved and registered with the authorities. To be eligible for registration, an NPO should have at least 50 individual or 30 group members. It should have a fixed office place. It should hire full time staff members. Organizations at national level should have a working fund of more than 100,000 Yuan. Local organizations should have more than 30,000 Yuan. It should function as a legal body that is able to take legal responsibilities concerning civil cases. These regulations have created barriers to the establishment and registrations of NGOs. First, not many NPOs are able to meet the funding requirements. Second, not all organizations need full time staff members; this requirement is particularly detrimental to self-organized workers who have full time jobs. Also, it is not practical for many organizations to have fixed offices. The requirements made it almost impossible for organizations aiming at confronting the authorities, such as independent trade unions, to register (Zhao 2001). Independent trade unions are still taboo in China (Amnesty International 2004). Independent organizations without government permission are suppressed.

However, self-organized groups are not always officially registered. A survey carried out by Xie (2003) shows that only 8–13 percent of NPOs were officially registered. There are various self-help groups operating under different names. For example, the Chinese Women Network in Hong Kong, the Nanshan District Woman Worker Service Centre in Shenzhen, and the Farmer Friends Cultural Development Centre in Beijing (Zhan and Han 2005). Compared with rural–urban migrants, informal workers from urban areas are even less organized, especially those working for private and small enterprises. There are no unions inside small enterprises and there are no labor-market-based unions for them to participate in. As a result, they are not really represented in the trade unions.

In India, impoverishment among poor working women, mostly own-account workers, has led to organizational strategies focused on securing the resources needed for *production*. There is no doubt of the need for such support in a country where there is no social security. However, for several reasons this strategy alone is unlikely to make much progress creating better forms of work in relation to the ILO agenda. First, credit- and savings-based organizations take time to build membership, and the need to correctly maintain the management of funds requires small group formation. Although there is nothing to stop these groups from coming together to increase their influence on government policy, they have tended to focus on securing production related resources for their members. Second, the ability of the members to actually negotiate production-related resources depends on how empowered the members are. If the collective is dependent on a single articulate person, this will constrain its reach. Third, there is the danger of the state realizing that, because of the manner in which the collective is seen to succeed, there is no need for changes in the structure that underpins the skewed balance in access to resources.

Combining unionization and self-organizing

The free membership of migrant workers' unions in urban China makes it difficult for them to be sustained and expand. Recognizing these unions' capacity to organize and support workers, the state now has the incentive to use them as supplementary to the formal union system and bring them under formal control. The allocation of working capital through the All China Federation of Trade Unions (ACFTU) is an incentive to rural–urban migrants' unions to become members of the ACFTU. For example, the Shenyang rural–urban migrant workers union recently received 100,000 Yuan from the municipal and district trade unions (Xinhua News Agency 2006).

Similarly in India, there are movements trying to combine unionization with self-provisioning. The largest of these is the Self Employed Women's Association (SEWA), based in the city of Ahmadabad, in the western state of Gujarat. In 2002, although SEWA membership is predominantly Gujarat based (its origin), accounting for 78 percent of its all India membership, the remaining 22 percent of its members are from seven cities in five Indian states (Madhya Pradesh, Uttar Pradesh, Bihar, Kerala and Delhi). Until 1994, SEWA membership was urban, due to its original base in the city of Ahmadabad. By 2000, its Gujarat membership stood at 38 percent urban and 62 percent rural. Most of SEWA's Gujarat members are manual laborers and service providers (56 percent), with home-based workers being the next largest category (35 percent), and the remaining made up of hawkers and vendors (9 percent) (SEWA web site).[2] SEWA has provided its members with the ability to save and obtain credit, housing, health care and child care. Since 1990, SEWA's activities have been broadened with a program of insurance in conjunction with public and private insurance companies (Vimosewa 2006).

However, unions for migrant workers have their limits. First, unions have to battle against the government's interest in protecting local businesses. Thus, even with stronger state support, it is not always easy to protect workers' rights. According to the statistics of the ACFTU, overdue salaries in enterprises, though 12.9 billion less than in 2004, reached 21.5 billion Yuan by the end of October 2005. Second, because they are not organized according to trade and are not involved in decision making inside businesses, unions are not able to engage in collective bargaining

(Zhou 2006). In this sense, the institutional innovation can at most provide a partial protection.

Organizations of informal workers tend to have two weaknesses. The first is the scale of coverage even within a trade or activity. This is due to several reasons, but the most significant one seems to be a question of incentive. Poor informal workers are so preoccupied with securing their livelihoods that there is a tension between short term "practical needs" and long-term "strategic needs" – a distinction made by Moser in relation to gender needs (see Moser 1993). The second is the lack of cross-trade or activity alliances under the banner of informal workers as a whole (Cohen *et al.* 2000: 19–20).

In summary, changes in the urban labor market have introduced more interactions between the state, individuals, and the nongovernment sector. At best, the efforts towards self-organization are likely to remain fragmented, with small gains being secured one step at a time. However, efforts should continue to be made in exploring ways to form coalitions of unorganized workers' organizations in order to strengthen collective voice and representation. Pressure also needs to be put on state governments to adopt and ratify legislative reforms if national level organizations of workers are to be more effective.

Conclusions

The changes in the urban labor markets of China and India pose two significant social protection challenges. The first relates to the increasing informal basis of working relationships. Given that informal work is assuming greater importance, and few newly created jobs offer full protection as they used to, the state needs to take a more active role in insuring that informal work is "decent." The second challenge relates to the role of state and nonstate actors in ensuring that workers can secure the guarantees and rights they are entitled to.

However, these challenges differ. First, in India the proportion of the urban labor force which is either self-employed or in casual work has increased gradually from 57 percent in 1994 to 61 percent in 2004. In the case of China, the proportion of those outside the salaried state and private sectors has increased sharply from just over 20 percent in 1994 to nearly 60 percent in 2004. Second, the comparison has highlighted the difference in the scale of self-employment: in India it increased from 39 percent in 1994 to 43 percent in 2004, whereas in China the proportion is much smaller at nearly 10 percent in 2004. As pointed out earlier, the social protection needs of those that are self-employed differ from those that are in either casual or piece-rate contract work. For some of the former, access to resources for "production" takes precedence, whereas for others it would also include the right to urban spaces for trade. For the latter, the important issues are related to wages, benefits and working conditions. In China, additional challenges are how to integrate rural–urban migrants into the urban social protection system, which is almost completely different from the rural system, and how the state can effectively engage nonstate actors to complement its efforts.

There can be no doubt that protection of social rights and guarantees against various risks needs to be institutionalized. Both the Chinese and Indian governments have been active in legislating on this front. However, in both countries, there has been limited success in enforcement due to a combination of weak state capacity and information asymmetries. While increasing resources would help, the main deficiency is "political will." In a globalized world, where the location of production and services is based on cost considerations, political will is likely to be biased towards those that generate work. The struggle by workers for equitable treatment from the polity will be a long one. The emerging interest in corporate social responsibility (CSR) may provide a platform for improved wages and working conditions for contracted factory and home-based workers. There is also a need to reflect on the nature of legislation. The Indian experience shows that legislation based on a traditional employer–employee relationship can work for informal workers in relation to securing rights related to wages. However, when it comes to legislating for social protection (e.g. unemployment, illness and retirement benefits) attention needs to be paid to the issue of incentives. The key to the participation of and contribution from informal workers lies in convincing them of the benefits and guarantees that any scheme has to offer. India could learn from China's guarantee of minimum living standard for urban residents, something that the welfare boards lack. This is a challenging task, given the varied nature and fragmented location of work in the informal economy. In relation to the other areas of social protection, India's greater experience in self-provisioning and the engagement of civil society may provide directions for China.

It is unlikely, at least in the near future, that the Chinese and Indian states will assume primary responsibility in either enforcing legislation or institutionalizing social protection for their urban informal workers. This chapter has shown that there have been attempts using a range of strategies to fill the gap in both the provision of social security (production and work-based) and the enforcement of legally constituted rights resulting from weak state capacity. India has been a forerunner in this area. The struggle to ensure guarantees and rights has been attempted in the form of self-provisioning, unionization or a combination of both. These mechanisms raise several issues and suggest areas where lessons can be learnt. First, while self-provisioning is important in meeting the social protection needs of urban "producers," it can in itself create a culture of dependency. Although this can be overcome through programs of empowerment there is a risk that self-provisioning can make the state complacent by removing pressures to institutionalize the required guarantees. Second, the Indian experience has shown the importance of collective action in the form of unionizing workers to bring about changes in social protection policies relating to urban informal workers. But the struggle is a slow and long drawn out one. Thus, there have been more successes in India when self-provisioning and unionization have been combined. Third, there are lessons to be learned from not only the benefits of having nationally active unions but also the weaknesses associated with the lack of cross-union activity. Notwithstanding the fact that the disparate trades or activities of informal urban workers generate different needs and priorities for social protection, there is one thing that these workers have in common – the lack of social protection. Federations of unions can enhance "voice" – something that is more important than the difference of interests between them. Fourth and finally, the Indian experience has shown that the success of unionization is highly dependent on its being independent from the state. In China, the state has taken on a dominant role in trying to provide and control the resources for protecting social rights and offering formalized guarantees for the informally employed. However, so far state sponsorship (implicit and explicit) and the onerous criteria for registration of NPOs effectively nullify the power of workers' unions. The newly established unions for rural workers are not yet able to be fully functioning trade unions. In China, the key issue facing labor protection is to persuade the state to allow nongovernment activities and self-organization to help to achieve a goal which the state's paternalistic approach has thus far not been able to fulfill.

Urban labor market changes in China and India entail challenges in social protection for self-employed and casual workers. This challenge is not only for the state but also confronts a range of civil society organizations. Neither is this challenge a question of who should be responsible. The challenge is essentially one of securing the guarantees and rights associated with decent work and sustainable livelihoods. There is room for partnerships. However, it is essential that any potential partnership does not unduly compromise the guarantees and rights of those who are struggling to make a living.

Notes

1 The terminology referring to the levels of government in India are: top level – central government (India) and state government (China); second level – state government (India) and provincial government (China); third level – municipal (urban India) and government below provincial level (China).
2 http://sewa.org/aboutus/index.htm

References

Agarwala, R. and Khan, Z. D. (2001) *Labour Market and Social Insurance Policy in India: A Case of Losing Both Competitiveness and Caring.* Washington, DC: World Bank.
Amnesty International (2004) "People's Republic of China: Human Rights Defenders at Risk." Available online at: http://web.amnesty.org/library/index/engasa170452004 (accessed on June 6, 2006).
Aziz, A. (1997) "Organising the unorganised labour: some issues," in R. Dutt (ed.) *Organising the Unorganised Workers,* New Delhi: Vikas Publishing House, 48–58.
Breman, J. (December 29, 2001) "An informalised labour system: end of labour market dualism," *Economic and Political Weekly,* 4804–4827.
Chan, A. (1998) "Labour standards and human rights: the case of Chinese workers under market socialism," *Human Rights Quarterly,* 20(4): 884–904.
Chikarmane, P. and Narayan, L. (October 7–13, 2000) "Formalising livelihood: case of waste pickers in Pune," *Economic and Political Weekly,* 3639–3642.
Cohen, M., Bhatt, M. and Horn, P. (2000) *Women street vendors: the road to recognition.* Working Paper SEEDS Paper No 1, New York: Population Council.

Cook, S. (2002) "From rice bowl to safety net: insecurity and social protection during china's transition," *Development Policy Review*, 20: 615–635.

Dasgupta, S. (2002) *Organizing for Socio-Economic Security in India*. Geneva: International Labour Office.

Dugal, R. (August 12, 2006) "Need to universalise social security," *Economic and Political Weekly*, 3495–3497.

Dyson, T. and Visaria, P. (2004) "Migration and urbanisation: retrospects and prospects," in T. Dyson, R. Cassen and L. Visaria (eds) *Twenty-First Century India: Population, Economy, Human Development and the Environment*, Oxford: Oxford University Press, 108–129.

Fan, Z. (2003) "The Status Quo and Development of China's Labour Legislation." [*Zhongguo Laodong Lifa Xianzhuang Yu Fazhan*] Available online at: http://www.usc.cuhk.edu.hk/wk_wzdetails.asp?id=3290 (accessed on June 6, 2006).

Ghosh, J. (2002) "Macroeconomic Reforms and a Labour Policy Framework for India." Available online at: http://www.networkideas.org/featart/feb2003/Macro_Labour.pdf (accessed on June 6, 2006).

Government of India (2001) *Report of the Task Force on Employment Opportunities*. New Delhi: Planning Commission.

Government of India (2002) "2nd Labour Commission Report": Government of India. Available online at: http://labour.nic.in/lcomm2/2nlc-pdfs/Chap-7finalA.pdf (accessed on August 10, 2005).

Hart, K. (1973) "Informal income earning opportunities and urban employment in Ghana," *The Journal of Modern African Studies*, 11(1) March: 61–89.

He, P., Liu, Y., Wang, Z., and Hua, Y. (2003) "Report on the social insurance of the flexibly employed," [*Linghuo jiuye qunti shehui baoxian yanjiu baogao*] in G. Zheng (ed.) *Changing Environment for Employment and Social Security (biange zhong de jiuye huanjing yu shehui baozhang)*, Beijing: China Labour and Social Security Press, 494–518.

Howell, J. (2002) *Good practice study in Shangai on employment services for the informal economy*. Working Paper Employment Paper 2002/06, Geneva: International Labour Office.

Howell, J. (2003) "Trade unions in China: sinking or swimming?" *The Journal of Communist Studies and Transition Politics*, 18(1): 102–122.

Jain, S. (1997) "Social security for the informal sector in India: Feasibility study on area-based pilot projects in Anand (Gujarat) and Nizamabad (Andhra Pradesh)," in W. van Ginneken (ed.) *Social security for the informal sector: Investigating the feasibility of pilot projects in Benin, El Salvador, India and Tanzania*. Issues in Social Protection, Discussion Paper No. 5, Geneva: International Labour Office, Social Security Department.

Jhabvala, R. (May 28–June 4, 2005) "Unorganised workers bill: in aid of the informal worker," *Economic and Political Weekly*, 2227–2231.

Jose, A. V. (August 12, 2006) "Is legislation the only solution," *Economic and Political Weekly*, 3480–3483.

Li, B. (2006) "Informal employment and its challenges to social policy in China." Paper presented at the Conference on *New World of Work, Asia Research Centre Discussion*, March 8, London: London School of Economics and Political Science.

Li, S. (2005) "China's Urbanization Rate to Reach 60% in 20 Years." Available online at: http://english.people.com.cn/english/200105/17/eng20010517_70205.html (accessed on June 5, 2006).

Lin, J. Y. and Liu, Z. (2000) "Fiscal decentralization and economic growth in China," *Economic Development and Cultural Change*, 49(1): 1–21.

Lu, L. and Yang, P. (2003) *Constructing Social Security System For Rural-Urban Migrant Workers* [*goujian mianxiang jincheng nongmin gong de shehui baozhang zhidu*], Nanjing: Nanjing Social Science.

Mathew, B. (January–March 2003) "A brief note on labour legislation in India," *Asian Labour Update*, (46): 2.

Meagher, K. (1995) "Crisis, informalization and the urban informal sector in Sub-Saharan Africa," *Development and Change*, 26: 259–284.

Mi, Q. (2004) "A Literature Review on Social Security of Rural-Urban Migrant Workers" [*nongmingong shehui baozhang wenti yanjiu shuping*]. Available online at: http://www.weiquan.org.cn/data/detail.php?id=4166 (accessed on June 1, 2006).

Ministry of Labor and Social Security (2002) "Flexible Employment: A Major Solution to Re-Employment." Available online at: http://www.china.org.cn/chinese/OP-c/149605.htm (accessed on June 5, 2006).

Moser, C. O. N. (1978) "Informal sector or petty commodity production: dualism or dependence in urban development?" *World Development*, 6(9–10): 1041–1064.

Moser, C. O. N. (1993) *Gender Planning and Development : Theory, Practice and Training*, London: Routledge.

Nair, R. P. (2004) *The Kerala construction labour welfare fund*. Working Paper 219, Sectoral Activities Programme, Geneva: International Labour Organisation.

National Bureau of Statistics of China (2005) "China Statistics Yearbook, 2005 Edition." Available online at: http://www.stats.gov.cn/tjsj/ndsj/ (accessed on June 1, 2006).

Neetha, N. (August 2006) "Invisibility' continues: social security and unpaid women workers," *Economic and Political Weekly*, 12: 3497–3499.

Rao, V. M., Rajasekhar, D. and Suchitra, J. Y. (August 2006) "Putting the cart before a non-existent horse," *Economic and Political Weekly*, 12: 3488–3491.

Ratnam, C. S. V. (1999) "India: collective bargaining – workers are less committed to any solidarity based on ideology and will readily shift their allegiance if unions do not deliver results," *Labour Education*, 1–2 (114–115): 84–91.

Sankaran, T. S. (August 12, 2006) "Can the best be the enemy of good, if the good is not good enough?" *Economic and Political Weekly*, 3491–3495.

Sassen, S. (1997) *Informalization in Advanced Market Economies*, Geneva: ILO.

Saunders, P. and Shang, X. (2001) "Social security reform in China's transition to a market economy," *Social Policy & Administration*, 35(3): 274–289.

Sundaram, S. K. G. (1997) "Organising the unorganised urban labour: Case studies from Maharashtra," in R. Dutt (ed.) *Organising the Unorganised Workers*, New Delhi: Vikas Publishing House, 95–105.

Tabak, F. and Crichlow, M. A. (eds) (2000) *Informalization: Process and Structure*, Baltimore, MA: The John Hopkins University Press.

Vimosewa (2006) "SEWA Insurance," Ahmadabad: SEWA. Available online at: http://www.sewainsurance.org/vimosewa.htm (accessed on June 6).

Wong, L. (1994) "Privatisation of social welfare in post-Mao China," *Asian Survey*, 34(4): 307–325.

Xie, H. (2003) "*The Dilemma of the Legal Status of Non-Government Organizations in China*" [*Zhongguo minjian zuzhi de hefaxing kunjing*]. Working Paper 280, Institute of Law, Beijing: Chinese Academy of Social Sciences [http://www.iolaw.org.cn/paper/paper280.asp].

Xinhua News Agency (2006) "The First Union for Workers from Rural Areas Received Funding Support": Xinhua News Agency. Available online at: http://news.xinhuanet.com/mrdx/2006-04/04/content_4381719.htm (accessed on June 1, 2006).

Zhan, S. and Han, J. (2005) "Non Profit Organizations for Rural-Urban Migrant Workers in China: Experiences and Challenges": Chinese Sociology Net. Available online at: http://203.93.24.66/shxw/shzc/t20050624_6321.htm (accessed on June 1, 2006).

Zhang, T. and Zou, H. (1998) "Fiscal decentralization, public spending and economic growth in China," *Journal of Public Economics*, 67: 221–240.

Zhao, L. (2001) "The non-profit sector and governance in China." Paper presented at the Conference on *International Forum on Governance in China*, September 11–13, Brighton: Institute of Development Studies.

Zhao, Y. H. and Xu, J. G. (2002) "China's urban pension system: reforms and problems," *Cato Journal*, 21(3): 395–414.

Zhou, Y. (2006) "Reducing pay in arrears and protecting labour interests," News for 14th session of Chinese People's Political Consultative Conference, June 1, 2006. Avabilable online at http://cppcc.people.com.cn/GB/3496/59086/59109/4183746.html

7 Ageing urban society
Discourse and policy

Ian G. Cook and Jason L. Powell

The experiences, representations and images of older people in China have increasingly become important in both the discipline and practice of social science. Indeed, social policy based on old age appears to be moving from its traditional concern with "public issues" in China to the question of how ageing is socially perceived and experienced by individual social actors related to consumerism on the one hand, and population control on the other (Powell and Cook 2000). Ageing identities have been grounded in policy discourses and professions of health and social care and the institutionalization of state care policy in China (Cook and Powell, 2005a). However, a perceived corrosion of these structures has led to an interiorization of the ground upon which a viable ageing identity can be constructed. There are two key issues that are important in exploring the relationship between personal experiences of ageing and policy discourse. Part of the seductive array of discourses centers on "active" lifestyles in urban society. Further, these discourses that impinge on ageing have thereby taken on a "normative" dimension, which mediates a daily understanding of what it is to "successfully" age through the life-course. It may be possible to critically assess social spaces created for older people in terms of the relationship allowed to exist between their inner world social identity and the outer world of China.

An examination of the relationship between China, urbanization and ageing policy must acknowledge the fact that social and economic discourses shape the perceptions of old age in the popular imagination. Ageing is a site upon which power is distributed and power games are played out mainly through "narratives." As Biggs and Powell (2001: 103) suggest

> narratives are not simply personal fictions that we choose to live by, but are discourses that are subject to social and historical influence. Narratives of aging [*sic*] are personal in so far as we apply techniques to ourselves, while the technologies and the ground on which they are told imply particular distributions of power that will determine the way and the what of the storyline.

Therefore, we need to take this into account when examining the assumptions that underpin gerontological discourse in China, while recognizing that

> "Discourse" itself is a phrase more often used to denote a relatively fixed set of stories that individuals or groups have to conform to in order to take up a recognised and legitimate role.
>
> (Powell 2005: 43)

When examining urbanization in China through the focus of ageing, social science needs to be seen as the product of one age group as it relates to another, and as such is intrinsically intergenerational in its social patterning and ramifications. China, of course, is on the move toward becoming a highly urbanized society, transformed from a peasant society over a period of decades rather than centuries. Although there is still a long way to go before urbanization levels reach those of such advanced capitalist societies as those of North America, Western Europe or Japan, the pace of change in China's emerging cities is truly remarkable. The contrasts with the Maoist era and its very tight controls over the population registration (*hukou*) system, without which migrants were unable to obtain such key necessities as food, access to jobs and healthcare, and shelter, are especially stark. From a situation in the 1950s through to the 1970s, in which China's cities and towns were relatively few in number, with urban centers characterized by austere values and a dominant production ethos, the country now has a burgeoning urban population largely focused on the more hedonistic pursuits of consumption. By 2004, official data from the *China Statistical Yearbook 2005* recognized 661 cities across China, with 41.8 percent of the total population classed as urban, compared to 28.5 percent in 1994 or 17.9 percent at the start of the reform era in 1978. And of course this recent figure of nigh on 42 percent is out of a population nudging 1.3 billion, so there are millions of people involved in, and affected by, this rapid socioeconomic transformation, both for good and ill.

Not only is China becoming highly urbanized, China's population is also rapidly ageing. The 2000 Census, for instance, showed that across the country the proportion of the elderly had reached nearly 7 percent, and it is well known that their numbers are increasing fast. Just over 88 million Chinese were aged 65 or over in 2000, compared to 25 million *less* in 1990, at 63.2 million, while there were only 26.2 million within the whole elderly category in 1953, the date of the first Census in the People's Republic (Cook and Powell 2005a: 74). Further, the distribution of the elderly is highly spatially uneven, including a mainly residual population in remote rural areas but more especially a growing proportion of the elderly within these burgeoning cities in China. Leading the way with nearly double the national average of elderly people is Shanghai, which "has become a society of the aged" according to the China Population Information Research Centre (CPIRC) in Beijing. The rapid growth in numbers of the elderly has led to great concerns among China's leadership, and such newspaper headlines in the West as

"Still-growing China faces crisis supporting ageing population" (Beck 2005). Our purpose in this chapter is to build on our previous published work on the elderly in China to explore the theoretical and policy dimensions interwoven between these two trajectories of rapidly emerging cities and rapidly ageing populations. We begin via consideration of the empirical parameters in more detail.

Urban and elderly trajectories

From the most recent Yearbook available at the time of writing, we have selected as a starting point the figures shown in Table 7.1, for cities with an official residential population of five million or more. Note that this data excludes significant numbers of the floating population (*liudong renkou*) within these cities, in the largest cities probably two to three million people according to best estimates. As Table 7.1 shows, 23 cities across the country have five million or more, even without the floating population, having nearly 200 million residents in total, an amazing number even by Chinese standards, especially given that in 1953 the *total* urban population was 78 million. These large cities have arisen largely as the result of policy decisions made by the central government, as a key part of China's drive to become a modern economy, fueled by dramatically high levels of investment, from the state and local state into infrastructure, and from Foreign Direct Investment (FDI) into manufacturing, retailing and the property market in particular. Today, the cities are themselves the drivers of fundamental socioeconomic change, not just at the local or national levels but also increasingly at the global level too (see e.g. the chapters in Wu 2006). Further, their growing linkages with neighboring cities are leading to the development of more embedded Extended Metropolitan Regions (EMRs) along the eastern seaboard, further deepening and widening the transformative structures and processes at work within China (Pannell 2002: 1584). And so, as we have calculated, the average GPD of these cities is 222.9 billion yuan, while that of Guangzhou and Beijing is nearly double that, and Shanghai is leading the way at around 3.5 times that figure. The revenue captured by local government mirrors such figures, contributing to a virtuous circle of further investment, while savings of individuals are also at a high level, averaging 82.6 billion yuan in these cities, and being especially high in Beijing and Shanghai; this too will be translated at some point into investment in consumer durables, housing and the like.

This is of course part of the upside of China's emerging cities. They are exciting dynamic locations in which to live and work. Many people are prospering within these cities and are gaining access to the fruits of their labor, as well as to the opportunities afforded by global links. The middle classes are growing both in numbers and in wealth. But there is also a downside. The speed of change stretches the social fabric enormously, for instance via large-scale annual migration, great social tensions between the haves and the have-nots, glaring contrasts in consumption between the wealthy and the poor, new health problems of obesity, smoking-related diseases, threats of epidemics such as HIV/AIDS, SARS, or Avian Flu – all within a built environment of continual demolition and large scale urban renewal. Many

Table 7.1 A comparison of socioeconomic indicators in large Chinese cities in 2004

City	Total hukou population (million)	GDP (billion yuan)	Local government revenue (billion yuan)	Total investment in fixed assets (billion yuan)	Fully employed staff and workers (million)	Savings deposits of residents (billion yuan)
Shanghai	13.524	745.0	112.0	289.7	2.680	696.1
Beijing	11.629	428.3	74.4	233.3	4.432	715.4
Guangzhou	7.377	411.6	30.3	125.4	1.865	425.7
Tianjin	9.326	293.2	24.6	86.8	1.726	211.7
Chongqing	31.442	266.5	20.1	147.7	2.048	219.0
Hangzhou	6.517	251.5	19.7	88.0	0.757	183.5
Chengdu	10.597	218.6	10.8	101.3	1.228	172.6
Qingdao	7.311	216.4	13.1	77.9	1.125	108.9
Ningbo	5.527	215.8	15.2	75.3	0.651	120.9
Dalian	5.615	196.2	11.7	58.0	0.819	145.3
Wuhan	7.859	195.6	10.4	79.7	1.363	145.3
Nanjing	5.836	191.0	17.0	99.0	0.855	128.7
Shenyang	6.939	190.1	11.0	93.8	0.951	167.2
Harbin	9.702	168.0	9.6	50.5	1.601	126.1
Jinan	5.901	161.9	8.9	54.8	0.788	87.1
Shijiazhuang	9.176	155.5	5.6	58.5	0.861	118.9
Fuzhou	6.094	154.8	7.5	47.4	0.782	99.6
Changchun	7.240	153.5	5.1	41.7	0.886	96.5
Zhengzhou	6.712	137.8	10.5	47.7	0.856	121.1
Changsha	6.104	113.4	8.1	59.1	0.629	80.1
Xi'an	7.250	109.6	7.5	60.6	1.142	143.3
Kunming	5.029	94.2	7.3	41.7	0.696	82.6
Nanning	6.489	58.9	4.3	25.4	0.537	51.6

Source: State Statistical Bureau (2005).

such pressures are familiar enough to those living in other urban societies, but it is the rapidity of urban change within the twenty-first century context of rapid social change at the global level that makes the Chinese situation almost unique, with perhaps only urban change in India being truly comparable in the contemporary era. But this process in China is happening within a one-party system in which the Chinese Communist Party dominates strategy and policy, making a fascinating contrast with urban change within the Indian democratic system.

Turning now to the elderly population of China, Table 7.2 updates and expands upon the data given for the year 2000 and for 2003 (Cook and Powell 2005a,b). The spatial pattern remains unsurprisingly very similar, with generally minor movements in the table. Thus, it is generally the heavily urbanized provinces of Eastern China that contain the highest proportions of elderly populations, with percentages generally over 9, contrasting with poor, rural, interior provinces in the mainland, with percentages less than 7. In this category is 15.4 percent of the population of Shanghai, while there are high proportions too for the other urban metropolises of Beijing, Tianjin and Chongqing, and also Jiangsu province.[1] We have also included for comparison data on the proportion of young children, and also "dependency rates."[2]

To conclude this section it is pertinent to briefly present the prognosis for future numbers of the elderly in China. Estimates vary, but analysts agree that later this century the proportion of the elderly will be at least double, and could even exceed triple, that of the current percentage, possibly to 27.1 percent by 2100 (Cook and Powell 2005a: 76). There will continue to be a broad regional disparity for some decades, with the Western region lagging in proportion behind the Eastern and central regions, but eventually convergence will be reached, by 2060 (ibid). The implication of this projection is that eventually urban–rural contrasts too will disappear, but much will depend on the resolution of sociospatial health disparities (Cook and Dummer 2004) which currently affect rural populations to a greater extent than urban ones, and hence longevity may continue to lag within rural areas. In an attempt to tackle such inequalities the Chinese government has just announced a substantial increase in funding for the rural health insurance system, but it is likely that the disparities between cities and countryside will continue for some time, including disparities in ratios of the elderly to the rest of the population.

The economic discourse

As we have noted in previous work, as in many other countries the official view of the growth in numbers of the elderly is driven by fear – that China's phenomenal economic success of recent decades will be undermined by the sheer volume and scale of economic resources that will be required to look after this elderly cohort. "Dependency rates" are widely referred to, rates that combine the numbers of children with the retired, as in Table 7.2. But we suggest that the concept of dependency is complex and requires some unraveling. Since the 1980s, the demographic success of the Single Child Family Program, notwithstanding the

Table 7.2 Demographic data by province in China in 2004

Province	Total population (million)	Gross dependency ratio	Children dependency ratio	Elderly Dependency Ratio	0–14 years old (%)	65 years old and over (%)
Shanghai	16.702	31.92	11.60	20.31	8.8	15.4
Chongqing	31.442	47.75	30.84	16.92	20.3	11.1
Beijing	14.213	26.71	12.62	14.10	10.0	11.1
Tianjin	9.868	31.40	17.23	14.18	13.1	10.8
Jiangsu	72.295	37.08	22.38	14.70	16.3	10.7
Zhejiang	45.682	34.04	20.92	13.11	15.6	9.8
Liaoning	41.100	30.49	18.14	12.34	13.9	9.5
Shandong	89.072	35.77	23.25	12.51	17.1	9.2
Hunan	65.041	37.58	25.50	12.08	18.5	8.8
Sichuan	84.919	39.63	27.40	12.23	19.6	8.8
Anhui	62.575	43.29	31.09	12.21	21.7	8.5
Fujian	34.048	38.46	26.67	11.78	19.3	8.5
Guangxi	47.408	41.62	29.68	11.94	21.0	8.4
Hubei	58.510	37.86	26.57	11.29	19.3	8.2
Henan	94.372	41.56	30.05	11.51	21.2	8.1
Jiangxi	41.524	42.07	30.67	11.40	21.6	8.0
Hebei	66.078	34.11	23.40	10.71	17.5	8.0
Guangdong	77.645	49.39	37.57	11.82	25.2	7.9
Yunnan	42.720	43.27	32.20	11.07	22.5	7.7
Shaanxi	36.022	37.85	27.31	10.55	19.8	7.7
Guizhou	37.780	49.37	38.11	11.25	25.5	7.5
Hainan	7.916	45.81	34.85	10.96	23.9	7.5
Inner Mongolia	23.233	32.61	22.70	9.91	17.1	7.5
Jilin	26.397	27.14	17.66	9.48	13.9	7.5
Shanxi	32.352	39.34	29.51	9.83	21.2	7.1
Heilongjiang	37.241	27.11	18.48	8.64	14.5	6.8
Gansu	25.409	40.24	30.97	9.27	22.1	6.6
Tibet	2.636	45.38	36.03	9.35	24.8	6.4
Xinjiang	18.880	39.53	30.79	8.74	22.1	6.3
Qinghai	5.213	41.26	32.94	8.32	23.3	5.9
Ningxia	5.662	45.97	37.70	8.28	25.8	5.7
National Total	1253065	38.63	26.76	11.87	19.3	8.6

Source: State Statistical Bureau (2005).

Notes
Data in this table are obtained from the Sample Survey on Population Changes in 2004. The sampling fraction is 0.966‰. Data for Beijing, Tianjin and Shanghai includes floating population. Figure for Chongqing appeared to be an error within the data source therefore the figure entered is the same as that in Table 1. Final two columns are authors' calculations.

ethical questions associated with it, has led to a *decrease* in dependency as far as the proportion of children is concerned. Again, this is similar to the outcomes in other countries too, even if the policy in China has been seen to be more draconian. Further, the decrease in number of children is spatially uneven, and it is well known, for example, that farmers were more likely to be allowed to have another child if the first one was female, that ethnic minorities were allowed to have more than one child lest the State be seen to be ethnically discriminatory, and that undercounting of female births is more likely in rural areas. Lou Binbin of CPIRC, cited by

Beck (2005), suggested that, in reality, in the cities there has been a one-child policy, but in the countryside fundamentally it has been two kids. This is the so-called one-and-a-half-child policy.

In all, therefore, if one considers Table 7.2, it is seen that the rates and patterns of dependency vary tremendously, and if anything it would seem that the urban areas are those in which dependency rates are less. The question of dependency, therefore, may well be one for the PRC government as a whole to consider, but at least in the short term it does not seem to be a particular problem for China's emerging cities. In addition, these cities are attracting huge numbers of migrant workers who contribute further to their vibrant economic expansion, and make the notion of dependency on only a few people of working age even more questionable. Also, note the savings rates in Table 7.1: these are urban entities in which wealth is rapidly accumulating.

But the issue of dependency refuses to go away. A recent article in *Beijing Today* notes that in Beijing the number of children has fallen by 283,000 from five years ago, but that the number of people aged over 65 years has by contrast risen, and now exceeds 1,660,000. This is 10.8 percent of the city's total population. The figure shows that every 100 working people are supporting 13 children and 14 seniors (Chen 2006). Also, Zhang (2002) notes, *inter alia*, "the paramount challenge for an ageing community is how to support and care for these *vulnerable people* (our emphasis) . . . the number of retired people is expanding rapidly and expenditure on pensions is growing even more quickly. In 1978, there was one retired person for every 30.3 employees. In 1999, the ratio had soared to one retired person for only 3.7 employees. If the current retirement ages remain unchanged at 55 for women and 60 for men, the ratio may climb further to one retired person for 2.4 employees by 2030" (Zhang 2002). But China in 1999 was a vastly different country from what it was in 1978 when poverty was widespread, and China in 2030 will be different again by an order of magnitude, in all probability. In other words, 30 employees in 1978 working in a commune situation would produce far less than 3.7 employees in 1999 working in a "town and village enterprise" and less than 2.4 working in a joint venture by 2030 for instance, especially if they were working in one of China's emerging cities.

We have suggested that ageist constructions underlie such common assumptions that older people are particularly vulnerable to the negative effects of economic urbanization. Many citizens across the life-course may feel vulnerable for a number of reasons. For example, where older people are identified as the most vulnerable in Chinese communities, it is in their relationship of dependency upon their family for essential daily care (Cook and Powell, 2005a). When older people feel vulnerable, their ability to withstand victimization may be substantially reduced. The level of vulnerability among older people is conditional upon their level of deprivation. The combined determinants of gender, poverty and age result in more vulnerability amongst elderly people than in other social groups.

Of course we acknowledge that it is certainly prudent to ensure that resources are available for one's retirement age But who exactly should pay for this? Deng Xiaoping sought to "smash the iron rice bowl" of welfare available for former employees of State-Owned Enterprises (SOEs). Today, welfare support rests upon a "multi pillar" approach (Williamson and Deitelbaum 2005) with the pillars being an individual contribution of 8 percent to mandatory individual accounts plus a 20 percent employer contribution to the first pillar in a pay-as-you-go defined benefit (PAYGO DB) scheme . Williamson and Deitelbaum note that the new system (modified in 2000) has proven to be difficult to develop and faces many teething problems, not least because of China's relatively underdeveloped financial markets, which are not yet best placed to handle large-scale pension funds. They question the origin of this partial privatization, and suggest that Chinese policymakers have sought to link into networks of experts around the world. Thus

> there have not only been extensive contacts between the World Bank and other such financial institutions, there have also been extensive contacts with various American think tanks, particularly those, such as the Cato Institute, espousing the partial or full privatization of the Chinese social security system.
>
> (Williamson and Deitelbaum 2005: 267)

The outcome has been the development of a system in which

> it is very likely that the most vulnerable (including recent immigrants from the countryside, unmarried women, low-wage workers, and those who have had irregular work histories due to mental health and other problems) are going to be put at the greatest risk and the most affluent workers are most likely to benefit. *The scheme is going to be much less redistributive than the scheme it is replacing* (our emphasis). This is a particularly serious problem for a nation with so many expected to be living at the economic margins during their retirement years.
>
> (Ibid: 268)

These are serious concerns. The authors suggest that there are three alternatives to the new system: first, to phase out the individual pillar completely; second, to replace the PAYGO DB pillar with a provident fund model as used in Singapore and several other ex-British colonies; or, thirdly, to replace the individual pillar with a pay-as-you-go or *notional* contribution model. This compromise system would offer greater protection to workers from market fluctuations of the type seen in the Asian Financial Crisis of the late 1990s, and is a system now being used in such diverse countries as Sweden, Italy, Poland or Mongolia.

The social discourse

The previous section illustrates the role of global experts, who operate from a neoliberal perspective in advising the PRC to offer privatized or semiprivatized alternatives to previous pension systems. This emphasis on the expert gaze dovetails neatly with much of our own work that similarly highlights the pernicious influence of the biomedical view and of a predominance of emphasis on biological ageing in the analysis and interpretation of an ageing "problem" in China's emerging cities. What Williamson and Deitelbaum attribute to economic globalization, we have linked to similar tropes of industrialization, Westernization and urbanization as the roots of rationalistic, positivistic and modernistic views of the ageing body.

> Biological and psychological characteristics associated with aging have been used to construct scientific representations of ageing in modern society. The characteristics of biological aging as associated with loss of skin elasticity, wrinkled skin, hair loss or physical frailty perpetuates [*sic*] powerful assumptions that help facilitate attitudes and perceptions of aging. It may be argued that rather than provide a scientific explanation of aging, such an approach homogenizes the experiences of aging by suggesting these characteristics are universal, natural and inevitable. These assumptions are powerful in creating a knowledge base for health and social welfare professionals who work with older people in particular medical settings such as a hospital or general doctors' surgery and also for social workers.
>
> (Powell and Biggs 2000: 17)

These new forms of social regulation were also reflected in the family and the community. Hence, modern systems of social regulation have become increasingly blurred and wide ranging (Powell 2001). Increasingly, modern society has regulated the population construct by sanctioning the knowledge and practices of the new human sciences – particularly psychology and biology. These are called gerontological "episteme" which are "the total set of relations that unite at a given period, the discursive practices that give rise to epistemological figures, sciences and possibly formalized systems" (Foucault 1972: 191; Cook and Powell 2005a: 79–80).

There has long been a tendency in matters of ageing and old age to reduce the social experience of ageing to its biological dimension, from which are derived a set of normative "stages" that over-determine the experience of ageing. Accordingly being "old," for example, would primarily be an individualized experience of adaptation to inevitable physical and mental decline and of preparation for death (Powell 2005). The paradox of course is that the homogenizing of the experience of old age, which the reliance on the biological dimension of old age entails, is in fact one of the key elements of the dominant discourse on ageing and old age.

Powell and Cook (2000) highlight how individual lives and physical and mental capacities which were thought to be determined solely by biological and psychological factors are, in fact, heavily influenced by urban environments in which people live in China. Biggs (1993) suggests that a prevailing ideology of ageism manifests biomedical models of ageing, suggesting that persons with such biological ageing traits have entered a spiral of "decay," "decline" and "deterioration." Along with this goes certain assumptions about the ways in which people with outward signs of ageing are likely to think and behave. These are "all explained away by "decline" and "deterioration": master narratives that comprise an ageing culture. The effects of the "decay, decline and deterioration" analogies can be most clearly seen in the dominance of medico-technical solutions to the problems that ageing and even an "aging population" is thought to pose. Here, the biomedical model has both come to colonize notions of age and reinforce ageist social preju-dices to the extent that "decline" has come to stand for the process of aging itself" (Cook and Powell, 2005b: 80–81).

It is interesting that comparative research on ageing in eastern culture highlights an alternative perception of the process; eighteenth century China indicates a rather different path than the conceptualization of ageing as a scientific process developed by Western rationality. For example, Powell and Cook (2001) observe that traditional Chinese society placed older people on a pedestal. They were valued for their accumulated knowledge, their position within the extended family, and the sense of history and identity which they helped the family to develop (Murray 1998). Respect for elderly people was an integral part of Confucian doctrine, especially for the family patriarch.

> The mixed love, fear and awe of the children for their father was strengthened by the great respect paid to age. An old man's loss of vigor was more than offset by his growth in wisdom. The patriarch possessed every sanction to enable him to dominate the family scene.
>
> (Fairbank 1959, in Powell and Cook 2001: 55)

This was a view that was also prevalent in Ancient Greece, with the notions of "respect" for older people, especially regarding gendered issues of patriarchy (Bytheway 1995). Prior to industrialization, in India, there was an acknowledg-ment that older people had responsible leadership roles and powerful decision-making positions because of their vast "experience," "wisdom" and "knowledge" (Katz 1996). It seems that, with the instigation of Western science and rationality, ageing began to be viewed in a different, more problematic context than that of the Confucian doctrine of ageing epitomized in China and issues of respect for ageing in India.

One of the ways to interpret populational ageing in China is through theorizing on what it means to age in society. There are concerns and social issues associated with ageing and these concerns are influenced by society whilst, at the same time, influencing society. The fear of crime is such a concern and operates on a myriad of emotional and practical levels, from making one feel vulnerable and isolated, to affecting one's personal wellbeing.

Many Chinese citizens may feel vulnerable for a number of reasons. Some may feel unable to protect themselves physically or economically, or feel themselves incapable of making a fast retreat. Three environmental clues – incivilities, neigh-borhood housing conditions, and neighborhood cohesion – all make a contribution toward vulnerability, particularly for older people, and tend to highlight people's feelings of dependency and vulnerability. Again, the themes of "decay, decline and deterioration" are pertinent, and, as Bytheway (1995: 37) has suggested.

> Although many of our older population are healthy and active, the physical
> consequences of a push, a shove or a fall are likely to be far more traumatic at
> an older than at a younger age. Even the problems of replacing pension books,
> library tickets, cheque books and other documentation ... may become more
> demanding and tiresome when we are older.

Such gerontological episteme as these, we argue, underpin the PRC's view of
the elderly in an ageist perspective in which being elderly, being disabled, and
being "vulnerable" are rolled together in one biomedical gaze under which the
ageing body becomes the object of government surveillance and the exercise of
power – points explored further in our earlier work (Powell and Cook 2000, 2001).
Ironically, the solutions to the "problems of ageing" are tractable to disciplines
such as gerontology, because they seem to promise answers to age prejudice and
marginalization. For example, the resulting "bio-medicalization of aging" (Powell
2005) socially constructs old age as a process of physical decline and places ageing
under the domain and control of biomedicine in such a way as to have influence
on societies such as the Chinese. Theories of ageing, albeit in contrasting ways,
see these phenomena as indicating particular sites of resistance in which dominant biomedical conceptualizations of ageing are to be contested and alternative
explanations can be intimated. Powell (2005) has claimed that social theories of
ageing are relatively uncultivated territory. Despite this, it would be somewhat
foolish to suggest that there are no social theories of ageing. One major issue for
social theorizing of ageing is the problematic of "successful" ageing (also known
as active ageing).

This was also influential in the development of the idea of active ageing as
"successful ageing" that has dominated discursive views of ageing in recent years.
Successful ageing attempts a strategic understanding of late-life issues, grounded
in psychological behavior that arises spontaneously amongst older people in particular (Baltes and Carstensen 1996). It sidesteps the issue of prescribing content
by engaging with psychological processes, and thus moving from questioning the
"what" of aging to the "how" (Baltes and Carstensen 1996). It is claimed that
older people are satisfied because they have found personal and existential strategies to minimize the losses and maximize the gains encountered as individuals age.
According to these authors, this model has the advantage of acknowledging socioe-
motional dimensions of ageing and multiple possibilities for self-development, and
is based on the meta-priority of mastering the challenges of ageing, whilst allowing
wide variety in the ways mastery can be achieved. Everyday existence is converted
into successful activities, which are converted into life-satisfaction through techniques applied to the self. Moody (1998) has quipped that the approach divides
the population into the "wellderly" and the "illderly" and that "successful ageing"
is essentially about "surviving" in urban spaces. Fundamentally, activity theory
maintains that any loss of roles, activities, or relationships within old age should be
replaced by activities to ensure happiness, value consensus, and well being; moral

positioning of ageing. Activity theories are a response to the problematization of older people as nonproductive. However, these have been criticized for being unreflective in their attachment to content over explanation (Powell 2005). Activity engages in a particular reductionism in presupposing that old age is defined entirely by the explanation of activity and engages in functional teleology in attempting to explain old age in terms of its effects on retirement.

This view has rich epistemological and ontological implications in terms of understanding the ageing self, China and urban reality. However, it also has important social policy ramifications. It both feeds and draws upon attempts to overcome the ageing body and, in the final analysis, death itself. In terms of identity, we are talking about the possibilities of reinvention and a denial of limits. In many ways this approach also reflects the "outside-looking-in" perspective in so far as, as theory, personal experience is also embounded by the external and the possibilities that the external (China) makes available for meaningful social action (ageing identity).

The discourse that comes to dominate the official agenda is one in which, because of their age, the elderly are universally vulnerable (as highlighted by Zhang above), and are subjects of inevitable decline and decay, with deterioration of performance in all areas as a direct consequence of their age. Age becomes the key single independent variable on which all other outcomes depend, rather than, for instance, location, social status, gender, ethnicity, wealth, family circumstances and a myriad of other attributes and characteristics that differentiate and heterogenize people one from the other. Nor is this to deny that *some* elderly are vulnerable, that *some* elderly require specific help and support in order to deal with their health and social circumstances, that *some* elderly can no longer live independently in the family home. But, we argue, the overriding emphasis on the biomedicalization of ageing leads to policies that are too broad-brush and sweeping to deal effectively with the myriad of circumstances in which the elderly, as with all others in society, find themselves.

Instead of this biomedical approach, we advocate the recognition and realization that age is primarily a social constructed problem and also "the symptomatic deep manifestation of underlying relations of power and inequality that cuts across and through age, class, gender, disability and sexuality" (Cook and Powell 2005a: 81). How absurd can it be that once an individual becomes 55, 60, 65, or some other socially defined age point, this person switches overnight to being "old," seemingly having a completely different, univariate, set of social and economic attributes from that of the day before? Note that, further, the biomedical model intertwines with the neoliberal model discussed above, to ensure that once this date arrives, the ageing body will be immediately targeted by an increasingly privatized army of care givers who wish to take this body under its purview – provided, that is, the ageing body does not prove to be too difficult to look after either economically or socially. Should the latter prove to be the case then the aged body will be transferred to state agencies for more expensive "treatment" to be applied.

Even the officially sanctioned *China Daily* has focused on this last issue via an article on care homes in Shanghai in 2004, confirming a point made in one of our earlier articles. Care homes are not set up to deal with the wide range of conditions that the elderly face. Instead, many prefer those still capable of independent living, although others may prefer bedridden patients. But, those with the relatively common condition of dementia "are generally excluded by the criteria" according to this investigative report. Also, changes in the patient's condition mean that he or she is forced to leave the home – which in any case is unlikely due to concerns for cost or accident liabilities to have a full range of preventive care, physical therapy or spiritual care available. Despite such concerns, the patients in such homes are the lucky ones, because the lack of government subsidies for such residential care means that many are excluded by financial circumstances from accessing even this relatively low level of care support. Where Shanghai leads, other emerging cities in China will follow. Unless greater resources are provided to improve access to such residential care, and then to improve the care within such homes, more elderly people will face a potentially miserable old age without sufficient support to assist them.

Who will these excluded elderly be? Concordant with the analysis of Williamson and Deitelbaum referred to previously, it will be the poorest elderly living in the poorest parts of the city. It is *these* elderly who are potentially vulnerable, not the elderly in general, while even within this category it will be specific elderly whose circumstances in terms of such parameters as impaired mobility, lack of access to family support or mental problems, or some combination of such variables, who are most in need of support. Others will not need such support. In this latter group will be those who remain fit and active, who can access family or community support more readily, who have a spouse, or who have greater financial resources, for example. We have reviewed the active elderly in China (Cook and Powell 2003). Here, we can summarize our main conclusions as being the need to regard the elderly as "invisible resources" to society rather than as burdens; to assist them to engage with others via use of their knowledge, accumulated experience and wisdom; to recover the traditions of veneration for the elderly within China and to provide facilities wherever possible for the elderly to remain physically and intellectually active. No picture of China's emerging cities would be complete without the images of the active elderly, engaged in *taijiquan* and *qigong*, ballroom dancing *en plein air*, exercising on roadside exercise machines, kite flying and other leisure pursuits, colonizing whatever tiny space is available beside the roadside, on areas flattened by bulldozers, or in linear and more conventionally rounded urban parks.

It is in these and similar images that the seeds of a more sophisticated policy and discourse will be found. Already there are signs that China's policymakers are engaging with the multidimensional facets of ageing via a range of initiatives. These range from the rather coercive "Law on the Rights and Interests of the Elderly," promulgated in late 1996, that, among other things, seeks to force families to offer financial support to their elderly parents, and encourages campaigns to "respect the elderly." The whole of society has to be involved in support for the elderly, according to Zhang Kaiti, vice-director of the China Research Center on Aging, cited by Wu (2003). Zhang argues that the elderly now have "higher and more special demands in their lives. First, they have to be out in society and that will help them not to be lonely. Second, children should return to see their parents often and communicate with them regularly. This is what is best for the elderly." High-quality services are also required, with 40 percent of the elderly interviewed in a major survey by the Center on Aging wishing for "someone to talk to" and assistance from the community when they had to go out. Such requests need not be expensive, and Zhang suggested that costs of providing this service and that of a medical service, life service and volunteer service is low, but it could have a better all round effect. All-in-all a better environment for the elderly could be created when society accepts that they need respect and help.

Theorizing ageing urban society

The elderly in China are being faced by a society undergoing rapid change. Nowhere is the pace of change more marked than in China's emerging cities, although in specific pockets of rural society change will also be fast. Traditionally in China, as we have shown above, the elderly were revered as the guardians of family tradition, as the fount of wisdom passed on from the ancestors. The Confucian tradition bolstered the standing of the family patriarch and he in turn upheld the virtues of Confucian tradition; but what of today, especially in an urban society in such a welter of transformation? The Chinese Communist Party (CCP) attacked and denigrated Confucian traditions in order to lead the change from an inward-looking tradition-obsessed feudal system toward an outward-looking modern society capable of dealing with the complex globalized world of today. However, in recent years the CCP has begun to change tack, recognizing that Confucianism can help stabilize the social system within such a maelstrom of change. There is a growing reemphasis on filial duty, on obligation to parents and grandparents – in part to dilute the selfishness of the "Little Emperors" and "Little Empresses" that are the outcome of the single child policy – and on looking out for the elderly. In our most recent work (Powell and Cook 2006) we have begun to theorize this via an emphasis on Judith Butler's concept of performativity, a concept originally developed to explain how dissent and opposition to norms of familial and sexual behavior can be subverted and opposed even where these norms seem to be at their most oppressive and rigid.

In this work is a "strong" conception of discourse, positing identity as discursively constituted, which treads between the extremes of the social constructivist debate, accounting for both constraint and potential for transformation through discourse. Butler is arguing for an "understanding of performativity not as the act by which a subject brings into being what she/he names but rather as that reiterative power of discourse to produce the phenomena that it regulates and constrains" (Butler 1993: 2). In doing so, Butler attempts a novel reworking of the tired structure/agency debate and offers a persuasive notion of subjectivity that is in no way predetermined but is nonetheless "always already" *compromised*. Or as Butler clarifies, "Social categories signify subordination and existence at once. In other words, within subjection the price of existence is subordination"

(Butler 1998: 20). In our latest article we cite a number of examples, including that in Mao Zedong's upbringing, of strong patriarchal traditions in China that, although at first seeming unbending and unbreakable, nevertheless offer the potential for dissent and overthrow.

The first example we provide is of the contradictory nature of the power of the patriarch, who even if he begins to become frail still retains the utterances of control and ritual within the family; but increasingly the utterances can become empty of power, even though the family will continue to pay lip service to his demands. The patriarch no longer has real power in the family, for it is his wife and sons who begin to wield this power rather than the patriarch himself. In this process is a link between performativity and rituals, institutions and ultimately social structures – "performative utterances" are institutionalized over time and hence become identifiable and carry meaning. Secondly, it is this circular, reiterative aspect to performativity that provides the space for adaptation and change and by the same token for a practical and pragmatic form of resistance (or perhaps, subversion). Age brought changing opportunities for resistance for different family members, and for combating the gendered aspects of Chinese social structure. And it is this latter point on (re)iteration which best encapsulates Butler's potential contribution to Foucauldian analyses of China. We also employ Mao's example to show that it was only when he stood up to the bullying of a teacher, and of his father too, that these elders "backed off," respecting him for what we would call "daring to dare" against their power and authority.

Today, in theory these patriarchal performativities of the type Mao opposed are no longer relevant, but in practice the elderly are still being faced with such concerns and are themselves developing new ones. As we put it elsewhere

> The elderly in China today are grappling with contrasting takes from that of the inbuilt patriarchic performativities of the pre-revolutionary period noted above. New conceptualizations of society, of aging, of social responsibilities, of material wealth, of rapid urban change are all combining to provide a context of remarkable social dynamism and challenge. But the concept of performativity helps us as social analysts to realize that China's elderly are not mere victims in a sea of turbulence; rather they are themselves an intrinsic part of this changing environment of the contemporary "Middle Kingdom".
>
> (Powell and Cook 2006)

Conclusion

In China's emerging cities lie a plethora of threats and opportunities for the future. There are threats of social exclusion and marginalization on the one hand, contrasting with opportunities for wealth creation and refined lifestyles on the other. China's growing number of urban elderly will face the same challenges faced by other urban dwellers, and although it may be tempting to see them more as potential victims due to their age we call upon researchers and policymakers alike to resist such facile stereotyping in order to develop specifically targeted sophisticated policies working with elderly residents themselves to discover their needs and wishes rather than assuming that all elderly wish the same outcomes because of their "age." In China, some elderly will not only be "illderly" or "wellderly," but "poorderly," "richderly," "femderly," "malederly," "Handerly" or "nonHanderly," for example. The survey conducted by the Center for Aging noted above showed that by 2000 the average income of the elderly across the country was four times that of 1992, and we have already shown in Table 7.1 the high rates of local authority revenue and savings within China's large cities. Contrary to dominant gloomy economist interpretations, therefore, we suggest that China's emerging cities at least will *not* be faced with a major resource deficit in consequence of their elderly population. Instead, they are likely to contain an active or fairly active group of elderly residents who can and will make a wider contribution to urban society rather than being dependent upon it. In terms of urban policy a pointillistic rather than broad-brush approach is required to ensure that the most vulnerable of the elderly receive the support that they require, while helping those who are less vulnerable to maintain their independence. If the latter policy is to bear fruit, the prevailing biomedical discourse must be resisted and replaced by one that shows that age is predominantly a social construct rather than a biomedical condition. In an era of "silver surfers" or "the grey pound," we would expect more such reinterpretations of the elderly within China itself, not just in the West.

Notes

1 Note that, as the footnote of the table suggests, we are not totally confident in the Chongqing percentage of the elderly, given that there is a question mark over the city's population recorded in the Yearbook table from which this information is extracted.
2 Whether this concept of dependency is proper or not in this context is still debatable.

References

Baltes, M. and Carstensen, L. (1996) "The process of successful ageing," *Ageing and Society*, 16: 397–422.
Beck, L (January 5, 2005) "Still-growing China faces crisis supporting ageing population," *The Scotsman*.
Biggs, S. (1993) *Understanding Ageing*, Milton Keynes: Open University Press.
Biggs, S. and Powell, J. L. (2001) "A Foucauldian analysis of old age and the power of social welfare," *Journal of Aging, Social Policy*, 12(2): 93–112.
Butler, J. (1993) *Bodies That Matter: On the Discursive Limits Of "Sex,"* London: Routledge.
Butler, J. (1998) *The Psychic Life of Power: Theories in Subjection*, Stanford, CA: Stanford University Press.
Bytheway, B. (1995) *Ageism*, Milton Keynes: Open University Press.
Chen, S. (March 24, 2006) "Beijing has fewer children and more seniors," *Beijing Today*. *China Daily* (April 5, 2004) "Tailoring health care policies for the elderly."
Cook, I. G. and Dummer, T. J. B. (2004) "Changing health in China: re-evaluating the epidemiological transition model," *Health Policy*, 67(3): 329–343.

Cook, I. G. and Powell, J. L. (Summer 2003) "Active aging and China: a critical excursion," *Syncronia*.

Cook, I. G. and Powell, J. L. (2005a) "China, aging and social policy: the influences and limitations of the bio-medical paradigm," *Journal of Societal and Social Policy*, 4(2): 71–89.

Cook, I. G. and Powell, J. L. (2005b) China and ageing: the influences of the bio-medical paradigm on population discourse and health policy, Paper presented in the China Session: "Continuity, transition and transcendence: urban development and reform in China (2)," *RGS/IBG Annual Conference*, September, London.

Foucault, M. (1972) *The Archaeology of Knowledge*, London: Tavistock.

Katz, S. (1996) *Disciplining Old Age: The Formation of Gerontological Knowledge*, Charlottesville, VA: Virginia University Press.

Moody, H. R. (1998) *Aging, Concepts and Controversies*, Thousand Oaks, CA: Pie Forge Press and Sage.

Murray, G. (1998) *China: The Next Superpower*, London: China Library.

Pannell, C. W. (2002) "China's continuing urban transition," *Environment and Planning A*, 34: 1571–1589.

Powell, J. L. (2001) "Theorizing gerontology: the case of old age, professional power and social policy in the United Kingdom," *Journal of Aging and Identity*, 6(3): 117–135.

Powell, J. L. (2005) *Social Theory and Aging*, Rowman and Littlefield: New York.

Powell, J. P. and Biggs, S. (2000) "Managing old age: the disciplinary web of power, surveillance and normalisation," *Journal of Aging and Identity*, 5(1): 3–13.

Powell, J. P. and Cook, I. G. (2000) "A tiger behind and coming up fast: governmentality and the politics of population control in China," *Journal of Aging and Identity*, 5(2): 79–89.

Powell, J. P. and Cook, I. G. (2001) "Understanding foucauldian gerontology: the Chinese state and the surveillance of older people," *International Journal of Society, Language and Culture*, 8(1): 1–9.

Powell, J. P. and Cook, I. G. (2006) "Unpacking patriarchy: a case study of patriarchy and the elderly in China" *International Journal of Sociology and Social Policy*, 26(7/8): 277–283.

State Statistical Bureau. (2005) *China Statistical Yearbook 2005*, Beijing: China Statistics Press.

Williamson, J. B. and Deitelbaum, C. (2005) "Social security reform: does partial privatisation make sense for China?," *Journal of Aging Studies*, 19: 257–271.

Wu, F. (ed.) (2006) *Globalization and the Chinese City*, London: Routledge.

Wu, N. (2003) "China improves life for the elderly," available online at: www.china.org.cn.htm (accessed May 23, 2006).

Zhang, B. (2002) "Ageing population requires new action," China Population Information Research Centre. Available online at: www.cpirc.org.cn/en/enews20020329.htm (accessed October 17, 2005).

8 Transition to homeownership

Implications for wealth redistribution

Si-ming Li

The twenty-plus years of urban housing reform has left marked imprints on China's urban sociospatial mosaic. In particular, the housing stock, which used to comprise essentially public rental housing, has now been more or less fully commoditized. Moreover, China has joined the rank of Great Britain, the United States and other advanced market economies to become a nation of homeowners. Accompanying the transition to homeownership have been massive housing construction programs, including the building of upmarket gated communities (Huang 2005), and large-scale out-migration of population to the suburbs (Li and Siu 2001). The rather dull and monotonous landscape that characterized the urban built environment in the Mao era has long given way to a vibrant and variegated scene. This chapter examines in detail the ownership transformation in urban China, trying to identify the major gainers and losers in different phases of the reform. I argue that the structure of inequalities in the socialist period has in fact strengthened under market transition in conjunction with the sale of reform housing and subsequent conferment of full ownership rights to the buyers.

Housing is more than consumption good. It is also an asset. To most home owners, the home is their single most important asset. Equally important, home purchase financed by mortgage loan is a form of leveraged investment, yet with reasonably low risk. As such, aside from its being a status symbol, homeownership also serves as a means of saving and investment as well as a hedge against inflation. Furthermore, the cost of housing consumption is not tenure-neutral. In China as well as in more developed market economies, the state has been actively promoting homeownership by offering taxation concessions and other policy incentives to homeowners. Thus, associated with the wholesale switch to homeownership are immense redistributions of wealth across different segments of the population.

Unlike the former Soviet Bloc countries which had adopted a "big bang" approach in transition to a market economy, China has preferred a more gradualist approach in its reform (Zhu 1999). While in the case of the housing reform, the objectives have been those of privatization and marketization from the very beginning, different stages of the reform were characterized by different emphases. Individuals and households responded to and were affected by the reform in different ways over different periods. The past few years have witnessed a surge of interest in the study of housing tenure in urban China. Recent works include, among others, Huang (2004), Huang and Clark (2002), Li (2000a), Li and Li (2006), and Li and Yi (2007). Building upon these works, the present chapter aims to answer the following questions. What kinds of measures were introduced in different periods to promote homeownership? Under what circumstances were such measures introduced, and how effective were they? Who were able to undertake the ownership switch and benefit from the policy changes? Who were left behind in the massive housing tenure transformation?

The switch to homeownership is not unique to China. Similar changes have taken place in advanced market economies as well as other former socialist countries. Below an overview of ownership transformation in different countries is provided, situating the Chinese case in a cross-country perspective. Then the reasons why owner occupation is generally the preferred mode are highlighted. Next the ownership transformation in urban China is examined in greater detail, in an attempt to identify the major gainers and losers in different phases of the reform. Data from three large-scale household surveys, two of which were conducted in 2001 in the cities of Beijing and Guangzhou, and the third in Guangzhou at the end of 2005, are employed to elicit the tenure switch trends in post-reform urban China.

Homeownership in the international context

Living in a home of one's own is often considered an intrinsic human value (Bramley and Morgan 1998). Homeownership has variously been labeled the "American dream" (Rossi 1980), the "Australian dream" (Bourassa *et al.* 1995), and part of a long tradition of English individualism (Saunders 1990). In these countries, owning a home is considered the ultimate aim of the householder (Kendig 1990). The postwar period witnessed rapidly rising homeownership. In the United States, the ownership rate jumped from 45 percent in 1940 to over 60 percent in 1960; thereafter it continued to exhibit a rising trend (Clark and Dieleman 1996: 5). In Great Britain, public rental housing under the name of council housing used to be of major importance. Yet the ownership rate nevertheless rose sharply from about 30 percent in 1950 to 65 percent in 1986 (Saunders 1990: 14). The "right-to-buy" policy of the Thatcher government in the early 1980s, under which sitting tenants of council housing were offered discounts of up to 60 percent to buy their own residences, encouraged the switch to homeownership. But the sharp rise in the ownership rate was observable long before such a policy was introduced.

In continental Europe, the public-rented sector has dominated the urban housing provision scene for many years. Nonetheless, rising ownership trends are also evident in Germany, the Netherlands and France, although renting public housing is still preferred by younger households (Clark and Dieleman 1996). In southern Europe, homeownership is even more prevalent than is in English-speaking countries. The ownership rate tops 80 percent in Greece, Italy and Spain (Stephens 2002). State provision of subsidized rental housing constituted an integral part of the socialist planned economy. It accounted for 67 percent of the total housing stock in the Russia Federation and 60 percent in Estonia in 1988. Within the former socialist countries, Bulgaria and Hungary were the only countries where the state was not actively involved in housing production and management (Struyk 1996: 8). Yet soon after the collapse of the communist regimes in the late 1980s and early 1990s, most former Soviet Bloc countries sought to privatize the public housing stock in the quickest manner possible, resulting in a sudden shift towards private ownership. In the Russian Federation, up to 11 million public housing units (36 percent of the state housing stock) were sold at heavily discounted prices between 1988 and 1994. In Estonia and Bulgaria, virtually all public housing units were sold over the same period (Struyk 1996: 24). Today, public rental housing in most former Soviet Bloc countries has virtually disappeared. In a number of these countries, the homeownership rate has reached 90 percent (Yasui 2002).

In China, the so-called ontological preference for homeownership (Saunders 1990) is perhaps no less strong than in Britain or the United States. Yet under the People's Republic such preference for owning homes and other landed property had to give way to the socialist ideology, which called for state ownership of all means of production. The early 1950s witnessed effective confiscation of all private rental housing. However, owner occupiers from the presocialist era were allowed to continue to dwell in their former residences, provided that the dwellings concerned were relatively small in size (Huang and Clark 2002). Aside from the small and dwindling private-owned sector, the socialist state, mainly through state work units, monopolized the production and allocation of housing in urban areas. Public rental housing dominated the housing provision scene.

China's reform began at the end of 1978. In the initial years the focus was on the agricultural sector, but, in 1985, the Chinese reformers shifted their attention to the urban industrial sector. In the same year China conducted a housing census which provided valuable information on the structure of housing provision under socialism and the early reform period. According to this source, municipal housing bureaus controlled 11.5 percent of all floor areas in cities, state work units owned and managed 70.4 percent, and urban collectives owned and managed 10.3 percent. In other words, almost 90 percent of the urban housing stock was public rental housing of various types. Private ownership accounted for just 10.3 percent (Li 1995: 332).

The 1985 Housing Census has never been repeated, but the 2000 Population Census did provide nationwide information on housing tenure. At the end of 2000, public rental housing comprised only 16.3 percent of the housing stock in cities. The private rental sector, which was eliminated in the early days of the People's Republic, resurfaced. But its relative importance was small, comprising only 6.9 percent of the stock. Various forms of homeownership accounted for 72.0 percent. The breakdown of the latter is as follows: ownership through purchase of former public rental housing, variously known as reform housing, 29.4 percent; self-built housing, usually located in small cities and suburban areas, 26.8 percent; commodity housing purchased in the open market, 9.2 percent; and "economic and comfortable housing," which was built with tax and land premium concessions and sold at a discount, 6.5 percent (NBSC 2003: 1866). Clearly, the structure of housing provision in urban China as revealed by the 2000 Population Census was very different from that in 1985. In particular, China has been transformed to a nation of homeowners.

Benefits of owner occupation

The massive housing tenure transformation first experienced in advanced market economies in the immediate postwar period and subsequently in China and other post socialist countries in the 1980s and 1990s was not merely a manifestation of the innate desire for homeownership. Without exception, it was achieved with the active involvement of the state, which has made owner occupation not only attractive but, more importantly, also financially feasible for the majority of households.

First and foremost, in the United States and other market economies the taxation system is structured so that owners are much more favorably treated than renters (King 1980; Olsen 1987). A house is an asset that yields rental income to its owner. An owner occupier can be seen as one who rents his own property. For a landlord, rental income net of depreciation and other expenses is subject to income tax. However, the rental income that an owner occupier implicitly receives from renting his residence is not subject to taxation. In addition, capital gains from selling owner-occupied properties are generally not subject to the capital gains tax. All these suggest that the monthly cost of using an owner-occupied dwelling, aside from the transaction costs involved in home purchase and sale, is lower than the cost of using an equivalent property in the rental market. In the United States, it has been estimated that the cost difference, which is in effect a subsidy to homeownership, is in the order of 10–15 percent (White and White 1977). In the United Kingdom, King's (1980) computation shows that the user cost of owner-occupied housing is slightly higher than that of public rental housing but less than one-half of the prevailing rent in the market.

It may be noted that the amount of ownership subsidy received depends on the marginal income tax rate. As the marginal taxation rate increases with household income, the ownership subsidy is also a function of household income. In other words, the comparative advantage of ownership, and hence the ownership rate, increases with income. Because the annualized cost involved in housing transaction decreases with the duration of stay, the annualized transaction cost involved in home purchase would be high for households with high mobility propensities. To these households, renting is probably a cheaper option. Hence, nonfamily households and young families who tend to have higher mobility propensities also tend to have higher propensities to rent; in contrast, households further advanced in the family life cycle are more likely to own.

Housing as an asset is highly expensive. Few can buy a housing unit outright without resort to mortgage finance. In many countries special financial institutions such as the savings and loans associations in the United States and building societies in the United Kingdom have been established to channel funds for the financing of home purchase (Bourne 1981; Maclennan 1982). The state often acts as a guarantor for deposits made with these institutions and for the mortgage loans extended. As such, mortgage loans are made accessible to households which otherwise would be denied such loans. The state's guarantee also allows the financial institutions to offer highly attractive mortgage terms: low lending rates and down payment requirements, and loan terms of 25 years or longer. With the state's support, households with minimal savings or assets can enter homeownership. For a given property, the monthly mortgage payment often differs little from the prevailing market rent. In fact, the effective payment, after all income tax-related deductions, is often lower than the rent. To a large measure, the rapid increase in the ownership rate in postwar Western societies can be attributed to the reforms in the financial sector.

As an investment good, housing also possesses other advantages. Many people are unaccustomed to the volatility of the capital market and are bewildered by the myriads of investment instruments such as stock options and other derivatives. To them, buying the home probably is the only form of investment that does not require much professional knowledge and time and energy to monitor market movements. Yet, investment in the home provides a reasonably good rate of return, especially in time of inflation. Although property prices do fluctuate and occasionally exhibit sharp falls, as in the United Kingdom in the early 1990s and Hong Kong after 1997, the overall trend in the postwar period in most advanced market economies has been one of rising property prices. Availability of mortgage loans with high loan-to-value ratios has made investment in the home even more attractive, as the very high leverage effect would many times magnify the return rate. Furthermore, monthly mortgage payment is a form of forced saving. It exerts discipline on the part of the mortgage holder, who might have otherwise spent the savings resulting from paying mortgage installments on consumption items. As such, home purchase is also a form of insurance, allowing the home owner – in fact the mortgage holder – to gradually accumulate wealth and hedge against aging. Differential access to homeownership implies differential ability to accumulate wealth.

In China to date, the taxation system is still rather rudimentary. In theory, the marginal taxation rate rises quite sharply with income, reaching 45 percent for people with earnings of 10,000 Yuan (1,250 US dollars) per month or above (SAT 2006). In reality, however, there lack formal guidelines in the computation of taxable income. It is the salary and wage income component that is subject to income tax. However, for many workers the bulk of earnings is in the form of bonus and housing and other subsidies, which often escape taxation. Imputed rental income derived from homeownership, of course, is not subject to taxation. But even landlords who are not business enterprises are unaccustomed to filing the tax form and paying tax on income generated by letting real properties. In such a highly irregular taxation regime, it is difficult, if not impossible, to compute the benefit derived from nontaxation of imputed rental income and other favorable taxation treatments accruing to owner occupation. Nonetheless, with further maturity of China's market economy, taxation considerations will surely play a more prominent role in housing tenure decisions in future.

If difference in taxation treatment between owning and renting is not a factor leading to the phenomenal transition to owner occupation, then what exactly has caused the tenure transition? Introduction to mortgage finance of course helps promote homeownership, but this came rather late in the reform period. Other measures, such as raising public housing rent and selling public housing to sitting tenants, have played more decisive roles in different phases of the reform. Below I discuss in greater detail the changing patterns of tenure composition in urban China over the course of China's housing reform.

Changing tenure composition: evidence from Beijing and Guangzhou

The 2001 Guangzhou and Beijing surveys

The 1985 Housing Census and the 2001 Population Census revealed sharply con-trasting tenure compositions. Fundamental changes had taken place. Yet how did these changes come about? What exactly did China's road to homeown-ership look like? To answer these questions, longitudinal data are needed. In 2001, with the help of mainland research institutes, a research team based at Hong Kong Baptist University conducted two household surveys, each com-prising 1500-plus households, in Beijing and Guangzhou. In both instances, the probability-proportionate-to-size approach was adopted to ensure sample repre-sentation. Population distribution based on household registration data was used to construct the sampling frame. Essentially identical questionnaires were employed in the two surveys. A major part of the questionnaire was made up of questions to solicit information on residential histories since 1980. Given the fact that some households might have moved but not yet reported the move to the relevant local authorities, in both surveys the recent movers could have been undersampled. Also, by design, migrants were underrepresented. Moreover, even though mov-ing house or purchasing a home is a highly important event, memory would fade as time progresses. There could be recall errors, especially for events that took place long time ago. These caveats aside, comparison with census and other data suggests that the surveys were of high quality.

The longitudinal data generated allow us to chart the path of tenure composition change in Beijing and Guangzhou over the period 1980 to 2001. Rather refined tenure classifications were employed in the questionnaire, but for inter-temporal comparisons, too much detail could obscure rather than elicit the overall picture. To more clearly depict the longitudinal trends, the different tenures are regrouped into three main classes.

1   *Rented*, which includes primarily housing managed by the municipal hous-ing bureau and housing owned and managed by work units. Both are public housing in the sense that the ultimate control rests with the state. The private rental sector was virtually nonexistent until only quite late in the study period. Because of this, it is subsumed under the general rented category;

2   *Owned-subsidized housing*: this mainly refers to housing bought from the municipal housing bureau or work units at highly discounted prices. Such

housing may be termed *reform housing*. It used to be subject to very stringent resale restrictions – that is, only the usage right but not the resale right was conferred to the buyer. Thus, owners of such housing in general were not able to benefit from capital gains arising from rising property prices;

3   *Owned-commodity housing*: the latter refers to housing purchased in the open market, which enjoys both usage and resale rights. Hence, this mode represents full private ownership.

4   According to Li and Yi (2007), Chinese housing reform can be divided into three major phases. First, the period 1979 to approximately 1992 may be termed the early reform stage, which encompassed a series of reform experiments. However, the main structure of housing provision remained largely unchanged. Second, there was the reform deepening or double track stage, lasting roughly from 1992 to 1998. This period was characterized by an emerging commodity housing sector which coexisted alongside the traditional system of bureaucratic housing allocation. Third, from 1998 onwards, with the cessation of welfare allocation of housing, a more or less fully marketized system of housing provision began to take shape. The following discussion of the tenure composition change as revealed by the Beijing and Guangzhou surveys is organized in respect to the three phases of the housing reform. The 2001 Beijing survey data also formed the basis of Li and Yi's (2007) study, which employed the Cox's proportional hazards model to analyze the ownership switch in different reform phases. The results of Li and Yi (2007) as well as those of previous works on housing decisions in urban China provide us with hints as to what kind of people would benefit from the phenomenal shift to home ownership in urban China as the reform progressed.

Early reform stage

Figures 8.1 and 8.2 respectively graph the Beijing and Guangzhou tenure split data given by the residential histories reported in the surveys. Broadly similar pictures emerge. At the beginning of the reform, the (public) rented mode dominated the housing provision scene. Probably reflecting the fact that Beijing, being the national capital, housed large numbers of Party organizations, government departments, research institutions and universities, the dominance of the rented mode there was even more prominent: 84.8 percent of the Beijing respondents indicated that they resided in (public) rented housing in 1980, as compared with 69.4 percent of the Guangzhou respondents. In the Guangzhou case, probably reflecting its close ties with Hong Kong and overseas Chinese communities, quite a sizeable percentage of the respondents – 27.8 percent – resided in private-owned housing at the beginning of the study period.

In theory, the housing reform began with experimental housing sales conducted in Xi'an and other cities in 1979. Under such schemes, the individual home buyer, the individual's work unit, and the state (central or local government) would each contribute one-third of the purchase price. Subsidized home ownership as housing tenure emerged. More favorable terms were offered for subsequent home sales,

150   *Si-ming Li*

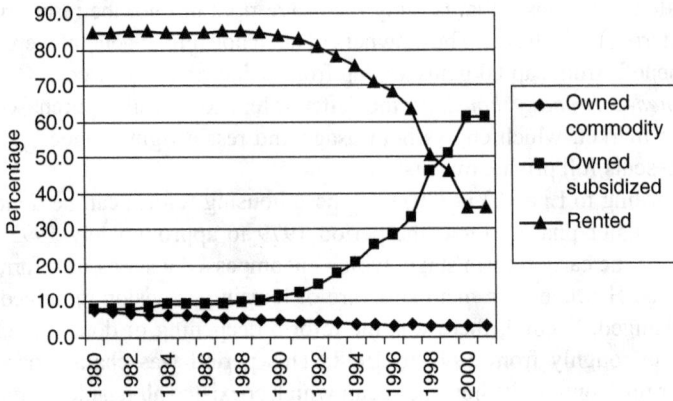

Figure 8.1 Tenure split in Beijing, 1980–2001.

Source: 2001 Beijing Survey.

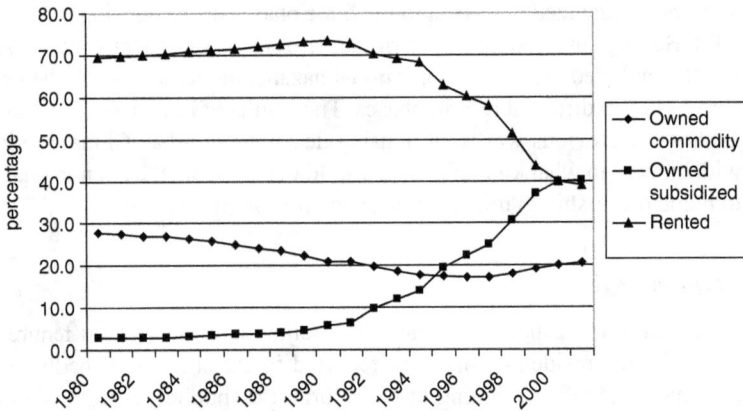

Figure 8.2 Tenure split in Guangzhou, 1980–2001.

Source: 2001 Guangzhou Survey.

but the scale of reform experiments was still limited. Relatively few were given the option to buy. The emphasis of the reform was on raising public housing rent to levels at least covering maintenance costs. Yet, in fact, in order to win workers' support in an increasingly turbulent and uncertain environment, throughout the 1980s work units – particularly state-owned enterprises (SOEs) – had made strenuous efforts to expand the scope of housing provision, including the provision of newer and better housing (Wu 1996), and continued to charge only nominal rents. The extremely low rents rendered the buy option unattractive (Chen 1996; Li and Yi 2007; Wang and Murie 2000).

While subsidized ownership gradually grew in importance, however, as of 1989 its share only reached 9.7 percent in Beijing and 4.6 percent in Guangzhou. Also, because of work units' drive to provide housing to an ever increasing number of workers, many who had previously lived in old and dilapidated private housing were for the first time offered public-rented accommodation. In the case of Beijing, rented housing's share stayed at about 85 percent throughout the 1980s. In the case of Guangzhou, it even exhibited a slightly increasing trend, reaching 73.4 percent in 1990. Underpinning the expansion of the public rental sector was a corresponding decline in (full) private ownership. In Beijing, between 1980 and 1989, the latter's share decreased from 7.4 percent to 4.9 percent. In Guangzhou, it decreased from 27.8 percent to 22.3 percent over the same period.

In market economies homeownership is associated with various economic benefits; however, in China this might not have been the case during the early reform phase, at least in relative terms. In fact, it might be argued that those who bought homes in this period could have suffered relative loss. Although the homes were priced at below cost, the degree of subsidy in public-rented housing was much higher. Moreover, people who made early purchase had to forego the opportunity of getting newer and better housing from the work units. In the Li and Yi (2007) study, the estimated equation for this period was not significant. The scale of home sale experiments was just too small to differentiate owners and renters. People who benefited most during this period included those workers who had previously lived in dilapidated housing of pre-1949 origin and who were for the first time offered cheap public rental housing. But those who were able to climb up the housing ladder by moving to newer and larger dwellings while continuing to pay nominal rents were the main beneficiaries of the expansion of public or work-unit housing. Previous works by Li (2000b) and Logan *et al.* (1999) indicate that, as in most socialist economies (Szelenyi 1983), these people were mainly the higher status workers, especially higher-rank cadres, and members of the Chinese Communist Party (CCP).

Reform-deepening phase

In 1988, after years of experimentation, China embarked on the launch of a nation-wide urban housing reform. But this initiative was interrupted by the Tiananmen Square Incident of 1989. At the end of 1991, the State Council issued the document *"On Comprehensive Reform of the Urban Housing System"* to reinstate the 1988 reform. In 1994, the State Council published the *"Decision on Deepening the Urban Housing Reform,"* which further elaborated the objectives and contents of the reform. In particular, the reform called for the establishment of a two-tier system of housing provision, comprising a partially subsidized sector of "economic and comfortable housing" targeted at the low and middle income group, and a fully marketized sector of commodity housing for higher income households (Li and Yi 2007; Wang and Murie 2000). In both sectors, the emphasis was on owner occupation. To channel funds to housing construction and to help finance home purchase, the State Council required all municipal governments to establish a mandatory Housing Provident Fund (HPF). All state work units were required to set up an account for their workers in the HPF. Every worker under this scheme would contribute 5 percent of his or her monthly income to the HPF account, and the work units concerned would contribute the same amount. HPF scheme holders could later draw on their account to help finance home purchase. They could also borrow mortgage loans from the HPF for this purpose. In addition to mortgage loans tied to the HPF, the country's four major state-owned commercial banks were also entrusted with extending mortgage loans to individual home buyers (Li and Yi 2006).

In the Third Plenum of the Fourteenth Central Committee of the CCP held in November 1993, China announced its intention of constructing a "socialist market economy." The state formally recognized the private sector. At the same time, SOEs were to be transformed into business undertakings in the true sense. SOEs could now identify their own development goals and strategies, formulate their own reward schemes, issue shares and become companies with limited liability, seek listing on the stock exchange, and engage in acquisitions and mergers (Li 2005). The operation environment became even more competitive and uncertain. Those that could not successfully adjust to the new situation suffered huge and long-lasting loss. Bankruptcy was a real possibility. Instead of finding ways to secure support from their workers, the priority for SOEs now was to control cost and cut loss. Disposing of their housing obligations was one way out. The home sales involved heavy discounts. Yet, to the SOEs concerned, the rental income foregone by the sale was minimal. Moreover, they would no longer need to maintain and manage the housing stock, which was costly.

The early- to mid-1990s witnessed the accelerated sale by work units of public-sector or reform housing to sitting tenants. As is evident from Figures 8.1 and 8.2, in both Beijing and Guangzhou, the relative importance of public-rented housing began to decline in the early 1990s, and the decline accelerated in the middle of that decade. At the same time, the subsidized owned sector grew in importance. By 1998, the year when China embarked on the next phase of housing reform, rented housing's share had decreased to 50.7 percent in Beijing and 51.4 percent in Guangzhou. Correspondingly, subsidized ownership's share in these two cities had increased to 46.0 percent and 30.6 percent, respectively. Previously it has been pointed out that the SOEs were under mounting cost-cutting pressure and eager to dispose of their housing obligations. In comparison, the financial pressure on government departments was much less stringent. A major taxation reform was introduced in 1994 to reassert the central government authority to access financial resources (Wong 1995). At the same time land leasing provided a major means for local governments to generate incomes. The enhanced financial positions of government departments and related institutions enabled them to continue to offer cheap rental housing to their workers. Under such circumstances, it may be expected that the increase in homeownership during this period took place mainly in SOEs instead of in government departments and other public organizations. The Li and Yi (2007) study found that in this period of reform deepening, people working in government and quasi-government institutions were

40 percent less likely to switch to ownership than were those who worked in SOEs.

The 1994 housing reform envisaged the development of a private housing market. Earlier, back in the late 1980s, work units were discouraged from constructing housing in their compound. In order to better plan and coordinate urban development, specialized development companies were formed to undertake housing production, often in the form of large residential estates. Work units would then buy the housing from the developers for subsequent allocation to their workers. Although the bulk of home purchase was made by work units, commodity housing was for the first time offered on the market. But in this period of reform deepening, only the very rich could afford it (Li 2000a). According to Lau and Li (2007), in Beijing, at market price, the price-to-income ratio stood at 14:2 in 1997, which was well above the World Bank guideline of 3:6. The 2001 surveys indicated that little commodity housing was sold to individuals. In both Beijing and Guangzhou, the share of (full) private ownership continued to fall. In Beijing, it dropped to 3.1 percent in 1999, the lowest in the entire observation period. In Guangzhou, the trend line hit the bottom in 1997, at 17.1 percent, before showing a modest rebound.

Clearly, in this phase of reform deepening the major driving force behind the transition to home ownership was the selling of reform housing by work units, especially SOEs. Purchase in the open market was of minimal importance. There could also be households who were forced to buy their residences. But many would welcome the opportunity to become homeowners, especially given the very low selling price. In this period older people, that is, people with substantial seniority in the workplace, were more prone to switch from renting to owner occupation. This would be expected, as the discount increased with years of service in the work unit. People with higher educational attainment and holding managerial positions were also more likely to make the transition to ownership. These were the people who could influence resource allocation in the work unit. The fact that they were more likely to buy reform housing suggests that to these higher status groups subsidized ownership was preferred to continuing renting from the work unit. It might be that after more than 15 years of reform, people began to realize the investment value of housing and other real property. Also, the rents of public-sector housing underwent a number of substantial increases, and further increases were on the horizon. People who could afford to buy and were able to choose the better dwellings would be likely to exercise their buy option. In a sense, then, the selling of reform housing perpetuated the structure of inequalities observed in earlier times. Subsequent developments, including the conferment of full ownership rights on owners of reform housing in the early 2000s and persistent rising housing prices, brought fortunes to these high-status groups, resulting in massive redistribution of wealth to those who were already on top of the socioeconomic ladder.

In this phase, membership of the CCP did not imply a higher likelihood of owning. But this was in line with the fact that most sales of reform housing took place in SOEs, rather than government and quasi-government organizations. In a SOE, under the enterprise reform, professionalism and the ability to generate new business and make money would be paramount, although undoubtedly the CCP continued to exert its influence on resource allocation.

Most recent trends and the 2005 Guangzhou survey

The year 1998 marked a watershed in China's urban housing reform. In his inauguration speech as the Premier of China, given in March 1998, Zhu Rongji proclaimed the end of welfare housing allocation. State work units would no longer offer cheap rental housing to their workers. In addition, subsidized home sales by work units would also be terminated. There would still be "economic and suitable housing"; however, the market would assume the preeminent role. Commodity housing would constitute the basis of urban housing provision. While in-kind subsidies were to be discontinued, cash subsidies were allowed. Individual work units having the financial means, which were likely to be government and quasi-government organizations, would offer cash housing subsidies to their workers to assist home purchase and mortgage payment.

Local governments were given some flexibility in deciding the date of implementation of the new policy. Most municipalities set 1999 or 2000 as the target implementation date. The last two years of the millennium witnessed a stampede of housing disposal by work units – the so-called catching the last train phenomenon. Government departments and quasi-government institutions, which had not been too enthusiastic about selling reform housing to sitting tenants in the past, were forced to do so under the new policy. In Beijing, the share of subsidized ownership jumped from 33.3 percent in 1997 to 61.2 percent in 2001. In Guangzhou, the stampede to catch the last train was also evident: subsidized ownership's share rose from 25.0 to 40.3 percent over the same period.

Again, the Li and Yi (2007) study shows that in the period 1998–2001 people most likely to make the renter-to-owner switch included those who were over 40 years of age, and those with higher education attainment and holding managerial positions (i.e. cadres). Interestingly, in this period of stampeding for subsidized ownership, the difference in the ownership switch ratio between SOEs and government and quasi-government organizations found in the previous period disappeared. On the other hand, membership of the CCP, which had been insignificant as a factor affecting the ownership switch before, became significant in the 1998–2001 equation. Quantitatively, CCP membership increased the likelihood of ownership switch by almost 60 percent. It may be argued that CCP membership is especially important in government and quasi-government organizations. Clearly, the "grace period" of the last years of the millennium enabled the CCP cadres in government and quasi-government organizations to "catch the last train" and enjoy the benefits associated with subsidized ownership, and, as a result, subsequently to receive the windfall gains in conjunction with the conferment of full ownership rights to owners of reform housing.

The change in policy in 1998 can be seen as a natural development of China's drive to build a market-based economy. But it can also be seen as an attempt to counteract the Asian Financial Crisis, which first struck Thailand in July 1997 and subsequently Indonesia, South Korea, Hong Kong and other East Asian economies. At about the same time as the policy of ending welfare allocation of housing was announced, the State Council also promulgated the idea of anchoring economic growth through the promotion of housing and related consumption, the latter including the private car. Commercial banks were strongly encouraged to offer mortgage loans. The down payment requirement was reduced from 30 to 20 percent, and guarantors were no longer required to secure mortgage loans. The HPF was extended to include all income earners and the focus of its use shifted to financing home purchase (Li and Yi 2006). The reforms in home finance have made purchase of commodity housing by individual households much more feasible, helping to promote the development of a thriving housing market.

The 2001 surveys were undertaken at a time when the new housing policy was just introduced. The effects of the policy initiatives on commodity housing purchase were still not evident at the time of survey. In order to better understand the full impacts of the 1998 reform, the Baptist University research team, in collaboration with the Centre for Urban and Regional Studies of Sun Yat-sen University, conducted another survey in late 2005. Broadly similar questionnaires and sampling strategies were employed.[1]

Data based on the 2005 survey showing the tenure split of Guangzhou for the period 1990–2005 are presented in Table 8.1. In the table, rented housing is further divided into rented-private and rented-public to take account of the increasing role of the market in recent years. As an integral part of the new housing policy, in the early 2000s the state permitted reform housing to enter the market. Many of the

Table 8.1 Changing tenure composition of Guangzhou as given by the 2005 survey

Year	% owned	Of which		% rented	Of which	
		% owned commodity	% owned subsidized		% rented-private	% rented-public
1990	45.9	35.0	11.0	54.1	10.8	43.3
1991	45.9	33.7	12.2	54.1	11.3	42.8
1992	47.9	33.0	14.9	52.1	11.7	40.4
1993	50.6	32.9	17.6	49.4	12.0	37.5
1994	51.9	32.8	19.0	48.1	11.8	36.3
1995	54.4	32.1	22.3	45.6	12.9	32.7
1996	56.3	32.0	24.3	43.7	13.2	30.5
1997	56.9	31.8	25.0	43.1	13.3	29.8
1998	60.0	33.6	26.4	40.0	13.2	26.8
1999	66.1	37.7	28.4	33.9	12.3	21.7
2000	71.0	41.8	29.2	29.0	12.3	16.7
2001	73.0	44.1	28.9	27.0	12.3	14.7
2002	73.4	45.4	28.0	26.6	13.2	13.4
2003	75.5	47.9	27.6	24.5	13.2	11.3
2004	76.1	50.3	25.8	23.9	13.3	10.6
2005	76.5	51.2	25.3	23.5	13.1	10.4

Source: 2005 Guangzhou survey.

resale restrictions on reform housing have since been lifted. In other words, full property rights are now conferred on owners of reform housing. Reform housing is instantaneously transformed into commodity housing. As was previously pointed out, such a move, in effect, has accorded owners of reform housing windfall gains, as the housing units they owned, which were bought with heavy discounts, can now be resold at full market price. In a sense, then, subsidized ownership as a tenure mode has ceased to exist, as almost all owned housing is now fully owned. However, for comparison purpose, Table 8.1 continues to make the difference between the owned-commodity housing and owned-subsidized housing modes, based on the conditions under which the purchase was made.

Probably because of the inclusion in the 2005 survey of Panyu, which until quite recently was rural in character, for the period covered by both Figure 8.2 and Table 8.1, the share of private ownership (owned-commodity) given by the latter was consistently higher than that by the former. Also, probably because the 2005 survey incorporated proportionately more migrants, the share of private-rented housing given by the 2005 sample was not insignificant even in the 1990s. But despite these differences the trends depicted by Figure 8.2 and Table 8.1 are quite similar. Both show an accelerated decrease of the rented mode, the drop being most drastic towards the end of the 1990s. Correspondingly, both sets of data show the owned-subsidized sector rising, especially in the late 1990s.

As for the trends in the first half of the 2000s, charted only by Table 8.1, the following observations can be made. First, the public-rented sector continued its declining trend. By 2005 its share had dropped to only 10.4 percent. Second, the relative importance of subsidized ownership started to decline in 2000. As of 2005, 25.3 percent of the respondents still resided in housing bought with heavy discounts. But this was some four percentage points below the figure in 2000, the highest on record. Clearly, people nowadays can no longer rely on work units to take care of their housing needs. Individuals and families who want to establish their own residence for the first time have to depend on the market to satisfy their housing needs. Similarly, people who want to move up the housing ladder have to search for appropriate opportunities in the market. In Guangzhou, according to Table 8.1, the share of owned-commodity housing shot up markedly from 33.6 percent in 1998 to 51.2 percent in 2005. Table 8.1 also indicates that despite the rapid increase in the owned-commodity sector, the increase in the total ownership rate has decelerated in the early 2000s, especially in the most recent years.

Obviously, in a system where the market prevails and where market institutions are firmly established, income, which is closely tied to education and occupational rank and which determines a person's position in the income tax ladder, plays an increasing role in tenure choice. Similarly, life-cycle considerations, which not only reflect personal and household preference and mobility inclinations, but also the portfolio positions at different stages of a person's life course, assume greater importance in the decision to own or to rent. Given the fact that cash subsidies are offered mainly to workers in government and related organizations, and such subsidies vary with occupational rank, it is likely that Party and government cadres will continue to outperform others in the quest for owner occupation in this era of market dominance. The fact that Party and government cadres tend to have better job stability and more predictable incomes implies that they also have better access to mortgage loans with attractive terms. As such, inequalities inherent in the former system of socialist resource allocation resurface in the current market system. But more research is needed to ascertain what kind of people and households are able to make the ownership switch when practically only commodity housing is available and when housing prices in all major cities in China are apparently beyond the means of all but the richest households.

Another observation evident from Table 8.1 is that in this period of market dominance, the private-rented sector has remained quite small. Its share stayed in the 12 to 13 percent range. To date, the policy emphasis has been on promoting private ownership. Only lip service has been paid to building the necessary institutional infrastructure for the development of the private-rented sector. In comparison with the rights stipulated in the sale and purchase agreement of housing (asset) transaction, the rights of buyers (landlords) and sellers (tenants) in rental deals are generally much less clearly defined. To the landlord, repossession of the let premises in case of rent arrears could be difficult and cumbersome. Recovering unpaid rent is almost impossible if the tenant absconds and disappears. In a time of heightened mobility this is a real possibility. Similarly, to the tenant, the tenancy agreement may not guarantee proper maintenance of the premises by the landlord. The legal means of upholding the tenancy agreement are either absent or unclear, and are likely to be beyond the means of the parties concerned to pursue. Moreover, the country's still irregular and ever-changing taxation system, which lacks clear guidelines as to how rental incomes are to be taxed and what deductions can be made, is also not conducive to the development of a thriving private-rented sector. A consequence of the underdevelopment of this sector is that people who cannot afford or prefer not to own, and people who are deprived of cheap public rental housing, are now trapped. The size of such groups will not be small, however, given the massive restructuring of SOEs and the continual huge influx of rural migrants to the major urban areas. To these people, the private-rented sector is just not large enough to provide them with adequate choices and decent housing at affordable rent. Their plight is even worse than in the socialist period, despite the huge improvements in the general housing provision scene.

Concluding remarks

China's urban housing reform has now more or less drawn to a close, with the cessation of welfare housing allocation and conferment of full ownership rights on buyers of reform housing. The rise in the homeownership rate was most spectacular in the mid- and late-1990s when SOEs were forced to get rid of their housing obligations under the enterprise reform and later when government and quasi-government organizations stampeded to "catch the last train." The speculative increase in the ownership rate was achieved primarily by the sale of reform housing at highly discounted prices.

People who were able to access resources in a socialist redistributive system were also likely to be those who were offered the best deals (in terms of price and quality of housing) when making the ownership switch. They include the managerial and professional staff of SOEs and the cadres of Party and government organizations. Conferment of full ownership rights in the early 2000s amounts to conferment of windfall profits to buyers of reform housing, resulting in huge redistributions of wealth in society. The main beneficiaries, of course, are the high-status workers who formerly got the best deals in reform housing sales programs. To a certain extent, the structure of inequalities in a socialist redistributive system is further strengthened under market transition. Today, housing essentially has to be obtained in the market. Yet, to certain extent, such a structure of inequalities persists, given that government organizations and other public institutions continue to offer cash housing subsidies to their workers.

Not every person can make the ownership transition, of course. Those who are left behind include those who were not offered the option to buy, and those who were offered the buy option but who did not have the financial means to do so even when offered huge discounts. Obviously, people who have never been offered work-unit housing, such as workers in underresourced urban collectives and migrant workers, belong to this category. But they also include people low on the job ladder and people who have been laid off by their work units. Obviously few of them can afford to own, especially in a fully marketized setting. But apparently renting is not a viable option either, as the public rental sector is dwindling – in fact disappearing while the private rental sector has remained undeveloped and offers few choices. The number of people in such a plight is by no means small. The heightened inequalities due to the sale of reform housing and subsequent conferment of windfall profits on the buyers, and the associated dwindling of public rental housing could be a major source of social unrest in the years to come.

Acknowledgments

This study is supported in part by Hong Kong Research Grant Council (Grant No. HKBU2135/04H). Dr Zheng Yi and Miss Carmen Lau assisted with the data analysis.

Note

1 However, the site coverage of the 2005 survey was extended to include Panyu District, which used to be a city on its own but was annexed by Guangzhou in 2000. Also, the sampling frame employed took account of the migrants. As such, the data provided by the 2001 and 2005 surveys may not be totally comparable.

References

Bourassa, S. C., Greig, A. W., and Troy, P. N. (1995) "The limits of housing policy: homeownership in Australia," *Housing Studies*, 10(1): 83–104.

Bourne, L. S. (1981) *The Geography of Housing*, London: Edward Arnold.

Bramley, G. and Morgan, J. (1998) "Low cost home ownership in the UK," *Housing Studies*, 13(4): 567–586.

Chen, A. (1996) "China's urban housing reform: price-rent ratio and market equilibrium," *Urban Studies*, 33(7): 1077–1092.

Clark, W. A. V. and Dieleman, F. M. (1996) *Households and Housing: Choice and Outcomes in the Housing Market*, New Brunswick, NJ: Rutgers University.

Huang, Y. (2004) "The road to homeownership: a longitudinal analysis of tenure transition in urban China (1949–94)," *International Journal of Urban and Regional Research*, 28(4): 774–795.

Huang, Y. (2005) "From work-unit compounds to gated communities: housing inequality and residential segregation in transitional Beijing," in L. J. C. Ma and F. Wu (eds) *Restructuring the Chinese City: Changing Society, Economy and Space*, London: Routledge, 192–222.

Huang, Y. and Clark, W. A. V. (2002) "Housing tenure choice in transition China: a multilevel analysis," *Urban Studies*, 39(1): 7–32.

Kendig, H. L. (1990) "A life-course perspective on housing attainment," in D. Meyers (ed.) *Housing Demography*, Madison, WI: University of Wisconsin Press, 133–135.

King, M. A. (1980) "An econometric model of tenure choice and demand for housing as a joint decision," *Journal of Public Economics*, 14: 137–159.

Lau, K. M. and Li, S-M. (2007) "Commodity housing affordability in Beijing, 1992–2001," *Habitat International*, 30: 614–627.

Li, S-M. (1995) *Zhongguo chengzhen de zhufang tizhi gaige* (Urban housing reform in China), in S-M. Li, Y-M. Siu and T-K. Mok (eds) *Zhongguo Shehui Fazhan (Social Development in China)*, Hong Kong: Hong Kong Education Press, 324–344.

Li, S-M. (2000a) "The housing market and tenure decisions in Chinese cities: a multivariate analysis of the case of Guangzhou," *Housing Studies*, 15(2): 213–236.

Li, S-M. (2000b) "Housing consumption in urban China: a comparative study of Beijing and Guangzhou," *Environment and Planning A*, 32: 1115–1134.

Li, S-M. (2005) "China's changing urban geography: a review of major forces at work," *Issues and Studies*, 41(4): 67–106.

Li, S-M. and Li, L. (2006) "Life course and housing tenure change in urban China: a study of Guangzhou," *Housing Studies*, 21(5): 655–672.

Li, S-M. and Siu, Y-M. (2001) "Residential mobility and urban restructuring under market transition: a study of Guangzhou, China," *The Professional Geographer*, 53: 219–229.

Li, S-M. and Yi, Z. (2006) *Financing housing purchase in China: with special reference to Guangzhou*. Hong Kong Baptist University, Centre for China Urban and Regional Studies, Occasional Paper No. 64.

Li, S-M. and Yi, Z. (2007) "The road to homeownership under market transition: Beijing 1980–2001," *Urban Affairs Review*, 42(3): 342–368.

Logan, J. R., Bian, Y. and Bian, F. (1999) "Housing inequality in urban China in the 1990s," *International Journal of Urban and Regional Research*, 23: 7–25.

Maclennan, D. (1982) *Housing Economics*, London: Longman.

National Bureau of Statistics of China (NBSC) (2003) *Tabulations on the 2000 Population Census of the People's Republic of China*, Beijing: China Statistical Press.

Olsen, E. O. (1987) "The demand and supply of housing service: a critical review of empirical evidence," in E. S. Mills (ed.) *Handbook of Regional and Urban Economics*, Vol. II, Amsterdam: Elsevier Science Publishers, 989–1020.

Rossi, P. (1980) *Why Families Move* (2nd edn), Glencoe, IL: Free Press.

Saunders, P. (1990) *A Nations of Homeowners*, London: Unwin Hyman.

State Administration of Taxation (SAT) (2006) *Zhonghua Remin Gonghe Guo Geren Soudeshui Fa (Personal Taxation Law of the People's Republic of China).* Available online at: www.chinatax.gov.cn/ (accessed July 6, 2006).

Stephens, M. (2002) "International models of housing finance: housing systems in the western and transition economies," in Organization for Economic Co-operation and Development (OECD), *Housing Finance in Transition Economies*, Paris: OECD Publications, pp. 175–182.

Struyk, R. (ed.) (1996) *Economic Restructuring of the Former Soviet Bloc: The Case of Housing*, Washington, DC: The Urban Institute.

Szelenyi, I. (1983) *Urban Inequalities under State Socialism*, Oxford: Oxford University Press.

Wang, Y. P. and Murie, A. (2000) "Social and spatial implications of housing reform in China," *International Journal of Urban and Regional Research*, 24(2): 397–417.

White, L. J. and White, M. J. (1977) "The tax subsidy to owner-occupied housing: who benefits," *Journal of Public Economics*, 7: 111–126.

Wong, C. P. W. (1994) "China's fiscal reform in 1994," in C. K. Lo, S. Pepper and K. Y. Tsui (eds) *China Review 1995*, Hong Kong: Chinese University Press, 20: 1–13.

Wu, F. (1996) "Changes in the structure of public housing provision in urban China," *Urban Studies*, 33: 1601–1627.

Yasui, T. (2002) "Housing finance in transition economies," in Organization for Economic Co-operation and Development (OECD), *Housing Finance in Transition Economies*, Paris: OECD Publications, pp. 17–36.

Zhu, J. M. (1999) "Local growth coalition: the context and implications of China's gradualist urban land reforms," *International Journal of Urban and Regional Research*, 23(3): 534–548.

Part III
Rebuilding residential space

9 Residential redevelopment and social impacts in Beijing

Hyun Bang Shin

Nowadays, people say that high-level cadres live around the second ring road, while paupers live around the fifth or sixth ring road . . .

(A resident subject to displacement from an inner city neighborhood)

Introduction

The ongoing reform practices in mainland China have dictated profound socioeconomic and political changes, altering the way of living for many urbanites. Housing reform and urban redevelopment were at the center of these changes, governing urban residents' housing consumption practices and transforming dilapidated neighborhoods into a modern, commoditized space. In social terms, urban redevelopment focuses largely on those dilapidated neighborhoods where residents have been increasingly marginalized in the process of implementing housing reform. Since the 1980s, various reform measures were centered on the promotion of homeownership through the commodification of urban housing (Wang and Murie 1999a; Zhou and Logan 2002). These included subsidized sale of public rental dwellings and new commercial units. Employees in state enterprises and institutions that could maneuver their budgets for such expenditure mostly benefited from the sale. Those residents in dilapidated neighborhoods, however, were excluded from enjoying such benefits. Dwellings therein were often too run-down to be considered for any subsidized sales. Most dwellings were owned by municipal housing bureaus or work units that were financially too weak to provide their employees with dwellings of better standard. Dilapidated neighborhoods were often loci of urban poverty as residents "remained in a peripheral position in the state occupation-based welfare system" (Wu 2004: 415). In short, those dilapidated neighborhoods have become the "space of marginality" in the midst of the reform process, eventually being subject to wholesale redevelopment and displacement.

In terms of urban development, such neighborhoods illustrate a different picture. They have been increasingly recognized by real estate developers for their valuable development potential (Wu 2002). This was possible with the implementation of urban land reform that allowed the transfer of land-use rights for commercial development (Zhang 1997). In Beijing, most redevelopment neighborhoods are

164   *Hyun Bang Shin*

located in and around the inner city districts that have become the major loci of
domestic and international business and financial activities (Gaubatz 2005).

For those residents in dilapidated neighborhoods, residential redevelopment
seems to provide differing degree of opportunities and costs. How likely is it for
the residents to find an affordable house in the market after their displacement?
What constraints would they face when entering the housing market for the first
time? Does the whole process of redevelopment and displacement shed any light
on our understanding of the housing reform and spatial changes? Based on the
findings from a case study of a redevelopment neighborhood, this chapter argues
that residential redevelopment is successful in transforming dilapidated neighborhoods into a more profitable space; that the residents therein are effectively
pushed towards the urban periphery upon displacement; that it is much less likely
for future displacees to become owner-occupiers due to various policy and market
constraints; and that their marginal position in both social and spatial terms is
predicted to continue.

Housing reform and residential redevelopment

Housing reform and the promotion of homeownership

Housing reform was introduced with an emphasis on sharing responsibilities
between the state, enterprises and employees to diversify sources of investment
(Li 2005). A strong emphasis was placed on introducing market components in
the housing sector so that housing was no longer treated as a welfare good but as a
commodity (Zhou and Logan 2002). The promotion of homeownership was at the
center of these reform policies. Homeownership was thought to release the state
and underperforming state enterprises from their overstretched burden of welfare
provision, and transfer the responsibility to the individuals. It largely progressed
on dual tracks: first, the supply of commercial and affordable housing; and second,
the privatization of existing public rental dwellings.

First, relatively better-off households were directed toward the commercial and
affordable housing sectors. The latter (known as *jingji shiyongfang*) was supplied at
a lower price than commercial housing, this reduction being made possible through
various government subsidies to developers (e.g. tax redemption) (Lee 2000). In
general, households whose income fell into the top 20 percent of the income deciles
distribution were expected to buy commercial housing at full market price. Those
households whose income was above the lowest 20 percent were considered as
potential buyers of both commercial and affordable housing. Over the years, the
sales volume of new residential units to individuals in urban China has increased
substantially. According to the National Bureau of Statistics, 88 percent of urban
housing sold in 2000 went to individuals instead of institutions, the sales volume
reaching 295.4 billion yuan (People's Daily 2001). In 2002, Beijing also witnessed
a high rate of market participation by individuals in housing purchase: 97 percent
of 16 million sq. mtr of residential dwelling space sold in the market was bought
by individuals (Beijing Municipal Bureau of Statistics 2003).

Second, the homeownership rate has also increased through the privatization of public rental dwellings, which were sold to sitting tenants at a discounted price based on employees' work history and ranks. The privatization was emphasized by the State Council as an essential component of housing reform policies. Throughout the 1990s, the sales volume had been rising steadily, and a big push came in 1998 when all kinds of welfare housing allocation were terminated. A case study on three cities, by Huang, found that nearly half of the homeowners became such in 1998, suggesting that many urban residents rushed into the queue for subsidized sales in order to "catch the last train" of welfare housing allocation (Huang 2004: 62–63). In August 2002, the then Deputy Minister of the Ministry of Construction was proud to announce that "since the mid-1990s, 80 percent of China's public housing has been sold to local residents" (Xinhua News Agency 2002).

In Beijing, the concentration of government institutions hampered the rise of homeownership during the early years of housing reform, but homeownership has been on the increase noticeably since 1998. Surveys by the municipal statistical bureau indicate that the proportion of owner-occupiers was just over 20 percent in 1998, but had reached 54.1 percent by 2001. The proportion of public rental tenants in 2001 was 44.5 percent (Beijing Municipal Bureau of Statistics 2002). It appears that the prereform dominance of public rental tenure has shifted towards a polarized system of owner occupation and public rental tenure. Private rental tenure was marginal and constituted less than 2 percent of the sample population. Although the strengthening of reform measures in the housing sector was intended to create diversity in the existing tenure structure, this much hoped for outcome seemed to have occurred only within the owner occupation sector, which was divided into homeownership with full and partial property rights. Although the public rental sector in Beijing occupies an important position in the tenure structure, its long-term prospects are not promising due to increasing urban redevelopment that replaces public rental units with commercial flats.

Deteriorating housing conditions in inner city districts

By 1978, the housing conditions in cities were in need of urgent attention. Per capita living space had declined from 4.5 sq. mtr in 1952 to 3.6 sq. mtr in 1978 (Kirkby 1990: 295). Despite the increased housing investment during the early years of reform implementation, the conditions of older dwellings in cities worsened. One of the major problems was the lack of maintenance and management funds. For instance, in Beijing, the maintenance and management fees in 1987 were, on average, 0.46 and 0.10 yuan per sq. mtr, respectively. The average rent of dwellings, however, was 0.11 yuan per sq. mtr in 1987, and the rent for *pingfang* dwellings was even lower, causing further deterioration due to near negligence (Sun and Zhang 1989: 7).

In Beijing, according to a nationwide survey on urban housing conditions in 1985, more than half of the residents (52.7 percent) did not have a private kitchen (Fan 1989). Nearly two-thirds (62.7 percent) had no access to private toilets, and only half (49 percent) had in-house tap water connection. Beijing's per capita floor space turned out to be 8.77 sq. mtr, placing the capital city as one of the regions with the worst conditions. One quarter of Beijing residents were classified as the housing poor, and the incidence of "housing poverty" was much more severe in inner city districts (Fan 1989: 32–33).[1]

Implementation of the Old and Dilapidated Housing Redevelopment Program

In 1991, the Beijing municipal government issued a plan to demolish and redevelop old and dilapidated dwellings. The specific program to initiate this work was known as the "Old and Dilapidated Housing Redevelopment Program" (hereafter ODHRP). The core idea behind it was to bring in real estate developers as the main financiers and project implementers, while local authorities provided administrative support. This was seen as an inevitable solution to the severity of dilapidated housing problems and the limits of public finance. According to Sun and Zhang (1989: 7), the total investment necessary to redevelop old and dilapidated dwellings in the Old City of Beijing in 1989 would be "more than 200 percent of total urban housing investment in the Old City since the Liberation."

The turning point was the speech by the mayor of Beijing on April 30, 1990, which emphasized the ripening opportunity for the redevelopment of inner city districts (Beijing Municipal Government 1990). It was stressed that a series of new estate developments in suburban districts was providing new dwellings that could be used for the relocation of inner city residents. In the ODHRP, demolition and wholesale redevelopment was the main method of transforming old and dilapidated neighborhoods. High-rise flats and commercial buildings were favored as the end products. To facilitate the program, an ODHRP office was opened at the municipal government to supervise and support the overall process. Furthermore, the municipal government set aside 200 million yuan to lend to those four inner city districts (namely Dongcheng, Xicheng, Chongwen, and Xuanwu), which were to receive particular attention due to the severity of their housing problems.

The progress of the ODHRP was also facilitated by land-use reform since the late 1980s, which created favorable conditions for real estate investment. Legislation such as the 1988 Amendment to the Constitution and the Land Administration Law enabled the transaction of land-use rights, leading to the establishment of a property market (Fang and Zhang 2003: 150). Furthermore, local governments in mainland China were given greater decision-making powers, and more incentives through fiscal reform, to manage and proceed with local investment to meet their regional needs and achieve local economic growth (Wei 1996). The sale of land-use rights by the municipal government was an effective means for securing extra-budgetary revenues to invest in elements of the urban infrastructure such as motorways, metro connection, electricity and water supply, all of which required immediate public intervention for the benefit of the growing population and economy.

By 1999, the number of ODHRP projects reached 279 (Fang and Zhang 2003). An official estimation suggested that by the end of 1999 160,900 households were displaced, of which 43.8 percent (70,500 households) were relocated elsewhere, and 29.8 percent (48,000 households) rehoused (UCCBMPPCC *et al.* 2003). Between 2001 and 2005, Beijing reportedly anticipated that another 340,000 households would be displaced as part of urban redevelopment projects (People's Daily 2002). Considering the number of inner city residents (Beijing Municipal Bureau of Statistics 2003), the scale of displacement indicated that approximately 14 percent would be affected by the redevelopment.

Field research and data collection

The discussion in this chapter is based on the author's research data collected from a series of field visits to Beijing in 2002 and 2003. The field research took place in Dongcheng, one of the inner city districts of Beijing. Within the district, a neighborhood called Xinzhongjie was selected as the main case study area. Xinzhongjie lies across the Workers' Stadium outside the eastern section of Beijing's second ring road. The dwellings subjected to redevelopment in Xinzhongjie showed the typical characteristics of old and dilapidated dwellings found in other redevelopment neighborhoods in Beijing (Figure 9.1). According to the director of the Dongzhimen street office that administered Xinzhongjie, most dwellings found in Xinzhongjie were public rental housing. The privatization of existing public housing units was not applied to these dwellings, as their condition was too dilapidated for them to be considered appropriate for such transfer of ownership.

The redevelopment of Xinzhongjie was phased in, presenting ample opportunities for examining the differing degrees of impact upon residents due to changing compensation policies. Xinzhongjie's first phase redevelopment started at the end of 1999 and was completed early 2002. In total, 550 households were displaced.[2] The end product of this first phase redevelopment was a commercial housing estate

Figure 9.1 A cul-de-sac in Xinzhongjie's second phase redevelopment area.
Source: Photo by Hyun Bang Shin.

Figure 9.2 The Sun City Estate, the end-product of Xinzhongje's first phase redevelopment.
Source: Photo by Hyun Bang Shin.

called the Sun City Estate (*Yangguang Dushi*) (Figure 9.2). At the time the author interviewed local residents, the second phase redevelopment was yet to be implemented. A household survey was undertaken in May 2003 by the developers in coordination with the local authority in order to estimate each household's level of compensation. Therefore, the remaining Xinzhongjie residents had all the reasons to anticipate demolition and redevelopment in the near future.

The research conducted was essentially qualitative, focusing on neighborhood conditions and residents' experiences under different compensation policies. For this chapter, the interviews with local officials and eighteen households were analyzed against the backdrop of housing and redevelopment policies in Beijing. The interviewed residents consisted of three different groups. The first consisted of those who were still residing in Xinzhongjie, awaiting displacement in the near future as part of the second phase redevelopment. The second comprised those who were displaced from Xinzhongjie as part of the first phase redevelopment. The third group consisted of those who were displaced from other redevelopment neighborhoods near Xinzhongjie within Dongcheng district. They were recruited to supplement the diversity of displacement experiences.[3]

The compensation practice in redevelopment

From in-kind to monetarized redevelopment compensation

From 1991, residents displaced from redevelopment neighborhoods were compensated in accordance with the State Council's Ordinance on the Management of Urban Housing Demolition and Relocation (hereafter 1991 State Council Ordinance). It called for in-kind compensation, combined with cash compensation if necessary, when residents were to become subject to demolition and relocation. Developers in charge were to provide rehousing or relocation dwellings elsewhere, guaranteeing the continuation of residents' existing tenure in a relocation dwelling. Such practice, however, led to high project costs and low profitability, eventually becoming a hindrance to the rapid expansion of redevelopment programs (Dowall 1994; Leaf 1995).

A major revision took place in 1998. While the 1991 State Council Ordinance was still in its place, the Beijing municipal government produced a revised compensation policy by announcing the implementation of the Measure for the Management of Urban Housing Demolition and Relocation (hereafter 1998 Compensation Measure). It became effective as of December 1, 1998 (Beijing Municipal Government 1998a). The key to this revision was the monetarization of redevelopment compensation by taking two factors into consideration: the number of registered household members, and formal dwelling space. The 1998 Compensation Measure did not rule out off-site relocation or on-site rehousing, but, in its actual implementation, cash-based compensation was accepted as the norm under the new regulation, as an official explained

> The biggest difference was that [redevelopment compensation] was not based on the allocation of relocation dwelling. All was monetarized... It also took the household element into consideration, but it mainly considered dwelling space . . .
>
> (Official from the Displacement and Relocation Department,
> Dongcheng district government)

Under the 1998 Compensation Measure, households were more likely to receive a larger amount of compensation if their household size was larger, and if they occupied a bigger dwelling space. Only those who were formally registered as Beijing residents were eligible for compensation. Informal self-built space was in principle not subject to compensation. If a household lived in a non-self-contained unit with no indoor kitchen or toilet facilities, the household was entitled to the receipt of an additional space subsidy of 25 sq. mtr (Beijing Municipal Government 1998b). For instance, when the 1998 Compensation Measure was applied, a three-person household living in a non-self-contained dwelling with a construction space of 20 sq. mtr would have received around 300,000 yuan as cash compensation upon displacement (see Table 9.3 later in this chapter for more details on the calculation method). For an average Beijing household whose annual household disposable income reached 37,391.7 yuan in 2002 (Beijing Municipal Bureau of Statistics 2003), this would be equivalent to nearly eight years' accumulation of their household income.

Rehousing difficulties

Due to the poor conditions of their dwellings, public rental tenants in redevelopment neighborhoods were excluded from taking part in the privatization process that swept the nation in the 1990s. When redevelopment takes place in their neighborhoods, residents would aspire to homeownership, as one of the interviewees vividly explained

> It's always no good to rent. In the end, you place this burden on your children, and it's not realistic either. Still want to have a place of one's own regardless of the size.
>
> (Middle-aged female in Xinzhongjie, subject to displacement)

Given the practice of monetarized redevelopment compensation, did the displaced residents manage to use the compensation to stay in their neighborhood and join the rank of homeowners upon redevelopment? The scale of displacement and the high prices of redeveloped flats in central Beijing suggests that this was not easy. A vivid example of how the compensation limits displacees' transfer to homeownership in inner city districts is the case of Xinzhongjie's first phase redevelopment that resulted in the construction of the Sun City Estate. As noted earlier, among the 550 households displaced from the neighborhood, only twenty of them were rehoused upon project completion – a rehousing rate of less than 4 percent.

At the planning stage, in-kind allocation of dwelling units was considered for residents' relocation, but the announcement of the 1998 Compensation Measure influenced the final decision to adopt cash-based compensation. This meant that those displaced residents had to buy a redeveloped flat on-site if they wished to be rehoused. The full market price of a redeveloped flat averaged 8,200 yuan per sq. mtr, but those returning residents were given a preferential price of 5,500 yuan per sq. mtr. This price, however, appears to have been still too high for most residents. The rehoused households interviewed by the author purchased two-bedroom flats with a construction space of between 107 and 116 sq. mtr. A 107 sq. mtr flat at full market price would cost 880,000 yuan. For average Beijing households, the price-to-income ratio (hereafter PIR) would reach as high as 25 to 1, making it difficult for them to buy a flat in the Sun City Estate. As for those rehousing households, the discounted price of the same flat would be 588,500 yuan, one-third cheaper than its full market price. This, however, would still lead to a PIR of about 28 to 1, as the displaced residents' annual disposable income was significantly lower than that of average Beijing households.[4] Given the high PIR, it was not surprising at all that few original residents returned to the neighborhood upon project completion. The Director of Dongzhimen street office recollected

> While carrying out the first phase of redevelopment [of Xinzhongjie], our original estimate was that about 10 to 20 percent [of the existing residents] would be able to return, but the final result was that the number was not as many as expected. At the time of initiating [this project], it was to demolish and carry out in-kind compensation. Afterwards, it was based on cash. In between, the policies have changed many times. I feel the policies change a bit too rapidly.
>
> (Director of Dongzhimen street office)

Suburbanization of displaced residents

Given the inability of displaced residents to purchase redeveloped flats for rehousing, the remaining option was to use their cash compensation to finance homeownership elsewhere. There were no available official statistics or registration data to reveal where the residents relocated, but interviews with some of the displaced households and neighborhood committee leaders all suggest that most residents moved to near suburban or outer suburban districts outside the fourth ring road. One of the Xinzhongjie neighborhood committee leaders recollected

> At the time of displacement [as part of the neighborhood's first phase redevelopment], after real estate developers heard about the news, they all came, each of them with a coach, pulling us into the car to take us to view their houses. So, for a while, because it was free of charge, all the residents got on the car everyday, taking a view of those houses, checking out which area has more convenient transportation, whether the sales price is relatively affordable, etc...[At that time] so many companies came. They came...from all over the city, but mostly from the [near and outer suburban] northeast, because we are geographically located at the north-eastern corner of the city ...
>
> (Xinzhongjie neighborhood committee leader)

In fact, the displaced residents were confronted with the acute affordability problem experienced in inner city districts. Table 9.1 summarizes the PIRs of commercial housing at various locations in Beijing by taking into account the annual household disposable income. According to the table, an average Beijing household would have to pay almost 20 years' accumulation of their household disposable income to buy a 80 sq. mtr self-contained commercial flat. In particular, the average housing price was highest within the second ring road, and dropped away toward suburban areas. The PIR outside the fourth ring road for an average household turned out to be 7.7 to 1, less than half of what it was within the second ring road. The displaced residents, having much lower incomes, experienced higher PIRs.

Table 9.1 Commercial housing prices and household income in Beijing

Location	Average price[a] (as of July 2001)	Interviewed residents	Beijing households		
Annual household disposable income (in 2002, yuan)		Average (N = 13) 21,003.7	Average 37,391.7	Bottom 20% of income decile 19,384.0	
Beijing as a whole	381,680	18.2 : 1	10.2 : 1	19.7 : 1	
Within the second ring road	620,240	29.5 : 1	16.6 : 1	32.0 : 1	
Between the second and third ring roads	561,600	26.7 : 1	15.0 : 1	29.0 : 1	
Between the third and fourth ring roads	414,480	19.7 : 1	11.1 : 1	21.4 : 1	
Outside the fourth ring road	288,000	13.7 : 1	7.7 : 1	14.9 : 1	

Sources: Household interviews by the author in 2003; Beijing Municipal Bureau of Statistics (2003); Xia (2002).

Note
a The average sale price of commercial housing in Beijing was based on the data produced by the National Statistical Bureau of China (Xia 2002), applied to a self-contained flat with a 80-square-meter construction space which was the average size of dwellings purchased by the interviewed households upon displacement.

The excessively high prices of commercial flats in central Beijing meant that most displaced residents from inner city districts had no choice but to move to near or outer suburban districts. This becomes more evident when the housing prices in Table 9.1 are compared with the cash compensation displaced residents actually received (Table 9.2). The interviewed residents received cash compensation which was 5 to 13 times the average annual household disposable income in Beijing (or 14 to 41 times the reported disposable annual household income of the interviewees), but the compensation was still far short of financing homeownership in central Beijing. Most interviewees were unable to find additional resources to bridge the affordability gap, and, thus unable to reap the benefits of their neighborhood redevelopment, were driven out of their neighborhoods to make way for more affluent members of society.

Constraints upon displacees

The previous section so far has focused on the affordability problem in the commercial housing sector in Beijing. There are, however, additional constraints that place greater pressure upon residents, further preventing them from staying in central Beijing and becoming owner-occupiers upon displacement. These constraints include the reduced cash compensation since 2001, high prices in the affordable

Table 9.2 Cash compensation received and housing price paid by displaced interviewees

| Interviewees | Displaced date | Reported annual household disposable income (yuan) ① | Cash compensation | | Proportion to Beijing's average annual household income[a] | Housing price paid (yuan) |
			Total (yuan) ②	Proportion to reported income ②/①		
Moved to a near suburban estate	Dec. 1999	n.a.	340,000	n.a.	9	315,000
	Jan. 2000	n.a.	275,000	n.a.	7	310,000
	Jan. 2000	19,800	300,000	15	8	320,000
Moved to an outer suburban estate	May 2001	20,400	280,000	14	7	210,000
	May 2001	5,040	205,000	41	5	210,000
	May 2001	17,448	490,000	28	13	215,000
Re-housed in the Sun City Estate	Jan. 2000	n.a.	295,000	n.a.	8	535,500
	Jan. 2000	n.a.	n.a.	n.a.	n.a.	580,000
Temporary residence after displacement	Dec. 2002	29,640	296,000	10	8	n.a.

Source: Household interviews by the author in 2003.

Note

a 37,391.7 yuan was the annual disposable household income by the end of 2002 in Beijing (Beijing Municipal Bureau of Statistics 2003: 179).

housing sector, limited formal financial opportunities, and the increased housing costs in redeveloped flats.

Reduced cash compensation since 2001

The 1998 Compensation Measure allowed developers and local authorities to go ahead with cash-based compensation instead of more time-consuming and expensive relocation of existing residents. In May 2001, the municipal government revised its compensation criteria (hereafter 2001 Compensation Measure), which stipulated that the estimation of compensation should be based solely on two factors: first, the construction space of one's formal dwelling; and second, the market-appraisal value of the occupied land (Beijing Municipal Government 2001a,b).

> The purpose of this [that is, 2001 Compensation Measure] is to follow the principle of market appraisal value. In other words, the dwelling space and the market appraisal value determine how much one gets. Basically, there is an evaluation company that completes the appraisal and submits a report to the Displacement and Relocation Department of the Housing Management Bureau. One copy is also given to the displacee.
> (Official from the Displacement and Relocation Department, Dongcheng district government)

The 2001 Compensation Measure would lighten the burden on developers by decreasing the total costs of residents' displacement and relocation at the expense of residents' benefits. Table 9.3 shows how much the total compensation would be reduced under the new measure when the 2001 Compensation Measure was applied to three-person households in non self-contained dwellings of different sizes. It suggests that the application of the 2001 Compensation Measure would result in as much as a 36 percent reduction of the total compensation. The table also shows clearly that the rate of reduction would be greater for those in smaller dwellings, disadvantaging those who had been allocated smaller dwellings in the prereform era.

Unaffordable "affordable housing" sector

The affordability problem in Beijing also engulfs the affordable housing sector, which was originally proposed by the government to make homeownership more affordable for low- and middle-income households. Affordable housing had its roots in the "comfort housing" (known as *anjufang*) program in the mid-1990s, and commenced in 1999 with the aim of building flats on government-allocated lands. A set of preferential policies, such as tax reduction, were implemented to set the sale price within the range of between 2,400 and 4,450 yuan per sq. mtr. In general, the price of an affordable housing flat was set to be 600 yuan lower than the price of other commercial flats nearby (*China Daily* 2001).

Table 9.3 Estimation of redevelopment compensation as per 1998 and 2001 Compensation Measures

Policy Doc.	Calculation method	Compensation	Non self-contained dwelling for a three person household with a construction space of		
			$20\ m^2$	$30\ m^2$	$40\ m^2$
1998 Compensation Measure	Cash compensation = (① + ②) × ③ ①: Dwelling construction space ②: Space subsidy for a non self-contained unit ③: Compensation unit price, determined by the local government	(① + 25) × 6300[a]	283,500	346,500	409,500
2001 Compensation Measure	Cash compensation = ① × (② + ③ × K) + ④ ①: Dwelling construction space ②: Base dwelling price ③: Base land price ④: Building replacement value K : Plot ratio adjustment co-efficient	① × $(1,000 + 5,600 \times 1.3) +$ $(24,255/29.66 \times ①)$[b]	181,955	272,933	363,910
	Rate of reduction (compared to the 1998 Compensation Measure)		36%	21%	11%

Notes

a The compensation unit price (6,300 yuan per square meter) was taken from an official at the Displacement and Relocation Department, Dongcheng district government.

b The values for ②, ③, ④ and K were from the compensation contract provided by an interviewee who was in temporary residence after displacement at the end of 2002. In the case of building replacement value ④, the author assumed for the sake of simplicity that the building replacement value was in linear proportion to the dwelling space. The building replacement value of the 29.66 square-meter dwelling occupied by the interviewee before displacement was 24,255 yuan.

The sale price of affordable housing was regulated by local governments, and differed from one district to another. In the case of Dongcheng district, according to a local housing official interviewed, its price in 2003 was 5,000 yuan per sq. mtr. For an affordable housing unit with a 70 sq. mtr construction space, the sale price would be equivalent to about 10 years' average household disposable income.

Major affordable housing sites were mostly located in outer suburban districts, and their availability within and around the second ring road was limited (People's Daily 2000). Moreover, although the total number of affordable housing flats completed between 1999 and 2002 in Beijing reached 71,731 units, this could only benefit less than three per cent of 2,472,000 households registered within inner city and near suburban districts (Beijing Municipal Bureau of Statistics 2002, 2003). Such limited supply of affordable housing stock spurred severe competition among Beijing residents (*People's Daily* 2001). Furthermore, the affordability problem in the affordable housing sector was fuelled by the developers' practice of building more spacious flats. The amount of profit a developer could retain from affordable housing development was set by the central government regulation at a fixed rate of three per cent of total housing costs (People's Daily 2000). Because of this, developers were lured into supplying more spacious flats in order to increase the transaction volume. For instance, the average construction space of an affordable housing unit turned out to be 95.3 sq. mtr in 1999, but had increased to 110.9 sq. mtr by 2002 (Beijing Municipal Bureau of Statistics 2002, 2003: 133).

Limits with formal financial opportunities

With the emergence and development of the housing finance system in mainland China, one would assume that the affordability gap could be addressed by housing loans. This requires a brief discussion of the Housing Provident Fund (hereafter HPF), which has been the backbone of mainland China's new housing finance system since its inception in Shanghai in 1991. The HPF receives monetary contributions from both employers and employees (World Bank 1992: 30–32). The HPF account holders are eligible to withdraw their accumulated funds when they retire or upon making a down-payment on a new house as a first-time buyer.

The HPF, however, has been criticized as having a serious equity problem. It is very much employer-based, which meant that those in nonregular jobs or out of work would likely be excluded. Workers with underperforming employers were also unlikely to receive employers' contributions, thus having their access denied (Rosen and Ross 2000). Moreover, because the contribution to the HPF is based on a fixed rate, the growing wage gaps in the labor market would lead to a situation in which a higher income earner would enjoy a higher contribution from his or her employer (Lee 2000).

When it comes to home buying, HPF account holders, if eligible, would be able to apply for HPF housing loans (Rosen and Ross 2000). This has been a completely new experience for urban residents in mainland China. To be eligible, an applicant must have a stable job and income, and have kept the HPF account for at least the preceding 12 months. The applicant must have also made contributions to the account consecutively during the last 6 months before making a loan application. Furthermore, before submitting a loan application, the applicant must have made a down-payment of at least 20 percent of the full price of a dwelling (*Beijing Daily* 2003). HPF housing loans thus provided are on preferential terms with lower interest rates (about 1 percent lower in 2002), offering advantages over commercial bank loans.

The HPF housing mortgage, however, would still be too much of a burden upon low-income households. According to the mortgage conditions at the China Construction Bank, for instance, for borrowing 100,000 yuan over a 15-year loan period at an annual percentage rate of 4.05 percent, an applicant would have to repay 742 yuan each month. This would be equivalent to about one quarter of the average monthly household disposable income in Beijing; but for those in the bottom 20 percent of the income decile distribution, the monthly repayment would reach three quarters of their household disposable income. It would also be a burden upon average Beijing residents if they were to become owner-occupiers by purchasing a new dwelling in central Beijing, where housing prices are far more expensive than elsewhere.

Reflecting such circumstances, a housing mortgage was regarded as an "unrealistic" option by displacees in redevelopment neighborhoods, as some of the interviewees from Xinzhongjie explicitly stated

> Who would provide you with mortgage? No way to take out a loan. ... My husband doesn't have a job, and I don't have one either. It's for sure that they wouldn't grant us any mortgage. I've never thought of that. Don't you ever say mortgage again!
> (Middle-aged female in Xinzhongjie, subject to displacement)

> Where would I get a loan from? Once you retire, then nobody gives you loan. If I have to get a loan, the only way is to depend on my elder son [who has a HPF account]. My second son doesn't have a job, and the third son is laid off. They all can't apply for a loan.
> (Retired couple in Xinzhongjie, subject to displacement)

Such concerns would be more prevalent if displaced residents did not have regular employees among their cohabiting household members; were dependent on the social safety net (i.e. Minimum Livelihood Security System); and did not have HPF account holders within the household either (see Table 9.4). In fact, when the interviewed households' occupational structure was examined, 16 per cent of all the household members (excluding students and children under schooling age) were found to be either laid-off or unemployed, and 27 percent, retired. The proportion of household members engaged in temporary or informal employment reached 20 percent.[5] Under these circumstances, many families would be unlikely to have employer-based HPF accounts and creditable income-generating activities, and therefore likely to experience difficulties in accessing the formal loans or housing mortgage opportunities that favor those with proven credit records.

Table 9.4 Household circumstances of Xinzhongjie residents subject to displacement in relation to their opportunities for housing loans

Number of households responded	Regular employee(s) among co-habiting household members?	Minimum Livelihood Security System beneficiaries?	Any Housing Provident Fund account holder(s) among co-habiting household members?	Any expectation for formal housing loan?
Yes	4	6	3	0
No	5	3	6	8
n.a.	0	0	0	1

Source: Household interviews by the author in Beijing in 2003.

Increased housing expenditure

Those interviewed households subject to displacement reported that their monthly rents averaged less than two per cent of their monthly household disposable income. This was much lower than reform policies anticipated. While the reform measures aimed at increasing the level of rent to reach 15 percent of household income, the rent level in Beijing had not risen to meet this target. The standard rent in the public housing sector at the beginning of reform policies in the late 1980s was 0.11 yuan per sq. mtr. It was increased to 1.3 yuan in 1999, and was further increased to 3.05 yuan per sq. mtr as of April 1, 2000, but this still constituted only about 6.3 percent of the interviewed households' monthly disposable income (*China Daily* 2000a,b).

While the residents expressed their desire to become homeowners to maintain their housing security, life as owner-occupiers in modern flats would require far more increased expenditure. Given the low level of household income and rents they experienced while residing in dilapidated public rental units, the increased monthly housing costs might turn out to undermine their ability to maintain their homeownership in the future. An interviewee who moved to a walk-up flat in an outer suburban district commented

> [Before displacement] we didn't have to spend much. Our rent was just over thirty yuan, and water and electricity bills were cheaper there. Now, things are not well. At the moment, I'm telling you, I just don't have the three hundred yuan [to pay for the bills]. I just don't eat or drink, but no three hundred yuan, and that's embarrassing.
>
> (Female retiree, moved to an outer suburban estate after displacement)

In order to examine how much pressure housing costs might have exerted upon residents after moving from their old neighborhoods, Table 9.5 made a summary of monthly housing costs incurred by the interviewed households in comparison

Table 9.5 Monthly housing costs and their proportion to household disposable income

Interviewees	Household disposable income (yuan) ①	Monthly housing costs reported by interviewees				% of household disposable income ②/①	% of Beijing's average household disposable income[d]
		Total (yuan) ②	Rent or management fee[a]	Utility bills[b]	Heating[c]		
Moved to suburban districts	4 households 1,306	375	51	179	145	28.7%	12.0%
Re-housed in the Sun City Estate	2 households n.a.	834	391	155	289	n.a.	26.8%
Displaced and in temporary residence	1 household 2,470	525	0	300	225	21.3%	16.8%
Xinzhongjie residents subject to displacement	7 households 1,866	216	28	149	39	11.6%	6.9%

Source: Household interviews by the author in 2003.

Notes

a Monthly management fees for the households re-housed or moved to suburban districts.

b Utility bills include electricity, water and gas bills.

c For the households re-housed or moved to suburban districts, this refers to the annual central heating costs, divided by twelve months.

d 3,116 yuan per household in 2002 (Beijing Municipal Bureau of Statistics 2003).

with their reported household income. The table only includes those households whose housing costs and monthly household disposable income were all reported to the author during the interviews.

In the case of households who were still residing in dilapidated dwellings in Xinzhongjie, the total housing costs incurred each month were on average 11.6 percent of their reported monthly household disposable income and 6.9 percent of Beijing's average monthly household disposable income in 2002. As for the households relocated to suburban districts, they experienced a significant increase in housing costs. The total housing costs of those four interviewee households constituted on average 28.7 percent of their monthly household income.

The proportion of housing costs to Beijing's average monthly household disposable income was highest in the case of those two households rehoused in the Sun City Estate. As mentioned earlier, these households are the wealthiest among the residents displaced as part of Xinzhongjie's first phase redevelopment. However, even for them, the monthly housing costs in redeveloped flats were beyond expectation. The high cost of living in the Sun City Estate caused most of the 20 rehoused households subsequently to leave the Sun City Estate. By August 2003, about 18 months after their rehousing, only six families remained in the estate, and they were also considering moving out in the near future.

Conclusion

Urban redevelopment in mainland China has been transforming dilapidated dwellings in prime locations into commercial flats, attracting wealthier sections of the urban population. Displaced local residents were in principle guaranteed a relocation dwelling in which they could continue their existing tenure and maintain housing security (before 1998) or offered cash compensation to become owner-occupiers elsewhere (since 1998). Homeownership, however, involved displacement to suburban estates. Inner city residents in dilapidated neighborhoods found it extremely difficult to be rehoused under the monetarized compensation policy. Most commercial flats, especially in central Beijing, were affordable only to the high income groups of urban residents (Wang and Murie 1999a,b; Wu 2002). For some displacees, suburban relocation might enable them to sustain their financial assets (i.e. redevelopment compensation) in the form of property assets (i.e. homeownership), which could then be used at a later stage as a bulwark (e.g. collateral) against any potential economic difficulties. For many others who became subject to displacement since 2001, this would no longer be applicable.

The new environment since the implementation of the 2001 Compensation Measure undermined residents' homeownership aspiration and their housing security. The new policy effectively reduced the total cash compensation, imposing harsher constraints upon public sector tenants who were facing entry into the housing market. Given the high prices in both commercial and affordable housing sectors, one alternative for the displacees would be to look for a private rental unit. This option, however, was also very much restricted due to the underdevelopment of the private rental market. As of 2001, private rental tenure was marginal in Beijing's tenure structure. One of the major reasons was the prohibition of resales or subletting for a certain period in the case of those properties with partial property rights. For instance, affordable housing was prohibited from resale or letting to a third party for a government-designated period (until homeowners gained full property rights) (Ministry of Construction China 1995, 1999). The same rule applied to those privatized former public housing units. The Ministry of Construction also prohibited subletting or leasing of state allocated public rental housing and any of those old and dilapidated housing units subject to redevelopment. Given the restricted supply of affordable rental units, private renting in inner city districts was often beyond the reach of most local residents.

In the reform process of realigning the role of the state, employers and individuals in housing provision, local governments and real estate developers have reaped the benefits of extensive urban redevelopment by generating revenues, "modernizing" cityscape and making development profits. In contrast, poorer sections of the urban population have become increasingly vulnerable in terms of financing and securing dwellings in the housing market. The development of the housing finance system (e.g. housing mortgage and employment-based Housing Provident Fund) would in principle fill the affordability gap and enhance poor residents' purchasing power, but their weak socioeconomic status keeps them from making use of such opportunities. With the shrinking public housing sector, residential redevelopment could no longer serve as a pathway to homeownership but simply force an exit to the much constrained private rental sector. This, however, could only be a short-term solution, as the limited income of poorer residents and their weak position in the urban labor market would pose a threat to their prolonged exposure in a private rental sector that demands much higher rents than the public rental sector.

Acknowledgements

The author would like to thank the Centre for Social Policy Research at the Chinese Academy of Social Sciences for kindly providing invaluable support for field research visits. The field research was partly funded by the Central Research Fund at the University of London. Thanks are also to Fulong Wu and anonymous referees for their constructive comments.

Notes

1 See Hong (1993) for the definition of "housing poor."
2 Unless otherwise stated, the information on the status and progress of Xinzhongjie redevelopment is from the web site of the Dongcheng district government, and also from the author's interviews with local officials and a former manager closely associated with the developer in charge of Xinzhongjie's first phase redevelopment.
3 The recruitment of residents for in-depth interviews was designed to maximize the opportunity to learn about the redevelopment processes and residents' differentiated displacement experiences unfolded in local contexts. For this, the author tried to ensure,

within the local constraints, the diversity of recruited residents in terms of their household income, employment status, and displacement and rehousing status. In this way, the research aimed at acquiring a comprehensive picture of the problems faced by local residents upon displacement, enriching our understanding of the social impact of Beijing's residential redevelopment.

4 Interviewees were asked to provide the actual disposable income of each cohabiting household member. This income mainly referred to the regular income, including monthly salaries if employed, social insurance and security benefits (if in receipt of such), and any other income generated from informal jobs claimed to have been engaged in. It is possible that income might have been underreported by the survey not being able to identify incomes from any concealed informal activities or financial support from social networks (e.g. next of kin). The reported income, however, would still serve the purpose of allowing comparison between relative differences in living expenses before and after displacement from dilapidated neighborhoods.

5 The high incidence of unemployment was characteristic of Xinzhongjie neighborhood. As of March 2002, the summary record of household registration data supplied by the neighborhood committee indicated that 29 percent of all the residents (excluding students and children under schooling age) turned out to have retired, and 10 percent lost their jobs by being laid-off or unemployed. This was in contrast with the official unemployment rate of Beijing, which was reported to be only 1.18 percent by the end of 2001 (Beijing Municipal Government 2002: 216).

References

Beijing Daily (March 6, 2003) "Beijingshi yiyou 65ge Loupan Keyong Zhengcexing Tiexi Daikuan Goumai" [Beijing already has 65 estates available for the purchase with loans at preferential rates], *Beijing Ribao.*

Beijing Municipal Bureau of Statistics (2002) *Beijing Statistical Yearbook 2002*, Beijing: China Statistics Press.

Beijing Municipal Bureau of Statistics (2003) *Beijing Statistical Yearbook 2003*, Beijing: China Statistics Press.

Beijing Municipal Government (1990) "Yinfa Chen Xi Tong Shichang Guanyu Weijiufang Gaizao Wenti Jianghua de Tongzhi" [Notice of Mayor Chen Xi Tong's Speech on Old and Dilapidated Housing Redevelopment]. Available online at: www.govfile.beijing.gov.cn/Govfile/front/content/21990043_1.html (accessed on December 27, 2005).

Beijing Municipal Government (1998a) "Beijingshi Chengshi Fangwu Chaiqian Guanli Banfa" [Measure for the management of urban housing demolition and relocation in Beijing]. Available online at: www.govfile.beijing.gov.cn/Govfile/front/content/01998016_0.html (accessed on December 27, 2005).

Beijing Municipal Government (1998b) "Guanyu Beijingshi Chengshi Fangwu Chaiqian Buchang de Youguan Guipifu" [Response in relation to urban housing demolition and relocation compensation in Beijing] Available online at: www.fw365.com.cn/zcfg/cqp/5.htm (accessed on April 20, 2005).

Beijing Municipal Government (2001a) "Beijingshi Chengshi Fangwu Chaiqian Guanli Banfa" [Measure for the management of urban housing demolition and relocation in Beijing]. Available online at: govfile.beijing.gov.cn/Govfile/front/content/02001087_1.html (accessed on December 27, 2005).

Beijing Municipal Government (2001b) "Beijingshi Fangwu Chaiqian Pinggu Guize" [Estimation rules for Housing Demolition and Relocation in Beijing]. Available online at: www.bjtd.com/article_view.asp?article_id=572 (accessed on May 15, 2005).

Beijing Municipal Government (2002) *Beijing Yearbook 2002,* Beijing: Beijing Nianjian Chubanshe.

China Daily (March 22, 2000a) "Capital to raise housing rent."

China Daily (June 22, 2000b) "More Beijingers want loans for homes."

China Daily (January 23, 2001) "Low-cost houses on horizon."

Dowall, D. E. (1994) "Urban residential redevelopment in the people's republic of China," *Urban Studies*, 31(9): 1497–1516.

Fan, Y. (1989) "Beijing Chengshi Zhuzhai Wenti de Xianzhuang he Renwu" [Current situation of Beijing urban housing problems and missions], *Beijing Guihua Jianshe [Beijing City Planning & Construction Review]*, 8: 30–33.

Fang, K. and Zhang, Y. (2003) "Plan and market mismatch: Urban redevelopment in Beijing during a period of transition," *Asia Pacific Viewpoint*, 44(2): 149–162.

Gaubatz, P. (2005) "Globalization and the development of new central business districts in Beijing, Shanghai and Guangzhou," in L. J. C. Ma and F. Wu (eds) *Restructuring the Chinese City: Changing Society, Economy and Space*, Oxon; New York: Routledge, 98–121.

Hong, M. (1993) "Zhuzhai Fazhan yu Shehui Gongneng" [Housing Development and Social Function], in X. Zhang and M. Hong (eds) *Zhuzhai Shehuixue Gaishu [Introduction to Housing Sociology]*, Beijing: Social Sciences Academic Press.

Huang, Y. (2004) "Housing markets, government behaviors, and housing choice: a case study of three cities in China," *Environment and Planning A*, 36(1): 45–68.

Kirkby, R. J. R. (1990) "China," in K. Mathéy (ed.) *Housing policies in the Socialist Third World*, London; New York: Mansell, 298–313.

Leaf, M. (1995) "Inner city redevelopment in China," *Cities*, 12(3): 149–162.

Lee, J. (2000) "From welfare housing to home ownership: the dilemma of China's housing reform," *Housing Studies*, 15(1): 61–76.

Li, B. (2005) "Urban housing privatisation: redefining the responsibilities of the state, employers and individuals," in S. Green and G. S. Liu (eds) *Exit the Dragon? Privatisation and State Control in China*, Oxford: Blackwell Publishers, 145–168.

Ministry of Construction China (1995) "Measures on the Management of Urban Housing Renting." Available online at: www.cin.gov.cn/law/depart/2000102006-00.htm (accessed on April 21, 2005).

Ministry of Construction China (1999) "Provisional Measures on the Management of Sales of Previously Sold Public Housing and Affordable Housing." Available online at: www.cin.gov.cn/law/depart/2000110911.htm (accessed on April 21, 2005).

People's Daily (June 4, 2000) "Economy housing gains favour."

People's Daily (March 19, 2001) "Building houses for low-income families."

People's Daily (April 1, 2002) "Beijingers concerned over house prices."

Rosen, K. T. and Ross, M. C. (2000) "Increasing home ownership in urban china: notes on the problem of affordability," *Housing Studies*, 15(1): 77–88.

Sun, H. and Zhang, W. (1989) "Jiashu Beijing Jiucheng Weifangqu Gaijian de Duice" [Countermeasure for the acceleration of the redevelopment of dilapidated housing districts in the Old City of Beijing], *Beijing Guihua Jianshe [Beijing City Planning & Construction Review]*, 11: 7–10.

UCCBMPPCC (Urban Construction Committee of Beijing Municipal People's Political Consultative Conference) *et al.* (2003) *Research report on the problems of old and dilapidated housing redevelopment in Beijing*, Internet. Beijing: China People's Political Consultative Conference. Available online at: www.beinet.net.cn/bjzx2003/report/report06.jsp (accessed on April 3, 2005).

Wang, Y. P. and Murie, A. (1999a) "Commercial housing development in urban China," *Urban Studies*, 36(9): 1475–1494.

Wang, Y. P. and Murie, A (1999b) *Housing Policy and Practice in China*, London: Macmillan.

Wei, Y. (1996) "Fiscal systems and uneven regional development in China, 1978-1991," *Geoforum*, 27(3): 329–344.

World Bank (1992) *China: Implementation Options for Urban Housing Reform*. A World Bank country study, Washington, DC: World Bank.

Wu, F. (2002) "Real estate development and the transformation of urban space in China's transitional economy, with special reference to Shanghai," in J. R. Logan (ed.) *The New Chinese City: Globalization and Market Reform*, Oxford: Blackwell Publishers.

Wu, F. (2004) "Urban poverty and marginalization under market transition: the case of Chinese cities," *International Journal of Urban and Regional Research*, 28(2): 401–423.

Xia, Y. (2002) "Analysis of the price of commercial housing in Beijing," in T. Jing (ed.) *Bluebook of Beijing 2002: Development Report of Chinese Capital City*, Beijing: Social Sciences Documentation Publishing House, pp. 135–139.

Xinhua News Agency (2002) "80 Percent of Urban Chinese Own Houses," August 12, 2002. Available online at: www.china.org.cn/english/China/39252.htm (accessed on October 25, 2002).

Zhang, X.-Q. (1997) "Urban land reform in China," *Land Use Policy*, 14(3): 187–199.

Zhou, M. and Logan, J. R. (2002) "Market transition and the commodification of housing in urban China," in J. R. Logan (ed.) *The New Chinese City: Globalization and Market Reform*, Oxford: Blackwell Publishers, 137–152.

10 Neighborhood changes and residential differentiation in Shanghai

Shenjing He and Fulong Wu

Introduction

Residential differentiation has long been a classic topic of sociospatial inequality studies. Research on residential differentiation revolves around different themes in different periods. In the 1920s, the Chicago School studied poverty, segregation and the inner city (Park *et al.* 1925). Although concern about class and segregation went quiet during from the 1940s to the 1960s, research interest resurfaced in the question of ethnic segregation and quantitative research on the patterns of residential differentiation since the mid-1960s, while in the 1980s the two themes of "underclass" and "social polarization" emerged and were closely linked to issues of race, ethnicity and segregation in globalizing cities (Hamnett 2001). In the 1990s, the issue of social polarization and duality in world cities received intensive research (e.g. Hamnett 2003; Marcuse and van Kempen 2000; Mollenkopf and Castells 1991; Sassen 2001). At present, under the forces of economic globalization and spatial reorganization, research in spatial differentiation has revived, with a particular interest in post-Fordist cities and globalizing cities. Recent studies on residential differentiation have several foci, for instance the concentration of poverty within particular neighborhoods, increasing division between races, greater segregation of immigrant groups, rich neighborhoods replacing poor neighborhoods in the central city, and increasing income disparities between neighborhoods (Hamnett 2003; Marcuse 1997; Marcuse and van Kempen 2000; Sassen 1991). Urban redevelopment has been recognized as an important factor leading to sociospatial differentiation. The notorious urban renewal in the United States of the 1960s was criticized for making the poor invisible by driving them out of the city (Gans 1967; Hartman 1964; Jacobs 1961). Sweeping neoliberal urban programs further intensified sociospatial division in North American cities, within which real estate development and property-led redevelopment have been prevalently employed to create the "revanchist city" (Smith 1996, 2002; Weber 2002).

Parallel to the divided city phenomenon in the post-Fordist globalizing cities, enlarged social division can be observed in a number of postsocialist countries, although presenting in a different pattern (Dangscht 1987; Gentile 2004; Kovacs 1994; Lehmann and Ruble 1997; Pickvance 2002; Ruoppila and Kahrik 2003;

Sykora 1999). In the context of market transition, evidence shows that urban China is undergoing housing stratification and greater residential inequality (Huang 2004; Li 2004; Logan 2005; Logan *et al.* 1999; Sato 2006; Wang 2000; Wang *et al.* 2005; Wu 2002). Through examining changing housing tenure, these studies suggest that housing inequalities in postreform China are mainly determined by three factors: market reforms, institutions, and historical legacies. However, these studies only analyze the static housing structure rather than the dynamic process of urban (re)development. In fact, extensive urban redevelopment in urban China has caused housing tenure changes and residential differentiation. Wang and Murie (2000) argue that the processes of urban redevelopment and residential displacement are likely to break up socially mixed areas in the inner cites. Although people who involuntarily moved from the central areas to peripheral estates have experienced a considerable increase in housing quality, their access to facilities and services is reduced, and the social mix of the inner city neighborhoods is lost. Marketization introduces a new mechanism of residential segregation associated with redevelopment. This is because, after the reemergence of land rent gradients, real estate developers prefer to redevelop old housing in good locations, through which they can easily capture high land rents (Dowall 1994). With selective gentrification and commercialization in good locations in the city centre, sociospatial differentiation is enlarged. Property-led redevelopment therefore has two implications (Wu 2002). First, while real estate development has made it possible to redevelop dilapidated areas, differentiation in price due to commodification has created new difficulties in redeveloping some of the worst residential areas. Second, through devaluing properties around derelict urban areas and industrial sites, marketization has made it more difficult for a large number of low-income groups, especially state industrial "laid off" workers, to draw benefit from their existing properties and relocate to other areas. Furthermore, under the new household sorting mechanism, which is based on housing affordability rather than the housing allocation system of state work units, only high-income and privileged groups can afford to stay in desirable locations in the central area (Wang and Murie 2000). Although redevelopment generally improves the housing conditions of relocated residents, the socioeconomic outcomes of redevelopment are not always optimistic (Logan 2005; Wang and Murie 2000). Urban redevelopment has brought about a number of negative impacts on low- to middle-income groups (Zhang 2002). Logan (2005) even suggests that large-scale urban redevelopment is one of the most influential factors leading to further residential differentiation in urban China.

Existing studies suggest that residential differentiation has enlarged under market transition, while urban redevelopment is an important factor accelerating the process. However, evidence is still lacking to illustrate the way in which urban redevelopment creates residential differentiation. Therefore, this study investigates how urban redevelopment affects housing tenure and determines different routes of housing tenure change. The research is based on a survey of 400 households and a number of interviews in both old and dilapidated neighborhoods and redevelopment neighborhoods.

Urban redevelopment and population redistribution in Shanghai

In Shanghai, a series of institutional changes, ongoing land and housing reform, and prosperous real estate development are turning the long-neglected inner city into a hotspot of urban redevelopment (Leaf 1995). In line with the institutional and political-economic transformations, the approach to urban redevelopment has also experienced significant changes in the postreform era. In present-day Shanghai, urban redevelopment has been adopted as a strategy to reimage the city and promote urban and economic growth. With the increasing involvement of private enterprise, property development has been significantly facilitating urban redevelopment and transforming urban landscapes. From the state-planned alleviation of old and dilapidated housing estates, to state-subsidized urban renewal, to state-sponsored property development, the approach to urban redevelopment in postreform China has changed a lot and brought about different impacts on urban neighborhoods (He and Wu 2007; Wu and He 2005). Property-led redevelopment has now become the prevailing approach to redevelopment (He and Wu 2005). The entire city, especially the old urban neighborhoods in the inner city, is under the tremendous influence of rampant redevelopment. With the booming real estate market, urban landscapes and population distribution have seen significant changes. Meanwhile, housing demolition and residential relocation occur. Extensive urban redevelopment has resulted in the clearance of dilapidated urban areas, increasing construction density, more high-rise/high-end properties, and the beautification of the environment.

The inner city has also seen decreasing population density and an increasing concentration of population with higher socioeconomic status – for example, higher education level. Based on the 1990 and 2000 census data (at the subdistrict level), two maps of population density in Shanghai in 1990 and 2000 have been produced (see Figure 10.1). As the figure shows, the population density of the inner city, especially for the four districts of Jing'an, Huangpu, Luwan and Hongkou, has significantly decreased over a period of ten years. Meanwhile, some subdistricts in the city fringe (e.g. some areas in Pudong, Minhang and Baoshan) have absorbed a large chunk of the population relocated from the central areas, resulting in an increase in population density. After a series of administrative adjustments since the 1980s, Minhang, Baoshan, Jiading and Pudong have experienced rapid development, which has greatly facilitated urban redevelopment in central Shanghai by providing spaces for relocated residents, factories, and work units.

Along with the decline of population density in the inner city, the socioeconomic profiles of inner city neighborhoods have also changed. Evidently, a population of higher socioeconomic status (people with higher level of education and income) is becoming more and more concentrated in the central area. Based on the 1990 and 2000 census data, Figure 10.2 shows the redistribution of population with higher education (two years of college education and beyond). The location quotient (LQ) of people with higher education level is shown at subdistrict scale. A higher LQ index suggests a higher concentration of people with higher education level.

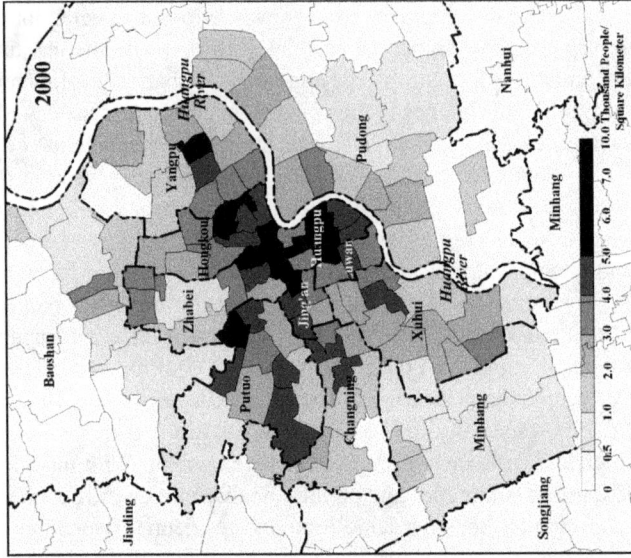

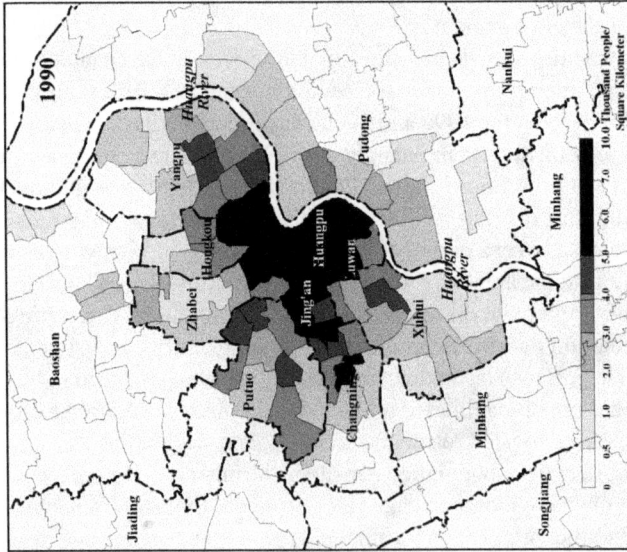

Figure 10.1 Changing population density in Shanghai (1990 vs. 2000).

Source: Produced based on 1990 and 2000 census data.

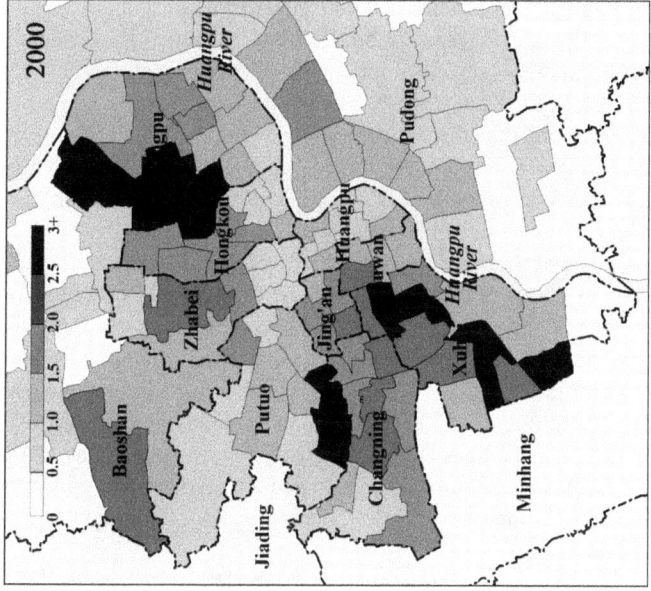

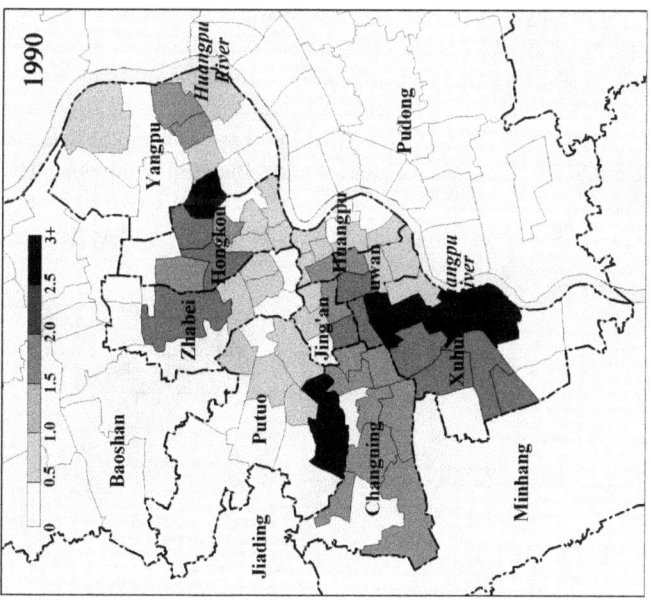

Figure 10.2 Changing location quotient of population with higher education level (1990 *vs.* 2000).

Source: Produced based on 1990 and 2000 census data.

In 1990, the proportion of people in the whole city who had gone through higher education was 6.54 percent. Except for some subdistricts in Yangpu, Xuhui and Putuo, the percentage of people who were educated to college level in the city central area was generally low. In many subdistricts of the inner city, especially old and dilapidated urban areas – for example, parts of former Nanshi (now merged into Huangpu district), Jing'an, Zhabei, Putuo and Yangpu – the LQ was even lower than 1.0, meaning that the concentration of highly educated people was lower than the average. In 2000, when the average percentage in the whole city had increased to 10.94 percent, the LQ of people who had gone through higher education in most parts of the inner city districts was higher than 1.0, which means a higher concentration of highly educated people than the average. Compared with 1990, in 2000, people who had gone through higher education had a considerably wider distribution and higher concentration in the inner city. In most parts of the inner city, and even in many areas in Baoshan and Pudong, the concentration of people who had gone through higher education was much higher. Parts of Xuhui, Changning, and Yangpu have the greatest percentage of highly educated population – more than 30 percent. However, in some areas of Luwan, Huangpu and Zhabei, because of the lack of redevelopment, the concentration of people who had gone through higher education was lower than in other inner city subdistricts.

With large-scale urban redevelopment through land leasing, Shanghai has experienced tremendous residential relocation from the inner city to the fringe, at an unprecedented speed and scale. According to statistical data, until the end of 1997 there were about 456,300 households, comprising more than 1.4 million people, who had moved out of the inner city (Fan 2004). According to the 1990 and 2000 census data, the population in the city core (i.e. Huangpu district, Jing'an district and Luwan district) declined by 691,700 or 36.4 percent. During the same period, the population in the six districts of Xuhui, Putuo, Pudong, Minghang, Baoshan and Jiading increased by 2,998,400 or 63.5 percent. As Figure 10.3 shows, if the People's Square is used as the centre point, the population has decreased by

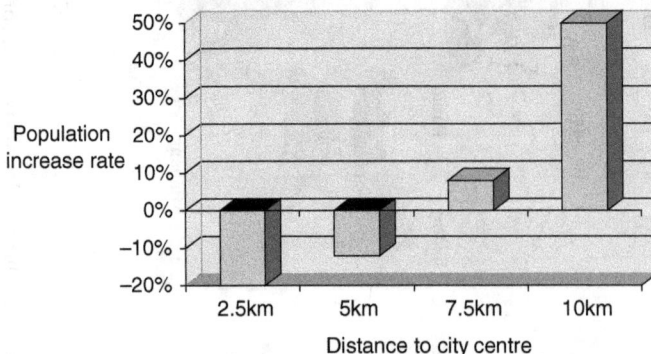

Figure 10.3 The redistribution of population in Shanghai (1990–2000).

20 percent and 12 percent respectively within radiuses of 2.5 and 5 kilometers, and has increased 8 and 50 percent respectively within radiuses of 7.5 and 10 kilometers (Gao and Jiang 2002).

Table 10.1 also shows the changing population distribution in different areas of Shanghai based on data from the five censuses between 1953 and 2000. Except for a slight increase between 1982 and 1990, there is a clear trend of decreasing population in the inner city area between 1953 and 2000, especially between 1990 and 2000. The population in the city centre (i.e. Huangpu, Luwan and Jing'an) decreased by nearly 50 percent from 1990 to 2000.

As for those people moved from the inner city to the periphery, many were involuntarily relocated. Urban redevelopment and work unit housing allocation are two major reasons for involuntary relocation (Wu 2004). In the last 15 years, the implementation of a series of urban redevelopment projects – for example, the "365 plan" (a plan for redeveloping 365 hectares of old and dilapidated housing estates before 2000 proposed by the Shanghai Municipality) – has resulted in a significant decrease in the population of the city centre. The comparatively lower housing prices on the outskirts attract some people who wish to purchase a larger house but lack the capability. However, the inconvenience of commuting and poor infrastructure greatly hamper large-scale voluntary relocation to the outskirts. In contrast, residential relocation towards the inner city is normally voluntary and based on personal choices (e.g. purchasing commodity housing) (Li and Siu 2001; Wu 2004). Considering the extremely high housing prices in the redeveloped inner city, people relocating to the inner city generally have comparatively higher socioeconomic status. On the one hand, extensive redevelopment in the inner city has pushed numerous low-income people to the outskirts. On the other, this has resulted in an influx of affluent people into the inner city through the redevelopment of dilapidated urban areas into more attractive places.

Evidently, urban redevelopment has significantly contributed to population redistribution and changing urban landscapes in Shanghai. High-value-added properties (e.g. high-rise buildings, luxury apartments, office buildings and commercial and recreational facilities) have replaced the old and dilapidated urban areas. Public green spaces have also been developed to beautify the city. Millions of people have relocated from the central areas to the periphery. Meanwhile, the inner city has become gentrified, in terms of people with higher socioeconomic status replacing those with lower socioeconomic status, and better housing replacing dilapidated housing. In sum, urban redevelopment has profoundly transformed the city in both physical and socioeconomic terms.

Study areas

In order to find out how urban redevelopment affects residential choices and housing conditions, this study focuses on two groups of people in the inner city of Shanghai, namely people in neighborhoods before and after redevelopment. Based on a questionnaire survey and semistructured interviews conducted in 2004, this chapter attempts to understand how urban redevelopment changes

Table 10.1 Population distribution in different areas of Shanghai (1953–2000) (unit: million people/percentage)

	The first census-1953		The second census-1964		The third census-1982		The fourth census-1990		The fifth census-2000	
	People	%	People	%	People	%	People	%	People	%
Whole city	8.98	100	10.82	100	11.86	100	13.34	100	15.57	100
Inner city[a]	5.28	58.8	6.29	58.1	5.89	49.7	6.86	51.4	6.68	42.9
in which	2.39	26.6	2.57	23.8	2.11	17.8	1.97	14.8	1.18	7.6
City centre[b]										
Outskirts[c]	3.7	41.2	4.53	41.9	5.97	50.3	6.48	48.6	8.89	57.1

Source: Compiled from Lu 2003.

Notes

a Includes nine districts: Huangpu, Luwan, Jing'an, Changning, Xuhui, Putuo, Zhabei, Hongkou, Yangpu.
b Includes three districts: Huangpu, Luwan and Jing'an.
c The rest of the city, including Pudong new district.

the socioeconomic composition of old neighborhoods. This study also tries to conceptualize how urban redevelopment creates different routes of housing change for different groups of people.

The study areas include three neighborhoods: one after redevelopment and two before redevelopment (see Figure 10.4). First, *Zhongyuan Liangwancheng*, also known as Brilliant City, is a redeveloped neighborhood located beside the Suzhou Creek, a major Shanghai waterway. It is a prominent project of the "365 plan." Jointly invested in by Shanghai COSCO (China Overseas Shipping Corporation) SALIM Group Ltd., COSCO Development Ltd., and COSCO Liangwan Ltd, the project has successfully redeveloped 50 hectares of dilapidated area into a modern condominium complex accommodating more than 6,500 households, or about 20,000 people. The project represents the new redevelopment approach of state-sponsored property development.

Second, *Shenjiazhai* is a dilapidated urban neighborhood located to the north of Shanghai railway station and the east of Liangwancheng, possessing a history and socioeconomic composition similar to those of Liangwancheng before the latter was redeveloped. It has long been a notorious old urban neighborhood concentrating high density and low quality houses, and lacking proper maintenance and redevelopment.

Third, *Jinganli* is an old-fashioned *lilong* (lane houses) neighborhood adjacent to Huaihai Road, one of the busiest commercial streets of Shanghai. Built in the 1930s, it became a declined inner city neighborhood suffering from an overcrowded living environment and lacking necessary sanitary facilities.

This study chooses both Shenjiazhai and Jinganli as study sites because they represent two types of old inner city neighborhoods in Shanghai. Shenjiazhai is a

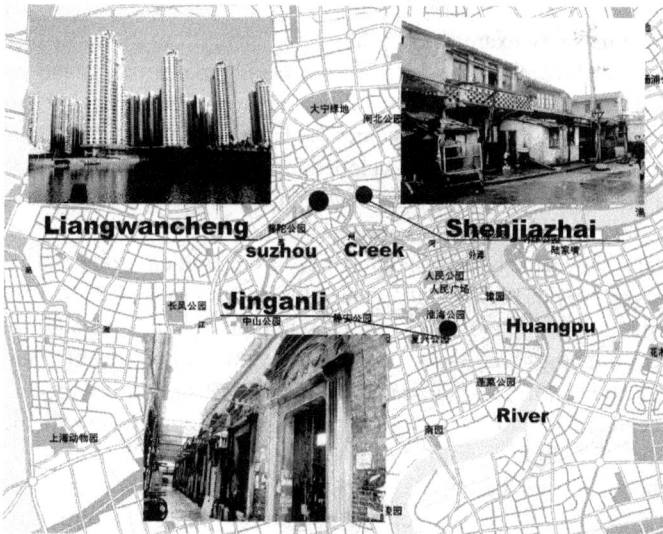

Figure 10.4 The locations and building styles of three neighborhoods.

typical dilapidated neighborhood that evolved from a shanty town existing before 1949, while Jinganli represents the typical old-fashioned *lilong* neighborhood, also built in the pre-1949 period. These old neighborhoods are declining in physical terms, due to the lack of proper maintenance and redevelopment in the past. Nevertheless, they will be redeveloped in the near future, since redevelopment plans have been made.

The questionnaire survey tried to cover roughly 3–8 percent of the households in each site. A total of 400 questionnaires was distributed to the three sites: 200 in Liangwancheng (about 6,500 households in total); 100 in Shenjiazhai (about 1,200 households); and 100 in Jinganli (about 1,500 households).[1] Sixteen interviews were also arranged with residents from different sites and different socioeconomic groups. The interviewees ranged from residents in preredevelopment sites (eight cases); residents in postredevelopment sites (four cases); and residents relocated to the suburbs (four cases). These semistructured interviews focus on residents' opinions on ongoing urban redevelopment, and its impact.[2]

Transforming the inner city neighborhoods

Based on the survey data, this study contrasts the built environment and socioeconomic composition of neighborhoods before and after redevelopment, and compares residents' different opinions on urban redevelopment. This section shows how urban redevelopment changes the neighborhood physically and socioeconomically and affects residents' access to different life chances (e.g. homeownership and employment).

Changing built environment and socioeconomic composition

First of all, this study examines neighborhood changes in the inner city through comparing the three sites. Lacking the necessary maintenance and redevelopment in the past, both Shenjiazhai and Jinganli display comparatively bad housing conditions. Once an old and dilapidated housing estate similar to Shenjingzhai, Liangwancheng has now been redeveloped into modern high-rise condominiums. There are great contrasts in the built environment between the preredevelopment and postredevelopment neighborhoods.

Table 10.2 shows the basic characteristics of the built environment. In terms of building style, Shenjiazhai sees dilapidated low-rise houses and Jinganli comprises overcrowded old-fashioned *lilong* houses, while Liangwancheng consists of high-rise modern buildings (see Figure 10.4). The average floor area in Shenjiazhai is 10.2 sq. mtr per capita, and in Jinganli it is only 9.9 sq. mtr per capita, while in Liangwancheng the figure is more than twice that. In comparison with the average level of Shanghai, 14.8 sq. mtr per capita at the end of 2004, the preredevelopment neighborhoods are far below the average, while the postredevelopment neighborhood is far above the average. The contrasts in housing conditions between Shenjiazhai and Liangwangcheng are also very impressive. Less than one-third of households in Shenjiazhai possess an independent living room, a private toilet and a private bathroom. The situation in Jinganli is comparable to this. Most residents

Table 10.2 Built environment in three neighborhoods (unit: percentage)

	Pre-redevelopment		Post-redevelopment
	Shenjiazhai	*Jinganli*	*Liangwancheng*
Building style	Dilapidated low-rise houses/ crude houses	Old-fashioned lilong houses	High-rise modern apartments
Average floor area* (m²/person)	10.21	9.97	35.04
Housing facilities			
Independent living room	19.0	29.0	100
Independent bedroom	71.0	54.0	100
Private kitchen	56.0	39.0	100
Private toilet	22.0	9.0	100
Private bathroom	11.0	5.0	100
Air conditioner	47.0	72.0	99.5
Gas	17.0	65.0	100
Broadband	8.0	0.0	72.5
Change of housing conditions in 10 years			
Greatly improved	0	1.0	47.7
Slightly improved	12.0	13.0	48.2
No changes	76.0	73.0	4.1
Deteriorated	9.0	10.0	0
Seriously deteriorated	3.0	0	0

Note
* Refers to the actual dwelling area.

do not have independent living rooms, private kitchens, toilets and bathrooms. In Liangwancheng, besides the basic facilities, most houses have other modern features, such as air conditioning, gas and broadband. Furthermore, three-quarters of respondents in Shenjiazhai reported that there has been no change in their housing conditions during the last 10 years, 12 percent of them even reporting that their housing conditions had either deteriorated or seriously deteriorated. The situation in Jinganli is similar. In contrast, most respondents in Liangwancheng reported that their housing conditions had either slightly or greatly improved.

The contrasts in the built environment between neighborhoods before and after redevelopment are evident. Table 10.3 shows that there are also great contrasts in socioeconomic characteristics between the residents of the three sites, in terms of respondents' age, education level, *hukou* status, occupation, working sector, annual family income and housing tenure. Jinganli and Shenjiazhai have similar age structures, with 26 percent elderly (over 65 years old). In comparison, Liangwancheng has more young people than the two preredevelopment neighborhoods. As for educational level, the majority of respondents in Shenjiazhai and Jinganli are poorly educated. Most people have not gone through higher education. There are only 3.0 percent in Shenjiazhai and 13.1 percent in Jinganli educated to college or university level. In contrast, respondents in Liangwancheng have a higher level of

Table 10.3 Socioeconomic characteristics of respondents in three neighborhoods (unit: percentage)

	Pre-redevelopment		Post-redevelopment
	Shenjiazhai	*Jinganli*	*Liangwancheng*
Age			
18–40	11.0	19.0	27.5
41–64	63.0	55.0	67.0
Above 65	26.0	26.0	5.5
Education level			
Primary school and below	19.0	10.1	52.0
Junior secondary school	41.0	40.4	8.0
High school	37.0	36.4	24.0
College/University	3.0	13.1	63.5
Master and beyond	0	0	2.0
Hukou status			
Local street office	95.0	100	65.0
Other street offices in Shanghai	3.0	0	25.5
Outside Shanghai	2.0	0	9.5
Occupation			
Government officer/ administrative personnel	9.0	10.0	30.2
Technological personnel	13.0	5.0	23.6
Clerk	18.0	20.0	13.6
Factory worker	29.0	41.0	4.0
Educational or medical care personnel	4.0	1.0	18.6
Services	10.0	6.0	1.0
Others	17.0	17.0	9.0
Annual family income			
<20,000 Yuan	44.0	40.0	3.0
20,000–50,000 Yuan	53.0	55.0	27.5
50,000–100,000 Yuan	2.0	5.0	52.5
100,000–200,000 Yuan	1.0	0	14.5
>200,000 Yuan	0	0	2.5
Housing tenure			
Government/work units owned, of which	**29.0**	**98.0**	**1.5**
Allocated by government	21.0	96.0	0
Allocated by work units	8.0	2.0	1.5
Private owned, of which	**70.0**	**2.0**	**94.0**
Inherited private housing	56.0	2.0	0
Purchase with subsidy	4.0	0	1.0
Commodity housing	10.0	9.0	93.0
Private rental	**1.0**	**0**	**4.5**
Owns more than one property	4.0	4.0	25.5

education, with 63.5 percent being college or university educated, and two percent educated to Master's level and beyond. In terms of *hukou* status, 95 percent of respondents in Shenjiazhai and 100 percent in Jinganli belong to the local street office, while in Liangwancheng 35 percent are not from the local street office.

More than half the respondents in Shenjiazhai work in low-end occupations, such as clerks, factory workers and services; in Jinganli, 61 percent of respondents work as clerks and factory workers. On the other hand, most respondents in Liangwancheng have better careers as government officers or administrative and technological personnel. The difference in annual family income between the three neighborhoods is remarkable. In both Shenjiazhai and Jinganli, the majority of respondents' annual family income is under 50 thousand Yuan. In great contrast, in Liangwancheng an annual family income is above 50 thousand Yuan is reported by 69.5 percent of respondents', of which 17 percent earn over 100 thousand Yuan.

In terms of housing tenure, 70 percent of properties in Shenjiazhai are privately owned, of which the majority is inherited private housing. However, despite a comparatively high percentage of private housing, only 10 percent are labeled as "commodity housing," and most of these are actually inherited houses sold by the original residents to people moving later. In Jinganli, 98 percent of houses are publicly owned with extremely low rents charged by the local housing authority (around 20–40 Yuan per month). However, in Liangwancheng 93 percent of houses have been purchased by residents as commodity housing. Furthermore, only 4 percent of respondents in both Shenjiazhai and Jinganli own a second property, while in Liangwancheng more than one-quarter of respondents own more than one property.

The great contrasts in the built environment and socioeconomic composition between neighborhoods before and after redevelopment not only indicate the problems of housing shortage and deterioration, but also suggest the existence of residential differentiation. Urban redevelopment has sorted people into different places according to their socioeconomic status: the better-off live in spacious houses in redeveloped neighborhoods, while low-income people still struggle with their appalling living conditions in neighborhoods lacking redevelopment.

Assessment of urban redevelopment

It is also important to learn people's own assessment of urban redevelopment to understand how redevelopment differently impacts their lives. Figure 10.5 shows residents from three neighborhoods with different evaluations of current redevelopment. Twenty-eight percent of respondents in Jinganli and 22.3 percent in Shenjiazhai consider that the current redevelopment approach does not benefit relocated residents. In Liangwancheng, nobody holds that opinion. In Jinganli 27.5 percent of respondents, and 17 percent in Shenjiazhai, criticize the way in which extensive redevelopment has resulted in rocketing housing prices. However, only 3.9 percent of respondents in Liangwancheng agree with this. Furthermore, a number of respondents in Shenjiazhai (22 percent) are anxious about damage to the historical and cultural heritage caused by redevelopment. Obviously, people

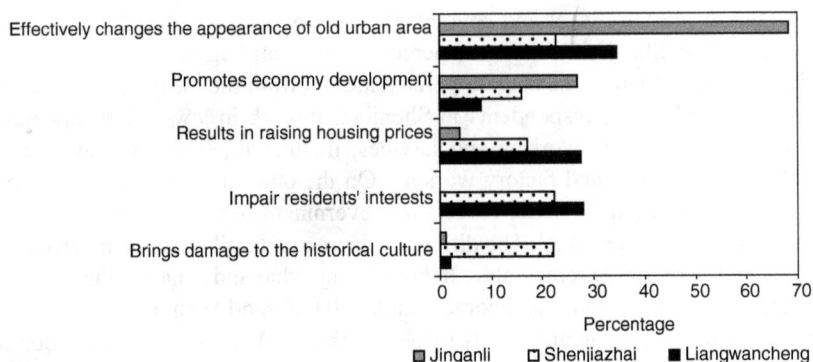

Figure 10.5 Residents' evaluation of the current redevelopment approach.

in Liangwancheng have evaluated the redevelopment activities more positively. In contrast, people in preredevelopment areas are less optimistic. A considerable proportion of respondents in Liangwancheng (68.2 percent) consider that redevelopment has effectively beautified the urban landscape. The percentages in Jinganli and Shenjiazhai are much lower: 34.6 and 22.7 percent respectively. As many as 26.8 percent of people in Liangwancheng agree that redevelopment has promoted economic development, whereas in Jinganli and Shenjiazhai only 8.1 and 15.9 percent have the same feeling. In general, people in the preredevelopment sites have a suspicious and even hostile attitude to ongoing urban redevelopment. Their comparatively low socioeconomic status suggests that they have less capability and thus less confidence in protecting their interests within redevelopment. In comparison, people in redeveloped sites have a more positive attitude towards redevelopment. Most residents in Liangwancheng have been able to obtain private housing ownership within the market-oriented reform, or have benefited from earlier redevelopment projects. Unsurprisingly, they are generally more positive about the current redevelopment approach.

Residents of different socioeconomic status have different assessments of ongoing urban redevelopment, which is also supported by correlation analysis between a series of indexes in the preredevelopment neighborhoods. These indexes include education level, family annual income, evaluation of redevelopment, and evaluation of monetary compensation. As shown in Table 10.4, residents' evaluation of monetary compensation is related to their education level, employment status, family annual income, and preference for remaining in the same neighborhood in the long term. Higher socioeconomic status, in terms of a higher education, more stable employment status, and higher family annual income, suggests a higher probability that people are positive about monetary compensation. Furthermore, people with a preference for staying in the same neighborhood in the long term (which means lower residential mobility) are more likely to be negative about monetary compensation. Different socioeconomic characteristics suggest different assessments of monetary compensation.

Table 10.4 Correlation between residents' evaluations of monetary compensation and their socioeconomic indexes (in Jinganli and Shenjingzhai)

		Education level[a] (low to high)	Employment status[b]	Family annual income[c] (low to high)	Whether prefer to stay in the same neighborhood long term (1. yes, 2. don't care, 3. no)
Evaluation of monetary compensation[d] (positive to negative)	Pearson correlation coefficient	−.168*	.152*	−.180*	−.187**
	Sig. (2-tailed)	.018	.032	.011	.008

Notes
** Correlation is significant at the 0.01 level (2-tailed).
* Correlation is significant at the 0.05 level (2-tailed).
a Education level: 1 = primary school and below; 2 = junior secondary school; 3 = high school; 4 = college/university; 5 = postgraduate.
b Employment status: 1 = permanent; 2 = short term contract; 3 = laid-off; 4 = unemployed; 5 = retired; 6 = self-employed.
c Family annual income: 1 = below 20 thousand Yuan; 2 = 20–50 thousand Yuan; 3 = 50–100 thousand Yuan; 4 = 100–200 thousand Yuan; 5 = 200–400 thousand Yuan; 6 = above 400 thousand Yuan.
d Evaluation of monetary compensation: 1 = reasonable and efficient compensation approach; 2 = neutral; 3 = inefficient and unfair compensation approach.

Potential impact of urban redevelopment

To assess the potential impact of urban redevelopment, respondents in Jinganli and Shenjiazhai were asked to predict what kind of impact redevelopment would have on their lives. As shown in Table 10.5, inconvenient access to public facilities, such as hospitals, schools, and cultural and recreational facilities, is the most significant change predicted by residents in Jinganli (34.1 percent) and Shenjiazhai (32.5 percent). Negative impact on employment status (i.e. rising unemployment due to increasing commuting cost and time) is the second significant change predicted by residents (24.8 percent in Jinganli and 28 percent in Shenjiazhai). A fragmentized social network is also another important change expected by residents (22.9 percent in Jinganli and 23.5 percent in Shenjingzhai). Evidently, the impact of redevelopment is vital for the life quality and employment status of residents.

In general, residents' opinions about potential urban redevelopment are rather negative and uncertain. The prediction of potential impact by respondents in predevelopment neighborhoods explains why residents in dilapidated neighborhoods are less confident about ongoing property-led redevelopment. This is because they

Table 10.5 The potential impact of redevelopment on residents' lives (unit: percentage)

	Jinganli	Shenjiazhai
Inconvenient access to public facilities	34.1	32.5
Risk of unemployment	24.8	28
Fragmented social network	22.9	23.5
Greater distance from the city centre	18.2	16

predict various undesirable outcomes of – for example, inconvenient access to the facilities in the city centre, insufficient compensation, the risk of unemployment, and disruption of social networks.

Interviews with relocated residents in the suburbs prove that residents' worries are reasonable. In one housing estate in Pudong which accommodates people relocated from the inner city, one officer from the residents' committee suggests

> Most people in this housing estate belong to low-income groups, with a considerable proportion of people accepting subsidies from the Minimum Living Standard Program (MLSP). Since they moved here, the problems of unemployment/laid-off have become more serious, because many cannot afford the high commuting costs and thus have to resign from their current jobs. Some used to earn a living by running a small business or renting rooms. Now it is impossible for them to do so because of the inconvenient location and underdeveloped infrastructure in this area.
>
> (Personal communication, April 1, 2004)

In sum, people in redeveloped sites have better socioeconomic conditions and enjoy benefits from redevelopment – for example, wider housing choices and a better built environment. Therefore, they are likely to be more positive towards the ongoing redevelopment. People in preredevelopment have lower socioeconomic profiles, and are anxious about the negative impact on their lives. They generally hold negative attitudes to urban redevelopment. People's evaluation of relocation compensation is highly related to their socioeconomic status. A higher socioeconomic status suggests a more positive assessment, and *vice versa*. Urban redevelopment not only sorts people according to their socioeconomic status, but also deprives low-income people of access to various sorts of life chances by relocating them to peripheral areas where facilities and infrastructures are underdeveloped. Despite the improved housing conditions, those peripheral neighborhoods with concentrated low-income residents are very likely to become enclaves of new urban poor. The process of urban redevelopment actually intensifies the differentiation between better and poorer neighborhoods.

Stratified housing status among affected residents

Differentiated housing status

The coexistence of market and nonmarket elements in China's gradualist market reform has resulted in a unique hybrid urban housing stock (Wang and Murie 1999; Zhang 2005). Commodity housing in China can be divided into four categories: commodity housing in the open market, work unit housing, resettlement housing, and housing-bureau housing (Li 2000; Li and Tang 1998). The latter three types of housing are beyond the logic of the housing market, and can be seen as a legacy of the centrally planned economy and the consequence of gradualist market reform. Local government and developers used to provide compulsory resettlement housing for affected residents in redevelopment projects (Li 2000). As a result, most of the original residents were relocated to standardized resettlement housing, although their housing space may have varied according to their previous housing conditions. However, market redevelopment and rising housing prices resulted in a shrinking resettlement housing stock, meaning that residents affected by redevelopment have been exposed to the emerging housing market. They have to participate in the process of housing privatization. Undoubtedly, this change will significantly affect residents' housing conditions after redevelopment.

Interviews with affected residents in different sites suggest a close connection between the outcome of redevelopment and residents' socioeconomic status (e.g. income, occupation and *hukou* status). Since the adoption of monetary compensation, resettlement housing is no longer offered to affected residents by demolition companies, except for infrastructure construction projects and important government-proposed redevelopment projects. Only limited resettlement housing is available, and the situation varies in different redevelopment projects. Since compensation for redevelopment has changed from resettlement housing to a certain amount of money, affected residents are pushed into the housing market. In other words, rather than moving to standardized resettlement housing, affected residents now have to relocate through purchasing or renting houses on the housing market. Therefore, the outcome of redevelopment in terms of residents' housing conditions varies significantly according to their socioeconomic capabilities.

The 16 interviewees may be roughly grouped into four categories: 1) better-off residents with higher mobility in housing relocation; 2) middle-income residents who managed to purchase commodity housing after accepting relocation compensation; 3) low-income residents who obtained considerable relocation compensation through bargaining in specific urgent redevelopment projects; 4) low-income residents who had great difficulty in improving their housing conditions due to their unfavorable socioeconomic status. The following four examples of interview excerpts represent these four types of residents.

1   Better-off resident

> My income and housing conditions are better than most people in Jinganli.
> Currently, my wife and I live in a *lilong* house of about 55 sq. mtr, which

is quite spacious. My daughter also has her own house in the city center. I really enjoy living in this neighborhood. If this area is redeveloped, I would like to move back or to some place around here. Obviously, the relocation compensation they (developers) offer will not be enough, since the housing price will dramatically increase after redevelopment. But I don't worry about that, I can afford a commodity house in this area anyway.

> (Interview with an old gentleman, current resident of Jinganli, February 20, 2004)

In this case, the interviewee has his own choice of relocation because he can afford commodity housing even after the housing price goes up after redevelopment. The redevelopment project does not have a negative effect on his housing status, since he has more housing choices and can afford the new housing in the redeveloped area.

2   Middle-income resident

I used to live in Changning district, close to the city centre. The floor area of my house was 50 square meters. In 2002, I was informed that I had to move due to underground construction. At that time, the compensation standard was 6,000 Yuan per sq. mtr., while the price of new housing in that area was 7,000 Yuan per square meter. The compensation standard was relatively high. Moreover, the government offered a reward of 20,000–30,000 Yuan for those residents who moved out by the deadline. Therefore, I got a total of 325,000 Yuan as redevelopment compensation. Adding part of my saving, I managed to buy a new unit of 92 square meters close to the outer ring road. Although the transportation condition is less convenient than before, my living conditions have been greatly improved.

> (Interview with a middle-aged gentleman, former resident of Changning district, who relocated to the vicinity of the outer ring road, March 29, 2004.)

This resident was lucky because he received comparatively high compensation, as the Shanghai government was making great efforts to expedite the underground construction, including offering high compensation. Middle-income residents greatly benefit from this kind of redevelopment project, and thus have more choices and advantages to purchase commodity houses than do low-income groups.

3   Low-income resident enjoying preferential compensation

I used to live in one room in an old-fashioned *lilong* house with my husband and one child. The floor area was only 14 sq. mtr. The housing quality and conditions were horrible, without sanitary facilities or private kitchen. The condition of my house has greatly improved after relocation. Now I own a two-bedroom flat. The construction area is 77 sq. mtr. I was supposed to pay the charge of 28,000 Yuan for the extra floor area. But my family can hardly afford that. Therefore I tried to bargain with the demolition company by all means to ask them to decrease the charge. Since the project was very urgent, after much bargaining, I had to pay 8,000 Yuan, but finally I negotiated a reduced rate of 4,000 Yuan.

(Interview with a middle-aged lady, former resident of Luwan district, adjacent to Jinganli, who relocated to Pudong new district, April 2, 2004.)

This lady obtained a great deal from the demolition company after much bargaining. However, this result was not attributed to her negotiation skills, but was due to a highly flexible compensation standard that reflected the urgent need of the developers and local government to implement the redevelopment project.

4   Low-income resident refusing to move

There are seven people who live together in our house: my husband, my son, my daughter, son-in-law and two granddaughters. The relocation compensation for us is extremely unfair. They (the demolition company) did not take my daughter's family into account because she does not have formal Shanghai *hukou*. She grew up in Shanghai, but her *hukou* problem hasn't been solved all along. That is ridiculous. My daughter and son- in-law have been to Beijing twice to appeal to the central government. The staff of the demolition company tried to stop them from appealing and took revenge on them because of their appeal. We are resisting moving out until we are offered a reasonable compensation. Now there are still about 20 households left on this site after most people moved out. My neighborhood is also resisting moving out due to the problem of unrea-sonable compensation.

(Interview with an old lady at a demolition site in Luwan district, April 7, 2004.)

Due to the disadvantage of non-Shanghai *hukou* status, the family of this old lady suffered from the unfair relocation compensation offered by the demo-lition company. With limited socioeconomic capability, they do not have any other choice but to struggle to obtain acceptable compensation.

Different routes of housing change

As a result of urban redevelopment through market operation, people are gradually required to improve their housing conditions through the housing market rather than through government/work units. Residents have to struggle to adjust them-selves to the transformation. That means in order to improve housing conditions and obtain commodity housing ownership, residents have to become involved in the process of housing commodification. Within the transformation from resettle-ment housing allocation to market participation, the situation of different groups of residents varies according to their diverse socioeconomic capabilities. According to the interviews, there are four routes of housing tenure change in urban redevelopment.

Route A: better-off residents generally have higher mobility and more relocation options through purchasing commodity housing from the market. In fact, some better-off residents have even left their old neighborhoods before redevelopment through selling or renting their houses to other lower-income people or migrants.

Route B: comparatively, middle-income people have fewer relocation options due to their limited socioeconomic capabilities. Redevelopment is a good opportunity for them to improve their housing conditions. Accepting a certain amount of monetary compensation, they are able to have more options for purchasing commodity housing from the market.

Route C: in some redevelopment projects within which developers apply highly flexible compensation standards to facilitate the relocation process, low-income residents who are good at bargaining may acquire better deals on relocation compensation – that is, better resettlement housing or even commodity housing ownership.

Route D: failing to adjust to the market transition, low-income groups have few relocation options: they can accept either the limited resettlement housing in some undesirable locations offered by the demolition company, or the monetary compensation – and look for cheap rental houses.

As shown in Figure 10.6, both better-off and middle-income groups have successfully adjusted to the market transition through participating in the housing

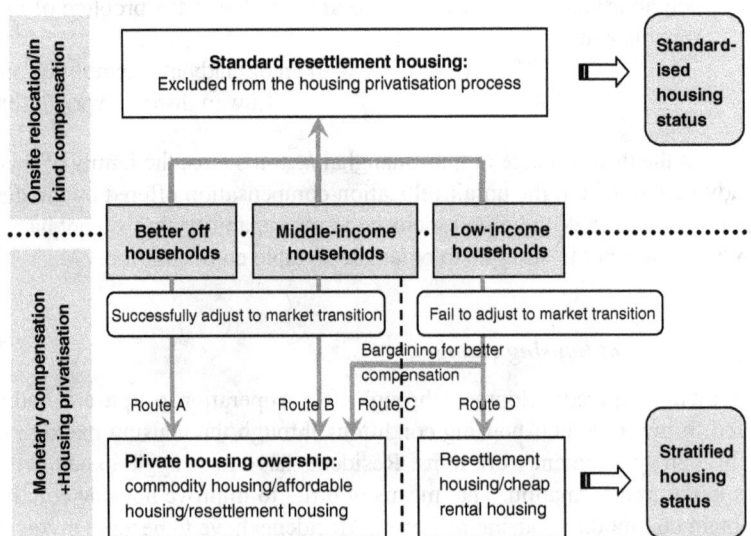

Figure 10.6 Affected residents' changing housing status after redevelopment.

commodification process and acquiring housing ownership. For the low-income groups, relocation compensation is far from resolving their housing problems, especially for large-size households, since property prices have constantly increased since the late 1990s. Therefore, they have not managed to obtain commodity housing ownership, even after receiving monetary compensation. Some of them refuse to move out of the redevelopment site and keep bargaining with the demolition company to struggle for better compensation. In some cases, local government and developers may deploy flexible rules of relocation compensation to promote rapid redevelopment. Therefore, a few low-income people have received considerable compensation through bargaining, which is actually unfair to relocated residents in general. But low-income residents are not always so lucky. For families with large households and nonlocal *hukou* status, purchasing commodity housing on the market is unrealistic. All they can do is resist relocation and struggle to get better/bigger resettlement housing. In one demolition site in Luwan district, people complained about the relocation compensation (personal communication, March 4, 2004).

> Those people who can afford commodity houses have moved out very quickly. If we had the capability, we would like to move as soon as possible. However, the compensation standard is too low, based on which we can never afford a house within a reasonable distance from the city centre. The alternative housing they (the demolition company) provided is too far away and lacking necessary local facilities such as banks, hospitals and schools. We don't want to accept that.

In routes A, B and C, people have benefited from urban redevelopment, while in route D the low-income residents are more vulnerable, and bear the cost of rapid redevelopment. Unable to benefit from market-oriented reform and no longer receiving the privileges provided by local state and work units (i.e. resettlement housing allocation), these low-income people are being gradually evacuated from the inner city. These people are becoming "invisible" in the city centre, and residential differentiation in the transitional city is enlarging as the redevelopment process increases the concentration of the urban poor and raises the risks of slum creation in the suburbs.

Conclusions

In Shanghai, rapid urban redevelopment over the last 15 years has significantly changed population distribution and urban landscapes. This study suggests that urban redevelopment has directly contributed to the creation and intensification of residential differentiation. Comparison between neighborhoods that have experienced redevelopment and those that have not, shows that the contrasts in the built environment and socioeconomic composition are significant. Residents' assessment of urban redevelopment varies according to their redevelopment experience and different socioeconomic status. Because of their limited socioeconomic capabilities, residents in old and dilapidated neighborhoods are uncertain about the outcomes of redevelopment. They are suspicious of, and even resist, urban redevelopment. Redevelopment is more likely to benefit middle- to high-income groups compared with low-income groups, although the needs of the latter for redevelopment are much more acute. Therefore, the evaluation of urban redevelopment by higher income groups is more positive than that by lower income groups. This research also indicates that urban redevelopment inflicts a number of undesirable impacts on low-income groups and affects their life chances, although their physical conditions are improved.

With urban redevelopment becoming more and more marketized (e.g. adopting monetary compensation) affected residents are no longer allocated standard resettlement housing. They have to struggle to obtain private housing ownership by adjusting themselves to market transition. As a result, the housing status of affected residents has been stratified according to their socioeconomic status. The better-off and middle-income groups who have successfully adapted themselves to the market transition and housing privatization acquire private housing ownership in the market after redevelopment. Within some redevelopment projects deploying flexible compensation standards, low-income residents who are good at bargaining may obtain better redevelopment compensation. However, most other low-income groups who fail to adjust themselves to the market transition have to accept limited relocation options.

Residential differentiation is emerging in urban China. Better-off residents who can afford the price of commodity housing have left the old neighborhoods, while people with low socioeconomic status, such as the aged, retired and unemployed/laid-off, are trapped in old and dilapidated areas and are waiting for redevelopment. However, sweeping urban redevelopment is acting as a device to sort different residents into different places, consequently increasing residential differentiation. As low-income residents are relocated from old neighborhoods to suburban housing estates through the mechanism of urban redevelopment, the concentration of underprivileged people is becoming even higher. Furthermore, inconvenient access to the inner city and the incomplete infrastructure in these suburban housing estates actually deprive low-income groups of some of the most essential life chances, leading to unaffordable commuting costs, little opportunity for small businesses, and lack of social networks.

Extensive urban redevelopment has involved different groups of residents in marketization and the housing commodification process. According to their capability for adjusting to the market transition, their housing status causes them to experience different routes of change. As the urban redevelopment process is gradually integrated into market transition, socioeconomic status has become one of the most important determinants for residents' housing status. Despite some specific cases in which low-income residents can acquire better compensation for relocation, in general low-income groups have been unfairly burdened with the social cost of ongoing property-led redevelopment. This will make the poor become poorer, and intensify residential differentiation. This study suggests that the impact of urban redevelopment on residential differentiation should be fully examined, and various measures should be taken to avoid its undesirable outcomes.

Notes

1 This questionnaire is composed of three parts. The first part is about basic information on the socioeconomic status of the head of household, including age, gender, education, *hukou* (household registration), occupation, income, etc. The second part is about the respondent's experience and opinions about redevelopment and relocation. Questions focus on respondents' experiences of redevelopment, opinions about the approach of urban redevelopment, and compensation. The third part of the questionnaire is about respondents' housing conditions, including housing floor area, housing quality, housing facilities, housing tenure, assessment of the neighborhood, and so on. The questionnaires were distributed to heads of households or their spouses. Questionnaires were distributed at weekends or in the evenings to ensure accessibility to target responders. In order to guarantee randomness, questionnaires were distributed along the streets at a fixed interval of 10 or 15 households. For example, numbers 1, 11, 21 ... or 1, 16, 31 ... on the same street were picked as the survey households. If there was no response from the selected household, the next household was visited. To ensure the accuracy and validity of the survey, the investigators helped the responders to fill in the questionnaires by asking and explaining the questions to them.
2 To reduce bias and enhance the effectiveness of interviews, particular attention has been paid to several issues. First, interviewees are carefully selected. Before arranging interviews, we went to the study sites to meet different residents to make sure they were appropriate informants. We also tried to develop trust with the respondents and therefore conducted the interviews in a friendly and informal atmosphere to increase respondents' motivation to answer the questions accurately. Some of the respondents were very supportive, in particular those residents in preredevelopment sites, because they regarded the interview as a good opportunity to express their opinions and feelings to "outsiders" and to the public.

References

Dangscht, J. (1987) "Sociospatial disparities in a 'socialist' city: the case of Warsaw at the end of the 1970s," *International Journal of Urban and Regional Research*, 11(1): 37–60.

Dowall, D. E. (1994) "Urban residential redevelopment in the People's Republic of China," *Urban Studies*, 31: 1497–1516.

Fan, W.B. (2004) *The Conservation and Renewal of Lilong Housing in Shanghai,* Shanghai: Shangai Science and Technique Publishing House. (In Chinese)

Gans, H. J. (1967) "The failure of urban renewal: a critique and some proposals," in M. Hausknecht and J. Bellush (eds), *Urban Renewal: People, Politics and Planning*, New York: Doubleday, Anchor Books, 464–484.

Gao, X. D. and Jiang, Q. Z. (2002) "Redistribution of population and suburbanization in Shanghai," *City Planning Review*, 26(1): 66–69. (In Chinese)

Gentile, M. (2004) "Divided post-Soviet small cities? Residential segregation and urban form in Leninogorsk and Zyryanovsk, Kazakhstan," *Geografiska Annaler B*, 86(2): 117–136.

Hamnett, C. (2001) "Social segregation and social polarization," in R. Paddison (ed.) *Handbook of Urban Studies*, London: Sage, 162–176.

Hamnett, C. (2003) *Unequal City – London in the Global Arena*, London: Routledge.

208 *Shenjing He and Fulong Wu*

Hartman, C. (1964) "The housing of relocated families," *Journal of American Institute of Planners*, 30(4): 266–286.

He, S. J. and Wu, F. (2005) "Property-led redevelopment in post-reform China: a case study of Xintiandi redevelopment project in Shanghai," *Journal of Urban Affairs*, 27(1): 1–23.

He, S. J. and Wu, F. (2007) "Socio-spatial impacts of property-led redevelopment on China's urban neighbourhoods," *Cities*, 24(3): 194–208.

Huang, Y. Q. (2004) "Housing markets, government behaviors, and housing choices: a case study of three cities in China," *Environment and Planning A*, 36: 45–68.

Jacobs, J. (1961) *The Death and Life of Great American Cities*, New York: Random House.

Kovacs, Z. (1994) "A city at the crossroads: social and economic transformation in Budapest," *Urban Studies*, 31(7): 1081–1096.

Leaf, M. (1995) "Inner city redevelopment in China," *Cities*, 12(3): 149–162.

Lehmann, S. G. and Ruble, B. (1997) "From 'Soviet' to 'European' Yaroslavl: changing neighbourhood structure in post-Soviet Russian cities," *Urban Studies*, 34(7): 1085–1107.

Li, S. M. (2000) "Housing consumption in urban China: a comparative study of Beijing and Guangzhou," *Environment and Planning A*, 32(6): 1115–1134.

Li, S. M. (2004) "Life course and residential mobility in Beijing, China," *Environment and Planning A*, 36(1): 27–43.

Li, S. M. and Siu, Y. M. (2001) "Commodity housing construction and intra-urban migration in Beijing – an analysis of survey data," *Third World Planning Review*, 23(1): 39–60.

Li, S. M. and Tang, Y. H. (1998) "Market segmentation and consumer characteristics of commodity honsingin Guangzhou: an analysis of household survey data," *Asian Geographer*, 17(1–2): 168–69.

Logan, J. R. (2005) "Socialism, market reform and neighbourhood inequality," in C. R. Ding and Y. Song (eds), *Emerging Land and Housing Markets in China*, Cambridge, MA: Lincoln Institute of Land Policy, 233–248.

Logan, J. R., Bian, Y. J. and Bian, F. Q. (1999) "Housing inequality in urban China in the 1990s," *International Journal of Urban and Regional Research*, 23(1): 7–25.

Lu, J. P. (2003) "Changing population distribution in Shanghai since the 1980s," unpublished thesis, Tongji University. (In Chinese)

Marcuse, P. (1997) "The enclave, the citadel, and the ghetto: what has changed in the post-Fordist US city," *Urban Affairs Review*, 32(2): 228–264.

Marcuse, P. and van Kempen, R. (2000) *Globalizing Cities: A New Spatial Order?* Oxford: Blackwell.

Mollenkopf, J. and Castells, M. (1991) *Dual City: Restructuring New York*, New York: Russell Sage Foundation.

Park, R., Burgess, E. and McKenzie, R. (eds) (1925) *The City*, Chicago, IL: University of Chicago Press.

Pickvance, C. (2002) "State socialism, post-socialism and their urban patterns: theorizing the Central and Eastern European experience." in J. Eade and C. Mele (eds) *Understanding the city: contemporary and future perspectives*, Oxford: Blackwell, 183–203.

Ruoppila, S. and Kahrik, A. (2003) "Socio-economic residential differentiation in post-socialist Tallinn," *Journal of Housing and the Built Environment*, 18: 49–73.

Sassen, S. (2001) *The Global City: New York, London, Tokyo,* 2nd edn, Princeton, NJ: Princeton University Press.

Sato, H. (2006) "Housing inequality and housing poverty in urban China in the late 1990s," *China Economic Review*, 17(1): 37–50.

Smith, N. (1996) *The New Urban Frontier: Gentrification and the Revanchist City*, London: Routledge.

Smith, N. (2002) "New globalism, new urbanism: gentrification as global urban strategy," *Antipode*, 34(3): 427–450.

Sykora, L. (1999) "Processes of socio-spatial differentiation in post-communist Prague," *Housing Studies*, 14(5): 679–701.

Wang, Y. P. (2000) "Housing reform and its impacts on the urban poor in China," *Housing Studies*, 15(6): 845–864.

Wang, Y. P. and Murie, A. (1999) *Housing Policy and Practice in China*, Basingstoke: Macmillan Press.

Wang, Y. P. and Murie, A. (2000) "Social and spatial implications of housing reform in China," *International Journal of Urban and Regional Research*, 24(2): 397–417.

Wang, Y. P., Wang, Y. L. and Bramley, G. (2005) "Chinese housing reform in state-owned enterprises and its impacts on different social groups," *Urban Studies*, 42(10): 1859–1878.

Weber, R. (2002) "Extracting value from the city: neoliberalism and urban redevelopment," *Antipode*, 34(3): 519–540.

Wu, F. (2002) "Sociospatial differentiation in urban China: evidence from Shanghai's real estate markets," *Environment and Planning A*, 34: 1591–1615.

Wu, F. (2004) "Residential relocation under market-oriented redevelopment: the process and outcomes in urban China," *Geoforum*, 35(4): 453–470.

Wu, F. and He, S. J. (2005) "Changes in traditional urban areas and impacts of urban redevelopment: a case study of three neighbourhoods in Nanjing, China," *Tijdschrift voor Economische en Sociale Geografie*, 96(1): 75–95.

Zhang, T. W. (2002) "Urban development and a socialist pro-growth coalition in Shanghai," *Urban Affairs Review*, 37(4): 475–499.

Zhang, X. Q. (2005) "Development of the Chinese housing market," in C. R. Ding and Y. Song (eds) *Emerging Land and Housing Markets in China*, Cambridge, MA: Lincoln Institute of Land Policy, 183–198.

11 Large urban redevelopment projects and sociospatial stratification in Shanghai

Ying Ying Tian and Cecilia Wong

Introduction

In 2005 China overtook the United Kingdom and became the fourth largest economy in the world. Economic growth has been accelerating following the gradual introduction of market forces into the Chinese economy since 1978. China now being one of the key global market players, the inflow of overseas capital for investment and joint-ventures and a strong export trade have contributed to urban growth, especially in large cities and coastal areas (Pannell 2002; Yeh 2000). The consequence of globalization and rapid economic growth have triggered the wider process of sociospatial restructuring in urban areas, especially in large cities such as Beijing, Nanjing, and Shanghai. The restructuring of the economic sector has concomitantly altered the urban landscape of these big cities. As Ma (2002) observes, the economic reforms are symbolized by the high-rise iconic office buildings, large shopping malls, and more varied housing styles. It is the changing sociospatial distribution patterns of large-scale housing redevelopment that this chapter aims to explore further.

There is widespread concern among researchers (e.g. Ma 2002; Wang 2002; Wu 2002, 2004a; Zhang 2000) that the interaction of market forces and large-scale property redevelopment has led to spatial stratification and inequitable development patterns in postsocialist China. Following the process of commodification of the socialist tenancy rights, in large-scale urban redevelopment local residents were dispersed from central areas and replaced by the wealthy (Lu 1997; Wu 2003). Freedom in choosing where to live by purchasing commercial housing has also led to high residential mobility in the city (Li 2004; Wang and Li 2004; Wu 2004b). Meanwhile, urban environments have become more and more dominated by gated communities with enclosed living spaces and amenities (Miao 2003). All these studies demonstrate that commodification of housing provision has changed the traditional social structure of Chinese cities. The economic status of different social groups, with differential market bidding power, has increasingly acted as the determining agent of housing property allocation. This trend of housing differentiation implies the threat of social segregation in the urban communities. However, while market-led urban redevelopment is generally regarded as the main driving forces of these changes, there is little knowledge about the actual process that leads to residential stratification.

The main purpose of this chapter is, therefore, to identify the key factors that underpin the dynamic process of large-scale housing redevelopment and to highlight the emerging sociospatial development trends from this process. The analysis particularly focuses on the production of upper-market residential properties and examines how such large-scale urban redevelopment projects impact on the sociospatial distribution of housing properties, and shape the overall urban landscape. These issues are explored via the case study of two housing redevelopment schemes in central Shanghai between 1998 and 2004. It was during this critical time period that the property market boom started and the government gradually shifted its attitude to urban redevelopment initiatives, introducing a whole array of urban reform policies.

Gentrification theory and institutional analysis of the housing redevelopment process

In order to analyze the dynamic process of large-scale housing redevelopment projects in China, there is a need to find a conceptual framework that can capture the complexity of the intertwining of political, economic, social, and cultural factors. The conceptual framework of this study is, therefore, informed by the gentrification theory of sociospatial restructuring and the institutional analysis of the property development process.

The concept of "gentrification" has been used widely in the Western literature to describe the spatial transformation outcomes of government regeneration policies in inner city areas as well as the wider processes of economic restructuring of cities. The crux lies in the negative outcome of the gentrification process, in that the newly restructured environment has displaced existing lower income residents in favor of the wealthy middle-class (Cameron 1992). In order to explain gentrification, Smith (1979a,b, 1996) argues that it occurs in places where there is a sufficiently large gap between existing rent and potential rent, created through underinvestment in the built environment (Smith 1996). Residents in these areas are, therefore, more likely to be relocated involuntarily. While the negative spatial differentiation outcomes of gentrification seem to fit well with the sociospatial restructuring patterns observed in postsocialist China, the underlying mechanisms of Smith's thesis have to be cautiously examined. There is a need to understand the underlying restructuring mechanisms by taking into account unique historical trajectories in different geopolitical situations (Darling 2005: 1030). Researchers such as Li (2000), Logan *et al.* (1999), Wang and Murie (2000), and Wu (2002) comment that analysis of the postreform restructuring of urban space in China has to take into account the legacy of socialist construction and, as a consequence, should not necessarily view the marketization of housing consumption as the sole determinant in the process. It is against this context that an institutionalist approach is introduced to examine the trajectories of the housing redevelopment process in Chinese cities.

Institutional analysis has been widely employed by researchers to understand the complex development process of the built environment (e.g. Ball 1998; Guy and Henneberry 2000, 2002; Healey 1997; Healey and Barrette 1990). Its application is, however, not unproblematic. First of all, there are different strands of institutional theory (see Scott 1995), ranging from those originating in the institutional approach in economics to the broader realm of "sociological institutionalism" (Gonzalez and Healey 2005: 2057). Second, the concept of institution has many meanings; it can be used loosely to embrace all kinds of institutions and organizations (e.g. Amin and Thrift 1995) or specifically to focus on the power structures of society (e.g. Paasi 2000: 6).

Institutional analysis in this chapter focuses on examining the housing redevelopment projects in Shanghai through the interaction of different actors with the existing structure of governance. In elaborating the institutionalist conception, Healey (1997: 37) argues that it is "the systems of meaning and frames of reference through which people in social situations shape their institutional practices." The emphasis on the dynamic process of the continual making of social life through interaction with others offers a useful framework for analysis of the changing governance dynamics and institutional settings of postsocialist property market development in China. As Wu (2004a: 9) observes, research on residential relocation has generally shifted from examining the demand factors of households to supply-side factors and the roles of developers, real-estate agents, and city planners. The analysis of the redevelopment case study in Shanghai, therefore, largely follows Healey's (1992) institutional model on *agency–structure* interactions. Institution can be seen as a network which includes resources, rules, and ideas that influence all actors and activities within the network. The outcome of the built environment is highly dependent upon the dynamic interaction between agency and structure, which can be empirically examined through relating the roles, strategies, and interests of agencies to the economic resources, institutional rules, and political organization and culture (Healey 1992; Healey and Barrett 1990). The advantage of this approach is to integrate the analysis of economic and social forces in the property development process and it can be applied to different economic and political regimes to avoid the problem of context-dependency (Guy and Henneberry 2000).

Case study methodology: two housing redevelopment projects in Shanghai

In order to track the changing relationship between political and socioeconomic circumstances, as well as the response of the key actors, the time dimension formed an important criterion in the process of selecting the case studies. Two housing redevelopment cases in central Shanghai, New Fukangli (see Figure 11.1) and International Ladoll City (see Figure 11.2), were chosen on the basis that they are directly comparable in terms of the scale of development, in the same neighborhood, and with the same developer, though there was a two-year time gap between the two projects. These two cases allow us to produce a more controlled

Figure 11.1 Two housing redevelopment projects in Shanghai. (1) New Fukangli (2) International Ladoll City.

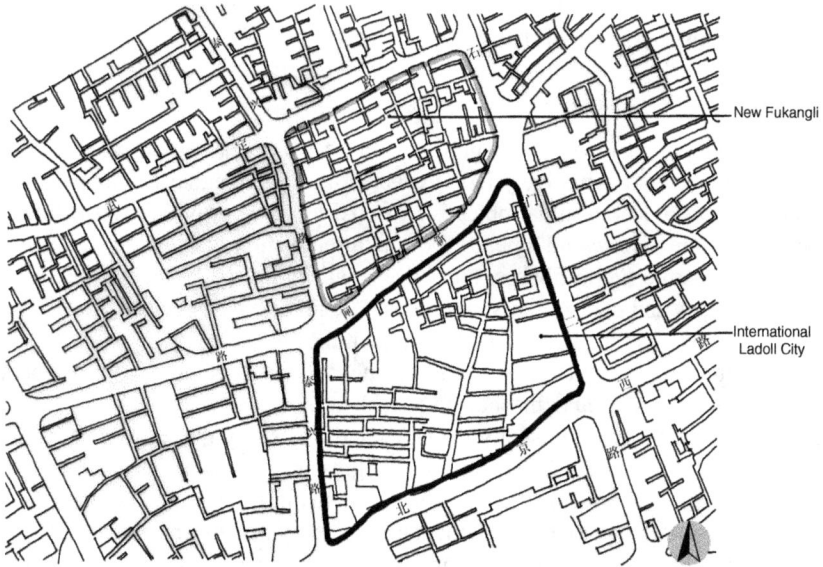

Figure 11.2 Location of New Fukangli and International Ladoll City.

analysis of the extent to which the changing political-economic circumstances have impacted upon the sociospatial restructuring outcome of housing differentiation and gentrification. Both New Fukangli and International Ladoll City are located in Jing'an District – one of the better-off areas of central Shanghai, with high land values and mature service provision (see Wu 2002). New Fukangli lies to the north of Xinzha Road, whereas International Ladoll City is situated just opposite, on the south of the road. Before the redevelopment, thousands of local residents were living in traditional *lilong*[1] houses which had been homes for generations of local residents. New Fukangli was developed between 1998 and 2001, and International Ladoll City between 2000 and 2004.

Primary data were collected in 2003 through face-to-face, semistructured, in-depth interviews with local residents, officials of the planning authority and other government departments, and development companies and street offices. Interview data was further augmented by site observations and documentary analysis. Comparative analysis of the empirical data was carried out to identify the key factors that underpin the dynamic process of housing redevelopment and to highlight the changing socio-spatial development trends from this process. To address this over-arching research question, the analysis focuses on examining the changing political and policy contexts of housing redevelopment and the fluctuations in the housing property market in respect of the two redevelopment schemes; the strategies adopted by the key actors and their relationships within the institutional network of housing redevelopment; their respective redevelopment objectives and built environment outcomes; and the tensions and conflicts arising from the pragmatic reform process and vague political ideology of a transitional society.

New Fukangli (1998–2000)

Policy and economic context

The redevelopment of New Fukangli was closely associated with the Housing Amenity Fulfilment Initiative (HAFI) enacted by the Shanghai Municipal Government (SMG). The original objective of HAFI was to provide local residents with basic living space and amenities through renovation of dilapidated housing stock, such as the *lilong* houses, that have small living space, lack of exclusive use of kitchens and poor sanitary amenities. The initiative has, however, changed its nature and delivery mechanisms throughout the years.

During the early period of 1991–1996, the housing improvement projects tended to be small in scale[2] and the housing stock was renovated to a limited standard. These projects were usually managed and funded by the property and land management bureaus. At this time, most original residents moved back to their neighborhoods and lived in the refurbished housing units.[3] However, in 1997 the SMG issued a circular "Implementation Comments on Speeding up Housing Amenity Fulfilment." The circular called for stronger involvement from both district governments and developers in housing improvement. In the next two years, housing improvement activities extended from renovation of housing units to larger scale renewal of entire housing blocks. Due to the lack of maintenance of many degraded houses with ageing building frames, demolition and rebuilding was seen as a cheaper option than refurbishment. The cost of renewal was funded from a package of subsidies from government and the work units of residents as well as the personal finance of residents. However, it was not until 1998–2000 that full-scale renewal was introduced to redevelop entire neighborhoods. There was a realization that in order to achieve good quality living, it was important to improve the wider physical environment of the neighborhood as well as the individual housing units and streets (*lanes*). This led to the strategy of demolishing the *lilong* houses and building new housing units with landscaped green communal spaces and community facilities. New Fukangli was one of the pilot projects of such redevelopment at the neighborhood scale. Under the banner of housing redevelopment, preferential policies were applied to these projects so that no land exchange fees and ancillary fees would be charged.

The redevelopment of New Fukangli unfortunately took place during the downturn of the property market and there was uncertainty over the investment return. As shown in Figure 11.3, Shanghai's property market cycle has experienced two upsurges and one downturn since the early 1990s. Between 1978 and 1992, the socialist ideology had changed and the property market started to take shape. With major political support behind the development of Pudong, a sharp increase in real estate investment was witnessed by 1993. Real-estate investment reached its first peak in Shanghai's property market after climbing to 65.8 billion yuan in 1996. However, due to the lack of real demand and purchase, many office buildings and apartments had no buyers or tenants, which resulted in high vacancy rates in the mid-1990s. A big gap between the completion of commodity buildings and their sales between 1996 and 1999 (see Figure 11.4) meant that there was a sliding property market in the late 1990s.

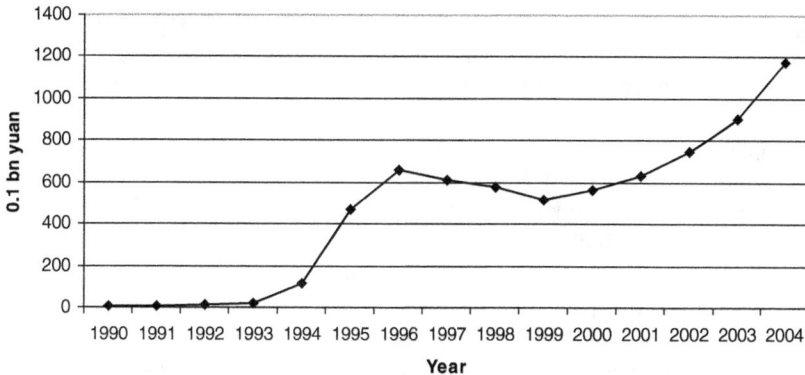

Figure 11.3 Real-estate investment in Shanghai, 1990–2004.

Source: Adapted from Sang, 2002; Shanghai Statistical Bureau, 2005.

Commodity Buildings Completed and Sold in Shanghai (1990-2004)

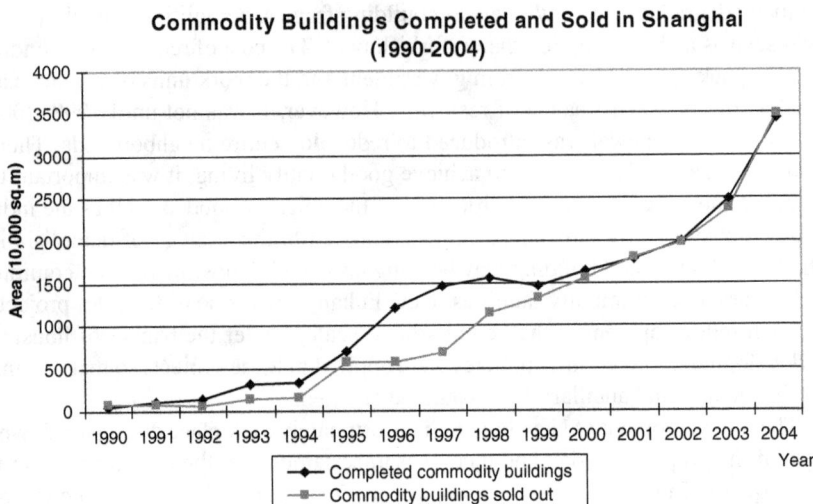

Figure 11.4 Commodity buildings completed and sold in Shanghai, 1990–2004.

Source: Shanghai Municipal Property and Land Management Bureau and Shanghai Statistical Bureau, 2002; Shanghai Statistical Bureau, 2005.

The redevelopment process and outcomes

Before the redevelopment of New Fukangli, the old community was made up of 48,000 sq. mtr of old style *lilong* houses which accommodated 1,504 families and 4,322 residents. According to a planning officer of Jing'an District Planning Bureau,[4] the original residents were slightly better off than the Shanghai average, as most of them had stable jobs and some had either family inheritance or support from overseas relatives. This *lilong* residential area was built in 1927, representing both traditional way of living in lanes and the strong architectural heritage of Shanghai (see Figure 11.5). The overcrowded living space and dilapidated amenities in these *lilong* houses were, however, no longer suitable for today's modern life. An original resident vividly described the living conditions at that time:

> I had lived in old Fukangli since I got married. We lived in a house of about 37 sq. mtr – it included a large room downstairs (about 20 sq. mtr) and a loft. Three generations lived in this house, including my mother-in-law and my son and daughter. The toilet was put in by ourselves, but there was no drainage, just a separate small room. … Our living conditions were so bad that we could not invite guests around. … We had to share the kitchen with three other families. It was very crowded at meal times and caused frictions and quarrels among the neighbors. Because of poor noise insulation, disputes with our neighbor downstairs were inevitable. I used to go straight back home

Figure 11.5 New Fukangli before the redevelopment. (a) The Entrance to Old Fukangli (b) The Lanes and (c) Shared Kitchen.

Source: Archive Photos, Jing'an Property Stockholding Co. Ltd.

from my school everyday just to avoid coming across our neighbors, and I rarely felt close to the old community.

(A retired middle-school teacher and an original resident,
November 14, 2003)

As the pilot of HAFI at the neighborhood scale, this project was progressed under the special attention of the Jing'an District Government and the leaders of the SMG. In 1997, Jing'an District Government commissioned Jing'an Property Group to carry out the renewal. A senior staff member of the developer explained that his enterprise was part of the Office of Jing'an Urban Renewal, affiliated to Jing'an Property and Land Management Bureau which was responsible for the management of state-owned properties and the living condition of local residents. The Group was initially established in the early 1990s to carry out renewal of state-owned housing, and has gradually grown as it gained experience. Since no public funding was attached to the New Fukangli redevelopment project, this group established the Jing'an Property Stockholding Co. Ltd. based on self-generated funding.⁵ Under the policy of the HAFI and the anticipation that most of the original residents would move back, this project did not need to be audited by the Economic Planning Committee in terms of socioeconomic impact. Meanwhile, the developer was exempt from various fees since there was no land exchange and the only involvement was the expansion of the water and power supplies.

At the beginning, Jing'an Urban Planning Bureau strongly advocated the physical and cultural conservation of this community by setting up the returning threshold of original residents to 80 percent. The restoration of three-storey terraced housing was also required. However, to the developer, the crucial challenge was to achieve an economic return as well as fulfilling the required political tasks. The delivery mechanism was that a substantial number of new properties would be sold back to the original residents at discounted rates, while the rest could be sold at market rates to offset the investment.

The residential area of New Fukangli was totally transformed by the redevelopment (see Figure 11.6a–d). Three rows of terraced houses were located in the south, multistorey buildings in the middle, and two tower blocks in the north. Residents were given the option of return or relocation elsewhere. The basic compensation principle was 1 sq. mtr of new flat to 1 sq. mtr of demolished floor space. If the resident had the ownership of the demolished house, the compensated floor space would be free. Tenants of state-owned housing could buy floor space at a discounted rate according to their number of working years for the state. Residents had to pay for any extra floor space, but at different price levels for different space thresholds. A resident explained his situation

> In my case, we paid 1,200 yuan per sq. mtr for the first 37 sq. mtr of the new flat, which was a discounted rate as our old house (with a total areas of 37 sq. mtr) was state-owned. Since our old living area was far below the set living standard of Shanghai, our new home is larger at 66 sq. mtr. We, therefore, had to pay for the difference of 29 sq. mtr at the price of full construction cost, that is, about 2,400 yuan per sq. mtr. If any resident needs more floor space than the set standard, one has to pay a commercial rate, that is 5,000 yuan per sq. mtr. I paid around 100,000 yuan for my flat. Our neighbors also bought their new flats for a similar price, paying between 100,000 and 200,000 yuan.
>
> (A returning resident of New Fukangli, November 14, 2003)

Given the promise of low-price flats at the site for the original residents, over half (52 percent) of the households chose to move back to the new development in New Fukangli. About 13 percent of the households moved to other residential areas in Jing'an District and the remaining 35 percent were relocated. Two options were offered to those who chose to relocate elsewhere: they were either provided with financial compensation to buy flats in locations of their choice or relocated to vacant flats in places at the city fringe such as Xinzhuang, Jiading, and Pudong. The promise to the original residents of discounted property prices meant that the developer did not need to allocate a large sum for compensatory

Figure 11.6 New Fukangli after the redevelopment. (a) Aerial Photo of New Fukangli (b) Terraced Houses and Multi-storey Flats (c) Medium High-rise Flats and (d) Friendly Communal Space-Fish Pond.

Source: Photos from Jing'an Property Stockholding Co. Ltd and the Authors' Photos.

payment. Instead, those who intended to return had to contribute a construction fee to the developers. Even taking into account the compensation fees made to other relocated residents, the developer admitted that not much investment was needed upfront. The redevelopment was carried out in stages. It first started with two high-rise apartment blocks; sales began after 30 percent of the main structure was finished. The remaining properties were developed in different phases. With financial contributions from the original residents, the developer successfully assembled the necessary capital without much initial funding or borrowing. The risk was very low, though the profit was modest.

Meanwhile, Jing'an Urban Planning Bureau and the developer tried to explore the possibility of retaining the vernacular architectural style as well as recreating quality communal spaces. It can be observed from Figures 11.6 a–d that a variety of high quality communal spaces, including fish ponds, gym, playground, tea house, gallery and meeting place, were planned for the residents. Special consideration was given to the needs of children and the elderly, as they tended to use these amenities more frequently. The planning officer explained that, due to the financial contributions made by local residents, they were also actively involved in making suggestions on the layout of individual housing units to reflect their own living style and needs. Drawings of the housing unit were shown to residents to seek suggestions with regard to the size and arrangement of the rooms. It is, therefore, not a surprise that local residents gained high satisfaction from their new homes, which gave them a strong sense of attachment to the community. The design and communal spaces also facilitated close interaction among neighbors, including those who had previously been in dispute.[6]

The redevelopment project of New Fukangli is renowned because it received numerous prestigious awards for achieving a successful partnership with the original residents to improve their living conditions as well as providing a vibrant and attractive community for both returning residents and new home buyers. It received visits from many government officials, developers and professionals and became a show case for government initiatives. Residents in central Shanghai regard New Fukangli as a "model" that expresses their hopes for a better living environment. In spite of the acclaimed success in public image and political terms, the developer claimed that it did not make much business sense as no profit was yielded from it. As the head of the Administration Section in Jing'an Property Stockholding Co. Ltd commented, "New Fukangli took place at the right time, in the right place. It is the only *one* in Shanghai and it is impossible to generalize its experience to other redevelopment projects now."

International Ladoll city

Policy and economic context

The redevelopment of International Ladoll City (immediately south of New Fukangli) was started two years later, in 2000, by the same developer. It proved to be the largest redevelopment project in Jing'an District under the New Round

Redevelopment Initiative (NRRI). This initiative was virtually the successor of HAFI after 2000. It aimed to redevelop the remaining 20 million sq. mtr of dilapidated housing areas, to improve 3.5 million sq. mtr of workers' flats, and to develop conservation measures for 10.2 million sq. mtr of garden houses, old apartments, and some newer style *lilong* houses. By the 1990s, the remaining undeveloped sites tended to be less attractive to developers, but the government still worked hard to facilitate the redevelopment. Of all dilapidated housing stock, the priority was to redevelop the old style *lilong* houses (14.3 million sq. mtr) in the central area that occupied 2,493 hectare of land.

In February 2001, the Shanghai Municipal Urban Construction Committee promulgated "The Provisional Methods of Encouraging Residents to Move Back to Boost New Round Redevelopment." This regulation continued the preferential policies of encouraging property-led redevelopment, which included

- Exemption from land grant fees for the approved sites under NRRI, on the condition that the original residents should be relocated or compensated.
- Exemption from primary service fees (about 320 yuan per sq. mtr).
- No charges on the existing value of the demolished state-owned properties.
- Exemption from air defense fees.
- Discount of/exemption from demolition and relocation management fees.
- Discount of the planning management fees.

The introduction of redevelopment initiatives, preferential policies, and housing provision reform policies coincided with an increasing housing demand. The property market therefore began to recover in 1999. The vacancy rates began to drop and investment began to increase (Figures 11.3 and 11.4). Housing prices started to rise steadily after 1999 and there was an upsurge of housing development and sales around 2003 and 2004.

The redevelopment process and outcomes

The site of International Ladoll City was dominated by old *lilong* houses, with four garden houses at the southeast corner. Residents there had very similar living conditions to those in New Fukangli. According to a senior staff member of the developer, their own survey showed that 70 percent of the residents had the capability of paying 100,000 yuan for the improvement of their living conditions. Considering this project as the continuation of HAFI, Jing'an District Government required that this project had to house 40 percent of returning residents. Meanwhile, as in the case of New Fukangli, there was no land exchange on this project and the developer enjoyed exemption from most taxes and fees applicable to new development projects.

Year 2000 was a crucial time for the wider institutional reform in Shanghai, when most commercial companies sought to divorce from their parent departments when the government department bodies. Although Jing'an Property Group was to be separated from Jing'an Property and Land Management Bureau, their close relationship and mutual trust permitted Jing'an Property Group to win this commission. Meanwhile, the separation also meant that the Group now had to operate as an enterprise, balancing costs and profits without resorting to public funding. Shanghai International Ladoll Property Co. Ltd (SILPC) was then established, with shares from several subcompanies under the Group.

Through its market and feasibility research, the developer found that it would definitely lose money if 40 percent of residents bought new properties at the site at discount rates. The solution was to find another site with lower land values at the fringe of the central city to develop cheaper relocation housing. Jing'an Property Group then collaborated with Xingye Real Estate Development Co. Ltd to develop a 70,000 sq. mtr residential area in Putuo District for the relocated residents. As a result, less than 200 newly developed flats at the original site were kept for sale to the 3,500 original residents. The Chief engineer and Manager of the development company explained the compensation and relocation scheme

> In additional to the discounted purchase of the total floor space in their previous rented property, there is a sliding charging scheme for different additional floor space thresholds: they only paid 3,000 yuan per sq. mtr for up to 8 sq. mtr per capita; 4,000 yuan from 8 to 12 sq. mtr per capita, and 6,000 yuan (the market price) for 12 sq. mtr or more per capita. The cheap housing we built in Putuo was very popular among the relocated residents. There were insufficient units to meet the demand. At the end, we paid them one-off compensation of 60,000 yuan per person and let them buy their homes wherever they wanted.
> (Chief Engineer and Manager, SILPC, November 2, 2003)

In the Spring Shanghai Property Fair held on May 1, 2002, International Ladoll City was unveiled as one of the foremost luxurious property developments in central Shanghai (Figures 11.7a–c). The project consists of one 27-storey apartment building for the original residents, seven 19–35 storey luxury apartment buildings, one serviced apartment block, one 33-storey officer tower, seven restored garden houses, and 30,000 sq. mtr of retail annex wings below the apartments along the roads. The housing units were priced at 8,000–10,000 yuan per sq. mtr at the outset. This property development was advertised as a residential area exclusively for the most successful entrepreneurs, managers, and professionals who deserved to enjoy the historic, international, and artistic atmosphere of this area; the relaxed ambience of Jing'an Park; and proximity to up-market consumer services in West Nanjing Road, where English bars, Starbucks, Chanel, and Versace are located. According to the Chief Engineer and Manager, the development of up-market apartments was not their initial objective. This had shifted several times in the development process to maximize the potential of the site by taking into account property market trends and customer requirements. As he explained

> In our initial proposal, there was no sign of any high price apartments at all. We planned 2,000–3,000 small housing units in multiple-storey and high-rise buildings, targeting medium-income families since the property market was

(a)

(b)

Figure 11.7 Visions and photos of the International Ladoll City after the redevelopment. (a) Masterplan of International Ladoll City (b) Frontage facing West Beijing Road and (c) High-rise Apartments and Elegant Landscape.

Source: Drawings from Shanghai International Ladoll Property Co. Ltd and the Authors' Photos.

(c)

Figure 11.7 Continued

less certain at that time. Later, when the property market began to pick up, we found that the location of this site was particularly unique in Shanghai – it was convenient, vibrant, arty, and with a rich sense of historic culture. Together with Zhongrui Real Estate Consultant (which owned 1 percent share of our development company), we developed a proposal for an up-market residential area. It was totally feasible for us to obtain good profits and enhance our reputation through this project. What we did were, first, to have more green space by reducing the floor space which then allowed us to set higher sale prices; second, to increase the number of large apartment units with en-suite bedrooms and servant bedrooms for three-bedroom and four-bedroom flats and to provide central air-conditioning to all flats; third, to design a glass lift for the high-rise apartments to promote a ground breaking sale point; and finally, to invite Ronald Lu & Partners (HK) Ltd and Belt Collins HK Ltd to enhance the elevation and landscape design for the upper market properties.

(Chief Engineer and Manager, SILPC, November 2, 2003)

The reconfigured scheme resulted in a modern and elegant design with high quality warm-colored cladding, large windows, and balconies. A large man-made lake was also created in the communal area to create a focal point. During the development process, planning officers strongly encouraged the developer to restore the garden houses for conservation purposes. Through their effort, not only were the four original garden houses at the southeast corner rebuilt, but three more were also added on the west side of the entrance (see Figures 11.7a and b). This was partly because the developer by then had bought into the idea that a rich cultural atmosphere would help to push up house prices. The restored garden houses in Beijing Road were unveiled soon after the project was started, and have attracted wealthy overseas and domestic buyers. However, these vernacular garden houses become specialist shops for top retail brands and high-class show houses rather than residences. The Chief Engineer and Manager of the project explained the reasons

> According to Jing'an Urban Planning Bureau and Shanghai Heritage Conservation Committee, these garden houses were listed and could not be demolished. However, HAFI at that stage [NRRI] aimed to improve the whole neighborhood rather than just refurbishing houses in several lanes. In order to ease the layout of new properties and achieve all the building regulations, the site had to be cleared and the residents had to choose where to live based on the equity rules. The reason for demolishing the garden houses was connected to the legitimate argument of relocation. We had to demolish them because you could not ask residents to move if the houses were just renovated.
> (Chief Engineer and Manager, SILPC, November 2, 2003)

In 2003, with a buoyant property market, the property price of International Ladoll City rose to 17,000 yuan per sq. mtr. New properties from the last phases were sold out in several weeks. According to the developer, only about 40 percent of the flats were purchased by Shanghai residents and less than 5 percent were purchased by returning local residents (the best-off in the old community). The remaining flats were purchased by overseas Chinese and buy-to-sell/let investors from Zhejiang and Jiangsu Provinces.

Changing institutional structure and sociospatial stratification

The two case studies exemplify the consequences of the transition from the socialist redevelopment legacy to the marketization of housing consumption. Table 11.1 compares the policy and economic contexts, resources, key actors and the development outcomes of the two housing redevelopment projects. Despite the fact that both projects are located in the same vicinity and were developed by the same developer, their very different socioeconomic outcomes show that the institutional structure of postsocialist China is in a constant state of flux. Within a mere two-year period between the completion of New Fukangli and the start of the International Ladoll City significant changes were found to have taken place in the institutional structures of housing development and the real-estate market. These changes have translated into very different development strategies, altered the institutional relationships between the key actors, and resulted in very different

Table 11.1 Comparison of the two case study housing redevelopment projects in Shanghai

	New Fukangli (1998–2001)	International Ladoll City (2000–2004)
Political context	HAFI – aimed to improve local residents' living conditions	NRRI – aimed to stimulate redevelopment with a more market-oriented approach
Economic context	Downturn of property market	Start of a buoyant market
Site conditions	Dilapidated lilong houses	Dilapidated lilong houses
Key actors	Institutional developer District government Property and Land Management Bureau District Urban Planning Bureau Residents who contributed finance (52%)	Institutional developer District government Property and Land Management Bureau District Urban Planning Bureau
Financial resources	Mostly from local residents and the developer's self accumulated funding	All from the developer
Social outcomes	Socially mixed community with original residents and private home buyers 52% of redeveloped flats are for original residents	Better-off residents were replaced by rich home buyers; Most original residents were relocated to the fringe of the central city
Property prices	Discount price for original residents; Commercial price: 6,000 yuan–9,800 yuan per square meter	Discount price for very few original residents; Commercial price: 13,000–18,000 yuan per square meter
Physical environmental outcomes	Flats for original residents and medium income buyers; and terraced housing for high-income buyers; good community facilities	Up-market luxury apartments with high quality landscaping and some conservation projects

styles of built environment, which in turn triggered a major process of sociospatial restructuring of urban land use across different parts of Shanghai.

New Fukangli was redeveloped as a socially mixed community for both original residents and private homebuyers. The design and provision of buildings, facilities and communal spaces were based on the needs and requirements of the residents. It created a community that the original residents could identify with. The redevelopment of International Ladoll City was, however, a rather different story as it was a commercial-led development influenced by the forces of the real-estate market. The arrangement of spacious apartments, high quality facilities, and elegant design and landscape fabricated an elitist and exclusive community. The result was a gentrified environment tailored exclusively for the rich. It was thus not surprising to find that the large majority of the original residents (even though they were relatively well-off) could no longer afford the newly developed luxurious apartments on the site and were forced to take up cheaper accommodation elsewhere. This phenomenon clearly fits well with the gentrification thesis in that the newly redeveloped environment has brought with it negative outcomes as the more affluent professionals and foreign buyers have displaced the existing less well-off residents in the most accessible central city location. The original residents have had, therefore, to relocate to cheaper sites in Putuo and other areas at the edge of Shanghai. This has resulted in a wider process of sociospatial restructuring of land use in different parts of the city. In order to analyze the interaction between the state and the real-estate market over different periods of time, and related impacts on the changing urban form, an institutionalist approach to the analysis of the dynamic process of sociospatial stratification was therefore found to be useful.

Since 1991, there have been continuous shifts in government policy toward housing renewal and redevelopment. In the early 1990s, the emphasis was on carrying out modest urban renewal that aimed to improve the quality of the housing stock and the immediate living environments of the residents. As time went by, the government's vision for urban renewal changed to embrace the wider agenda of full-scale urban redevelopment. The increase in scope and scale of housing redevelopment in the late 1990s was nonetheless constrained by a lack of matching resources. The government no longer had the capacity to offer a large package of subsidies and thus had to look for alternative strategy and policy instruments. After a brief attempt in seeking financial contributions from the original residents, the government eventually resorted to free market enterprise. The only incentive the government could offer the private developer was tax exemptions.

The private sector, on the other hand, is fully driven by market signals. During the downturn of the real-estate market in the 1990s, sales of domestic and commercial properties in Shanghai had been sluggish. Given this uncertainty in the market, the developer could not see any prospect of reaping much profit from the rent gap, as suggested by Smith, even in a central location such as New Fukangli. Once the market recovered in the early 2000s, the developer's entrepreneurial instinct was to maximize potential profits by pushing the upper end of the property market in central locations such as International Ladoll City. This meant that even where the redevelopment was carried out by the same developer at the same location in Jiang'an District, the mindset was now totally different. The social objective of rehousing 40 percent of the former residents was replaced by the priority of relocating existing residents to other cheaper areas.

The institutional framework used to carry out housing renewal and redevelopment has dramatically changed in China over the last two decades. From this analysis, it is clear that the redevelopment trajectory of New Fukangli was still very much in line with the socialist ethos of renewing the dilapidated housing stock in inner city areas to improve the living quality of existing residents and the local neighborhood. In order to achieve this resident-oriented objective, an entrepreneurial approach of drawing in private finance from the residents was introduced to accumulate investment capital to kick-start the redevelopment process. The outcomes have been widely deemed as desirable by the local community and the redevelopment has not brought with it any major sociospatial restructuring of the urban form. However, the lack of financial capability to implement large-scale urban redevelopment forced the government to look for alternative strategies to fulfill its aspirations. That meant resorting to market forces and private sector resources. This change in policy ethos and the maturing of the real-estate market means that the role of the government has shifted from being the active enabler to being a symbolic partner. Meanwhile, the changing role of the developer has paralleled that of the government: from being the agent in delivering housing redevelopment on behalf of the state, to being the key driver of sociospatial restructuring in the city, largely through the development of upper-market properties in prime sites and cheaper properties on the edge of the city.

The inability of the state to realize its urban development visions has increasingly led it to seek partnership with the private sector to access market resources. This has altered the relationships between the government and the developer. The developer was the agent or the subsidiary of the government when developing New Fukangli and was seen as an operation arm of the government. By the time International Ladoll City was developed, the developer had become an independent private property company fully driven by profits, though it still enjoyed some tax exemptions from the government. The power relationship between the government and the developer has thus shifted and rebalanced during this period of time, and it is not surprising to see that there were tensions between these two actors. This tension was clearly manifested over the issue of the conservation of the garden houses in Beijing Road during the redevelopment of International Ladoll City. As admitted by the Chief Engineer and Manager of the developer, despite the fact that these garden houses were listed buildings, they had to be demolished to avoid legal wrangling over the legitimacy of relocating original residents (if these houses were renovated, then there was no excuse to relocate the residents). This episode epitomized the conflict between the wider social objective of conservation as articulated by the Jiang'an Urban Planning Bureau and Shanghai Heritage Conservation Committee and the narrow, profit-making mindset of the developer which would remove any obstacles (in this case, the original residents) that were in its way. It is also interesting to note that, subsequently, these garden houses were rescued from the bulldozers because their existence would enhance the ambience of the area which could then translate into higher house prices and bigger profits.

The consequence of this changing institutional framework of housing redevelopment in Shanghai has been a rapid transformation of the urban landscape. The velocity of redevelopment, starting from the prime central locations, is slowly rippling out to the edge of the city through the relocation of the original residents from the center to the periphery. One can apply Smith's rent gap argument to explain this process of gentrification. With the rising property market in the early 2000s, the gap between the existing and potential value of this prime development site in central Shanghai widened, thus providing significant incentives to the developer to maximize the capital yield by developing upper-market properties. To pursue its profit the developer employed more calculative instruments, including the use of a sliding charging scheme for different additional floor space thresholds to put off the original residents from buying the properties. The final decision to renovate the garden houses in Beijing Road was profit-driven rather than a victory for the Planning Bureau. These lend further support to Smith's gentrification thesis.

Conclusion

The contrasting changes to the built environment between the two case studies in Shanghai can be regarded as a miniature reflection of how housing inequalities are generated in a transitional society. One can argue that the invisible hand of the market through land rent has restructured the land use of Shanghai and enhanced property development through the city, both in the central sites and the less developed peripheral locations. The question is: how does this process of spatial restructuring affect the outcome of sociospatial stratification? In the case of International Ladoll City it was to displace the medium-income group in favor of super-wealthy elites – the implications of which are more significant given that the government has been instrumental in this process by offering tax exemptions to a purely profit-making real estate project. The lack of public resources to fund major redevelopment projects to realize the state's ambition of competing in the global world means that market forces will continue to dominate the urban landscape and the state will have to make concessions to lure in private sector resources. Under this trend of joint-venture development, it is not difficult to envisage that the phenomenon of spatial displacement and sociospatial stratification will be widely seen in different parts of China, especially in the main cities. In the case of International Ladoll City, it was the medium income group that was pushed out; however, the implication of this spatial restructuring process is that the lower income groups will be pushed even further out from the city to the least desirable locations. The issues are whether there are employment opportunities and social infrastructure to support the needs of these disadvantaged groups and whether they can afford the commuting costs to take up employment in the city center. At the macroeconomic level, Smith (1996) argues that gentrification is a result of the movement of capital into and out of the built environment to yield profits, and this capitalist mode of production tends to create the boom-and-bust cycle witnessed in many Western cities. Certainly, there is a role to be played by planners in mitigating the negative outcomes of the stratification process and to address the uneven development created by gentrification at local, regional and national levels. However, as shown in the case studies, the power of planners in China is rather limited. These are big questions to be answered and merit further research in the future.

Notes

1   "Li" and "Long" are two Chinese words meaning neighborhoods and lanes, respectively. *Lilong* settlements have low-rise, ground-related housing patterns and a hierarchical

spatial organization network separating public and private spaces that evoke a strong sense of neighborhood. *Lilong* houses characterize the traditional urban housing form of the City of Shanghai.

2 Housing units were renovated and refurbished to a limited standard as the projects were small in scale. Later on, when larger-scale projects were introduced, there was full scale housing renewal and redevelopment.

3 According to Shanghai Municipal Urban Planning Bureau (1998), 94.3 percent of 1,165 households moved back in HAFI projects at the outset.

4 Personal interview of Ying Ying Tian with the Head of the Building Management Section of Jing'an District Planning Bureau, November 5, 2003.

5 Based on personal interview with the Head of the Administration Section of Jing'an Property Stockholding Co. Ltd on November 7, 2003.

6 Personal interview by Ying Ying Tian with a returned resident (a retired middle-school teacher) on November 14, 2003.

References

Amin, A. and Thrift, N. (eds) (1995) *Globalization, Institutions, and Regional Development*, Oxford: Oxford University Press.

Ball, M. (1998) "Institutions in British property research: a review," *Urban Studies*, 35(9): 1501–1517.

Cameron, S. (1992) "Housing, gentrification and urban regeneration," *Urban Studies*, 29(1): 3–14.

Darling, E. (2005) "The city in the country: wilderness gentrification and the rent gap," *Environment and Planning A*, 37: 1015–1032.

Gonzalez, S. and Healey, P. (2005) "A sociological institutionalist approach to the study of innovation in governance capacity," *Urban Studies*, 42(11): 2055–2069.

Guy, S. and Henneberry, J. (2000) "Understanding urban development processes: integrating the economic and the social in property research," *Urban Studies*, 37(13): 2399–2416.

Guy, S. and Henneberry, J. (2002) "Approaching development" in S. Guy and J. Henneberry (eds) *Development and Developers: Perspectives on Property*, Oxford: Blackwell, 1–17.

Healey, P. (1992) "An institutional model of the development process," *Journal of Property Research*, 9: 33–44.

Healey, P. (1997) *Collaborative Planning: Shaping Places in Fragmented Societies*, Basingstoke: Macmillan Press.

Healey, P. and Barrett, S. M. (1990) "Structure and agency in land and property development processes: some ideas for research," *Urban Studies*, 27(1): 89–104.

Li, S. M. (2000) "Housing consumption in urban China: a comparative study of Beijing and Guangzhou," *Environment and Planning A*, 32: 1115–1134.

Li, S. M. (2004) "Life courses and residential mobility in Beijing, China," *Environment and Planning A*, 36: 27–43.

Logan, J. R., Bian, Y. J. and Bian, F. Q. (1999) "Housing inequality in urban China in the 1990s," *International Journal of Urban and Regional Research*, 23: 7–25.

Lu, J. H. (1997) "Beijing's old and dilapidated housing renewal," *Cities*, 14(2): 59–69.

Ma, L. J. C. (2002) "Urban transformation in China, 1949–2000: a review and research agenda," *Environment and Planning A*, 34: 1545–1569.

Miao, P. (2003) "Deserted streets in a jammed town: the gated community in Chinese cities and its solution," *Journal of Urban Design*, 8(1): 45–66.

Paasi, A. (2000) "Europe as a social process and discourse: consideration of place, boundaries and identity," paper presented at the Third European Urban and Regional Studies Conference, Voss, September 14–17, 2000.

Pannell, C. W. (2002) "China's continuing urban transition," *Environment and Planning A*, 34: 1571–1589.

Sang, R. L. (2002) "Some issues regarding the trend of Shanghai real-estate market," *Shanghai Real-Estate Association*, 7: 12–19. (In Chinese)

Scott, W. R. (1995) *Institutions and Organizations*, Thousand Oaks, CA: Sage Publications.

Shanghai Municipal Property and Land Management Bureau and Shanghai Statistical Bureau (2002) *Shanghai Real Estate Market, 2002*, Beijing: Chinese Statistics Press.

Shanghai Statistical Bureau (2002, 2005) *Shanghai Statistical Year Book 2002; 2005*, Beijing: China Statistics Press.

Smith, N. J. (1979a) "Towards a theory of gentrification: a back to the city movement by capital not people," *Journal of the American Planning Association*, 45: 538–548.

Smith, N. J. (1979b) "Gentrification and capital: theory, practice and ideology in society hill," *Antipode*, 11(3): 24–35.

Smith, N. J. (1996) *The New Urban Frontier: Gentrification and the Revanchist City*, London: Routledge.

Wang, D. and Li, S. M. (2004) "Housing preferences in a transitional housing system: the case of Beijing, China," *Environment and Planning A*, 36(1): 69–88.

Wang, Y. (2002) "A case study on urban community in Shanghai – community classification, spatial distribution and changing tendencies," *Urban Planning Forum*, 142(6): 33–40. (In Chinese)

Wang, Y. P. and Murie, A. (2000) "Social and spatial implications of housing reform in China," *International Journal of Urban and Regional Research*, 24: 397–417.

Wu, F. (2002) "Sociospatial differentiation in urban China: evidence from Shanghai's real estate markets," *Environment and Planning A*, 34: 1591–1615.

Wu, F. (2003) "Residential relocation under market-oriented redevelopment: the process and outcomes in urban China," *Geoforum*, 35: 435–470.

Wu, F. (2004a) "Intraurban residential relocation in Shanghai: modes and stratification," *Environment and Planning A*, 36: 7–25.

Wu, F. (2004b) "The rise of 'foreign gated communities' in Beijing: between economic globalisation and local institutions," *Cities*, 21(3): 203–213.

Yeh, A. G. O. (2000) "Foreign investment and urban development in China," in S. M. Li and W. S. Tang (eds) *China's Regions, Policy, and Economy*, Hong Kong: The Chinese University Press, 34–64.

Zhang, X. (2000) "On the population movement and the residential pattern in Shanghai," *Urban Planning Forum*, 5: 72–75. (In Chinese)

Part IV

Emerging leisure, retailing, and consumption practices

12 Spaces of leisure

Gated golf communities in China

Guillaume Giroir

Introduction

Luxury gated communities in China now number in the hundreds. For example, 250 luxury villa estates have appeared around Beijing in the last 20 years; the number reaches 145 on the outskirts of Shanghai; Chengdu, the capital of the distant province of Sichuan, has 52 gated communities.[1] Nevertheless, private and secured residential communities centered on a golf course are much rarer here than they are in the United States. The gated golf communities occupy the most luxurious sector of the market. In addition, these gated golf communities represent a very particular type of territory in the context of China: large-sized spaces with particularly low residential density and low forms of housing in a country which is, on the contrary, characterized by very high population densities, an extreme rarity of available land (notably in eastern China and around large cities) and a general verticality in urban shapes. These communities consume not only land but also water to an excessive degree.

In such conditions, these territories, which combine residential and recreational functions, bring up serious issues in numerous domains such as urban planning and the environment, and thus lead to debates in the press. The objective of this study is to analyze these Chinese gated golf communities with a principally geographic approach.[2] First, the study presents the phenomenon of gated golf communities and shows that it fits into a wider historical evolution. Examples of gated golf communities in the United States and in France will be discussed in order to put the Chinese case into perspective. Then, the chapter identifies the specificities of this type of community in China and brings to light the multiple property, political, and environmental issues that they involve (Wu 2006a,b). The chapter also presents a typology of gated golf communities in China, contrasting the golf villas in intra-urban settings, then in suburban and outlying areas, and finally in rural (or perimetropolitan) settings.

The phenomenon

The phenomenon of gated golf communities is the territorial product of the merging of two distinct historical processes: the tendency towards privatization of residential space and the growing role of the leisure economy in developed societies.

Theoretical framework

As private, secured residential spaces, golf villas represent a particular form of gated community.[3] They are thus part of the larger movement which tends towards the production of private, enclosed, secured residential forms. While certain European and North American residential complexes dating from the nineteenth and early twentieth centuries constitute the first historical manifestations of this process, the movement towards gated communities produced particularly numerous forms, first in the United States, starting in the 1950s, before spreading to the rest of the world in more or less specific forms depending on the local context. These gated communities also fuel debate, most often critical of the consequences for the future of the city of this process of privatization of urban space.

Yet gated golf communities are not ordinary enclosed communities. The luxury villas here are located in leisure space. This integration of residential and recreational functions into a single closed and private ensemble constitutes a particular kind of entity. In developed countries, where urban economies are largely specialized, leisure activities contribute more and more to the development of urban space.[4] This leisure economy proceeds through multiple factors, as much through supply as through demand: the increase in the amount of leisure time (decreasing work, increased life expectancy), increased mobility, the will of elected officials to redevelop former industrial or dockside sites, the desire for entertainment, but also an enrichment of the forms of leisure activities offered by businesses. This evolution is a reversal of the paradigm. While before, tourism and leisure activities were byproducts of urbanization, they are today producers of specialized urban development. This process operates in three phases: in the first, tourist space is an appendix, a superfluous and parasitic organ; then, it creates specific communities, such as seaside or mountain resorts; today, tourism and leisure activities are at the center of many urban planning initiatives.

In rare cases, leisure activities contribute to the essential growth of urban structures: this is notably the case with certain theme parks or large-sized sports facilities. One of the most notable examples is provided by the Disney Company, whose theme parks have represented one of the forces of development of the new city of Marne-la-Vallée. Similarly, the construction of the *Stade de France* (France's national stadium) has played a major role in the reorganization of the *Plaine-Saint-Denis*. Also, on a smaller scale, multiplexes, sports or recreational complexes, video game arcades, or other installations such as the Hard Rock Café, more or less profoundly transform the landscape, the sociology and the image of certain isolated neighborhoods. These 'fun enclaves' tend to multiply, either in central neighborhoods – as at Navy Pier in Chicago, where the public space is in reality invaded by a mix of recreational activities (Children's Museum, skating rink, carousel, Ferris wheel, open-air theater) and commercial ones (restaurants, conference centers) and greatly shaped by large American corporations (Gravari-Barbas 2001) – or in surrounding areas like Universal City Walk in Los Angeles, which is a half-commercial, half-fun space of a couple hundred meters linking a theme park to a multiplex. The urban space is thus more and more molded by large companies, specialized in the leisure industry. This leisure economy tends to transform cities into fun cities.[5]

Turning the city's territory into tourist and/or leisure centers, which is at the same time a more or less radical and direct form of privatization, sometimes attracts negative reactions. Many observers have a critical view of this evolution, even if this point of view does not always escape caricature or bias: some would speak of the "disneylandization" of urban space (Davis 1996, 1998). The future Val d'Europe Center in Marne-la-Vallée has been nicknamed "Mickeyville" by critics. Criticism points in several directions. The leisure activities offered are considered as mass activities, based in standardized products, without any true cultural content. This could be a sterilized type of urbanism – that is, unrepresentative of society in its diversity. In addition, leisure activities are often pretexts for more commercial or real-estate-focused strategies. Gated golf communities are clearly part of this movement. Yet leisure activities, as territorial phenomena, present a major distinction between developed spaces (multiplexes, streets) and undeveloped or open spaces (sports fields). Among the latter, golf courses have the essential particularity of being artificial landscapes of large size, most often several dozen, even hundreds, of hectares.

In the United States, simple, concise but evocative formulas are proposed: "golf homes" or "villas on golf courses." This expression underlines the association of individual-type housing and a particular kind of leisure space, which is the basis for this type of locality. In other cases, the term "community" introduces an extra precision: it is then a question of a "golf course community" or of a "residential golf resort community." These areas appear as particularly organized social entities, and not just as juxtapositions of individual villas integrated into golf courses. Certain expressions like "golf community with luxury homes" clearly highlight the luxurious character of these complexes. In France, the most often used term is "domain," which adds a reference to the feudal era to the other characteristics in order to better underline the exclusive nature of these places. Yet the descriptive American names such as "luxury homes in a private gated golf community," "private golf community" or even simply "gated golf community" show that in these private, enclosed and secured places are a particular type of gated communities. In fact, the United States is both the cradle of gated golf communities and is the focus of their largest global concentration. It is therefore necessary to describe the phenomenon in the United States in order to put the Chinese example into perspective.

The United States

Private gated golf communities have become an important sector of the general real estate market in the United States (Sorkin 1992), particularly in the market for gated communities.[6] Florida has more than 500 gated golf communities, while they number 375 in California and 210 in Arizona. While these communities enclose a rather limited population, their land hold is often quite significant: for example, Grand Haven, on Florida's eastern coast, spreads out over 546 ha. The success of such a formula in the United States, joining golf and generally luxurious villas, is explained by a series of factors: vast land availability, attractive bioclimatic zones (notably the Sunbelt), elevated buying power, the long-standing popularity of golf, the presence of great golf course developers like Jack Nicklaus and Robert Trent Jones, and/or the population's receptiveness towards enclosed residential forms.

These particular forms of private, secured communities also show a large diversity. Certain gated golf communities are intended for active retired people (Indian River Colony Club in Florida), others are joined with a marina (Mission Inn's Las Colinas in Florida) or situated in the mountains (Mountain Air in North Carolina, or, even with private ski trails, Queechee Lake in Vermont), or on a lake (Lake Ridge in Texas) or even on an island (Spring Island in South Carolina). While these enclaves are generally intended for a wealthy clientele, the level of luxury is nevertheless rather variable. Certain developments are very luxurious (e.g. the 4 million US dollars plus villas at Wakefield Plantation in North Carolina) while others are home to middle class residents (villas of 80,000 US dollars maximum at Leatherwood Landing on Kentucky Lake in Tennessee).

France

Outside of the United States, this type of development appears to be much more recent. In Europe, the gated golf community is present in the Mediterranean region, notably Spain, France, Italy and Portugal. However, the rarity of land and water resources, the hilly character of the relief in Mediterranean zones, political pressure from ecologists, and some of the population's hostility towards this kind of private, secured, elitist residential enclave limits their spread. In France, only a few examples truly correspond to the definition of gated golf communities.

The *Domaine de Pont-Royal en Provence*, in the township of Mallemort and halfway between Aix-en-Provence and Avignon, 9 km from the A7 highway, was built in 1991 and inaugurated in 1992. Enclosed and accessible only by the single guards' post, the ensemble includes many typical elements. A 47 ha. golf course, designed by Severiano Ballesteros, was placed on calcareous and occupied by former hunting grounds, scrubland and a pine forest. Tourist and leisure facilities are provided by a 1,200 sq. mtr clubhouse, with gourmet restaurant, a *Pierre et Vacances* hotel, and tourist apartments. Inside the "domain," luxury villas are grouped together in "Le Clos du Golf," an ensemble of several types of Provencal houses with personalized and private entrances. On the Côte d'Azur, the *Domaine de Terre Blanche* also presents itself as "a great luxury resort." This golf club resort, opened to the public in April 2004 and situated in the township of Tourettes, includes an ensemble of 266 ha. entirely enclosed by a 2 mtr high compound wall and a single entrance with a rising barrier. The development is protected by surveillance cameras placed every 25 mtr, infrared radar detectors and a computerized, central post which ensures security 24 hours a day.

Another recent example is the *Domaine de Gassin* Country Club, a few kilometers from Saint-Tropez (Drouin 2003). Opened in 2004 thanks to French and American investors, this gated golf community spreads out over 115 ha., divided between an 18-hole course, a 9-hole compact course, 171 homes (60 individual homes with private pools), a luxury hotel with 38 suites, and a club house, as well as a fitness and beauty center. The price of homes ranges from 900,000 to 3.2 million US dollars. Other projects are near Paris. Notably, Marriot's *Village d'Île-de-France*, located near Disneyland Resort Paris, presents itself as an eventual ensemble of 275 villas set around a vast stretch of water and a 27-hole golf course, all being offered as time-shares for a partly North American clientele.

Gated golf communities in China

In China, there are not many gated golf communities, but they are distinct because of strong land hold, their level of luxury, and their diversity. Their spread in China is carried out in a particular territorial, socioeconomic and political context, characterized by an accelerated transition – powered by globalization and money-making – but also strong constraints of government control.

Methodological difficulties in identifying the phenomenon in China

Spotting and counting this kind of territory in China is problematic. There are villa zones (*bieshu*) and golf courses (*gaoerfu*) respectively in China, but areas that join the two have not yet been the subject of a proper account. In some cases, certain gated golf communities are indeed identifiable by their names: "gaoerfu bieshu" (villas on a golf course), like the Beijing Xiangcun Gaoerfu Bieshu or the Yintao Gaoerfu Bieshu and Tianma Huayuan Gaoerfu Bieshu in Shanghai. Elsewhere, the term *bieshu* is replaced by another, generally more poetic or evocative term: "Zhuangyuan," "Shanzhuang" (e.g. Qingchengshan Gaoerfu Shangzhuang in Chengdu, Gaoerfu Chengshi Huayuan in Wuhan). Yet numerous villa zones with golf courses are only titled "bieshu," without other qualifications. Moreover, many gated golf communities include neither the term "golf" nor the term "villa" (or their equivalents).

The difficulty in identifying gated golf communities in China also comes from publicity: certain real estate developments announce the creation of a golf course to come on adjoining undeveloped land, without specifying a timeframe or making a definite promise. The prospect of having a golf course at their disposition is used to attract buyers for the villas. Some villa zones are presented as villas with a golf course, when in reality the course is only bordering the residential development. Although here we have a development close in form to the golf course villa complex, it nevertheless seems that this category should be excluded because of the spatial disassociation and the institutional differences of these two entities. In addition, significant disproportion can exist between the number of villas and the surface area of the golf course. Some villa zones only have a practice course; others have a small outdoor putting green. It has been decided not to count these kinds of development because of the limited surface area of the land reserved for golf.

The question of marking the object of study's boundaries also arises for certain golf courses centered on a large hotel complex but including a few, often quite luxurious, villas in a generally distinct zone. Here, the number of villas must be taken on a case by case basis. In the case of Fuchun Resort, 25 km from Hangzhou, the development of 120 ha. includes an 18-hole course, a hotel and only five large luxury villas. The extremely small number of villas stretches the limit of the definition, and leads to this case being excluded from the gated golf community category. When these criteria are adopted, there appear to be very few Chinese gated golf communities. Their spatial distribution largely follows the geography of development in China, and strongly favors large cities. In Beijing, we can estimate their numbers at 21, while there would only be nine in Shanghai, and five in Guangzhou and Shenzhen. More recently, a few other large or medium cities (e.g. Hangzhou, Harbin, Chengdu, Wuhan, Zhuhai) have begun to have one. Overall, we can estimate the total number of gated golf communities as at least 50. Such a number needs constant updating, given the strong dynamics of gated communities in China.

In general, we can distinguish two large types of spatial configuration. In certain cases, we have numerous villas around a central golf facility, as in the Tomson Golf Villas in Shanghai. Elsewhere, the villas can be concentrated in a separate zone inside a vast golf facility. For example, the Beijing Xiangcun Gaoerfu Bieshu spreads out over only 4.4 ha inside a large golf course of 240 ha., but it contains 55 villas. The extreme example is Mission Hills in Shenzhen where a golf course of 20 sq. km is shared by owners of just 200 villas. The villas, concentrated in the Mission Hills in Residence, thus occupy a surface area that is totally disproportionate in relation to the course.

Luxury villas and golf courses

The parallel rise of both luxury villas and golf courses is part of the most significant phenomena in the emergence of postcommunist land-use practices on the outskirts of large Chinese cities. These two types of developed and undeveloped space did not necessarily appear only with the politics of reform. Precommunist villas can be found in China: for example, in the center of Nanjing, an ensemble of villas housed members of the nationalist government. On the contrary, during the Maoist period, the very notion of an individual villa was inconceivable in a regime that swore by collective living and proletarian ideology. Similarly, golf may have ancient origins in China, which is one of the countries that claims the invention of this leisure activity. A Chinese form of golf was supposedly created around 300 B.C.[7] Nevertheless, the rise in golf playing owes much to foreign presence, notably in the colonial period. The British army introduced golf to Hong Kong in 1890, but the first golf course in China was created in Shanghai in 1917, on land that is today the location of the city zoo. However, under Mao golf was considered a bourgeois, decadent leisure activity, and for this reason prohibited. Many golf courses in the province of Guangdong, the inland area surrounding Hong Kong, were thus converted into rice paddies. These two kinds of development – the villa complex and the golf course – in a way symbolic of capitalism, saw a renaissance starting in the 1980s, and most of all in the 1990s. Their spread took place through marked cycles which were linked to the political climate, but also to the economic, and notably the stock market, situation.

The market for luxury villas has evolved in three successive growth phases, separated by more or less severe declines. The first phase took place in the early 1990s and the second towards the end of the decade, but with a limited number of developments. The third phase is in progress at the moment, with larger and more numerous developments; it has been greatly stimulated not only by China's entry in the WTO, the 2008 Olympic Games in Beijing, and the Universal Exposition of 2010 in Shanghai, but also by the emergence of a class of the new rich. The first post Cultural Revolution golf course opened in 1984 in Zhongshan Hot Spring thanks to the famous American player Arnold Palmer. It was only in 1986 that Beijing received its first golf course, the Beijing International Club, an 18-hole course which was created along the Ming Tombs reservoir. For the last couple of years, golf courses have tended to multiply across China. The exact number in unknown: there are about 200 operational golf facilities, but more than 500 to 1,000 facilities could be under construction (Ng 2004). While the phenomenon of golf has become almost ubiquitous in China, the majority of courses are located around large cities in eastern China, notably in the province of Guangdong, which takes advantage of the lack of space in Hong Kong.

Both types of territory occupy large, even very large, surface areas, in general on the outskirts of metropolises. They cater for the same wealthy groups. Two types of clientele are partially shared: some golfers live in villas, while some villa residents play golf. In spite of these common points, these two types of complex are generally spatially disassociated.[8] Gated communities, golf facilities, as well as horse clubs and international campuses form a veritable "club system" which tends to give structure to the outskirts of large cities (Giroir 2002, 2003a,b, 2006a,b,c,d). Many of them show golf facilities and villa zones in close proximity, if not bordering – as in Yushu Linfeng, a villa zone of about 22 ha. in the Haidian district of Beijing, which has a 27-hole course but separated from it by a highway. Many other villa developments have been built in more or less immediate proximity of golf facilities: this is the case in Beijing with He'an Huanyuan (Venice Villa), south of the Huatang international course, the Wanshu Huafu near the Wanliu course, or Shuise Shiguang, near the Beijing country golf club. Integration of a golf course and a complex of luxury villas is rare, but this integration itself appears in complex territorial configurations.

The order of construction for villas and golf facilities is variable. Generally, the two are offered simultaneously. Yet in certain cases the villas have been finished after the creation of the golf course: either a residential program had been planned from the start and develops gradually, often in a specified zone of the golf facility or around a centralized course, or, as in Mission Hills, the installation of a number of villas was decided afterwards, and, as it seems, without any advanced planning. The opposite scenario also exists: certain promoters promise to create a course on the land reserves of the villa zone in order to make the existing villas more attractive to buyers or to justify the high prices. It is also sometimes a way to first pocket the profits before creating a facility which is generally unprofitable.

Reasons for associating golf courses and villas

Why do gated golf communities exist in China? Why is there such an association between luxury villas and golf? This particular type of private, secured enclave is produced by multiple factors. Some are specific to China, other are not. Each player in this micromarket has a particular interest in promoting this kind of residential and recreational enclave. For promoters, the association between villas and golf is an optimal commercial and financial configuration. The presence of golf facilities is a powerful selling point. It allows a differentiation between offers in a highly competitive luxury real estate market. Compared to other gated communities, gated golf communities offer not only the opportunity for recreational activity, but also a clear added landscape value. By creating very low density, golf courses give the feeling of large spaces in urban outskirts where open territory is rare and where developed forms, often vertical, are omnipresent and oppressive. They avoid the pitfalls of developments which are too dense, where the inevitable face to face settings go against the idea of the private space which motivates residential choices in this kind of enclave. The criterion of environment has indeed become determinant in this segment of the market. In addition, in a very monotonous delta area, like the one around Shanghai for example, the creation of a golf course produces a rather strongly differentiated microlandscape. Sand pits, waterways, small hills and diverse ways of treating the vegetation (the closely mowed surface of the greens, the grassy zones on the fairways, and dense, unmowed grass in the rough) produce a landscape which is certainly artificial but different from its immediate surroundings.

Promoters also see in the establishing of a golf course a way to create and secure precious land reserves. Thus, it is not uncommon that the planned size of the course is reduced to make way more or less surreptitiously for the construction of villas. We then witness a progressive densification of the open space. While golf courses help to sell villas, they are themselves generally unprofitable because of the heavy maintenance costs. As such, almost half of golf courses in China may be in deficit.[9] In other words, while golf facilities help villa sales, the villas themselves ensure the profitability of this kind of development. The rarity of this kind of private enclave indeed allows the fixing of sale prices well above the average: the sale price per sq. mtr. often reaches 10,000 to 15,000 yuan, even 20,000 to 25,000 yuan for the most expensive villas, instead of the average 5,000 to 10,000 yuan per sq. mtr for those without golf facilities. Substantial membership fees are added to the sale price, which ensures constant revenue for the directors of golf villas. These fees can sometimes reach up to 12 yuan per sq. mtr. per month in a development such as Bihai Fangzhou in Beijing – for villas of 630 sq. mtr an annual expense of more than 90,000 yuan. In the luxurious Shunjingshan development, also located in the capital, the fees do not go over 8 yuan per sq. mtr per month, but, attached to villas of 2,000 sq. mtr, they add up to a total sum of 192,000 yuan per year. Similarly, villa residents make up the majority of golf club members: thus the registration fees for these exclusive clubs often reach considerable sums (47,000 US dollars at the Tianma Golf Club in Shanghai, and even 315,000 US dollars at Mission Hills in Shenzhen). The residents themselves invite outside golfers (clients, personal acquaintances) who must pay substantial sums in order to play – for example, 1,800 yuan in Tomson Golf Villas for a weekend (not including club rental, 210 yuan, and shoe rental, 40 yuan); this sum does not include additional expenses such as restaurants or other leisure activities. The resident golfer generates a cash flow, directly or indirectly, which contributes to the financial balance of these residential entities.

For large municipalities like Beijing and Shanghai, the creation of such gated golf communities brings some political risks, but also some strong advantages. The sale of high priced land rights makes up a major source of revenues which permits continued urban growth. Golf courses, with or without villas, also serve as support for authorities' urban marketing policies: indeed, all the large Chinese metropolises are attempting to improve their image abroad, and trying to appear to be 'green cities' or "eco-cities." This is the case not only in Beijing in view of the 2008 Olympic Games (cf. the slogan, "Green Beijing"), but also in Shanghai ("Green Shanghai"). This green-focus is a response to a preoccupation with sustainable development as well as an economic promotion strategy. Here, it is a question of creating an attractive, worthwhile setting for investment, notably from abroad. The authorities often use it in order to promote economic development zones, notably on the Internet. In part thanks to golf facilities, Shanghai received the title of "National Garden City" from the central government in January 2004. With 35.78 percent of surface area dedicated to green space and 9.2 sq. mtr of green space per capita, it has gone beyond the required amounts (35 percent and 6.5 sq. mtr, respectively) needed in order to obtain this nationally envied award. The city also plans to organize a "Green World Expo," a vast media operation. Similarly, the green-focus helps ensure price stability for luxury real estate programs, guaranteeing future fiscal results. As for the host districts or neighborhoods, they also see several advantages in these operations. When the developments are of large size, they are often a major source of fiscal revenues and a significant element in the diversification of the local economy. They also represent an important boost in the service job market (caddies, security guards and gardeners). The interested parties themselves appreciate this kind of employment, which provides decent pay often accompanied by free meals and uniforms. The local political representatives see in these developments as well the opportunity to meet decision-makers with greater influence.

For rich, private buyers, the association of villas and golf facilities offers an exceptional lifestyle which is characterized by a natural-style environment. Taking into account the abundance of green and waterfront spaces, these areas are blessed with a highly appreciated microclimate, especially in summer. This allows rich residents, of whom a remarkable number are retired or semi retired, to practice as often as possible and on foot (or by golf cart) an outdoor leisure activity which sometimes becomes a passion. For the often recent and avid elite, it is a sign of distinction to rise to a certain social status and an international openness. It is also an ideal framework for reinforcing one's social network: some observers have forged the expression "guanxi golf-style" (relations based on playing golf) in order to label this phenomenon. Buying a luxury villa located on a golf course represents a perfectly rational investment as well: the almost structural rarity effect of this kind of luxury enclave allows a securing and valuing of the considerable sums invested. Nevertheless, a number of buyers wish to have access to golf facilities without at all wanting to play. Others would like to begin playing this sport but are not able to achieve a satisfactory level. Some developments have even instated restrictive rules: for example, at Tomson Golf Villas in Shanghai, players with a handicap over 36 are not allowed to access the course;[10] beginners are only allowed to practice at the driving range so as not to disturb the other players.[11]

Problems of gated golf communities

While the creation of golf facilities is the product of a large blend of interests, their excessive and partially unchecked spread is sometimes in contradiction to the interests of the community. Thus, in recent years the phenomenon of gated golf communities both as golf spaces and as large luxury villa zones has become the subject of intense public debate, even in the official media.

In a context of high population density and rarity of agricultural land, the land question is central for golf facilities, with or without villas. According to the official press, land availability in China is extremely limited: 0.13 ha. in 12 provinces and municipalities and 0.06 ha. in seven of them. The province of Guangdong, and notably the Pearl River Delta, one of the most densely populated regions in the world, nevertheless has 54 golf facilities. In addition, urban spread is particularly accelerated around large cities, precisely where gated golf communities are located. Some golf villas are spread out over vast areas: this is notably the case in Dongfang Taiyang Cheng (Oriental Sun City) (234 ha.) northeast of Beijing, in Tianma Huayuan Gaoerfu Bieshu, east of Shanghai (184 ha.), or in Yushan Gaoerfu, southwest of Shanghai (150 ha.). We could also add the special example of Mission Hills, a giant golf villa zone of 20 sq. km, located about 35 km north of Shenzhen.

The issues of overconsumption of land brought on by golf facilities, with or without villas, are severe. Such a waste of land is one of the elements compromising the country's food self-sufficiency, and in particular accelerates the destruction of agricultural belts surrounding large cities. Taking into account the sensitivity of the land question in China and the necessity of removing, and paying compensation to, hundreds, even thousands of country-dwellers before creating a course, golf facilities have become a political issue. Gated golf communities, most often characterized by a small number of imposing and luxurious villas, make the elites' life style and sociospatial disparities especially visible. The increase of private space also elicits criticism from those who remain attached to the notion of public space. In particular, these developments feed a debate on the politics of urban planning. Is the multiplication of golf facilities the optimum use of land in urban space or its outlying areas? Would it not be better to instead create high technology zones, commercial spaces, or even other, yet public, green spaces?

These different questions have provoked reaction from some experts as well as from ordinary people. According to the official press, numerous telephone calls and letters of protest against the violation of agricultural land use rules have been addressed to the Minister of Land and Resources. This situation has driven the government to show its willingness to regulate these excesses and take back control after what is presented as local authorities' mistakes. According to the official figures quoted by the official English-language *China Daily,* China has 176 golf facilities spread out over 26 provinces and municipalities. Yet, in reality, only one of them was approved by the central government, according to the Minister of Land and Resources, the only State organization which normally authorizes nonagricultural use for areas larger than 1,000 *mu* (70 ha.) (Anonymous 2004a). Yet an 18-hole golf course corresponds to about 80 ha. Thus almost all golf courses have been illegally authorized by the local authorities only, including those of simple small towns or even village committees. Presented as "image projects" intended to improve the economic environment, the golf courses have almost always been approved. Hundreds of courses, sometimes augmented by real estate programs, may be under construction with only the approval of local governments.

Golf facilities are also accused of wasting water resources. Obtaining perfect greens indeed necessitates intensive watering, in the order of 10,000 cu. mtr per ha. This overconsumption of water appears to be particularly inappropriate in urban regions that often suffer from water shortage. In spite of the lack of water, Beijing still allowed the creation of 24 golf facilities. In addition, in order to obtain functionally and visually perfect greens and fairways, as well as to maintain the health of these completely artificial places, it is necessary to resort to the intensive use of chemical fertilizers, herbicides and fungicides (Jenkins 1994). However rainwater washes pollutants into the waterways and underground reservoirs used by agriculture. These diverse types of pollution could have effects on the health of local residents and wildlife.

Faced with this situation, the Bureau of Resources, Land and Housing of Shanghai decided in August 2002 not to approve the creation of new golf courses. Similarly, the Bureau of Environmental Protection of Shanghai made the systematic treatment of waste water from golf courses mandatory, and outlawed the use of herbicides (Anonymous 2002a). The ban on new golf facilities in favor of the environment could also be explained by a wish to improve the management of existing courses, which have extremely underutilized capacities (Anonymous 2002b): in reality, it may be a question of regulating the expansion of golf facilities in order to raise the number of visitors to existing ones and reduce their deficit. However, in addition, it seems that these measures are not effective, if judged by the large number of courses opened since the regulation. Several gated communities were opened in 2004 in Beijing and in Shanghai, while, in 2005, the extremely luxurious golf villas of Shunjingyuan were inaugurated inside the capital's fourth ring road.

Typology of Chinese gated golf communities

Gated golf communities in China form a group of complexes which vary greatly in size, location, the level of luxury, the ratio of developed to undeveloped space, or even landscape morphology. Taking into account their strong spatial hold, it seems that distance from the city can be chosen as the main criterion in order to establish a typology. Indeed, the location factor is revealed to be determinant: those communities which are within immediate proximity to the urban space fall into a spatial context characterized by high density and intense competition for scarce land; on the other hand, those located several dozen kilometers away occupy spaces with much lower density and do not come into direct conflict with the metropolitan dynamic. Between the two cases, we can observe diverse variations.[12]

Shunjingyuan in Beijing: an intra-urban golf community

Gated golf communities in true intra-urban locations are particularly rare; in this respect, the case of Shunjingyuan Shishang Qingquan (Shunjingyuan, for the sake of simplicity) is without a doubt unique in large Chinese cities. The field work was carried out in November 2003, while this golf villa complex was still under construction. Work was completed in September 2004 with a grand opening in June 2005. Administratively, Shunjingyuan falls under the jurisdiction of the Chaoyang district, and not one of the four central districts of the capital. Yet this gated golf community is the only one located inside the fourth ring road, near the Siyuan interchange where the fourth beltway and the major northeast road towards the international airport cross. Shunjingyuan is thus found in the area between the third and fourth beltways – an area whose northern and eastern parts show an almost integral urbanization of space.

The community consists of a microterritorial enclave oriented northeast and southwest, the borders of which coincide with roadways of varying importance: in the northwest, the highway to the airport; to the north, the Siyuan exchange; to the northeast, the fourth ring road; and to the southeast, the Xiaoyun road. It is therefore an example of an interstitial gated golf community – that is, one that has come to occupy a space which is for the most part undeveloped, all in a dense and continuous urban fabric. In reality, maps and satellite images show that, originally, the zone was partially occupied by a piece of urban fabric, which was therefore bulldozed to make room for this intra-urban golf villa development. Overall, the villas occupy a zone of 3.5 ha. inside a nine-hole golf course of 20 ha., which makes for a total green space of about 80 percent (see Figure 12.1).

Adaptation, not only to land constraints but also to urban ones, was achieved through daring optimization of available space and positioning in the market for great luxury. Shunjingyuan has three imposing villas in "château style" of 2,000

Figure 12.1 The Shunjingyuan Villas in Beijing.

Source: Photograph by G. Giroir, November 2003.

sq. mtr. each on three levels. The price is 25,000 yuan per sq. mtr., plus cooperative fees of 8 yuan per sq. mtr. per month. There is also a 12,000 sq. mtr. villa zone linked to the hot spring; it has six parts, all representing a particular foreign style. 93 apartments of a minimum of 500 sq. mtr. each are added, at a price of 22,000 yuan per sq. mtr. Apartments and villas are sold for 10 to 60 million yuan. In total, the program presents abundant housing space with a developed area of 11 ha. In order to leave as much undeveloped space as possible, notably the golf course, large collective facilities (the pool and parking) are semiunderground. In order to protect residents from noise pollution from the fourth ring road, and also to ensure privacy, the villas and apartment buildings are at the center of the golf course. Located at the very heart of the villas, a "sun palace style" garden with a vast, 140,000 sq. mtr aquatic area gives the feeling of being outside of the city. The Chinese style garden includes a zigzagging wooden path, strange-shaped stones and a fish pool; its purpose is to bring peace and serenity, while in the heart of the city. A curtain of willow trees gently helps close the ensemble.

Tomson Golf Villas: suburban gated golf community

Suburban gated golf communities make up the most represented category since the suburban is a type of gated community which achieves a certain balance between proximity to the city and the size of golf facilities, the whole in a territorial context marked by a strong dynamic of urban spread, and therefore intense competition for land use. In this regard, they depend on a compromise which could perhaps also be an optimum situation, as much for the resident golfer as for the managers of the villas themselves. They are situated between a few and 30 km distance from the city and in this way have a number of unique characteristics which make them intermediary types between intra-urban and perimetropolitan golf villas. It is nevertheless useful to establish the distinction between suburban and peri-urban-type gated golf communities in that their relation to the city is quite different.

Nevertheless, these residential enclaves will be in the mid-term integrated in the urban fabric. The extreme rarity of such underdeveloped spaces inside an urban fabric which is little by little becoming more dense and continuous explains their commercial placement. In general, the rarity and high price of real estate, the cost of irrigation and the relatively low number of villas creates enclaves of great luxury, in spite of some diversity in the supply. For example, this is the case in the Bihai Fangzhou, whose villas (of at least 630 sq. mtr) are offered from 15 to 38 million yuan. As for the most expensive of the Tomson golf villas in Shanghai – they sell for 22,000 yuan per sq. mtr. Some entrances to the gated golf communities are built in a monumental style. The complex of Bihai Fangzhou in Beijing forms a true "golf city" (see Figure 12.2).

Located in the New Zone of Pudong, 3.6 km from the Yangpu bridge and 5 km from the Nanpu bridge, the Tomson golf villas constitute the golf facility closest to the center of Shanghai. The villas are representative of gated golf communities in the inner suburbs. Open to the public in 1995, only a few years after Pudong's launch, they occupy a central undeveloped space in Pudong, between several areas

Figure 12.2 Bihai Fangzhou's monumental entrance. Notice the bronze statues of golfers.

Source: Photograph by G. Giroir, November 2003.

Figure 12.3 The clubhouse of Tomson Golf Villa.

Source: Photograph by G. Giroir, July 2002.

under construction: the Luijiazui financial and trade zone to the west, the Jinqiao Export Processing Zone to the north, and the Zhangjiang High Technology Park to the south. Here we have a rectangle of about 140 ha. (of which 100 ha. are for the golf course itself) marked off in the north and west by two waterways, and to the south and east by two major roadways (Longdong Avenue and Yunshan Street) (see Figure 12.3).

The Tomson golf villas show a process of progressive densification, the only solution to compensate for the financial losses of the golf course itself. Surrounding the golf course, nine phases of development have created residential subcomplexes, each comprising between 40 and 75 free-standing villas (from 180 to 702 sq. mtr. with garden) or sometimes semi-detached ones (except for phase III, which consists of apartments of 140 to 190 sq. mtr.): in total, a residential development of several hundred villas. Most of the villas are intended for rent at a price of 23 US dollars per sq. mtr per month. The largest villa takes up 1,277 sq. mtr on two floors, for a sale price of 28 million yuan. Villas with a direct view of the golf course are sold for twice the price of the others.

The ratio of developed to undeveloped space constitutes a major issue. Yet the interests of developers and of residents are extremely divergent. While the residents would like to take advantage of the largest undeveloped space possible, the developer would like to maximize the profitability of the land available. This contradiction created an incident all the more significant in that it was reported in the official press. In June 2003, a group of Tomson golf villas residents created the first homeowners' association in order to file an official complaint for false advertising. It accused the developer of having changed construction plans without their permission (Anonymous 2004b). According to them, the developer did not build, as promised, the service center which was to include a restaurant and sports and leisure facilities, and the size of lawns and gardens was reduced in relation to the original plan. On September 15, 2003, the residents' committee sent a letter to the developer, stating their demands. Several acts of protest were also carried out: a concert featured 300 car horns, posters and banners declared, "Protest against the Tomson developer for having used false advertising in order to fool clients" or "Protest against the Tomson developer for arrogantly having changed the original plans for the community." After having met with the Pudong authorities, the protesters agreed to take down the banners.

Mission Hills: the gated golf community in outer metropolitan areas

A certain number of gated golf communities are located clearly at the periphery of metropolitan areas while remaining functionally linked to them. Around Beijing, communities such as Beijing Xiangcun Gaoerfu Bieshu, Tixiang Caotang and Dongfang Taiyang Cheng have been created. There are also a number of enclaves of this type in the outskirts of Shanghai: Tianma Golf Villas, Shanghai Links, and Taiyangdao, for example. Linked to different degrees with Hong Kong, Guangzhou, and Shenzhen, many developments have taken place in the province of Guangdong, notably Mission Hills in Shenzhen. Out of the reach of urban spread, often of large size, set in zones with relatively low population density and exceptional locations, true centers of local development, these gated golf communities in outlying areas have very specific qualities.

In general, the distance from these golf villas to the city is more than 30 km but less than 100 km. Taking into account their centering on one or several large cities, most of them are located near the important networks which spread out from urban centers: for example in Shanghai, the Taiyangdao Villas and the Tianma Golf Villas are accessible by the new A9 motorway. Most developments offer bus services: at Mission Hills, around 100 shuttles daily link the Center of Hong Kong and the golf course, taking about one hour's travel time. Located far from the outer limit of urbanization, these gated golf communities escape from the pressure of developed spaces. They thus have vast available real estate since they colonize natural spaces (protected or not) or agricultural space. Therefore they are large-size golf courses. Mission Hills, the largest golf course in Asia, or even the world with its 20 sq. km, even falls under the category of giant golf courses.[13] For golf villa buyers, the tops of hills or low mountains are particularly appreciated sites because of such qualities as cool weather in the summer, the technical aspects of the golf course, and privacy.

Mission Hills clearly stands out (see Figure 12.4). Also known as Guanlanhu Gaoerfu Julebu ("Lake Guanlan Golf Club," the name of the nearest town) it occupies a huge area of land between the Bao'an district to the north of the Shenzhen Special Economic Zone and the municipality of Dongguan. It is conveniently

Figure 12.4 The main entrance at the Mission Hills in Shenzhen.

Source: Photograph by G. Giroir, August 2004.

linked to Shenzhen and Hong Kong by a north–south motorway. With its 20 sq. km, and ten 18-hole golf courses, or 180 holes in total, such an area comprises the largest golf course in the world. Opened in 1995, its clientele was originally almost exclusively from Hong Kong; today, out of 4,000 club members, half are Chinese and half are from the rest of the world. This vast complex has multiple facilities: 52 tennis courts, a five-star hotel, a luxurious spa, and a large selection of boutiques and restaurants. Initially, villa construction was not planned. This decision was reversed both to benefit golfers wishing to pursue their passion daily and to make the golf course profitable (Taylor 2004). The planned real estate development of 200 villas is concentrated in Mission Hills in Residence, a zone of 4.6 ha. opened in May 2004. It goes without saying that the land reserves of this giant golf facility would allow the creation of a large-scale real estate development.

Luxury villas occupy an area of 400 to 900 sq. mtr (not including garage, terraces and garden) for a sale price of 20,000 yuan per sq. mtr. Some of them reach 2,200 sq. mtr on three stories, with a direct view of the golf course – designed by Jack Nicklaus for the World Cup – and are sold for 30 million HK dollars (see Figure 12.5). Some of them are intended for rent, notably for the very wealthy from all over the world, who arrive in helicopters, play a round of golf and then leave the same day or a few days later. Such concentration of wealth explains why this gated golf community is protected by five levels of security: a compound wall surrounding the complex, infrared motion detectors on the golf course, security barriers around each zone, including on doors and windows in each villa; active

Figure 12.5 The Mission Hills in Shenzhen has a great luxury villa with pool and a direct view of the golf course.

Source: Photograph by G. Giroir, August 2004.

security is ensured by 400 guards, former officers of Zhongnanhai (the compound of the top central government officials) who make up the military elite in Beijing, and 60 dogs. While the golf villas set in dense urban areas make up one of many centers of development, they are also a major stimulus for the local economy when in rural areas. In this way, the economy of the town of Guanlan was greatly stimulated by the creation of the large Mission Hills golf course. This region of red clay hills situated north of Shenzhen was traditionally quite poor. Then, in the 1990s, David Chu, the owner of a small Hong Kong sports club and former University of Toronto law student, had the idea of buying this land in order to create a giant golf course. The peasants living on the land were compensated by the developer and the local government. Today, the town of Guanlan uses Mission Hills in order to attract investors. This powerful complex provides hundreds of more or less qualified jobs for the local population. Mission Hills employs no less than 4,000 people, including about 2,000 caddies, for the most part young girls. The displaced peasants were rehoused in apartment buildings; some of them sublet their apartment to golf course employees. Nevertheless, the eruption of this luxury oasis in a poor region has made for sharp social contrasts.

Conclusion

Gated golf communities clearly indicate the enormous divide between not only incomes but also lifestyle and place of residence that exists between ordinary people and economic and political elites in China (Webster *et al.* 2006; Wu 2006a; Giroir 2006b, 2006c). As a territory, gated golf communities fit an organizational model which is largely standardized and with reoccurring motifs (golf courses, clubhouses, spas, five-star hotels, and luxury villas). Nevertheless, these basic elements make room for multiple spatial combinations, depending on various differentiating factors: the natural site, the distance from the city, the size, the level of luxury or even the relation of the golf course to the villas. While this type of gated community was invented and largely developed in the United States, their construction in a country like China shows the difficulties of their transposition to a profoundly different sociodemographic, economic, political and cultural context. These gated golf communities also demonstrate the presence of deeply rooted cultural factors, as shown by the search for certain types of natural site and sometimes landscape. The recent installation of homes with a strong spatial hold, intended for elites, in the Chinese context of high-density, low-availability land, is responsible for an inevitable structural contradiction. This contradiction is so much stronger in the case of gated golf communities in that landscapes with high added-value are rare and are the subject of a systematic strategy of appropriation and colonization.

The very particular case of gated golf communities helps focus a critical point of view on the recent emerging "garden cities," "green cities," "eco-friendly cities" or "eco-cities." Many city-makers from China or abroad are imagining a "new Chinese urbanism" allowing an escape from the side-effects on the environment of the American dream. Yet, the existence of gated golf communities around big Chinese cities reveals a big gap between these avant-garde theories and experiences and the reality of existing urban spaces. It raises various questions. One is, who are the customers of these "eco-cities?" In the case of gated golf communities the new green areas represent private spaces belonging to and benefiting a very small minority. Environmental improvement of cityscapes is not always in line with democratic governance. Another question which could be considered as quite incongruous is, does the creation of green areas necessarily favor the environment? The example of gated golf communities in China shows that the extension of a landscape mimicking nature may represent an overconsumption of land, water, and chemical products. Paradoxically, the greening process of urban space can lead to an aesthetic improvement of the landscape but may be in contradiction to the principles of sustainable development

Notes

1 According to the web site www.villas.com.cn (in Chinese), accessed on November 21, 2004.
2 The study is essentially based on field work carried out in November 2003 and August 2004 on various sites in Beijing, Shanghai, Nanjing, Guangzhou and Shenzhen.
3 For the general presentation of the phenomenon of gated communities and case studies, see for example the journals *Urbanisme* (n 312, 2000 and n 337, 2004) and *Etudes foncières* (n 101, 2003).
4 Here, we will not refer to tourism as such, which is sometimes the origin of large-size organizations as in Nice or in Las Vegas.

5 A ranking of American cities in terms of leisure activities is published every year by an American company. In 2003, Minneapolis was therefore "the most fun city in the United States" (Anonymous 2003).
6 From www.golf-homes-guide.com.
7 During a visit to the Suzhou golf course in November 2003, I was able to see two large mural paintings in the basement, one representing the Saint Andrews course, founded in Scotland in the sixteenth century and reputed to be the oldest in the world, and the other, of the Ming period, featuring players in a game close to golf using wooden clubs.
8 Here, we will not refer to the cases of golf courses with luxury hotel complexes, like the Spring City Resort in Kunming, Yunnan province.
9 Other sources speak of 80 percent, even 100 percent. See "Golf courses devouring land illegally in China," *Xinhua,* 03-07-2004.
10 A golf handicap is a numerical measure of an amateur golfer's playing ability. It can be used to calculate a so-called net score from the number of strokes actually played, thus allowing players of different proficiency to play against each other on equal terms. (Wikipedia)
11 *Tomson Golf Villas* brochure, July 2002.
12 For the most part concentrated on the mega cities of Beijing and Shanghai, except for the perimetropolitan-type gated golf communities, as in the example of Mission Hills in Shenzhen.
13 *Mission Hills* is larger than the famous, 100-year-old course, Pinehurst (US).

References

Anonymous (August 13, 2002a) "Shanghai limits golf courses for environmental protection," *Xinhua News Agency.*
Anonymous (August 14, 2002b) "City Bans New Golf Links." Available online at: *www.eastday.com.*
Anonymous (November 07, 2003) "Milwaukee named to top 15 'fun cities'," *Business Journal.*
Anonymous (March 07, 2004a) "Golf courses devouring land illegally in China," *Xinhua.*
Anonymous (October 28, 2004b) "Villa owners tee off at developer," *Xinhuanet.*
Davis, S. G. (1996) "Theme park: global industry and cultural form," *Media, Culture and Society*, 18: 399–422.
Davis, S. G. (January 1998) "Quand les parcs à thème gangrènent les villes. L'espace urbain perverti par les loisirs," *Le Monde diplomatique.*
Drouin, P. (June 05, 2003) "Colbert Orco aménage un golf haut de gamme à Saint-Tropez," *Les Echos.*
Giroir, G. (December 2002) "Le phénomène des *gated communities* à Pékin, ou les nouvelles cites interdites," *Bulletin de l'Association de Géographes Français*, Paris, 423–426.
Giroir, G. (2003a) *Transition et Territoire en Chine. Le Cas des Périphéries de Pékin.* Habilitation à diriger des recherches (unpublished). University of Orléans.
Giroir, G. (2003b) "Gated communities, clubs in a club system. The case of Beijing (China)," in *Proceedings of the International Conference on Gated Communities*, Glasgow, September 2003.
Giroir, G. (2006a) "Yosemite Villas-Mirror of Emerging Capitalism? An American-style gated community in Beijing," *China Perspectives*, Hong Kong, March–April, no. 64: 13–23.

Giroir, G. (2006b) "The Purple Jade Villas (Beijing), a golden ghetto in red China," in K. Frantz, G. Glasze and C. Webster (eds) *Private Cities: Global and Local Perspectives,* London: Routledge, 142–152.

Giroir, G. (2006c) "The Fontainebleau Villas (Shanghai), a Globalized Golden Ghetto in a Chinese Garden," in F. Wu (ed.) *Globalization and the Chinese City*, London: Routledge, 208–225.

Giroir, G. (2006d) "Hard enclosure and soft enclosure in the gated communities: some theoretical perspectives and empirical evidence in China," *Proceedings of the International Symposium on Territory, Control and Enclosure: The Ecology of Urban Fragmentation,* Pretoria, South Africa, February 28–March 3, 2006.

Gravari-Barbas, M. (2001) "Les enclaves ludiques: Le cas du Navy Pier à Chicago," in C. Ghorra-Gobin (ed.) *Réinventer Le Sens De La Ville: Les Espaces Publiques A L'heure Globale*, Paris: L'Harmattan, 159–168.

Jenkins, V. S. (1994) *Le Gazon, ou l'histoire d'une obsession américaine*, Washington, DC: Smithsonian Institution Press.

Ng, S. (May 06, 2004) "At golf, China swings and misses," *Asia Times.*

Sorkin, M. (ed.) (1992) *Variations on a Theme Park: The New American City and the End of Public Space*, New York: Hill & Wang.

Taylor, M. (March 30, 2004) "Luxury living in Shenzhen simply par for the course," *South China Morning Post.*

Webster, C., Wu, F., Zhao, Y. J. (2006) "China's modern gated cities," in G. Glasze, C. Webster and K. Frantz (eds) *Private Cities: Global and Local Perspectives*, London: Routledge, 153–170.

Wu, F. (2006a) "Globalization and China's new urbanism," in F. Wu (ed.) *Globalization and the Chinese City*, London: Routledge, 1–19.

Wu, F. (ed.) (2006b) *Globalization and the Chinese City*, London: Routledge.

13 A tale of two cities

Restructuring of retail capital and production of new consumption spaces in Beijing and Shanghai

Shuguang Wang and Chongyi Guo

Introduction

Retailing always has been a prominent element of urban morphology. As a city evolves and expands, so does its retail sector. Historically, the spatial pattern of urban retail growth has experienced a centrifugal shift of activity from central city locations outward to more peripheral areas. Typically, the forces that are associated with this shift include the suburbanization of population, increasing personal mobility, greater disposable income, changes in transportation technologies, and favorable government land use policies (Hartshorn 1980; Simmons *et al.* 1998; Yeates and Garner 1976).

Since the economic reform began in 1978, Chinese cities have experienced enormous transformation. Many including Beijing and Shanghai are also striving to become world cities. Although neither Hall (1966) nor Friedmann (1986) include retailing as a defining characteristic of a world city, all world cities have a robust and sophisticated retail sector, as is evident in New York, London, Paris, Tokyo, Singapore and Hong Kong. As Yeates (1998) points out, while retail activities occupy only a small proportion of the developed urban land, they play several important roles, including the generation of large amounts of employment while serving as the centers of consumption. The level of retail development also reflects the standard of living in the host cities, especially the world cities. Even more important, the main commercial districts shape the city's image and provide the city's face to the world.

For 30 years before 1978, retail in Chinese cities was a simple yet rigid distribution system. The entire retail system was either state-owned or collectively owned, with the department store being the predominant retail format. Private business ownership was banned and retail chains were non existent. Since the economic reform, the retail sector has undergone profound changes: business ownership has diversified considerably, international retailers have been allowed into the city, and various contemporary retail formats have been introduced. In essence, the sector has moved away from a centrally planned system towards a market-oriented retail economy. Along with this shift there has been significant restructuring of retail capital and production of new consumption spaces.

Bradshaw (1996) theorized a model of economic transition for the postsocialist states, of which China is one. While not retail specific, this model provides a useful framework for examining restructuring of retail capital in China. Based on the experiences of the former Soviet Union and the Eastern and Central European countries, Bradshaw identifies four dimensions in the economic transition process: macroeconomic stabilization, economic liberalization, privatization, and internationalization. These dimensions have no particular sequence and often take place simultaneously.

First, macroeconomic stabilization refers to the need to bring the economy into balance, with two components: to balance the level of monetary income with the supply of goods, and to balance the difference between government expenditures and revenues. The planned economy had typically been characterized by a shortage of consumer goods. This often resulted in considerable personal savings, which Bradshaw (1996) describes as "repressed inflation." A major corrective action in the transition process is to improve the supply of consumer goods and, at the same time, implement controlled wage increases.

Second, economic liberalization refers to the gradual removal of government restrictions on economic activities in general and on price control in particular. Initially, the process of price liberalization may produce a severe price shock; but, in the end, it makes the inefficient state-owned enterprises no longer economically viable and leads to the creation of new and more efficient enterprises (Nakata and Sivakumar 1997).

Third, liberalization is to legalize private economic actors and to eventually create a private sector. Privatization is achieved in two ways: by selling off state-owned enterprises, and through the creation of new, privately owned businesses. Privatization introduces new sources of capital and gives companies freedom in business decision-making, both necessary for the transition towards a market economy.

In need of economic stabilization, and under international pressures as they strive for membership in international treaties or trading blocks, postsocialist states have begun to open up their national borders to FDI to capture the opportunities afforded by the globalization of the world economy. Internationalization enables these states to obtain much needed capital, technology, and managerial know-how, as well as high-quality consumer goods. Through innovation diffusion, foreign investors play a catalytic role in the economic transition process for postsocialist states (Dawson 2003; Lever and Daniels 1996).

It should be emphasized that accompanying the economic transition is a fundamental change in the role of the state, manifested by the replacement of antiquated socialist plans with promarket economy policies, and by the shift from owning enterprises and setting prices towards regulating business operations by legal means. The challenges for the governments of postsocialist states include establishing new rules and new institutions for stronger governance (United Nations Development Programme 1999), balancing between public-interest and private-interest (Wrigley and Lowe 1996), and minimizing the various impacts of the economic transition on the well-being of their citizens (Green and Ruhleder 1995).

Local governments are also being forced to be much more competitive with each other as they attempt to protect their economic base and exploit new competitive edge with which to attract global financial capital and foreign technologies. This intergovernmental competition has bred so-called entrepreneurial cities (Knox *et al.* 2003), or in a few cases, global islands of prosperity (Heredia 1997).

Using the Bradshaw model as a conceptual framework, this chapter examines the restructuring of retail capital and production of new consumption spaces in Beijing and Shanghai – two global islands of prosperity in China. Changes take place so frequently that most statistics are out of date shortly after their publication. Instead of attempting to capture the latest counts of stores and amount of retail space, we emphasize the patterns of change in the last two decades, especially since the early 1990s. The main data sources are the 1998 Census of Commercial Activity in Beijing (Beijing Statistics Bureau 1999) and the 1999 Census of Commercial Activity in Shanghai (Shanghai Office of Commercial Activity Census 2001). They are supplemented by the recent editions of *Almanac of China's Commerce* (China Chamber of Commerce 2001 and 2004) and a number of reputable websites. We have also collected our own data through field survey and personal interview.

The two cities

Beijing, the capital of China, is a modern city of historical significance. Consist-ing of 11 districts and 7 counties, Beijing occupies a total area of 16,800 square kilometers (Table 13.1). In the official statistics, the city of Beijing is differen-tiated into three geographical zones: the Inner City, the Inner Suburb, and the Outer Suburb. The Inner City is comprised of four districts: Xicheng (West City), Dongcheng (East City), Xuanwu, and Chongwen (Figure 13.1). The Inner Suburb is composed of four other districts: Haidian, Chaoyang, Fengtai, and Shijingshan. The remaining three districts and seven counties form the Outer Suburb. The Inner City and the Inner Suburb together form Central Beijing (also referred to as the Central Area in this chapter). This is a continuously built-up area of high popu-lation density (especially the Inner City). While Central Beijing comprises only 8 percent (or 1,370 square kilometers) of the entire city in area, it accounts for 62 percent of the city's total population (Table 13.1). As documented in Zhou and Ma (2000), since 1980, the Inner City has witnessed a slight population decline, while both the Inner Suburb and the Outer Suburb have experienced significant population gain, a clear indicator of population suburbanization. Until the early 1980s, a grid network served all transport in Central Beijing. To cope with the rapid expansion that occurred after the economic reform began, the road network has been transformed, and the new system is now dominated by a series of five ring roads and several radial highways. During the same two decades, the single-line subway system was expanded not only in length but also with a new loop constructed to coincide with the northern half of the Second Ring Road. Several Light Rail Transit (LRT) lines have also been added to the system.

Shanghai is known as China's business capital and center of consumption. The city consists of 19 administrative divisions. Nine urban districts form the Central

Table 13.1 City profile of Beijing and Shanghai

Attributes	Beijing	Shanghai
Administrative divisions	18	19
Central Area	8 (Xicheng, Dongcheng, Xuanwu, Chongwen, Haidian, Chaoyang, Fengtai, Shijingshan)	9 (Changning, Hongkou, Huangpu, Jing'an, Luwan, Putuo, Xuhui, Yangpu, Zhabei)
Suburb	10 (Changping, Daxing, Fangshan, Huairou, Mentougou, Miyun, Pinggu, Shunyi, Tongxian, Yanqing)	10 (Baoshan, Chongming, Fengxian, Jiading, Jinshan, Minhang, Nanhui, Pudong, Qingpu, Songjiang)
Area (km²)	*16,800*	*6,340*
Central Area	1,370	289
Suburb	15,430	6,051
Population size (in millions)	*13.6*	*16.4*
Central city	8.5	6.9
Suburb	5.1	9.5
Urban residents	10.5	12.7
Rural residents	3.1	3.7
Population density (persons per km²)	*807*	*2,588*
Central Area	6,200	23,944
Suburb	330	1,566
Per capita income (in yuan)		
Urban residents (% change 1998–2004)	15,640 (+84.6)	16,683 (+90.2)
Rural residents (net)	6,170 (+56.1)	7,066 (+30.7)
Estimated consumer market size (in billions of yuan)*	186.5	283.0

Source: National Bureau of Statistics of China, 2006.

Note
* Estimated consumer market size = per capita income * population.

Area, and the others the suburbs (see Table 13.1 and Figure 13.1). The Central Area occupies only 5 percent of the total land of Shanghai, but includes 42 percent of the total population. Population density in the Central Area is therefore extremely high, with 23,944 persons per square kilometers, compared to 1,566 in the suburbs and to 6,200 in central Beijing. Over the past 20 years, Shanghai has also undergone unprecedented urban renewal and expansion. The most significant urban expansion is the development of the Pudong New Area. To facilitate intra-urban movement and to unify Pudong with the rest of the city, a series of key transportation links were built, among which are two ring roads (the Inner Ring and the Outer Ring) and five LRT lines (two underground, three at the surface).

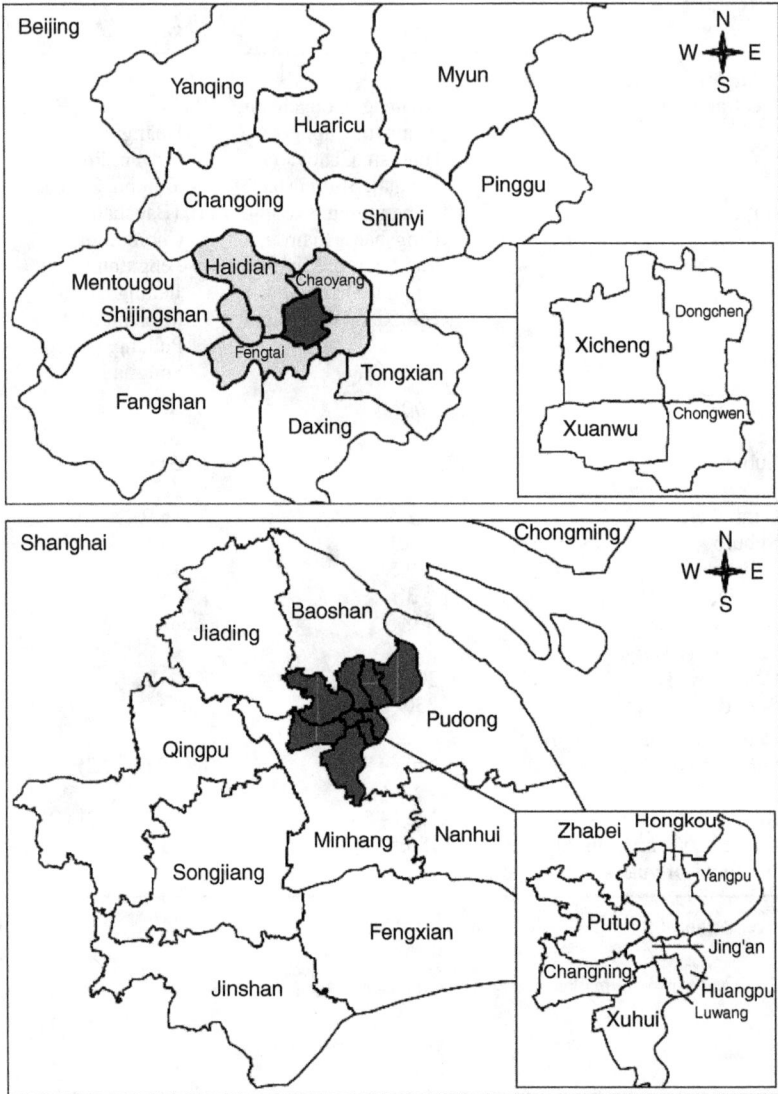

Figure 13.1 Administrative divisions of Beijing and Shanghai.

Urban development stimulates retail growth in two ways: opening up new locations and sites for construction of large retail facilities, and reinforcing accessibility to the new consumption spaces by providing efficient transportation networks. Two decades of reform and economic stabilization have also nurtured affluent consumer markets in both Beijing and Shanghai, a necessary condition for retail growth and addition of consumption spaces. Per capita income for urban residents nearly doubled in both cities between 1998 and 2004. In the same period, per capita income for rural residents increased by 56 percent and 31 percent in Beijing and Shanghai, respectively (Table 13.1). Despite a much smaller land area, Shanghai has a larger population and higher per capita income than Beijing; accordingly, its consumer market is much larger as well: 283 versus 186 billion yuan.

Retail deregulation and restructuring of retail capital

Retail capital is fundamental to the production of consumption spaces. Certain retail facilities such as shopping centers require large sums of investment in the form of sunk cost. The level of development of the retail sector is therefore closely associated with the availability of retail capital. Before 1978, the entire retail system in China was either state- or collectively owned, meaning that retail capital was concentrated excessively in the hands of the state. Yet, the state capital available for creation of consumption spaces was very limited, resulting in a simple and rigid distribution system in the country. In the last 20 years or so, and with state deregulation, sources of retail capital have diversified considerably, and the total amount of retail capital available to create new consumption spaces has been increased enormously.

Retail deregulation

At the same time as the economic reform began to bring improved income to its ordinary citizens in the 1980s (the result of *macroeconomic stabilization*), a series of policy changes were instituted by the state government to reform the country's distribution system, and retail deregulation occurred (Sun 1997, 2002; Wang and Jones 2001, 2002), resulting in significant ownership diversification. First, it permitted the entry of individual retailers into the distribution system. Soon after, it began to give up its monopoly in procurement of commodities, and relaxed price control (i.e. *economic liberalization*). Beginning in 1984, small, state-owned stores were allowed to be leased or sold to private operators (*privatization*). In 1993, the Chinese Parliament passed a new law that both encouraged and legitimized the transformation of the large- and medium-sized state enterprises into joint-stock companies (Wan 1999).

China also opened up its long-protected retail sector to foreign investment (*internationalization*). In 1992, China designated six cities (Beijing and Shanghai included) and five Special Economic Zones to experiment with investment of foreign retail capital. To control the experiment process effectively, the Chinese government cautiously imposed a series of restrictions on the operation of foreign retailers. The entry of foreign retailers must be approved by the state government: local governments were prohibited from admitting foreign retailers independently. Approved foreign retailers must operate in joint ventures with at least one Chinese partner: whole foreign ownership was prohibited. In joint ventures, foreign investors' stakes must be less than 50 percent. With regard to format, joint ventures were strictly limited to single-store retailing: retail chains and wholesaling were prohibited. With the designation of the experimental cities, the state government approved 15 foreign retailers to establish joint ventures in China. In June 1998, the experiment was expanded to all provincial capitals and the cities that are independent of their provinces in economic planning (State Council 1998). While still insisting on joint ventures, the state government began to allow foreign retailers to hold majority ownership (Wang 2003). After 15 years of prolonged negotiation and a series of concessions, China was finally admitted to the World Trade Organization (WTO) in 2001. As promised to the WTO at the time of its accession, China removed all remaining trade barriers and completely opened its retail market to foreign capital, from December 2004.

In order to take the advantage of the favorable political environment created by the state-introduced deregulation, the governments of Shanghai and Beijing wasted no time and spared no efforts in reforming their obsolete retail system. For example, the government of Shanghai in 1993 alone made a number of significant changes ("Shanghai strives to become an international city of commerce" 1994), including a comprehensive ownership reform of state- and collectively owned retail enterprises. Specifically, it granted 700 or so large and medium-sized enterprises autonomy in business decision-making, and either sold or contracted all small retail stores to private operators. It also authorized the establishment of 19 joint-stock companies. The development of Shanghai into an international center of commerce requires the participation of international retailers. The Shanghai government went out of its way to attract FDI. To overcome the restrictions imposed by the state government in the 1990s, the Shanghai government took the liberty of approving foreign investors independently, despite the great political risks. In 1993 alone, it approved 179 foreign-investment retail licenses, worth 66 million US dollars of FDI ("Shanghai strives to become an international city of commerce" 1994). In 1996, it approved another 62 business contracts worth 220 million US dollars (Shanghai Academy of Social Sciences 1997).

The government of Beijing took similar measures. In 1987, the city contracted many large- and medium-sized retail firms to private operators. In 1994, 19 large state-owned firms were reformed into joint-stock corporations, and 70 small enterprises were converted to joint-stock-cooperatives. In 1995, another 48 large firms were reorganized into joint-stock corporations (Beijing Commercial Activity Development Research Group 1999). In 1996, the government of Beijing eliminated its Bureau of Commerce (the administrative body that oversaw all the state-owned retail stores in Beijing) and turned it into a limited liability company group (He 1997). In 2001, it accelerated withdrawal of state capital from the entire commercial sector including retailing (Hong *et al.* 2002).

Government-assisted business consolidation occurred in both Beijing and Shanghai to nurture indigenous retail conglomerates to combat foreign competition. Typical examples in Beijing are the creation of Beijing Wangfujing-Dong'an Group Ltd. and Capital Group. The former was created in 2000 (Dou 2004), the latter in 2002 through a merger of 10 local companies (China Chain Store Association 2004). Shanghai created Brilliance Group in 2003 through the merger of four state-controlled joint-stock corporations, instantly making it the country's largest retail conglomerate. These mergers led to further restructuring of retail capital in both cities.

Restructuring of retail capital

Without detailed investment data, restructuring of retail capital is examined through an analysis of changes in store/enterprise ownership, which is the catalyst for retail capital restructuring. As Table 13.2 illustrates, by the late 1990s, state- and collectively owned enterprises were still predominant in the retail sector in both Beijing and Shanghai. Together, they accounted for 64 percent of all retail establishments in Beijing and 50 percent in Shanghai. However, other types of ownership had not only occurred but expanded rapidly, especially joint-stock and privately owned enterprises. In Beijing, joint-stock ownership accounted for 16 percent of the total retail businesses, and the privately owned businesses accounted for 19 percent. In Shanghai, joint-stock ownership was much smaller in proportion, accounting for less than 2 percent of the total retail businesses, but privately owned retailers reached a remarkable 47 percent.[1]

Foreign-invested retail establishments include those operated by the overseas Chinese from Hong Kong and Taiwan, as dictated in state regulations. While they constituted less than 1 percent of the total retail enterprises in both cities in the late 1990s, they were expanding steadily, given that they only began to operate in the mid-1990s. Mostly in big-box format, their stores were much larger in size, thus providing more consumption spaces than most domestic retailers.

Table 13.3 shows the ownership composition of the large retailers in Beijing and Shanghai in 2003. Clearly, the state-owned and the collectively owned continued

Table 13.2 Legally-registered retail enterprises in Beijing and Shanghai by ownership

	Beijing (1998)		Shanghai (1999)	
	No.	%	No.	%
State-owned	2,589	22.1	9,480	20.3
Collective	4,882	41.7	13,955	29.9
Co-operatives	133	1.1	357	0.8
Joint-stock	1,818	15.5	593	1.3
Private	2,206	18.8	21,799	46.7
HK, TW*	32	0.3	160	0.3
Foreign	45	0.4	231	0.5
Others	7	0.1	112	0.2
Total	11,712	100.0	46,750	100.0

Source: (a) Beijing Statistics Bureau, 1999; (b) Shanghai Office of Commercial Activity Census, 2000.

Note
* HK = Hong Kong; TW = Taiwan.

Table 13.3 Large retailers* in Beijing and Shanghai by ownership, 2003

Type of ownership	Beijing			Shanghai		
	No. of stores	%	2000–03 % change	No. of stores	%	2000–03 % change
Domestic	1120	97.1	−12.5	9497	95.3	190.8
State-owned	256	22.2	−17.1	710	7.1	−34.9
Collectively-owned	159	13.8	−16.1	140	1.4	−82.8
Co-operatives	20	1.7	−0.6	5	0.1	−54.5
Joint stock	48	4.2	0.6	2893	29.0	7132.5
Joint stock / co-operatives	76	6.6	−0.7	25	0.3	−83.3
Limited liability	280	24.3	10.4	4701	47.2	309.5
Private	280	24.3	10.9	1008	10.1	7100.0
Others	1	0.1	0.1	15	0.2	
HK-TW	16	1.4	0.1	161	1.6	101.3
Foreign	18	1.6	−0.1	304	3.1	−18.7
Total	1154	100.0	−12.5	9962	100.0	167.8

Source: Almanac of China's Commerce 2004.

Note
* Large retailers are defined as those that have annual retail sales of at least five million yuan (US$625,999) and with 60 or more employees.

to decline in proportion, as did cooperatives (see the columns of percentage change between 2000 and 2003). At the same time, joint-stock, limited liability and private companies were all on rise. In fact, they have now exceeded state- and collectively owned retail businesses by large margins.

Two important observations can be generalized from Tables 13.2 and 13.3. First, as a direct result of retail deregulation, the traditional ownerships – both state- and collectively owned stores – have lost their long-established monopoly. Modern types of companies, such as joint-stock, private, and the overseas-owned expanded significantly, a fundamental indicator of retail capital restructuring in China. They have been promoted by both the state and the municipal governments of Beijing and Shanghai as new sources of retail capital. More importantly, they are better able to respond to changing consumer demands and enjoy a higher degree of freedom in business decision-making, including decisions on production of consumption spaces. Second, Shanghai has a much larger retail sector, with eight times as many retail enterprises as in Beijing, indicating that Shanghai has access to much more retail capital. As well, many more foreign retailers choose Shanghai over Beijing to ground their retail capital. This contrast is further revealed in the following sections, that deal with consumption space production.

Production of new consumption spaces

In retail geography, consumption space is a term used to refer to various types of retail facilities. From the retailer's point of view, merchandise is considered consumed when it is sold to consumers in retail stores (Wrigley 2002). Before the 1980s, all retail outlets in Chinese cities belonged to seven types: department store; grain/flour store; grocery store; book store; stationery/sports goods store; hardware/electrical supplies store; and coal store. The largest spatial clusters of consumption space were the traditional retail strips usually anchored by large department stores, which also performed the highest-order retail functions. Since the early 1980s, a variety of new consumption spaces have been created along with the restructuring of retail capital. In a nutshell, all new retail formats that had been created in the Western economies were introduced. These include supermarkets, hypermarkets, factory outlets, warehouse retail stores (including membership clubs), and shopping centers. Even prototype power centers consisting of a cluster of large-format stores have begun to emerge. These new facilities dramatically altered the retail structure and landscape in Beijing and Shanghai. In this section, we examine the creation of three large types of new consumption space – modern department stores, hypermarkets, and shopping centers – whose development all requires large sums of capital.

The department store boom

The first wave of new consumption space creation began in the late 1980s and lasted for nearly 10 years. It was characterized by the development of modern department stores. Unlike their obsolete cousins, these new department stores were much larger and more glamorous, all equipped with elevators and escalators. The 1998 Census of Commercial Activity in Beijing shows that only 19 percent of the existing department stores existed before 1978; 18 percent were opened between 1978 and 1989, and 63 percent in the 1990s. In 1987, Beijing had only six department stores larger than 10,000 square meters of floor space. This number increased to 40 in 1994, and 70 in 1996 (Beijing Almanac Compilation Committee 1997; Zhang 1997). A similar boom occurred in Shanghai. Before 1978, the retail market was dominated by 12 state-owned large department stores, scattered in different districts. The 1999 Census of Commercial Activity in Shanghai revealed the existence of 77 department stores of 5,000 square meters or larger.

It should be pointed out that not all buildings that house department stores were constructed by retailers. Some were built by real estate developers in response to the needs of retailers for new consumption spaces. Lured by the potential for high profit in the late 1980s and the early 1990s, both retailers and commercial real estate developers invested heavily in these large retail facilities, and most of the modern department stores are concentrated in the central areas of Beijing and Shanghai. Located either along the ring roads or radial highways, or at major road intersections, these department stores acted as intervening opportunities and intercepted suburban shoppers. They also anchored major shopping districts as part of city center revitalization.

These modern department stores, which became major retail destinations and generated substantial sales volumes in the late 1990s, were built mainly by the newly created joint-stock corporations. Yet, it is difficult to examine the investment patterns because, unlike in the United States and Canada (and possibly in the European countries as well) where a few retail chains own most of the department stores, the ownership and operation of department stores in China are highly fragmented, and there is no systematic information on the numerous retailers that own and operate them. To illustrate the role of the transformed state enterprises in the development of modern department stores in Beijing and Shanghai, a brief description of the Beijing Wangfujing Group Ltd. and the Shanghai Brilliance Group is presented below.

The predecessor of Beijing Wangfujing Group Ltd. was Beijing Department Store. First opened to shoppers in 1955, the department store had been the largest of its kind in Beijing for more than 30 years. In 1993, it was transformed into a joint-stock enterprise, the state being the controlling share holder, but with all employees having the option of purchasing and owning shares. In 1994, it went public and began to be listed in Shanghai Security Exchange, when it was also renamed Beijing Wangfujing Group Ltd. By far it is Beijing's largest department store chain with 15 locations, but only 4 of the 15 stores are in Beijing, and 3 of these 4 were acquired through merger with Beijing Dong'an Group.[2]

Shanghai Brilliance Group was created in 2003 through the merger of four large state-owned enterprises, each itself being an independent corporate group: Shanghai No. 1 Department Store (Group) Co. Ltd.; Hualian (Group) Co. Ltd.; Shanghai Friendship (Group) Co. Ltd.; and Shanghai Materials (Group) Co. Ltd. The original Shanghai No. 1 Department Store was built in 1949 as the first state-owned large retail outlet in Shanghai (with eight stories and 25,000 square meters). In 1992, it was transformed into a joint-stock enterprise, and entered into a joint venture with the Japanese Yaohan to develop Shanghai's largest department store. The new 180,000 square meters store opened in 1995 in Pudong District, but in only two years Yaohan went bankrupt, and withdrew from the operation in 1997. Since its creation in 2003, Brilliance Group has been operating more than 10 department stores in Shanghai, but under five different banners (i.e. Shanghai No. 1, No. 1 – Yaohan, Yong'an, Dongfang, and Hualian), and none of these controls more than four stores.

Foreign retailers also played an important role in the creation of modern department stores. Four observations can be made from Table 13.4. First, all foreign retailers are from East and Southeast Asia (particularly Japan, Malaysia, Hong Kong and Taiwan), and none from North America and Europe. Second, it seems that foreign retailers favor Shanghai more than Beijing, as more foreign-invested department stores have been developed in the former than in the latter. Third, unlike those from Hong Kong, Taiwan and Malaysia, which invested in both cities, the Japanese retailers tended to focus on either Beijing or Shanghai, possibly to avoid competition among themselves. Three Japanese-invested department stores in Shanghai were closed due to the economic difficulties encountered by their parent companies in Japan. In 1997 when the Japanese Yaohan went bankrupt, the management of its store in Pudong District was transferred to its Chinese partner – Shanghai No. 1 Department Store; its second store in Minhang District was converted to a shopping center (now called Brilliance South Mall); and the Jusco

Table 13.4 Foreign operators of major department stores in Beijing and Shanghai, 2006

Foreign retailers	Beijing	Shanghai
SOGO (Japan)	Xuanwu store (80,000m^2)	(no presence)
Ito Yokado (Japan)	Chaoyang store (15,000m^2)	(no presence)
Isetan (Japan)	(no presence)	Jiang'an store Luwan store
Jusco (Japan)	(no presence)	Zhabei store (closed)
Yaohan (Japan)	(no presence)	Pudong store (180,000m^2)* Minhang store (closed)
Parkson (Malaysia)	Xicheng store (30,000m^2) Haidian store (n/a)	Luwan store (28,000m^2) Changning store (n/a)
Pacific (Taiwan)	Xicheng store (37,800m^2)	Xuhui store (30,000 m^2) Luwan store (30,000 m^2) Zhabei store (50,000 m^2)
New World (H.K.)	Chongwen store 1 (n/a) Chongwen store 2 (n/a)	Luwan store (n/a) Changning store 1 (n/a) Changning store 2 (n/a) Hongkou store (n/a) Minhang store (n/a)

Source: Various corporate websites.

Note
* After Yaohan's bankruptcy, the ownership of the store was transferred to Shanghai No. 1 Department Store.

Department Store near Shanghai Railway Station in Zhabei District was turned into wholesale market. Finally, except for the recent development of Hong Kong's New World in the Minhang District of Shanghai (opened in 2005), all the foreign-invested department stores are located in the central areas of the two cities (see Table 13.4 with reference to Figure 13.1).

The department store boom was short lived in both cities. General merchandise discounters and large-format specialty stores began to be introduced in Beijing and Shanghai in the mid-1990s. As these retailers began to set their stamp on the retail market, the position and dominance of the department stores were put under increased pressure. Starting in 1997, large department stores began to experience declines in both sales and profits. According to information collected by the Beijing Commission of Commerce ("Will wholesaling of high-grade goods be profitable" 1999), 30 department stores in Beijing suffered losses in 1998, and 19 made no profit at all. A number of them had to be closed (Han 1998; Li 1998).[3] Some of them were converted to wholesale markets with spaces leased to individual merchants. Oversupply had been cited as the direct cause, but oversupply itself could be attributed to ineffective government planning. In 1993, the government of Beijing announced that Beijing should have 100 large department stores with 10,000 square meters of floor space or more by the year 2000 (Li 1998). In support of this plan, state banks were instructed to issue loans to both retailers and developers, contributing further to the overheating department store boom.

In Shanghai, many department stores suffered as well. For 50 years after 1949, Shanghai No. 1 Department Store was the city's largest retailer with the most sales. In 1999, it lost the title to a supermarket chain – Lianhua.[4] A survey of 20 major department stores found that 12 of them experienced negative growth in sales between 2001 and 2002, and another three had less than 1 percent increase (Shanghai Commerce Information Center and Sona Consulting Ltd. 2003). Of the 12 state-owned large department stores that had served Shanghai residents for 40 years, all but one had been closed or converted to other uses. Three Japanese-invested modern department stores were also closed, as mentioned earlier in this section.[5]

The hypermarket boom

Hypermarket is the European name for large-format stores that combine a super-market with a discount department store under one roof. In North America, it is known as a supercenter, typically associated with Wal-Mart operations. The hyper-market was introduced to China in the mid-1990s by foreign retailers. Soon after, it was copied by domestic retailers and flourished in both Beijing and Shanghai, leading to the second wave of production of new consumption space. These stores are much larger (typically ranging from 10,000 to 20,000 square meters) than most other formats, and are in direct competition to the modern department stores.

The French firm Carrefour was the first to transplant hypermarkets to Beijing and Shanghai (Table 13.5). In 1995, Carrefour opened its first hypermarket in Beijing but without state approval. With permission from the municipal govern-ment, Carrefour teamed up with a Chinese company (Zhongchuang Commerce) to establish a business management firm named Carrefour-Zhongchuang Busi-ness Management. This same firm then created a retail subsidiary with Carrefour holding controlling shares. While the retail subsidiary was registered under the name of Zhongchuang Commerce, it was actually operated by Carrefour, with the Carrefour brand (Chen 2004), and was hence a de facto Carrefour hypermarket. This allowed Carrefour to bypass the state restrictions effectively. Shortly after, it negotiated with and obtained approval from Shanghai municipal government to open stores in Shanghai. In 1999, Carrefour established its China HQ office in Shanghai and entered a new partnership with the Shanghai-based Lianhua Group.

The German company Metro opened its first Chinese store in Shanghai in 1996 (in partnership with the local Jinjiang Group). Unlike Wal-Mart and Carrefour, Metro focused exclusively on the membership club format, open only to registered members – mostly institutions and small retailers. Until 1999, Metro's operation was limited to Shanghai and the neighboring Jiangsu and Zhejiang provinces, while awaiting state approval. It was not until 2006 that Metro opened its first store in Beijing.

Wal-Mart was among the first 15 foreign retailers approved by the state gov-ernment in 1992 to set up an experiment operation in China, and it was the only one from the Western hemisphere. This should have given Wal-Mart a huge first-mover advantage over its principal European competitors Carrefour and Metro. However, despite the tremendous market opportunities, retail regulations in China

Table 13.5 Major hypermarket operators in Beijing and Shanghai in 2006

Retailer	HQ location	Beijing		Shanghai		% of stores in Central Cities
		Years of entry	No. of stores	Years of entry	No. of stores	
Lianhua (domestic)	Shanghai	2003	5	1991	13	–
Hualian GMS (domestic)	Shanghai	2001	0	1993	14	64
NGS (domestic)	Shanghai	–	0	1993	29	17
Wu-Mart (domestic)	Beijing	1994	10	–	0	58
Chaoshifa (domestic)	Beijing	1999	17	–	0	82
Jingkelong (domestic)	Beijing	1994	4	–	0	n/a
Wal-Mart (U.S.)	Shenzhen	2003	3*	2005	2	75
Carrefour (France)	Shanghai	1995	6	1996	11	65
Auchan (France)	Shanghai	2003	2	1999	4	33
Metro (Germany)**	Shanghai	2006	1	1996	4	80
Makro (Netherlands)**	Beijing	1997	2	–	0	100
Lotus (Thailand)	Shanghai	2003	7	1998	20	43
RT-Mart (Taiwan)	Shanghai	–	0	1998	6	n/a
Trust-Mart (Taiwan/U.K.)	Shanghai	n/a	4	n/a	9	n/a
Hymart-Hymall (Taiwan)	Shanghai	–	0	1997	15	47
E-Mart (S. Korea)	Shanghai	–	0	1997	3	66

Source: various corporate websites.

Notes
* Including one membership club.
** Warehouse retail/membership club.

were very restrictive, the distribution system chaotic, and the retail channels fragmented (Chan *et al.* 1997). Like all other foreign retailers, Wal-Mart was looking for "islands of prosperity" with affluent consumers, to ground its first retail capital. At first, it targeted Shanghai as the beachhead for its landing in China. While the Shanghai government welcomed Wal-Mart, negotiations failed for undisclosed reasons. This cost Wal-Mart one of the largest and the wealthiest consumer markets in China until 2005. It subsequently went to Shenzhen and established its China base there. However, Wal-Mart never gave up its desire to enter the large cities of Shanghai and Beijing. In October 2002, after patient negotiations with both the state and Shanghai governments, Wal-Mart finally obtained permission to operate in Shanghai. This was achieved through establishing a new division: the East China Wal-Mart Store Ltd in partnership with the Beijing-based China International Trust & Investment Corporation (Shanghai Almanac Compilation Committee 2003). With the formation of the new division, Wal-Mart was given the green light to open three super-centers in Shanghai. For various reasons, but at least partly due to its loss of first-mover opportunities to Carrefour and Metro, only two of the three announced stores in Shanghai have opened so far. Indeed, after a decade of delay, Wal-Mart's entry into Shanghai has become much more difficult and costly. The retail market has become congested. Other foreign and domestic retailers have populated Shanghai with more than 100 hypermarkets (see Table 13.5). The existing hypermarkets have preempted Wal-Mart from many premium locations.

Similar difficulties were encountered in Beijing. While Carrefour was suspended from expansion in 2001 for violating state regulations, Wal-Mart won approval from both the state and the local government to open five stores in Beijing – a Carrefour stronghold (Kynge and Young 2001). To date, however, only three of the five planned stores have opened, suggesting difficulty in finding suitable locations or obtaining profitable real estates. In fact, when Wal-Mart announced its plans, Beijing was already served by four Carrefour hypermarkets, two Makro membership clubs, and many others that are operated by domestic retailers.

While Auchan has made a comparable degree of market penetration as Metro in both Beijing and Shanghai, the role of Makro is much limited. Since its entry into Beijing in 1997, it still has only two stores in the capital city and still has no presence in Shanghai. The six Asian retailers also played an important role in the development of hypermarkets, but they are heavily biased towards Shanghai. The Thai-based Lotus has 20 stores in Shanghai, as opposed to 7 in Beijing. RT-Mart, Hymart, and E-Mart has made no investment in Beijing at all.

Both Beijing and Shanghai have nurtured their own hypermarket operators. In Shanghai, they are represented by Lianhua, Hualian GMS, and NGS (i.e. Agro Business). In Beijing, the largest operators are Wu-Mart, Chaoshifa and Jingkelong. They are all joint-stock corporations either transformed from former state-owned enterprises or newly created during the economic reform. These domestic operators attempted to lay down a network of stores as quickly as possible to preempt their foreign competitors, even at the cost of reducing profit margins by carrying unproductive stores. Nonetheless, they are so far largely regional players with business operations limited to their home city, as indicated in Table 13.5.

The shopping center boom

Another wave of consumption space production in Chinese cities is represented by the boom of shopping center development that took place at the same time as the hypermarket boom. China did not have shopping centers until the mid-1990s; but since then, there have been considerable development and construction. The boom has led to competition among the large cities of Beijing, Shanghai, Guangzhou and Shenzhen to build the largest shopping mall in China (Li 2004; "China's largest shopping center to be completed in Beijing" 2004). These municipal governments enthusiastically welcome investment from all sources, but particularly FDI, in construction of large shopping centers to raise their city's profile.

Once again, Shanghai leads Beijing in shopping center development. The first shopping center in Shanghai opened in 1993, but in the next three years, the pace of development was slow and project scale was moderate. After 1997, however, development accelerated and projects became progressively larger. By the end of 2005, 37 shopping centers were operating in Shanghai, with a total of 2.5 million square meters of consumption space. They range from 7,000 to 320,000 square meters, with an average of 65,000 square meters (see Table 13.6). Twenty-four of them readily qualify as regional and superregional shopping centers by Western standards.

The 37 existing shopping centers are concentrated in nine districts (Figure 13.2). Except for Pudong and Minhang, all the other host districts are part of the densely populated central area. A closer look shows that the shopping centers are concentrated around traditional commercial nodes (i.e. retail strips), and subway/LRT stations. It should be noted that subway and LRT lines in Shanghai are laid in such a way that they pass through most of the municipal-level commercial nodes. As such, many shopping centers are located both in a commercial node and at a subway station. This signifies that access to shopping centers depends heavily on public transit, especially rapid transit. Only in the past two to three years have shopping centers begun to appear in suburban districts. Because suburban districts are not as well served by public transit as are the districts in central areas, almost all suburban shopping centers provide their own shuttle buses, free of charge, to bring in shoppers.

Table 13.6 shows clearly that overseas investment has played an important role in the development of shopping centers in Shanghai. Of the 37 existing centers, 24 (65 percent) were developed with overseas capital. The table also reveals that all the overseas investments are from Southeast Asia, particularly Hong Kong (16 centers), Taiwan (5), Thailand (1), and Singapore (2). Participation from North American and European investors and developers is so far absent, a very different pattern of investment than for the hypermarket. Furthermore, almost all the overseas investors/developers are ethnic Chinese well-connected to Mainland China, with close political and business ties with the state or local governments,[6] which made negotiation for favorable land use rights easier.

Domestic capital began to flow into shopping centers in 1999 from two distinctive types of sources: state-controlled joint ventures, and private enterprises. State investment is best represented by Brilliance Group. Shortly after its formation in 2003, Brilliance Group established a distinct subsidiary solely responsible for shopping center development and management – the first known professional shopping center developer in China. Typical private investors are Wenfeng Group and Shanghai Summit Property Development Corporation. The former invested 42.5 million US dollars to develop the 84,000 square meters Wenfeng Mall in Pudong District in 2003; the latter built Shanghai's largest shopping center, the Summit Mall, in 2005 (see Table 13.6).

There are clear differences in shopping center development patterns between the overseas and domestic investors, and among the overseas investors themselves. As Table 13.6 illustrates, investors from Hong Kong and Singapore favor construction of ancillary malls, which form part of a larger complex including office towers or apartment buildings, while other overseas investors and most domestic developers tend to engage in the development of freestanding malls. For example, both Grand Gateway Plaza and Plaza 66, developed by the Hong Kong-based Hang Lung Properties, have twin office towers soaring above them. Westgate

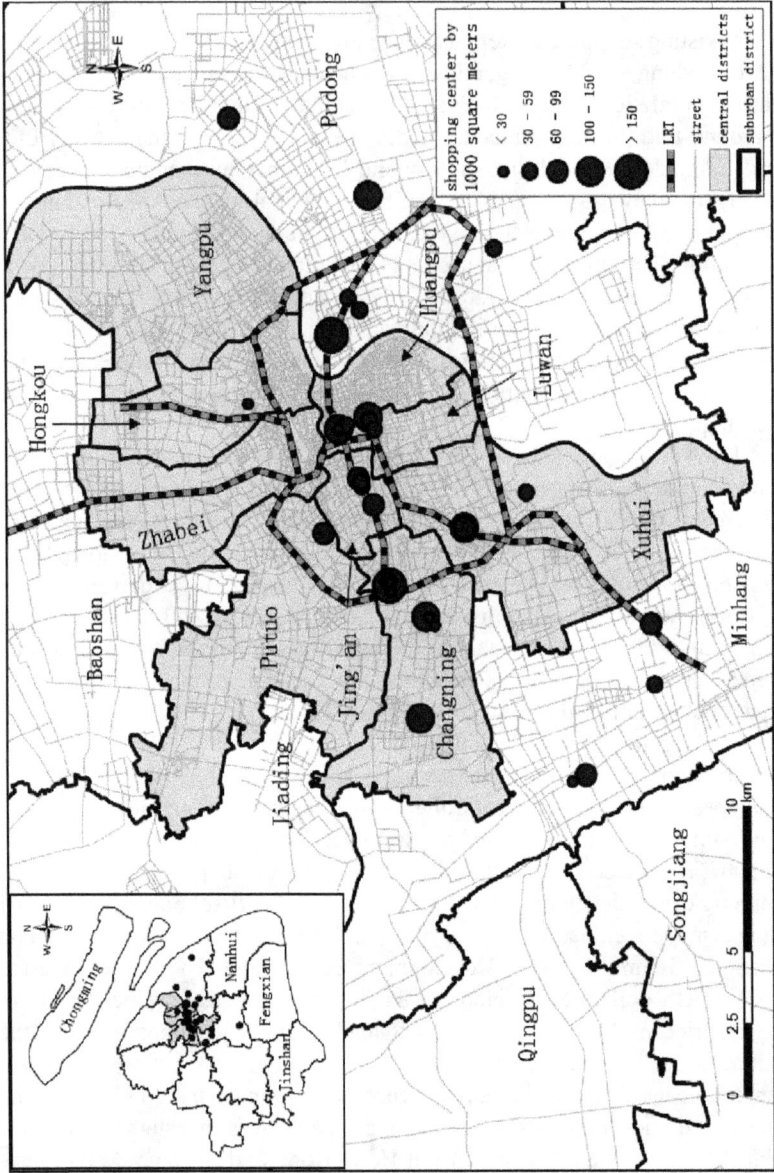

Figure 13.2 Existing shopping centers in Shanghai in 2005.

Table 13.6 Existing shopping centers in Shanghai

Physical form	Domestic-invested	Overseas-invested
Free-standing	• Brilliance South Mall;100,000m²; 1999 • Hualian Community Shopping Center ; 23,000m²; 2002 • Asia-Pacific Plaza; 55,000 m²; 2002 • Wenfeng Mall; 70,000 m²; 1998 • Millennium Plaza; 54,000m²; 2003 • Qibao Nextmall; 30,000m²; 1999 • Landmark Square; 38,000m²; 2003 • Jinhui Plaza; 55,000m²; 2004 • Brilliance West Mall; 111,000 m²; 2005 • Thumb Plaza; 110,000m²; 2005 • New World City; 120,000m²; 2005	• Friendship Shopping Center; 21,000m²; 1994 (HK) • Qibao Hymall; 30,000m²; 1999 (Taiwan) • Pudong Hymall; 40,000m²; 1999 (Taiwan) • Longhua Hymall; 20,000m²; 2000 (Taiwan) • Tungtay Leisure Square; 7,000m²; 2002 (Taiwan) • Super Brand Mall; 240,000 m²; 2002 (Thailand) • Join Buy City Plaza; 92,000m²; 2004 (HK) • Metro Town; 17,000m²; 2004 (HK) • CEPA Mall; 36,000m²; 2005 (HK)
As podium of office tower (Ancillary malls)	• Beethoven Plaza;* 20,000m²; 2003 • Summit Mall; 320,000m²; 2005	• Shanghai Square; 45,000m²; 1993 (HK) • MM21; 42,000m²; 1996 (Taiwan) • Hong Kong Plaza; 38,000m²; 1998 (HK) • Westgate Mall; 70,000m²; 1998 (HK) • Metro City; 67,000m²; 1998 (Singapore) • Grand Gateway Plaza; 140,000m²; 1999 (HK) • Shanghai Times Square; 109,000m²; 2000 (HK) • CITIC Square; 34,500m²; 2000 (HK) • China Resources Times Square; 51,000m²; 2001 (HK) • Plaza 66; 52,000m²; 2001 (HK) • Xin'ning;* 25,000m²; 2002; (HK) • Hongqiao Shopping Mall; 80,000m²; 2002 (HK&Macau) • Maxdo Mall; 20,000m²; 2002 (HK) • Raffles City; 50,000m²; 2004 (Singapore) • Brilliance-Shimao International Plaza; 58,000m²; 2005 (HK)

Source: Compiled by the authors from various sources and field work.

Note
* Podium of apartment towers.

Mall is also attached to an office tower hosting many well-known multinational corporations. These investors favored this form of development for three strategic reasons. First, land cost for building the shopping center is greatly reduced, because the same land is also used for high-rise office buildings, and rent generated by leasing office spaces constitutes a significant portion of the investment returns. Second, each tower houses thousands of office employees, mostly white-collar professionals, who themselves are frequent and affluent shoppers. Third, as Shanghai becomes an international economic, financial, and trade center, there will be even greater demand for quality office space in the city. As office towers at strategic locations have great potential for property value appreciation, many of the developers have the intention of selling these commercial properties to other interested international real estate investment trusts (REITs) to make a one-time profit.

The Taiwanese developers seem to focus on development of freestanding and community-oriented shopping centers in suburban districts, which could be the result of their inability to obtain favorable land use rights in the central area of Shanghai. In general, investors from Taiwan do not have the same capital, both monetary and political, as those from Hong Kong. Accordingly, they may lack bargaining powers. In fact, three of the four shopping centers that were built with Taiwanese investment were developed by the same investor, Ting Hsin International Group, which is also the parent company of Hymart. This is the only overseas investor that intends to develop a chain of community shopping centers with a distinct brand – Hymall (meaning Happy Shopping Mall).

With the exceptions of Beethoven Plaza and Summit Mall, all of the centers that were built by domestic developers are freestanding malls (see Table 13.6); and, except for New World City, all the freestanding malls are located in suburban districts. They range from flea-market style centers with no anchors, to full-sized regional malls. Completed in 2005, both Brilliance West Mall and Thumb Plaza represent a new trend of shopping center development. Unlike the earlier centers that are enclosed malls, they are built as semienclosed malls with such elegant landscaping and amenities as fountains, wading pools, resting areas, and open-air performing stages.

While Beijing has a much smaller number of shopping centers, 13 in total (see Table 13.7), it has the country's largest mall – Golden Resources Mall, completed in 2004, in western Haidian District. The 680,000 square meters mall was developed by a domestic real estate developer – Century Golden Resources Group – at a cost of 3.8 billion yuan or 475 millions US dollars ("The future of the world's largest mall is uncertain" 2004). Other than the differences in number and center size, the development patterns are similar to those in Shanghai. For example, all 13 centers are located in the central city (one in Xicheng, four in Dongcheng, one in Chongwen, three in Haidian, three in Chaoyang, and one in Fengtai). Overseas investments have also played an important role, and five of the six overseas developers are from Hong Kong: Cheung Kong Holdings Ltd. (for The Malls at Oriental Plaza); Sun Hung Kai Properties (for Sun Dong'an Plaza); New World Group (for New World Shopping Mall); Henderson Land Development Company Ltd. (for

Table 13.7 Existing shopping centers in Beijing

Physical form	Domestic-invested	Overseas-invested
Free-standing	• Golden Resources Mall; 680,000m^2; 2004 • Four Seasons Plaza: 132,000 m^2; 2003	• Xidan Cultural Square Plaza; 35,000 m^2; 1999 (H. K.) • Auchan-Leroymerlin Plaza; 65,800 m^2; 2004 (France)
As podium of office tower (Ancillary malls)	• COFCO International Plaza; 60,000 m^2; 1996 • Full-link Plaza; 16,000 m^2; 1997; • China World Shopping Mall; 60,000 m^2; 2000 • Qinchun-Huamei;* 25,000 m^2; 2005 • Zhongguangcun Shopping Center; 200,000 m^2; 2006	• Sun Dong'an Plaza; 200,000 m^2; 1997 (H. K.) • Henderson Shopping Center; 80,000 m^2; 1998 (H. K.) • New World Shopping Mall; 70,000 m^2; 1999 (H. K.) • The Mall on Oriental Plaza; 1999; (H. K.)

Source: Compiled by the authors from various sources and filed work.

Note
* Podium of apartment towers.

Henderson Shopping Center); and China Resources (for Xidan Cultural Square Plaza). The only Western investors are the French Auchan and LeroyMeilin, but the plaza that they developed in Fentai District is more like a prototype power center, as its only tenants are two large-format "big box" stores operated by Auchan and LeroyMeilin, respectively. For the same reasons as in Shanghai, most of the shopping centers were developed as ancillary malls attached to office towers. It should be mentioned that a domestic developer – Aika Investment (Group) Ltd. – built a 160,000 square meter mall in 2005, but the project went terribly wrong due to the inexperience of the developer in managing and operating the mall. To begin with, it was never able to fill the retail spaces with enough tenants. Only nine months into business, it had to cancel all the leases and vacate the existing tenants, transforming the building into a wholesale market ("Beijing Aika Shopping Center undergoes transformation" 2006). It should also be noted that shopping centers are not separated from modern department stores and hypermarkets. The latter often anchor shopping centers, becoming the centers' largest space takers.

Challenges to the urban planning and management regime

Development of large retail facilities, particularly hypermarkets and shopping centers, has also posed unprecedented challenges to the existing planning and management systems in Beijing and Shanghai. While both cities have encouraged investment from all sources of retail capital in development of new consumption spaces, neither Beijing nor Shanghai has instituted an effective planning process and approval mechanism. Their existing systems are inconsistent and not as transparent as they should be. For instance, neither Beijing nor Shanghai has a detailed land use bylaw, as most North American cities do, to guide the development of large retail facilities. As a result, irrational concentrations at a few locations have occurred, causing undue competition. Nanjing Road E. in Huangpu District – Shanghai's "main street" for nearly a century – is anchored by five large department stores and two shopping centers. Xujiahui of Xuhui District, a shopping district of 0.74 square kilometers, contains six large department stores. The construction of four large shopping centers was allowed within a 1-kilometer stretch of Nanjing Road W – namely Westgate Mall (42,000 square meters), Plaza 66 (52,000 square meters), CITIC Square (355,000 square meters), and Join Buy City Plaza (91,000 square meters). The first three are actually within 50 meters of one another. Unlike in American and Canadian cities, where different types of big box stores cluster to form a power center, hypermarkets in Shanghai are often close to one another to compete among themselves. As illustrated in Figure 13.3, 13 hypermarkets cluster in mid Minhang District, a reflection of poor planning and control on the part of the city. Not surprisingly, two of them, both operated by domestic retailers, became victims of cannibalization and went bankrupt; they were replaced by Carrefour and Lotus stores, respectively (Zheng 2005). Similar clusters occurred in Beijing. For example, between 1990 and 2000, six large retail

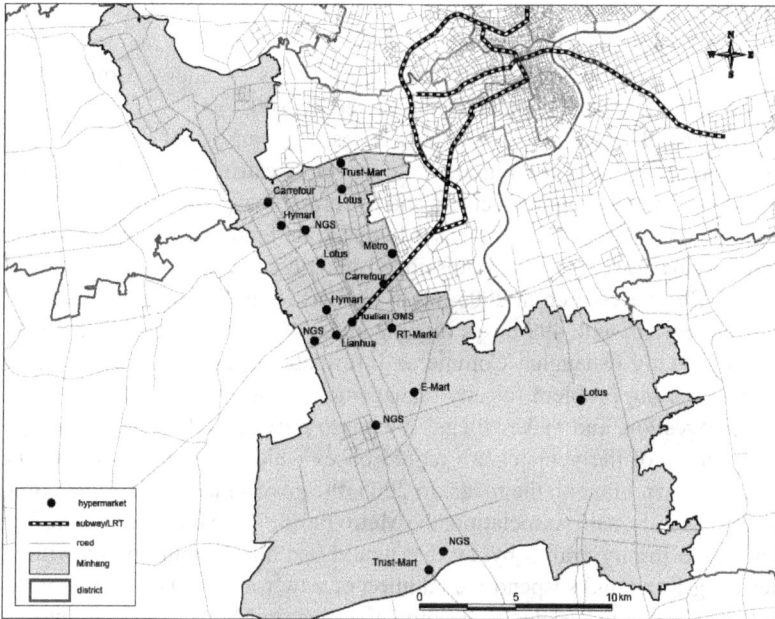

Figure 13.3 A cluster of hypermarkets in Shanghai's Minhang District.

facilities were constructed along a short stretch of Xidan Street in Xicheng District: Xidan Shopping Plaza (1991), Xidan Emporium (1995), Xidan-Scitech Shopping Plaza (1996), Zhongyou Department Store (1998), Capital Times Square (1999), and Xidan Cultural Square Plaza (2000). Such high concentrations would not have been permitted in North American cities.

Corrective measures were introduced much later, and sporadically. In 2001, the Shanghai government issued a bylaw with two important clauses: (1) construction of new hypermarket within the Inner-Ring Road is banned unless a special permit from the municipal government is granted; (2) development of future hypermarkets (10,000 square meters or larger) outside the Inner-Ring Road must go through a public hearing (an urban management exercise common in most Western cities), and all approved projects must be at least three kilometers away from any existing hypermarket (Shanghai Commission of Commerce and Shanghai Development and Planning Commission 2001). The Shanghai Retail Chain Association is delegated the authority to preside over such hearings; pertinent government officials, industry leaders, interested retailers and representatives of the affected communities (who are often handpicked by government officials) are invited to comment on the business proposals. Yet, the public hearing process is hardly effective and does not apply to shopping center development. The first Wal-Mart store in Shanghai, which opened in 2005, did not observe this requirement (Guo 2006). In October 2006, the Korean E-Mart obtained approval to open its fourth hypermarket in

Baoshan District of Shanghai on a site less than 500 meters from an existing Carrefour store (Zhou and Li 2006). The 10th Five-Year Plan for Commercial Activity Development in Shanghai (2001–2005) capped the number of hyper-markets at 60 for the entire city including suburbs (Shanghai Commission of Commerce 2000), but the total has now exceeded 100.

Another challenge is posed by shuttle buses. To compete for market shares and to overcome the restricted mobility of consumers caused by the lack of private automobiles, many shopping centers and hypermarkets provide free shuttle buses to bring in shoppers,and use the buses to penetrate their competitors' trade areas. According to a government-commissioned study conducted by Shanghai Institute of Retail Chain Research in 2005, 60 hypermarkets in Shanghai were providing such free service, with 499 buses running along 499 different routes and making 4,795 trips daily (Shanghai Commerce Information Center 2005). These buses have posed a big problem for city management. Not only do they contribute to traffic congestion, and make "illegal" stops (to pick up and discharge shoppers), but also most of the vehicles are retired buses which emit excessive pollutants and break down often on the roads. In 2005, the government of Shanghai ordered Shanghai Retail Chain Association, the Metro Police and Municipal Public Transit Authority to jointly draft a bylaw that would ban all shopping buses within the Inner-Ring Road and suspend the addition of new routes outside the Inner-Ring Road. The bylaw was slated to become effective on May 1, 2005, but has never been implemented due to resistance from the hypermarket operators (Liu 2005; "Shanghai encounters resistance" 2005). While such problems also exist in Beijing, the Beijing government has neither introduced public consultation in its planning and approval process, nor attempted to issue any bylaw to curb the operation of shuttle buses.

The chaotic development patterns have also prompted the state government to introduce new forms of intervention. In 2004, the state government ordered that all municipalities make and announce their own land use bylaws for commercial facil-ity development, and that their municipal plans be revised accordingly (Ministry of Commerce 2004). After a nationwide survey jointly conducted in 2005 by the Ministry of Commerce and the People's Bank of China, which revealed a worrying amount of vacancy in recent commercial property developments, the state govern-ment ordered state-controlled banks to tighten their lending policies towards large shopping center projects. In April 2006, the central bank – the People's Bank of China – raised its lending rate to further dampen the overheating economy (Berman 2006; Bradsher 2006). In addition, the state government stipulated that all land must be publicly bid for at the market price, eliminating under-table deals between bribing developers and corrupt government officials. This makes it more difficult and more expensive for most domestic developers and some foreign developers, who rely on Chinese bank loans, to develop new shopping centers. In its 10th Five-Year Plan for Commercial Activity Development (2000–2004), the government of Beijing prescribed construction of four large shopping centers (each with 200,000 square meters) outside the central city in its northeastern, northwestern, southeast-ern and southwestern suburbs, respectively (Beijing Development and Planning

Commission and Beijing Commission of Commerce 2001). Five developers, all domestic, responded with enthusiasm (Zhao 2001). These proposed projects are now all suspended because the loans that the developers had secured from state banks are no longer forthcoming as a result of state auditing. As well, the land has become much more expensive now that it must be obtained through public bidding at the market rate.

Concluding remarks

As Shanghai and Beijing strive to become world cities, a new retail economy has evolved accordingly. Clearly, the retail sector has been transformed from a state-dominated distribution system to a market-oriented economic entity, with significant restructuring in retail capital provision. The retail transformation in post-reform Beijing and Shanghai is a clear demonstration of the Economic Transition Model depicted by Bradshaw. Indeed, all four dimensions of the transition process took place in retail capital restructuring and the production of new consumption spaces. Retail liberalization began as early as the late 1970s by permitting the entry of individual retailers into the distribution system. However, it was only the early 1990s that saw the implementation of major reforms such as the transformation of large- and medium-sized state enterprises into private or joint-stock companies, and the opening up of the retail sector to international retailers.

While the wealthy consumer market and increased levels of consumption nurtured by the two decades of economic reform constitute the necessary condition for sustained retail growth, it is retail deregulation that has been the fundamental driving force behind the structural changes in Beijing's and Shanghai's retail sectors. At the core of the retail deregulation was ownership reform: the abandonment of state monopoly and the mobilization of different sources of retail capital including private funds, capitals raised on the stock market, and FDI. This resulted in a proliferation of retail enterprises and stores, which expanded the distribution system significantly with vast new consumption spaces – particularly modern department stores, hypermarkets, and shopping centers. They play an important role in improving the retail economy in general and in satisfying changing consumer tastes in particular.

While the trend of reform and development is similar in the two cities, Shanghai leads Beijing by a large margin in the production of new consumption spaces (see Tables 13.4, 13.5, 13.6 and 13.7), indicating that the Shanghai government is more entrepreneurial than the government of Beijing. For instance, the government of Shanghai took extraordinary initiatives to maintain or regain its competitive edge in the country to lure global financial capital that was flowing into China in the 1990s. One such initiative was to approve the entry of foreign retailers without state endorsement. This would seem to be a politically risky initiative, as the central government did issue a circular in 1997 to reiterate that local governments had no independent authority to approve the entry of international retailers ("Local governments are prohibited from approving foreign invested retail enterprises"

1997), and it admonished Carrefour in 2001 for flouting the state rules in expanding businesses in China. Nonetheless, the state government did not close any stores that had already been opened, nor did it take any punitive actions against the municipal government of Shanghai. Indeed, when China opened its borders to international retail capital, there existed virtually no rules and laws. Rules and laws were written and revised constantly as foreign retailers moved in and expanded their operations. If Shanghai had followed the state policies to the letter in the 1990s, it would not have attracted such international retailers as Carrefour, Metro, Auchan, Lotus, and many others, which also located their China HQ offices in Shanghai. These retailers have made significant contributions to the production of new consumption spaces in Shanghai through capital investment. While the Beijing market is equally attractive to FDI, and Beijing also approved the entry of foreign retailers without state permission, the number is much smaller due mainly to the cautiousness of the Beijing government in minimizing political risks. This signifies that in the early stages of economic transition, when new national policies and corresponding governing institutions were still incomplete and were still evolving, those local governments that had the courage to take bold initiatives, despite political risks, could emerge as clear winners. Shanghai is just such an entrepreneurial city.

Notes

1 There were thousands more individual retailers in both Beijing and Shanghai, but they are excluded from our analysis due to lack of detailed data.
2 The four stores in Beijing are: Beijing Department Store (the original store); Chang'an Department Store (17,000 square meters, opened in 1990); Shuang'an Department Store (22,000 square meters, opened in 1994); and Dong'an Department Store (opened in 1998).
3 These include Yashi, Kama, Wanhui-Shuang'an, Tianyun, Wangtong New World, Qiancun, and Hailan-Yuntian (Han 1998).
4 Lianhua is now also part of the newly created Shanghai Brilliance Group.
5 In 1998, the Japanese Yohan went bankrupt. As a result, its store in Pudong was transferred to its Chinese partner – Shanghai No. 1 Department Store. Its second store in Minhang District was converted to a shopping center (now called Brilliance South Mall). The Jusco Department Store near Shanghai Railway station was turned into a wholesale market.
6 For instance, Hutchinson Whampoa Real Estate Ltd., the developer of Westgate Mall, is owned and controlled by Hong Kong billionaire Lee Ka-Shing, who is known to be a friend of such state leaders as Deng Xiaoping and Jiang Zemin. CITIC Pacific Ltd. is a subsidiary of CITIC Hong Kong (Holdings) Ltd., chaired by the son of late Chinese Vice President Rong Yiren. The Rong family is historically rooted in Shanghai and still enjoys close relations with the Shanghai municipal government ("The red capitalist Rong Yiren passed away" 2005). Hang Lung Properties is another that enjoys extensive connections in mainland China. The developer entered China in the early 1990s when real estate prices were at rather low levels and opportunities abundant, and was granted favorable land use rights by the Shanghai Municipal Government in late 1993 to construct two luxury shopping centers, Grand Gateway Plaza and Plaza 66. Even the Thai-based developer of Super Brand Mall, Chai Tai Group, is a business conglomerate owned by an overseas Chinese family. Many of these overseas investors and developers are also known to be generous donors to local governments. For instance, the Chairman of Hong Kong's Shimao Group, a Mainland Chinese immigrant, has donated 10 million US dollars in the

past 10 years for various causes, including 2 million US dollars to help Shanghai with its bid for the 2010 World Expo.

References

"Beijing Aijia Shopping Centre undergoes transformation" (2006) retrieved on May 18, 2006, from http://i18.cn/newscenter/news/guoneinews/2006-5-18/27914.shtml

Beijing Almanac Compilation Committee (1997) *Beijing Almanac 1997*, Beijing.

Beijing Commercial Activity Development Research Group (1999) "A 10-year retrospect of commercial activity development in Beijing," *Journal of Beijing College of Finance and Trade Management* (1): 27–32.

Beijing Development and Planning Commission and Beijing Commission of Commerce (2001) *The 10th Five-Year Plan for Commercial Activity Development in Beijing*, Beijing.

Beijing Statistics Bureau (1999) *Census of Commercial Activity in Beijing*, Beijing: China Commerce Publishing House.

Berman, D. (April 28, 2006) "China hikes rate to dampen growth," *National Post*, FP1.

Bradshaw, M. J. (1996) "The prospects for the post-socialist economies," in P. W. Daniels and W. F. Lever (eds) *The Global Economy in Transition*, Essex (England): Addison Wesley Longman Limited, 263–288.

Bradsher, K. (April 28, 2006) "China's first rate change in 18 months jars markets," *Toronto Star*, F3.

Chan, W. K., Perez, J., Perkins' A. and Shu, M. (1997) "China's retail markets are evolving more quickly than companies anticipate," *The McKinsey Quarterly* (2): 206–211.

Chen, G. (2004) *Carrefour Strategies*, Guangzhou: South China Daily Publishing House.

China Chain Store Association (2004) "Retail chain development and growth in China, 2002–2003," *China Chain Store Almanac 2003–2004*. Beijing: China Commerce Publishing House.

China Chain Store Association (2005) *China Chain Store Almanac, 2005*. Beijing: China Commerce Publishing House.

China Chamber of Commerce (2001) *Almanac of China's Commerce*, Beijing: China Almanac Publishing House.

China Chamber of Commerce (2004) *Almanac of China's Commerce*, Beijing: China Almanac Publishing House.

"China's largest shopping mall to be completed in Beijing" (April 28, 2004) *Ming Pao*, p. 25.

Dawson, J. (2003) "Towards a model of the impacts of retail internationalization," in J. A. Dawson, M. Mukoyama, S. C. Choi, and R. Larke (eds) *The internationalization of Retailing in Asia*, London: RoutledgeCurzon, 189–209.

Dou, H. (December 11, 2004) "General manager of Wangfujing Group explains purchase of Shuang'an and Dong'an," *Beijing Daily*.

Friedmann, J. (1986) "The world city hypothesis," *Development and Change* (1): 69–83.

Green, C. and Ruhleder, K. (1995) "Globalization, borderless worlds and the Tower of Bagel," *Journal of Organizational Change Management*, 8(4): 55–68.

Guo, C. (May 20, 2006) "The public hearing process for large commercial facilities loses its credibility," *China Commerce Daily*.

Hall, P. (1966) *The World Cities*. London: Weidenfeld and Nicolson.

Han, J. (1998) "New challenges for department stores in Beijing," *Science and Technology Think Tank* (2): 22–23.

Hartshorn, T. A. (1980) *Interpreting the City: An Urban Geography*, New York: John Wiley & Sons.

He, T. (1997) "Operation and reform of Beijing 1st Bureau of Commerce," *Almanac of China's Domestic Trade 1997*, Beijing: Ministry of Domestic Trade, VIII, 1–2.

Heredia, B. (1997) "Prosper or perish? development in the age of global capital," *Current History*, 96(613): 383–388.

Hong, T., Wang, Q. and Yao, X. (2002) "Government of Beijing accelerates withdraw of state capital from the retail sector," *Almanac of China's Domestic Trade 2002*, Beijing: China Chamber of Commerce, 61–63.

Knox, P., Agnew, J. and McCarthy, L. (2003) *The Geography of the World Economy* (4th edn), New York: Arnold.

Kynge, J. and Young, E. (November 8, 2001) "Wal-Mart gets go-ahead to open stores in Beijing: U.S. company's fortunes rise while rival Carrefour's fall," *National Post*, PF16.

Lever, W. F. and Daniels, P. W. (1996) "Introduction," in P. W. Daniels and W. F. Lever (eds) *The Global Economy in Transition*, Essex (England): Addison Wesley Longman Limited, 1–10.

Li, F. (1998) "What should China's retail industry remember from 1997?" *Science and Technology Think Tank* (1): 6–8.

Li, M. (March 15, 2004) "Property rent at premium business location in Shanghai is soaring: department stores are doomed to suffer," *People's Daily* (overseas edition), p. 10.

Liu, J. (March 28, 2005) "Free shuttles are to be banned within Inner-Ring Road beginning May 1," *Labour News*.

"Local governments are prohibited from approving foreign invested retail enterprises" (August 11, 1997) *People's Daily* (overseas edition), p. 2.

Ministry of Commerce and Ministry of Construction (2004) *Guidelines for Municipal Commercial Activity Development Plans*. Beijing.

Nakata, C. and Sivakumar, K. (1997) "Emerging market conditions and their impact on first mover advantages: an integrative review," *International Marketing Review*, 14 (6): 461–485.

National Bureau of Statistics of China (2006) *China Statistics Yearbook 2005*. Beijing.

Shanghai Academy of Social Sciences (1997) *Shanghai Economic Yearbook 1997*, Shanghai: Shanghai Economic Yearbook Publishing House.

Shanghai Almanac Compilation Committee (2003) *Shanghai Almanac 2003*, Shanghai: Shanghai Almanac Publisher.

Shanghai Commerce Information Center (2005) "Free shuttle buses are to be banned, different interest groups present varying arguments," retrieved on April 4, 2005, from http://www.commerce.sh.cn

Shanghai Commerce Information Center, and Sona Consulting Ltd. (2003) *The White Book of Shanghai's Retail Development*. Shanghai: Shanghai Commerce Information Center.

Shanghai Commission of Commerce (2000) *Outline of the 10th Five-Year Plan for Commercial Activity Development in Shanghai*. Shanghai: Shanghai Commission of Commerce.

Shanghai Commission of Commerce, and Shanghai Development and Planning Commission (2001) *Announcement of Introducing Public Hearing Process for Development of Hypermarket*. Shanghai.

"Shanghai encounters resistance for its decision to ban free shuttle buses within the Inner-Ring Road" (April 8, 2005) *First Financial Post*.

Shanghai Office of Commercial Activity Census (2001) *The 1999 Census of Commercial Activities in Shanghai, Summary Statistics*. Shanghai: Shanghai Office of Commercial Activity Census.

"Shanghai strives to become an international city of commerce" (January 12, 1994) *People's Daily* (overseas edition), p. 1.

Simmons, J., Jones, K. and Yeates, M. (1998) "The need for international comparisons of commercial structure and change," *Progress in Planning*, 50(4): 207–216.

State Council (1998) *Announcement of State Policies with regard to Foreign Retailers That Do Not Have State Approval*. Beijing.

Sun, Y. (1997) *Retail Opportunities in the People's Republic of China*. Toronto: Centre for the Study of Commercial Activity, Ryerson University.

Sun, Y. (2000) *Urban Development and Retail Structure in Beijing* (unpublished Ph.D. dissertation), Saskatoon: University of Saskatchewan.

"The future of the world's largest mall is uncertain" (November 18, 2004), *Economic Observer.*

"The red capitalist Rong Yiren passed away" (November 5, 2005), *Chinese Canadian Post*, p. 4.

United Nations Development Programme (1999) *Human Development Report 1999*. New York: Oxford University Press.

Wan, D. (1999) "Fifty years of commerce development in New China" Almanac of China's Domestic Trade, 1999 (A special issue to mark the 50th anniversary of the People's Republic of China). Beijing: Almanac of China's Domestic Trade Publishing House.

Wang, S. (2003) "Internationalization of retailing in China," in J. A. Dawson, M. Mukoyama, S. C. Choi, and R. Larke (eds) *The Internationalization of Retailing in Asia*. London: RoutledgeCurzon, 114–135.

Wang, S. and Jones, K. (2001) "China's retail sector in transition," *Asian Geographer* 20(1–2): 25–51.

Wang, S. and Jones, K. (2002) "Retail structure of Beijing," *Environment and Planning A* 34(10): 1785–1808.

"Will wholesaling of high-grade goods be profitable?" (January 28, 1999), *China Consumers*, p. 3.

Wrigley, N. (2002) *Reading Retailing: A Geographical Perspective on Retailing and Consumption Space*, London: Arnold; New York: Oxford University Press.

Wrigley, N. and Lowe, M. (1996) *Retailing, Consumption and Capital: Towards the New Retail Geography*, Essex: Longman Group Ltd.

Yeates, M. (1998) *The North American city* (5th edn). New York: Addison Wesley Longman, Inc.

Yeates, M. and Garner, B. (1976) *The North American City* (2nd edn). New York: Harper & Row Publishers.

Zhang, Z. (1997) "Seventeen large department stores opened for business," *Almanac of Beijing 1997*, Beijing: Beijing Almanac Compilation Committee.

Zhao, A. (2001) "Domestic and overseas capital compete to build large shopping malls in Beijing," *China Business and Trade* (19–20): 10–14.

Zheng, J. (September 7, 2005) "Lotus enters town of Qibao, excebating market saturation," *Economic Daily News.*

Zhou, G. and Li, W. (October 26, 2006) "E-Mart's latest store in Shanghai to be constructed in Baoshan District, less than 500 meters from Carrefour," *21st Century Economic News.*

Zhou, Y. and Ma, L. J. C. (2000) "Economic restructuring and suburbanization in China," *Urban Geography*, 21(3): 205–236.

14 When local meets global

Residential differentiation, global connections and consumption in Shanghai

Jiaming Sun and Xiangming Chen

To decipher and deconstruct the multifaceted relationship between globalization and local transformation in Chinese cities, especially Shanghai (Chen and Sun 2007; Sun and Chen 2005), this chapter focuses on the residential differentiation of global oriented consumption in Shanghai as a function of socioeconomic variables and personal global connections (PGCs) (e.g. having worked for a foreign company locally). Data[1] from Shanghai reveal a considerable variation among different residential categories with regard to residents' socioeconomic status, and that while social economic divisions are prevalent among residential categories, PGCs significantly affect global oriented consumer behaviors such as eating McDonald's or KFC (Kentucky Fried Chicken), purchasing and wearing foreign brand clothes, and using foreign brand household appliances. That is, people in better or higher-end residential spaces with certain global connections are more likely to purchase foreign brand goods, while rural residents and those with fewer global connections are attracted more by the symbolic meaning of foreign products. The findings suggest that residential categories reflect people's socioeconomic status and external connections, both of which influence the extent to which people are oriented toward consuming global brand products, especially in a globalizing city like Shanghai where residential patterns and lifestyles have become more differentiated.

Residential differentiation: the focus of the study

The residential pattern of a city reflects a sorting process by which people settle in and move between neighborhood areas based on a variety of individual demographic and socioeconomic characteristics and community and neighborhood features. These factors drive residential differentiation in a market economy in which people tend to end up living where they live in response to varied conditions and constraints. China's booming coastal metropolis of Shanghai has experienced dramatic residential transformation since the early 1990s as both a transitional city moving away from socialist planning and a globalizing city becoming integrated with the outside world. This process is characterized by, on the one hand, rapid real estate development in place of traditional government control of the housing sector, and, on the other, the penetration of global capital, which in turn has fueled a "hot" housing market.

First of all, scholars have studied the causes and consequences of spatial differentiation in major Chinese cities by focusing on reform policies and market mechanisms in land and physical infrastructure development (Lin 2001; Wu 1999; Wu and Yeh 1999; Yusuf and Wu 1997; Zhu 2000). This focus has provided a broad context for understanding the extent and type of spatial differentiation bearing on characteristics of and changes within the urban housing sector. Research on urban housing itself began with a focus on the macro reform policies and practices plus their local variations and how they affected the types of housing investment and provision (Chen and Gao 1993a,b; Chen and Hua 1996; Lee 1988; Wang 1990; Wu 1996; Song *et al.* 2004). While some studies (Wang and Murie 1996; Zhou and Logan 1996) examined the commodification of urban housing as a result of market reforms, others have shown that housing inequalities within cities and work units persisted due to the unequal control and allocation of valuable resources within the entrenched redistributive system and power hierarchy (Bian 1994; Bian and Logan 1996; Bian *et al.* 1997; Logan *et al.* 1999).

With better data, research on urban housing inequality has become more refined and varied at and across district, community, and neighborhood levels, especially in the case of the largest metropolises like Beijing, Shanghai, and Guangzhou where large-scale morphological transformation has already taken place and created multiscaled spatial parameters for residential differentiation (Gaubatz 1999; Wu and Yeh 1999). The more fine-grained spatial analysis of housing inequality has focused on the increasing individual residential mobility and choices within cities in response to more varied housing types, housing tenures, traditional and shifting values of certain inner-city locations, and different income levels (Li 2003 Li and Siu 2001). Most recent studies (Wang and Li 2004) have found income, social status, differential price, neighborhood security, living convenience, and the lingering *hukou* system to be important determinants of residential choice and the lack of housing options for rural migrants. As these factors become more important, they are more likely to create serious residential segregation (Gu and Liu 2002; Huang 2005).

As research has moved from housing reform and inequality at the national level with aggregate data to increasingly detailed local studies of residential differentiation, scholarly attention has also turned to the impact of globalization on local residential space (Wu 2001). Having examined the high-end townhouse development projects carrying the names of transplanted cityscapes such as "Cambridge" and "Orange County" in suburban Beijing, Wu (2004) has argued that this phenomenon reflects a local image and social construction of globalization or a global lifestyle that developers have promoted and sold to the new rich consumer in a niche property market.

Although many studies have touched on the market-driven urban spatial differentiation, there have been few efforts to uncover the spatial and cultural effects of globalization on local consumers, and how their lifestyles, to the extent they are globally oriented, are displayed residentially. In a paper discussing the impact of PGCs on residential choices in Shanghai, Sun and Chen (2005) provide a new perspective on spatial differentiation in this globalizing city. As a follow-up and complementary analysis here, we explore residential differentiation in Shanghai further by examining the relationship between differentiated residential spaces and their occupants' consumer behaviors, as they are associated with income, education attainment, and PGCs.

Unpacking the global-local nexus

Despite the myriad conceptualizations of the global-local relationship such as "glocalization" (Robertson and Khondker 1998) and "grobalization" (Ritzer 2003), it is not always clear how the global and local are linked and interact in different empirical contexts. According to Robertson and Khondker (1998), globalization refers both to the compression of the world and the intensification of consciousness of the world as a whole. They posit that globalization involves the structuring of a social system at the global level and that there is an intensification of global consciousness in the sense that individuals are increasingly oriented toward the world as a whole. From a cultural perspective, Appadurai (2001) argues that global cultural flows are shaped by the multiplicity of perspectives generated by flows of people, money, ideologies, media technologies, and symbols. Local cultures incorporate global symbols but in ways specific to the local context. There is no pure local culture that is untainted by global culture but rather a variety of local cultures that are increasingly interpenetrated and constantly remade out of elements of global cultural flows (Held 1999).

Focusing on consumption, Ritzer (1996) used *The McDonaldization of Society* to describe the process by which the principles of the fast food chain have become globally influential. Treating McDonald's as the "paradigm case" of social regimentation, Ritzer argues that "McDonaldization" may be an inexorable process as it sweeps through seemingly impervious institutions in different parts of the world. However, firms, including McDonald's, that produce and market "globally" also develop necessary local connections. That is, their production and selling must be able to stand on local feet, and globally marketable symbols must be "creamed" off local cultures. In this sense, global business not only involves "delocation" but also "relocation" or translocation (Bocock 1993).

In reality, the global-local nexus of consumption is often a two-way street involving both changes in local consumption and local modifications of a global company's standard products and operating procedures. While the key standard elements of the McDonald's system – queuing, self-provisioning, and self-seating – have been accepted by consumers throughout East Asia (Watson 1997), some aspects of this model have been rejected, notably those concerning time and space, particularly in local settings. A mall in one part of the world (London or Hong Kong) may be structured much like that in another location (Chicago or Mexico City, for example), but there will be some differences in their specific contents (Ritzer 2003). In many parts of East Asia, consumers have turned their local McDonald's into leisure centers, after-school clubs, and social and dating places

(Yan 2000). The meaning of "fast" has been subverted in these settings where it refers to the delivery of food, not to its consumption. An interesting case in which the global adapts to the local is that McDonald's introduced rice dishes in Hong Kong to broaden its appeal during the economic downturn, taking business away from some traditional chain rice restaurants (Yu 2002).

In consumption, globalizing and localizing dynamics do not necessarily conflict with each other, but unfold simultaneously; and when they interact, they do so in different ways at different times in different parts of the world. While traditional societies may experience the powerful impact of global consumer culture and thus change quite drastically, they exhibit continuities that may be reflected in mixed values and adaptable behaviors of individual consumers. In this chapter, by exploring how consumption in Shanghai has evolved and differentiated along both spatial and social dimensions, we focus on the interaction between the increasing penetration of global consumer culture and varied responses and adaptations of local residents. The following analysis of consumer culture will allow us to make some sense of the nuanced texture and varied outcomes of the new urbanism of globally oriented local consumption in Chinese cities, as exemplified by the cutting edge of that consumption in rapidly globalizing Shanghai.

Consumption as a mirror of spatial and cultural differentiations

McCracken (1990) describes consumption as a thoroughly cultural phenomenon and argues that in Western developed societies culture is profoundly connected to and dependent upon consumption. Without consumer activities, modern societies would lose key instruments for the reproduction, representation, and manipulation of their culture. Thus, how we consume and why we consume influences how we construct our everyday lives. If culture changes with consumption, it does so slowly in a general sense but unevenly across space depending on how consumers react to new and different products. As globalization stretches the boundary of the world market to include more local places, new and different consumer goods of global brands have become more available to local consumers. Global brand products have become available in many Chinese cities, especially those coastal cities like Shanghai. Take foreign fast foods as an example. The number of KFC restaurants in China has already exceeded 1,000 in 230 cities of all provinces and regions except Tibet, while McDonald's has been adding about 100 restaurants annually over the last few years, with over 600 outlets in approximately 170 Chinese cities today, and a projected 1,000 restaurants to be opened by the 2008 Beijing Olympics. In 2003, McDonald's and KFC accounted for eight percent of the total income of fast food restaurants in China, which stood at 22 billion US dollars.[2] Shanghai alone hosts over 100 KFC and McDonald's restaurants, which have spread throughout the city and penetrated local residential areas since their early clustering in the downtown and busy commercial areas. The American fast food chains are betting on the growing purchasing power and open-mindedness of consumers in Shanghai.

As American fast foods have caught on, Shanghai consumers have also been chasing global clothing brands. The city has become a shopping haven for such brands as Nike, Pierre Cardin, Puma, Tommy Hilfiger, and Valentino. While faked clothes with these labels can be bought along the well-known Xiangyang Street in Shanghai for much less than the real thing, the fancy stores on Nanjing Road and Huaihai Road carrying the authentic wear attract a growing number of affluent local consumers. It appears that the relatively small number of people with high incomes can afford to purchase foreign brand-name clothes, whereas more people and families go to McDonald's and KFC restaurants as mass consumers. In reality, why people choose to spend money on different global brands, say American fast foods versus brand-name clothes, is much more complex. While all global brands have certain general appeal to local consumers, the latter choose the former for a variety of different reasons based on individual characteristics and their niches in the local. Furthermore, in the rapidly globalizing city of Shanghai, factors reflecting growing global-local connections are likely to influence people's decisions on consuming global brands. More important, one of the most salient features of a rapidly globalizing city like Shanghai is its increasingly visible functionally and symbolically differentiated and fragmented economic and social spaces within and across different urban areas. The data in this study reveal that these new local residential spaces vary in the pattern of globally oriented consumers of brand-name foods, clothes, household items, and recreational activities. It behooves us to find out how much personal characteristics and resources versus global connection matter to globally oriented consumption in Shanghai.

Gauging differentiation in Shanghai

A city with a rich historical and current mix of Western and Chinese cultures, Shanghai provides an excellent case for studying the complex and multifaceted relationship between global connections and global consumption behaviors. Shanghai is the largest and the economically most important city in China. Since China introduced the economic reform and open-door policy in 1979, especially since the launch of the Pudong development in 1990, Shanghai has made great achievements in economic and social development through increasing economic and cultural "connections" with foreign countries. An increasing number of large multinational companies have set up enterprises in Shanghai, facilitating the city's economic development and its integration with the world economy. Shanghai has experienced accelerated local transformations by reshaping its urban culture towards that of an outward-oriented, multifunctional world city.

We have collected the needed data in Shanghai's Pudong New Area, whose takeoff in the early 1990s marked the beginning of Shanghai's "renaissance" and remarkable rise to the position of global city. Pudong itself has undergone arguably the most remarkable transformation of any part of any urban area in the world over the 1990s. Besides the symbolic aspect of its skyline, Pudong has developed different areas for Shanghai's new financial district (dubbed "the Manhattan of China") and high-tech manufacturing. The modern bank and factory buildings aside, a number of McDonald's and KFC restaurants have opened up and so have upscale department stores like Yaohan and other commercial outlets. Residents in Pudong district do not need to cross the Huangpu River to consume varied foreign brand goods and services.

The rapid transformation of Pudong from a backwater of Shanghai to the latter's "crown jewel" is reflected in demographic, urbanization, and economic trends and weights, which have translated into a booming consumer market. In 1990, Pudong had 1.3 million people with permanent residence; the number rose to 1.8 million in 2003, accounting for 13.2 percent of Shanghai's total registered population, even though it only occupies 8.4 percent of the city's land area.[3] Despite this rapid urbanization in Pudong, in 2001 it administered 13 towns (*zhen*) which were officially defined rural areas, in addition to 13 wards (*jiedao*) in urban areas. To obtain a representative sample revealing the residential types and differentiation across the Pudong area, we employed a three-layered sampling procedure with three steps. First, we selected nine wards and three towns to give more weight to the larger urban population. Second, we selected two neighborhood committees in every ward, one neighborhood committee in two of the three towns bordering or close to the urban wards, and one community in the third and more rural town located farther away from central Pudong. This spatial coverage of our sample gave us a broad spectrum of residential differences, knowing that rural residents in Pudong were exposed to the influence of rapid urbanization and globalization. Third, we randomly selected 25 households in every chosen neighborhood committee for interviews using a questionnaire. We ended up conducting 450 interviews in the urban wards and 150 interviews with officially rural households in the more and less urban towns for a total of 600 cases.

In this chapter, we use a number of observed variables to explore how the global consumption pattern varies by different residential types and according to some socioeconomic attributes of the surveyed residents. The variables measuring global consumption are: Have you eaten in McDonald's or KFC? Have you purchased and worn foreign famous brand clothes? Have you been to a bowling alley? Do you own a personal credit card? Have you watched any Western movie in the recent three months? In addition, we have constructed an index to measure global consumer behaviors (GCB) (0–100) from the above dummy responses, that can be used in multiple regression analysis.

Besides the focus on residential category as the main independent variable, there is a variety of independent variables to be used, such as age, education, income, and so on. While the independent variables above are expected to have differential effects on GCB across residential categories, we are much more interested in measuring and modeling the influence of PGCs on where people end up residentially net of the demographic and socioeconomic attributes. Since PGCs represent different ways in which local (Shanghai) residents are linked to the outside world, we conceptualize them as *relational social assets* that can help bring about social and economic advantages including living in an up-scale neighborhood area. These relational assets may function in a way similar to the ways social networks, in general, have been shown to generate economic returns like good jobs, higher salaries, access to materials and markets for officials and entrepreneurs (Bian *et al.* 1997; Lin 2001). Since PGCs provide local connections with people, resources, and information in an extra-local or global network, they permit people who are more strongly globally connected to have a better chance of living well locally than those who have no or weak global connections.

To measure PGCs as relational assets, we use four dummy variables: 1) having worked for a foreign company locally (1 = yes); 2) having been abroad (1 = yes); 3) having relatives and friends overseas (1 = yes); and 4) often surfing foreign Web sites (1 = yes).[4] However, we avoided treating these as restrictive or mutually exclusive categories in the survey by allowing the respondents to choose up to four categories if they had all four PGCs. The extent of overlap across the four dummy variables is indicated by their moderate bivariate correlations, which range from 0.13 to 0.30. For example, about one-third of the people who have worked for a foreign company either have been abroad or have overseas relatives

Household appliances by socioeconomic attributes and global connections

As shown in Table 14.1, 79.6 percent of residents in agricultural villages are edu-cated to "below senior high school" level; whereas 75.7 percent in luxury flats and villas have a university or graduate degree. Per capita income at 4,000 yuan and over accounts for 97.2 percent of those in luxury flats and villas, whereas only 10.2 percent of those in agricultural villages earn that much. In luxury flats and vil-las, 35.1 and 29.7 percent are "company executives," and "technical/educational personnel," respectively. However, "manufacturing workers," and "office clerical workers" are more likely to live in "urban residential villages," "old urban set-tlements," and "new commercial housing complexes." Residents in "luxury flats and villas" and "new commercial housing complexes" have strong PGCs, which are much weaker in the other residential categories. The overwhelming majorities in luxury flats and villas, and new commercial housing complexes have property rights to their residences (94.4 and 90.6 percent). However, only 49.2 percent of respondents in old urban settlements are houseowners.

If the differences in occupation and education attainment across the residential categories provide a clear picture of social differentiation, the variation in house-hold appliances offers additional information on spatial differences in consumption in Shanghai. Table 14.2 shows foreign brand household appliances as a percentage of all household items by the residential categories. This percentage is very high for households in luxury flats and villas, where some foreign brand household items (such as motorcycle, video recorder, movie camera, cell phone, etc.) reach almost 100 percent, while people in the other residential categories own much smaller percentages. The gaps between "luxury flats and villas" and "agricultural villages" range from 30 to 90 percent. More importantly, people with more global connections own a much higher percentage of foreign brand appliances than the average. The larger proportions of owners of such luxury items as pianos and pri-vate cars live in luxury flats and villas. Overall, people with global connections are

Table 14.1 Education attainment, household income, occupations, and global connections across residential types in Shanghai (in percentage)

	Agricultural villages	Town centers	Urban residential villages	Old urban settlements	New commercial housing complexes	Luxury flats and villas	Total
Education Attainment							
Below senior high school	79.6	48.8	59.2	60.7	37.5	13.5	56.3
Vocational school, college	18.4	41.5	25.3	18.0	18.8	10.8	23.8
University, graduate school	2.0	9.8	15.5	21.3	43.8	75.7	19.8
Per capita Income (yearly)							
300–1900 yuan	48.9	35.0	27.5	35.7	16.7	0	28.4
2000–3900 yuan	40.8	47.5	53.4	46.4	40.0	2.8	47.3
4000-over yuan	10.2	17.5	19.1	17.9	43.3	97.2	24.3
Personal Global Connections							
Have you worked for a foreign company	4.08	12.5	11.62	21.05	30.00	59.46	15.95
Have you been abroad	2.04	5.00	12.47	5.08	35.48	59.46	14.5
Do you have relatives and friends overseas	14.58	12.82	23.31	23.73	29.03	61.11	24.57
Do you often surf foreign Web sites	14.29	31.71	35.79	39.34	59.38	78.38	38.00
Rent or Own One's Residence							
Rent one's apartment	10.20	5.00	12.47	32.20	6.25	2.78	12.82
Having use right to one's residence	12.24	10.00	25.20	18.64	3.13	2.78	19.90
Owning one's residence	77.55	85.00	62.33	49.15	90.63	94.44	67.28

Table 14.2 Foreign brand household appliances as a percentage of all household items in Shanghai

	Agricultural villages	Town centers	Urban residential villages	Old urban settlements	New commercial housing complexes	Luxury flats and villas	Have global connections	None global connections
Radio	5.9	28.6	19.6	27	27.3	61.9	29.3	11.0
Color television	11.6	54.3	41.6	42.9	55.2	73	50.0	32.9
Stereo system	28.6	50	40.3	36.7	35	84.8	54.8	21.2
Microwave oven	12.5	22.2	24	14.9	25	62.9	30.3	17.1
Washing machine	3.7	12.9	17.3	16.7	20.7	47.2	24.5	9.7
Refrigerator	10.8	20.6	22	16	31	48.6	30.4	11.7
Camera	23.8	43.5	39.4	30.3	73.9	77.1	53.7	25.4
Video recorder	60	52.9	53.1	52.2	53.8	96.6	62.7	48.5
VCD or DVD	0	33.3	19.9	22.6	8.7	62.9	28.3	12.7
Movie camera	33.3	0	61.8	25	66.7	95.5	71.7	41.7
Personal computer	20	37.5	28.3	25	27.8	80.6	38.6	24.6
Air conditioner	10	47.4	31	10.3	24	44.4	35.9	21.0
Motorcycle	0	0	27.8	0	25	100	38.8	3.7
Piano	0	0	33.3	50	50	76.9	53.3	25.0
Cell phone	45.5	58.8	65.2		76	94.6	71.4	61.8
Private car	0	25	57.1	0	0	65.4	61.8	16.7

more likely to buy foreign brand household items, as they are more informed of the availability of foreign products locally and more appreciative of the functional values embodied in these products.

How do individuals differ in consuming globally?

The question to be addressed further is: How do individual consumers differ in pursuing a global life-style as a result of their varied positions in residential categories, income, education attainment, and global connections? We begin the analysis by looking at consumers' consciousness of foreign brands through responses to the statement "I always pay attention to famous foreign brand goods when shopping."

Figure 14.1 shows that 41 percent of residents in luxury flats and villas either strongly agree or agree with the statement about foreign brands, whereas only 6 percent of agricultural villages' residents respond the same way. It is interesting to note that except for those in luxury flats and villas, half of the respondents did not favor foreign brands in their buying decisions. The preference of residents in "luxury flats and villas" for foreign brands reflects a tendency of the housing rich to at least equate foreign brands with social status. It indicates both spatial and social differentiation in terms of local consumers' varied responses to global brand products and fashions.

The next analytical step involves looking at the relations between residential categories and consumer activities (see Figures 14.2–14.6).

Eating at McDonald's has become increasingly popular for Shanghai residents, although different people may do so for different reasons. Our survey shows that people who choose to eat McDonald's or KFC as opposed to traditional fast Chinese foods vary distinctively by residential categories. Figure 14.2 shows that in agricultural villages 63.3 percent of the respondents answer "yes" to the fast food question, which received 100 percent response in luxury flats and villas. Figure 14.3 shows a gradually increasing percentage of people wearing foreign brand clothes: from agricultural villages' (20.4 percent), to luxury flats and villas (97.3 percent). All residents in luxury flats and villas have been to a bowling alley, whereas only 26.5 percent of people in agricultural villages have (see Figure 14.4). Figure 14.5 indicates that most people in agricultural villages, town centers, and urban residential villages have not watched a Western movie recently, while half of the residents in commercial housing complexes and 64.9 percent in luxury flats and villas have done so. Another striking difference among different residential categories is the owning of a credit card. Figure 14.6 demonstrates that 91.9 percent of the residents in luxury flats and villas do so, while credit card owners in agricultural villages, town centers, urban residential villages, old urban settlement, and new commercial housing complexes range from 27.7 to 56.5 percent.

Modeling global consumer behavior

Assuming that demographic and socioeconomic attributes have different effects on the neighborhoods, we focus on a number of these important variables including

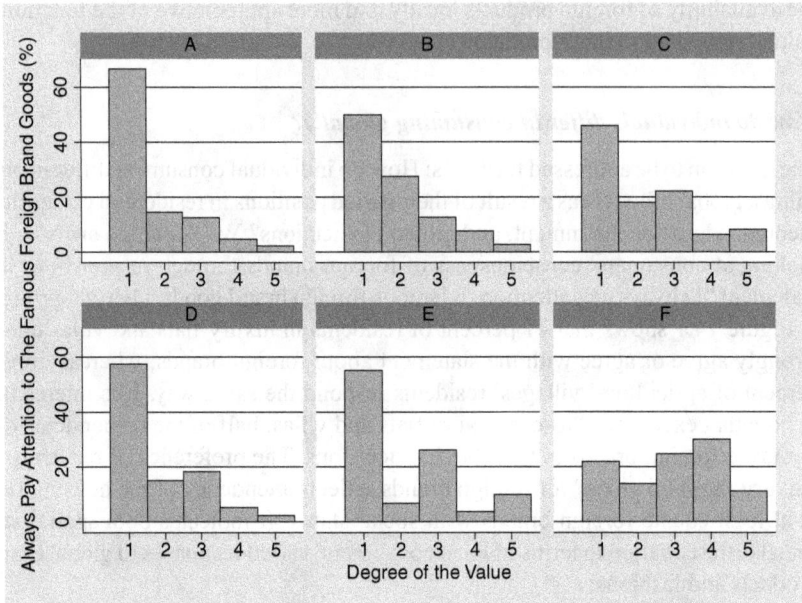

Figure 14.1 Always pay attention to famous foreign brand goods when shopping.

Notes

The horizontal axis is a Likert scale from 1 to 5 indicating strongly disagree, disagree, neutral, agree, and strongly agree respectively. The six residential categories are represented by letters from A to F where A = Agricultural villages, B = Town centers, C = Urban residential villages, D = Old urban settlements, E = New commercial housing complexes, F = Luxury flats and villas. The same residential categories also are used in the following figures.

GENDER, AGE (in years), EDUCATION, and PER CAPITA INCOME (logged) with residential categories and global connections. EDUCATION is measured as an ordinal variable (1 = below primary school, 2 = primary school, 3 = junior high school, 4 = senior high school, 5 = vocational school, 6 = two − year [community] or television colleges [*dazhuan* or *dianda*], 7 = four − year college or university, and 8 = post graduate study). PER CAPITA INCOME is logged to normalize its skewed distribution.

First of all, we expect younger people to be more avid global consumers. Higher education and income provide more human and economic resources that allow people to consume more global products. The index of GCB, which is based on the multidependent variables,[5] has a scale of 0–100, with zero indicating no GCB and 100 denoting a full set of GCB.

Table 14.3 presents the results from three regression models predicting GCB. First, we examine the effects of gender, age, education, and income on GCB (model 1) without controlling for residential category and global connections. The model shows that all independent variables are significant at p value <0.01 level

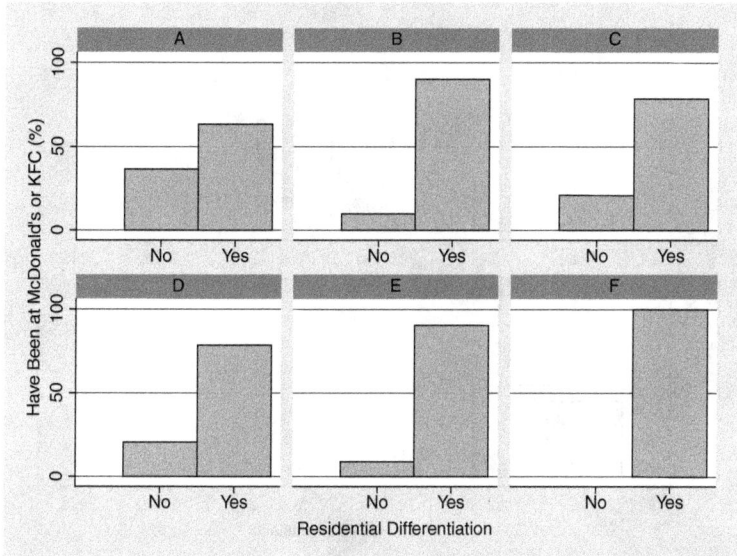

Figure 14.2 Have Been to McDonald's or KFC by residential differentiation.

Note
For residential types A to F, see the notes in Figure 14.1.

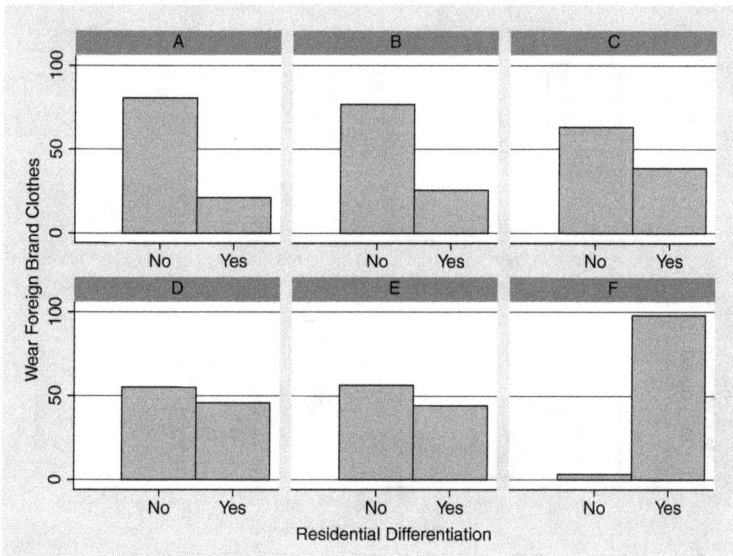

Figure 14.3 Have worn foreign brand clothes by residential differentiation.

Note
For residential types A to F, see the notes in Figure 14.1.

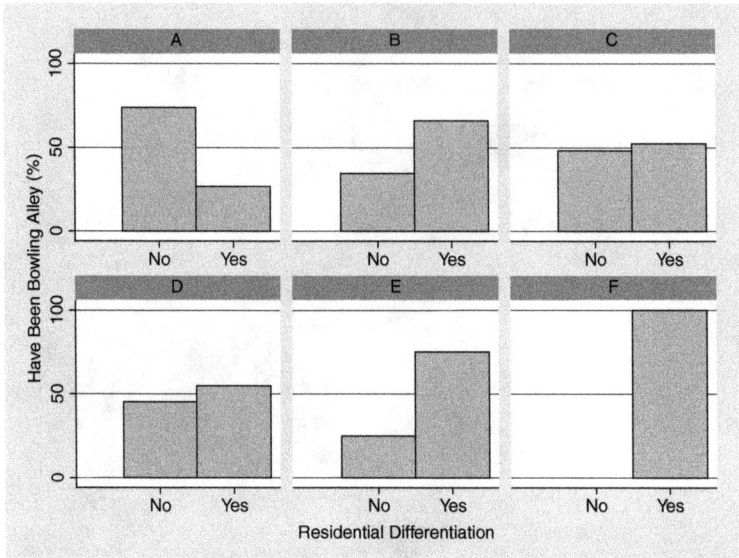

Figure 14.4 Have been to a bowling alley by residential differentiation.

Note
For residential types A to F, see the notes in Figure 14.1.

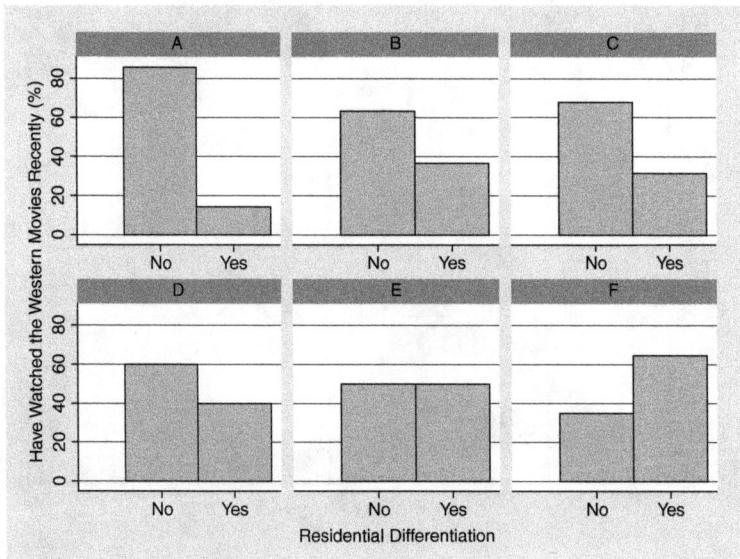

Figure 14.5 Have watched a western movie recently by residential differentiation.

Note
For residential types A to F, see the notes in Figure 14.1.

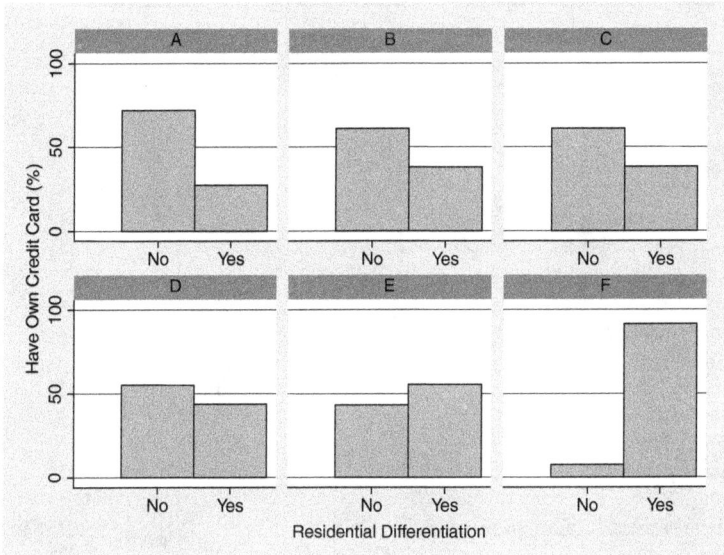

Figure 14.6 Owning a credit card by residential differentiation.

Note
For residential types A to F, see the notes in Figure 14.1.

except gender (p value < 0.1 level). Females are more engaged in GCB as opposed to males. The negative coefficient for age confirms that younger consumers are more globally oriented. As expected, both education and income have a strong positive effect on GCB.

Model 2 reveals the additive effect of residential differentiation on GCB. People living in luxury flats and villas are most likely to engage in GCB, while those in the other two residential categories are also more likely to consume global products relative to those in agricultural villages and town centers. It is important to note that despite the effect of residential differentiation, the demographic and socioeconomic predictors continue to have their expected effects on GCB. In Model 3, we have added global connectivity as four dummy variables to assess their relative effects on GCB. It turns out that all four global connections have more or less equally strong influences on GCB. While the strong effect of global connections has crowded the weak effects of living in urban residential villages and old urban settlements, living in luxury flats and villas remains a strong positive predictor for GCB. Since Model 3 has the highest R-square, we feel confident that it approximates to a complete model of GCB by including both residential differentiation and personal connections.

Discussion and conclusion

In the last two decades, Shanghai has experienced the local touch-down and spread of globalization, which we have tried to capture by examining the relationship

Table 14.3 Regression models predicting global consumer behavior (GCB)

	Model 1	Model 2	Model 3
	GCB	GCB	GCB
Gender (Female = 1)	2.64*	2.45*	3.08**
	(1.39)	(1.35)	(1.30)
Age	−0.46***	−0.48***	−0.42***
	(0.04)	(0.04)	(0.05)
Education levels	2.84***	2.37***	1.47***
	(0.48)	(0.47)	(0.47)
Annual income per capita	13.65***	10.67***	8.06***
(logged)	(1.04)	(1.12)	(1.14)
Urban residential villages and old urban settlements#		3.74**	2.86
		(1.89)	(1.81)
New commercial housing complexes#		6.01*	3.04
		(3.41)	(3.30)
Luxury flats and villas#		22.47***	17.72***
		(3.69)	(3.61)
Have worked for foreign company			5.01***
			(1.93)
Have been abroad			6.15***
			(2.10)
Have friend/relative on abroad			4.39***
			(1.58)
Often surf foreign website			7.46***
			(1.60)
Constant	−55.53***	−37.02***	−22.38***
	(6.85)	(7.46)	(7.55)
Number of observations	600	600	600
R-squared	0.51	0.54	0.58

Notes
Standard errors in parentheses.
* Significant at 10%.
** Significant at 5%.
*** Significant at 1%.
# Agricultural villages and town centers were combined as a new omitted category for comparison.

between residential differentiation and GCB and by modeling this behavior as a collective function of both individuals' characteristics and their global connections. The analysis has uncovered striking evidence that local residents' GCB is embedded in a complex global-local nexus, which consists of varied external linkages and differentiated socioeconomic and residential conditions.

To the extent that urban differentiation has a spatial, horizontal aspect and a social, vertical dimension, they are closely related in local settings. As localities become increasingly globalized, both spatial and social differentiations are influenced by specific channels that bring individuals and the outside world closer together. This means that the local impact of globalization can be measured and modeled not only through the extent of residential differentiation but also through globally oriented consumer behavior as it is shaped by individuals' demographic and socioeconomic attributes, residential positions, and global connections. Since consumer behavior reflects a socio-cultural choice of certain locally available products, it takes on a global orientation when these products bear an external and global brand and reputation. As a result, external or global connections are expected to induce locals to consume globally.

The emergence of GCB among locals may also be analyzed as a process of cultural diffusion that originates from the outside and gradually takes root inside or locally. The speed and spread of this process depend on individuals' responses to global brand products, and people in differentiated socioeconomic and residential spaces respond differently to diffused material items.

The analysis in this chapter has focused on the crucial relationship between residential differentiation and GCB. Since GCB is the dependent variable and residential differentiation by itself cannot fully account for the former, we have examined how local consumers' demographic and socioeconomic attributes and their global connections are related to their residential spaces and to their engagement in various globally oriented consumer activities. Finally, we have organized the independent variables into a set of regression models, which demonstrate the additive effects of demographic and socioeconomic attributes, residential positions, and global connections on GCB. The full model (3) yields the most important finding that even when demographic, socioeconomic, and residential variables are all controlled for, PGCs still have a great deal of influence on GCB.

By explaining local Shanghai residents' globally oriented consumer behavior using their demographic and socioeconomic characteristics, residential locations, and PGCs, we have "sliced" through and opened two connected layers of the interstitial spaces around the global-local nexus, so to speak. First, we have revealed an extensive relationship in Shanghai between differentiated residence and consumption of global products. Those who have climbed up and settled into the luxury flats and villas – the top residential category – have also lived a globally oriented lifestyle featuring fast food, brand clothing, and Western leisure and entertainment activities. This layer of the global-local nexus, in a way, features differentiated local residential spaces that have become unevenly globalized spaces of consumption and lifestyle. Second, we have established the relative and independent effects of residential differentiation and PGCs on global consumption, controlling for the demographic and socioeconomic variables. This finding exposes a thicker layer of the global-local nexus where personal global connections have entered and function as a relational mechanism for transmitting global social and cultural influence to local consumer behavior. Establishing this explicit global-to-local channel of influence on consumer behavior has taken the study on the local impact of globalization a step further. It also may move us in a new theoretical direction of seeing and interpreting global influence as a local socialization mechanism.

Notes

1 The data used in this chapter came from a survey in Pudong, Shanghai supported by a grant from the CCK Foundation for International Exchange to Xiangming Chen during 1999–2001. We thank Yuan Ren and his team at Fudan University for carrying out the survey in 2001. Comments by Fulong Wu on an earlier draft of this chapter are appreciated.
2 "KFC and McDonald's – a model of blended culture," *China Daily*, June 1, 2004, available online at: www.chinadaily.com.cn/english/doc/2004-06/01/content_335488.htm (accessed on October 1, 2004).
3 Shanghai Year Book 2004 published by Shanghai Statistical Bureau.
4 The proportions of the sample having zero, one, two, three, and four personal global connections (PGCs) are 46.1, 31.6, 13.3, 6, and 3 percent, respectively. With regard to the distribution of PGCs, 15.6 percent of the respondents have worked for a foreign company; 14.3 percent have gone abroad; 23.8 percent have relatives and friends overseas; and 37.9 percent have surfed foreign Web sites. Unfortunately, we could not separate overseas relatives from friends in our sample; this however is not a problem because we used the PGCs as a scale instead of as categories in the multivariate regression analysis.
5 To compose the index several variables related to global consumption are selected, including: Have you had McDonalds' or KFC? Have you purchased and worn foreign brand clothes? Have you been to a bowling alley? Do you own a credit card? Have you watched Western movies in the recent three months?

References

Appadurai, A. (2001) "Grassroots globalization and the research imagination," in A. Appadurai (ed.) *Globalization*, Durham, NC: Duke University Press, 1–21
Bian, Y. (1994) *Work and Inequality in Urban China*, Albany, NY: State University of New York Press.
Bian, Y. and Logan, J. R. (1996) "Market transition and the persistence of power: the changing stratification system in China," *American Sociological Review*, 61: 739–758.
Bian, Y., Logan, J. R., Lu, H., Pan, Y. and Guan, Y. (1997) "Work units and housing reform in two Chinese cities," in X. Lu and E. Perry (eds) *Danwei: The Chinese Work-unit in Historical and Comparative Perspective*, New York: M.E. Sharpe, 223–250.
Bocock, R. (1993) *Consumption*, London: Routledge.
Chen, X. and Gao, X. (1993a) "China's urban housing development in the shift from redistribution to decentralization," *Social Problems*, 40: 266–283.
Chen, X. and Gao, X. (1993b) "Urban economic reform and public-housing investment in China," *Urban Affairs Quarterly*, 29: 117–145.
Chen, X. and Hua, X. (1996) "Housing reform and private housing investment in urban China," in G. Tolley, S. Y. Hao, and M. Occomy (eds) *Urban Land and Housing Reform in Socialist and Formerly Socialist Countries*, Mount Pleasant, MI: Blackstone Books, 298–329.
Chen, X. and Sun, J. (2007) "Untangling a global-local nexus: sorting out residential sorting in Shanghai," *Environment and Planning A* (in press).
Gaubatz, P. R. (1999) "China's urban transformation: patterns and processes of morphological change in Beijing, Shanghai and Guangzhou," *Urban Studies*, 36: 1451–1521.
Gu, C. and Liu, H. (2002) "Social polarization and segregation in Beijing," in J. R. Logan (ed.) *The New Chinese Cities: Globalization and Market Reform*, Oxford: Blackwell, 198–211.

Held, D. (1999) *Global Transformations: Politics, Economics and Culture,* Stanford, CA: Stanford University Press.

Huang, Y. (2005) "From work-unit compounds to gated communities: housing inequality and residential segregation in transitional Beijing," in L. J. C. Ma and F. Wu (eds) *Restructuring the Chinese City: Changing Society, Economy and Space,* London: Routledge, 192–221.

Lee, Y.-S. (1988) "The urban housing problem in China," *The China Quarterly,* 115(September): 387–407.

Li, S.-M. (2003) "Housing tenure and residential mobility in urban China: a study of commodity housing development in Beijing and Guangzhou," *Urban Affairs Review,* 38: 510–534.

Li, S.-M. and Siu, Y.-M. (2001) "Residential mobility under market transition: a study of the newly constructed commodity housing of Guangzhou?" *The Professional Geographer,* 53: 219–229.

Lin, G. C. S. (2001) "Metropolitan development in a transitional socialist economy: spatial restructuring in the Pearl River Delta, China," *Urban Studies,* 38: 383–406.

Logan, J. R., Bian, Y. and Bian, F. (1999) "Housing inequality in urban China in the 1990s," *International Journal of Urban and Regional Research,* 23: 7–25.

McCracken, G. (1990) *Culture and Consumption,* Bloomington, IN: Indiana University Press.

Ritzer, G. (1996) *The McDonaldization of Society,* Thousand Oaks, CA: Pine Forge Press.

Ritzer, G. (2003) *The Globalization of Nothing,* Thousand Oaks, CA: Pine Forge Press.

Robertson, R. and Khondker, H. H. (1998) "Discourses of globalization: preliminary considerations," *International Sociology,* 13(1): 25–40.

Song, S., Chu, G. and Chen, X. (2004) "Housing investment and consumption in urban China," in A. Chen, G. Liu, and K. H. Zhang (eds) *Urbanization and Social Welfare in China,* Aldershot: Ashgate, 87–106

Sun, J. and Chen, X. (2005) "Personal global connections and a new residential differentiation in Shanghai, China," *China: An International Journal,* 3(2): 301–319.

Wang, D. and Li, S.-M. (2004) "Housing preferences in a transitional housing system: the case of Beijing, China," *Environment and Planning A,* 36: 69–87.

Wang, Y. (1990) "Private sector housing in urban China since 1949: the case of Xi'an," *Housing Studies,* 7: 119–137.

Wang, Y. and Murie, A. (1996) "The process of commercialization of urban housing in China," *Urban Studies,* 33: 971–989.

Watson, J. L. (1997) *Golden Arches East: McDonald's in East Asia,* Stanford: Stanford University Press.

Wu, F. (1996) "Changes in the structure of public housing provision in urban China," *Urban Studies,* 33: 1601–1627.

Wu, F. (2001) "Housing provision under globalization: a case study of Shanghai," *Environment and Planning A,* 33: 1741–1764.

Wu, F. (2004) "Transplanting cityscapes: the use of imagined globalization in housing commodification in Beijing," *Area,* 36(3): 227–234.

Wu, F. and Yeh, A.G.-O. (1999) "Urban spatial structure in a transitional economy: the case of Guangzhou, China," *Journal of the American Planning Association,* 65: 377–394.

Wu, W. (1999) "Reforming China's institutional environment for urban infrastructure provision," *Urban Studies,* 36: 2263–2282.

Yan, Y. (2000) "Of hamburgers and social space: consuming McDonald's in Beijing," in D. Davis (ed.) *The Consumer Revolution in Urban China,* Berkeley, CA: University of California Press, 201–225

Yu, V. (August 20, 2002) "McDonald's sets its sights on rivals in Hong Kong," *Arlington Heights Daily Herald*: 1.

Yusuf, S. and Wu, W. (1997) *The Dynamics of Urban Growth in Three Chinese Cities*, New York: Oxford University Press.

Zhou, M. and Logan, J. R. (1996) "Market transition and the commodification of housing in urban China," *International Journal of Urban and Regional Research*, 20: 400–421.

Zhu, J. (2000) "Urban physical development in transition to market: the case of China as a transitional economy," *Urban Affairs Review*, 36: 178–196.

Index

For Product Safety Concerns and Information please contact our EU
representative GPSR@taylorandfrancis.com
Taylor & Francis Verlag GmbH, Kaufingerstraße 24, 80331 München, Germany

www.ingramcontent.com/pod-product-compliance
Lightning Source LLC
Chambersburg PA
CBHW060145280326
41932CB00012B/1644